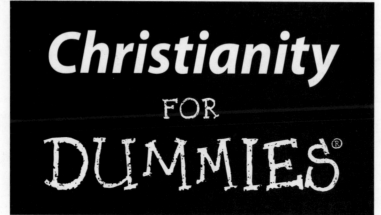

by Richard Wagner

Foreword by Kurt Warner
Super Bowl and NFL MVP

WILEY

Wiley Publishing, Inc.

Christianity For Dummies®

Published by
Wiley Publishing, Inc.
111 River St.
Hoboken, NJ 07030-5774
www.wiley.com

Copyright © 2004 by Wiley Publishing, Inc., Indianapolis, Indiana

Published by Wiley Publishing, Inc., Indianapolis, Indiana

Published simultaneously in Canada

For general information on our other products and services or to obtain technical support, please contact our Customer Care Department within the U.S. at 800-762-2974, outside the U.S. at 317-572-3993, or fax 317-572-4002.

Wiley also publishes its books in a variety of electronic formats. Some content that appears in print may not be available in electronic books.

Library of Congress Control Number is available from the publisher.

ISBN: 0-7645-4482-9

Manufactured in the United States of America

10 9 8 7 6 5 4 3 2

1O/QV/QW/QU/IN

WILEY

About the Author

Richard Wagner is author of numerous books, including *Christian Prayer For Dummies*, and is publisher of *Digitalwalk* (www.digitalwalk.com), a Web-based Christian discipleship magazine. He has been a guest on Christian radio programs across the country discussing prayer and Christian discipleship issues. Rich has served in church leadership and teaching roles for more than a dozen years. He graduated with a bachelor of arts degree from Taylor University and pursued graduate studies at The American University in Washington, D.C. He lives in Princeton, Massachusetts, with his lovely, quirkless wife and three terrific, though zany boys. You can e-mail Rich at rich@digitalwalk.net.

Dedication

To Joe Wagner — my father, teacher, and friend

Acknowledgments

In the process of writing this book, I was blessed with a superior editing team: Alissa Schwipps, who did a splendid job of managing the project from start to finish; Kristin DeMint, for her terrific ideas and editing prowess; and Dr. Winfried Corduan, for his wisdom, thoughtful insights, and keen suggestions to help ensure the accuracy and representative nature of the book's text. What's more, special thanks to Alissa and Kristin, the duo who always seemed to know just the right tweak to make to improve the flow or readability of the book.

Thanks to Kathy Cox at Wiley for her enthusiasm about the book, from the proposal stage to the finished product.

I'd also like to thank my father, Joseph Wagner, who provided helpful, honest feedback on the chapters. I'd also like to thank Pastor Eric Hartlen and everyone at Heritage Bible Chapel for their consistent prayers and encouragement.

Heartfelt thanks to Kurt Warner for his participation in this project and to Marci Moran at Kurt's First Things First foundation for the work she performed to make it all happen.

Finally, I'd especially like to thank my wife, Kim, and my three sons, Jordan, Jared, and Justus. No author has ever had a homefield advantage like I have; their 24/7 prayer support and unbridled enthusiasm for this book were the fuel that the Lord used to help get it from page one to the back cover.

Publishers Acknowledgments

We're proud of this book; please send us your comments through our Dummies online registration form located at www.dummies.com/register/.

Some of the people who helped bring this book to market include the following:

Acquisitions, Editorial, and Media Development

Senior Project Editor: Alissa D. Schwipps

Acquisitions Editor: Kathy Cox

Copy Editor: Kristin DeMint

Assistant Editor: Holly Gastineau-Grimes

Technical Editor: Winfried Corduan, PhD, Professor of Philosophy and Religion, Taylor University

Senior Permissions Editor: Carmen Krikorian

Editorial Manager: Jennifer Ehrlich

Editorial Assistant: Elizabeth Rea

Cover Photos: © Philip Gould/CORBIS

Cartoons: Rich Tennant, www.the5thwave.com

Production

Project Coordinator: Maridee Ennis

Layout and Graphics: Andrea Dahl, Denny Hager, Rashell Smith, Melanee Wolven

Proofreaders: Laura Albert, Brian H. Walls, TECHBOOKS Production Services

Indexer: TECHBOOKS Production Services

Special Help: Christina Guthrie, Laura Miller, Chad Sievers, and Esmeralda St. Clair

Publishing and Editorial for Consumer Dummies

Diane Graves Steele, Vice President and Publisher, Consumer Dummies

Joyce Pepple, Acquisitions Director, Consumer Dummies

Kristin A. Cocks, Product Development Director, Consumer Dummies

Michael Spring, Vice President and Publisher, Travel

Brice Gosnell, Associate Publisher, Travel

Kelly Regan, Editorial Director, Travel

Publishing for Technology Dummies

Andy Cummings, Vice President and Publisher, Dummies Technology/General User

Composition Services

Gerry Fahey, Vice President of Production Services

Debbie Stailey, Director of Composition Services

Contents at a Glance

Table of Contents

Foreword

●●●

1 love a good road trip. It's a chance to jump into the car by myself with no
particular destination, just enjoying the drive and whatever else comes
my way. I've taken many of these rides during the course of my life, but they
were all small-time compared to the one I'm on now — my *spiritual road trip*.
This life-long excursion has just a single purpose: getting to know God
through Jesus Christ.

My journey began in a small Iowa town over thirty years ago. I trekked all
over Iowa, through most of the United States, and even across the Atlantic.
I rose from the unknown valleys of Arena Football to play and win on the
center stage of all American sports — the Super Bowl. Through my professional football and private life, I've experienced spectacular mountaintops,
passed through low valleys, and narrowly escaped horrendous storms.

I'm not alone on this road trip; God's right there with me. Of course, being the
control freak that I am, I started off by assuming control of the driver's wheel.
I had my mind made up on where I was going to go and how I was going to get
there. I didn't need God's help or want his company, so I quickly threw him into
the trunk and started on my way. It didn't take long, however, before I hit a few
snags, had a blowout in the rear tire, and heard a loud rattle under the hood.

During these times of crisis, I'd rush to the trunk, let God out, and ask him to
bail me out. Like a spare tire, I saw God as my backup plan, on call 24/7 for
whenever I had trouble. I let him fix everything and, after things were fine and
dandy again, I'd quickly stuff him back into the trunk.

But after I'd been traveling down the road solo for a while, the scenery
became less exciting and the radio tunes grew stale. I started to feel lonely
and empty inside and longed for something more. I'd routinely ask God to
take a seat in the back and keep me company for a while; we even got to
know each other a little bit, sang a few songs, and shared advice. But when
he started to tell me where to go and what to do, I'd shove him right back
into the trunk and carry on alone.

Eventually, as surroundings became less and less familiar, I discovered that
I wasn't able to rely on my instincts anymore. I kept getting lost and was
unable to find my way to a life of meaning and peace. Realizing that I could
use some navigation help after all, I invited God to join me in the front pas-
senger seat as my copilot. I threw him the atlas, pointed to where I was going,
and asked him to chart the way. I soon discovered that God had quite a knack
for plotting a course. He always seemed to select the best route, even if it

wasn't the fastest or most convenient. Many times I didn't agree with his routing, however, and simply chose to take off on my own. *I* was in the driver's seat, after all. Yet, time after time, my plans never worked out. In the end, after 26 years of detours, diversions, and dead-ends, I finally realized that I was better off in the hands of God and decided to let him take over the wheel. So, I got out of the car, tossed the keys to God, and slid into the back-seat. Yes, I sometimes act like a backseat driver, firing my thoughts and opinions at him, telling him what he should and shouldn't do. But he always seems to look back at me with a smile, responding with grace and love.

Regardless of your situation or background, you're at some point on your own spiritual road trip. Perhaps you're well into the drive, or maybe you haven't even started the engine. But wherever you are along the way, pull over at the next rest area and turn the page.

When you do, you'll discover that Richard Wagner is waiting for you there. Rich will lead you on a journey to discover Christianity and what it's all about. As you turn the pages, I promise you that there'll be times you'll laugh out loud at his offbeat approach, but the humor will never quench the truth and significance of his words.

So buckle up, grab the wheel, and set the cruise for the ride of your life. But I must warn you — by the time you're done discovering what the Christian faith is all about, you might find yourself sliding into the backseat and tossing your keys to a new driver just like I did.

Kurt Warner
Super Bowl and NFL MVP

Introduction

_{. . . . .}

When I start to rattle off the host of names ascribed to Christians, I begin to feel like Bubba, the Alabaman shrimp farmer from the Oscar-winning film *Forrest Gump*. In one of the film's memorable moments, Bubba explains to Forrest Gump a bazillion different ways you can prepare shrimp, be they barbecued, scampi, gumbo, and so on. I suppose if you were to ask Bubba about the variety of Christians, he might say something like this:

> *Anyway, like I was sayin', there are born-again Christians, evangelical Christians, Roman Catholics, Protestants, Anglicans, mainline denominational Christians, non-denominational Christians, charismatics, Pentecostals, and Calvinists. There are Greek Orthodox, Russian Orthodox, Serbian Orthodox, Lutheran, Methodist, Free Methodist, Baptist, Southern Baptist, Presbyterian, Assemblies of God, and African Independent. You've also got your Shakers, Quakers, Amish, Coptic, Plymouth Brethren, Congregationalist, Episcopalian, Christian and Missionary Alliance, and Evangelical Free Christians. That — that's about it. . . .*

Although the taste differences between Bubba's shrimp burger and coconut shrimp are great, each dish has the same primary ingredient. Similarly, Christians have a multitude of names with as many shades of belief, but the centerpiece for each Christian, no matter the label, is the same — Jesus Christ, a Jewish carpenter who lived some 2,000 years ago.

Christianity For Dummies is a friendly, approachable guide that introduces you to Jesus Christ, the Christian faith, and the Christian Church. This book is written for people who are curious about Christianity and wonder what exactly it means to be a "Christian." It's intended both for people who aren't Christians and for Christians who are interested in discovering more about their faith.

Keep in mind that any author brings to a book his or her background, experiences, and a specific set of beliefs. From the outset, let me make it clear that I'm a born-again, evangelical and Protestant Christian. However, my overriding goal for *Christianity For Dummies* is to be unbiased, fair, and respectful toward all branches of the Christian Church, so that a Christian from any of these backgrounds can point to the book and claim, "Yeah, that's my faith."

About This Book

If you want to know absolutely, positively all the nitty-gritty details of Christianity, I recommend getting a semi, driving to your local university

library, and persuading some students to help you load up racks of books into the semi trailer. But if you want to discover what you *need* to know about the Christian faith, then you've come to the right book. *Christianity For Dummies* provides a hearty exploration of the Christian faith, but does so without requiring a semi or a band of starving students. This book also approaches the subject matter in an easy-to-understand manner, without overloading you with a lot of theological mumbo-jumbo.

If you read *Christianity For Dummies* from cover to cover, you find the topics logically ordered, with each succeeding chapter building upon what you read about in earlier chapters. However, the book is a reference book, so don't feel like you must read it from start to finish. Instead, you may wish to open up the Table of Contents and find a topic that suits your fancy. Or flip through the pages 'til you find a section that jumps out at you. Or perhaps you want to peruse the index for the subject that you've been curious to explore.

Conventions Used in This Book

To help you navigate through this book, I've set up a few conventions:

- ✔ *Italics* are used for emphasis and to highlight new words or terms that I define.

- ✔ **Boldfaced** text is used to indicate the keywords in explanatory bulleted lists and the action part of numbered steps.

- ✔ `Monofont` is used for Web addresses.

As you read, keep in mind the following additional conventions and definitions:

- ✔ **Capitalization:** Several Christian terms mean different ideas depending on capitalization:

  - *Church* with a capital *C* refers to the worldwide body of Christians, while *church* with a small *c* means a local or individual church congregation, building, or parish. Another common name for the Church is the *Body of Christ* or simply the *Body*.

  - *Orthodox* with a capital *O* refers to Eastern Orthodox Christians, a division of the Christian Church, whereas *orthodox* with a small *o* refers to traditional, historical Christian beliefs.

  - *Catholic* with a capital *C* refers to the Roman Catholic Church, while lowercase *catholic* means "universal."

- ✔ **Two global Churches:** Based on how the Christian Church developed through the centuries, people often draw a line of distinction between the Western and Eastern Churches. The *Western Church* refers to the Catholic and Protestant Churches, while the *Eastern Church* is another term for the Orthodox Church.

✔ **Referring to Christian groups:** In this book, I refer to Roman Catholics as _Catholics_. Likewise, I call Eastern Orthodox Christians simply _Orthodox Christians_.

✔ **Referring to God:** Christians refer to God with many names, but in this book, I generally use "God" and "Lord." Also, in accordance with historical Christian beliefs, I make use of the traditional masculine pronoun "he" to refer to God.

✔ **Referring to Christianity:** Christianity sounds like a generic enough word to define, but even this term can mean radically different ideas to different people both inside and outside of the Christian Church. Therefore, when I speak of _Christianity,_ keep in mind that I use the term in three respects:

- **"Mere" Christianity:** Christian author C.S. Lewis used the term "mere Christianity" to describe the core essentials of the Christian faith that any believer, regardless of his or her background, agrees on. _Christianity For Dummies_ focuses on this common ground across the Christian Church, be it Protestant, Catholic, or Orthodox. However, many important differences of belief that one can't just sweep under the table exist among these branches of the Church. So when there is disagreement on a given topic, I point out these differences.

- **"Historical" Christianity:** When I claim an idea as a Christian belief, I speak of a belief that has historically been upheld by the Church for some 2,000 years, not by the latest fashionable flavor of Christian thinking that may be in vogue for the moment.

- **"Biblical" Christianity:** Christians have always believed that the Bible is the inspired, authoritative, and reliable written Word of God. Following in this mold, this book treats the Bible as the legitimate "instruction manual" for Christians and the "bottom line" for matters pertaining to the Christian faith. (See Chapter 2 for more on why Christians believe the Bible is reliable.)

✔ **Bible references:** Because 1,001 different kinds of Bibles and translations are available at your local bookstore, I don't want to use a page number when I reference a Bible passage. Therefore, when I quote from the Bible, I use the standard way to cite passages. For example, John 3:16 refers to John as the book of the Bible, 3 as the chapter number, and 16 as the verse.

✔ **Bible translation:** Speaking of the Bible, each Bible passage in this book is from the World English Bible translation (on the Web at www.worldenglishbible.com). On occasion, I paraphrase the text to make it more readable.

What You're Not to Read

Although this book focuses on what you need to know about Christianity, I do deal with some topics that, though useful, are less essential for you to know, at least during your first read-through. This "skippable" material is identified as follows:

- **Text in sidebars:** Sidebars are shaded boxes that pop up here and there in the chapters. They deal with subjects related to the chapter, but aren't necessary reading.

- **Anything with a Technical Stuff icon:** This information is technical or historical stuff that you may find interesting, but you won't miss out on anything critical if you want to pass over them.

Foolish Assumptions

As I wrote this book, I made a few assumptions about you. Whether the assumptions are foolish or not, here they are:

- You may or may not call yourself a Christian, but, regardless of your experience or background, you are curious to discover more about the Christian faith.

- You've likely seen the Catholic pope on television and heard the terms Protestant and Orthodox before, but you'd probably like to know more about the differences among what Catholic, Protestant, and Orthodox Christians believe.

- You may go to church every Sunday, just once a year, or perhaps you've never once entered a church sanctuary.

- You've probably heard Christian jargon — such as *born again*, *evangelical*, *Catholic*, or *orthodox* — through the media or in conversations and want a better understanding of what all these buzzwords mean.

- You keep catching reruns of *Jesus of Nazareth* on TV and you'd like to know what it's all about.

How This Book Is Organized

Christianity For Dummies covers the key topics of the Christian faith in five parts.

Part I: Uncovering What Christianity's All About

In the first chapter, you discover the basics of what Christianity is, what it's not, and how it fits into the context of the world's religions. This part then dives into the issue of whether Christianity's a "blind faith" or a faith that history and reason support. Next, you center on the heart of Christianity and discover what the Good News of Jesus Christ is all about.

Part II: Exploring the Basic Principles of the Christian Faith

Part II delves into the essentials of the Christian faith. You look at the human predicament of sin and God's graceful response — Jesus Christ. You then explore the Bible, who the Christian God is, and what sacraments and ordinances are. This part is rounded out by looking at what Christianity says happens after people die.

Part III: Here's the Church, Here's the Steeple: Peeking into the Christian Church

You discover in this part how the early Church began with Jesus' original disciples and survived through some tough times, as well as explore the Church's relevance in the modern era. I know what you're thinking — history's boring. Don't worry, I avoid the "yawning syndrome" often associated with Church history as I show you the distinct backgrounds, traditions, and beliefs of Catholics, Orthodox Christians, and Protestants. You then discover what Christian worship's all about.

Part IV: Christian Living in a Postmodern World

This part discusses what happens when a person makes a decision to believe in Christianity and how one lives out its teachings. If you're a Christian, this discussion provides a roadmap for your "Christian walk." If you're not, this dialogue helps provide a fuller understanding of how Christians aim to live out their faith in the world around them.

Diving headfirst into the briar patch, this part also deals with some tough theological questions, such as: Why does a loving, all-powerful God allow bad things to happen? Why would I want to join a church filled with hypocrites? How can Jesus be the only way to God? *For Dummies* books are never shy, and so, in that tradition, this part tackles these thorny subjects head on.

Part V: The Part of Tens

In Part V, I provide several handy-dandy resources to help in your exploration of the Christian faith. If you feel like celebrating, check out a listing of ten holidays, holy days, and seasons. If you're in need of inspiration, flip to the discussion of ten great Christians. Finally, if you're searching for God's truth, check out ten key passages in the Bible.

And don't forget to check out the two helpful appendixes at the back of the book. Appendix A is a glossary that guides you through the world of Christian buzzwords, and Appendix B is a handy timeline of important events in Christian history.

Icons Used in This Book

The icons in this book help you find particular kinds of information that may be of use to you:

Keep a close eye out for the Remember sections; they highlight important ideas for you to keep in mind to deepen your understanding of Christianity.

The Technical Stuff icon highlights information that's interesting but not critical to your understanding of the topic at hand. So, reading these sections can provide useful tidbits of information, but feel free to skip them on the first reading.

This icon draws attention to key points that help you make sense of the Christian faith or apply it to your life.

Take special note of the cautions I provide in the Warning sections. These will save you from falling into the Pit of *M*s — misconceptions, misunderstandings, and mistakes.

Where to Go from Here

So where do you go from here? (Well, considering that this is a book about Christianity, there's one place I *won't* tell you to go.) If you're already captivated by the book's prose and consider it a page-turner like the latest Grisham thriller, then please turn the page and continue. But if you have a specific topic that you're eager to dive into, check out the following points of departure:

- ✔ For the basics of Christianity, see Chapters 1 and 3.

- ✔ For an exploration of why Christianity claims to be true, see Chapters 2, 15, and 16.

- ✔ For a discussion of who Jesus Christ is, see Chapter 5.

- ✔ If you've ever read one of those *Left Behind* books and want to make sense of this "End Times" business, see Chapter 9.

- ✔ Want to know what a Protestant or a Catholic believes? Or what an evangelical is? See Chapters 10 and 11.

- ✔ Wonder what it means when some say that Christianity's a personal relationship with God? See Chapters 3 and 13.

- ✔ Let's get practical. How should a Christian live in the 21st century? See Chapters 13 and 14.

Part I

Uncovering What Christianity's All About

The 5th Wave — By Rich Tennant

In this part . . .

*I*f you've ever left your car out in ice or snow, you know that before driving, you first have to scrape off the windshield to have a clear view of the road. This first part helps act as that ice scraper by creating a clear picture of what Christianity is and showing you how the Christian faith compares to other world religions. Here I give you a backdrop on what Christianity claims as truth, so you can delve into the details that I discuss later in this book and understand why Christians do what they do. In that light, this section explores how Christians answer questions about the existence of God and the reliability of the Bible. I also introduce you to that which is responsible for Christianity's existence: the message of God's grace.

Chapter 1

Good News in a Bad News World

*W*hen you click the remote and watch the nightly news broadcast, good news is sure hard to come by. Instead, other people's bad news always seems to take center stage: A burglar steals an elderly couple's life savings, a fire rips through an apartment building, or a hijacked plane crashes in Siberia. You visit the checkout aisle at your local grocery and see that other people's bad news sells tabloids: a celebrity's failed two-week-old marriage, a politician's scandal, or a mystery illness that causes an Olympic gold medalist to grow a second nose.

You and I are inundated with bad news, but it's the yearning for good news that keeps us getting out of bed each day: a marriage proposal, a job promotion, the expectancy of a child or grandchild, the winning ticket of the Super Lotto. Good news not only makes your day, but it also gives you hope and optimism for the future.

Christianity is a faith that's all about good news. The heart of the Christian message is called the *gospel,* which means — you guessed it — the "good news." The Christian faith, therefore, claims to offer meaning and hope to people, not just for a day, but also for all eternity.

So what exactly is this so-called good news that Christianity claims? How is it different from other religions? And if Christianity is supposed to be about good news, why does it seem that so much bad news — scandalous priests, corrupt televangelists, and so on — flows from the Christian Church these days?

In this chapter, you discover the essence of Christianity and how it compares to other world religions. You also explore some popular misconceptions of the Christian faith so that you can discern what Christianity is and is *not.*

Packing Christianity into a Nutshell

Trying to define Christianity in a single sentence is kind of like trying to cram my family's luggage into the back of our minivan when we go on vacation — an impossible task until you start throwing many bags, even seemingly important ones, out the window. I spend this entire book diving into what the Christian faith is, but if I had to pack it into a nutshell, I'd say that Christianity is the belief that God chose to create and love humans, and — at an incredible cost to himself — frees them from a tight spot if only they, in response, choose to reach out for his helping hand.

I dive into the cut-and-dry basics of Christianity later in this chapter, but first I give you the scoop on the whole shebang — from beginning to end (as briefly as possible!) so you know what you're dealing with. So kick back, get a mug of java or tea, and read on for the story of Christianity. (If you want to get to the nitty-gritty, flip ahead to the section, "Understanding how Christians define their faith.")

Going back to the beginning: People choosing, God responding

Christians believe in what they call the one True God, who is perfect, has existed forever, and created the world and all its itty-bitty little creatures (see Chapter 7). But when God created humans, he came up with something extra special; he not only gave people pinky toes and eyebrows, but also the one-of-a-kind gift of *free will* (choice).

God gave people the ability to choose whether to follow him and have a relationship with him or to go our own separate ways. The reason he did this seems pretty obvious to me: Suppose you desired a relationship with a special someone. Would you prefer a person who decidedly picked you out of a crowd, or would you rather have a robot that was programmed to do nothing else? Personally, I prefer the chooser. I often wonder why my wife decided on me, but I won't argue; I'll just enjoy the voluntary, albeit semi-crazy, decision she made. So too, God opted for a humanity with free choice. But when he did so, he took a risk, because people can decide to go their own ways and forget about him.

God made it clear from the get-go that following him meant letting the good times roll, while going against him would be a major bummer for all parties involved — yucky stuff like eternal death and judgment, as I discuss in Chapters 4 and 9.

The first folks to live out this experiment in freedom were Adam and Eve. The couple had some good times with God for a while. But as the Bible talks about in the Book of Genesis, curiosity got the better of them, and they soon wanted to know what it was like doing what they wanted to do instead of what God wanted them to do. They disobeyed God, setting off a chain reaction of disobedience (or *sin*) that has spiraled through every generation since them. See Chapter 4 for more on Adam and Eve's escapade.

When people recognize sin in their lives, their natural response is to try to do something to make up for it. Humans have continually tried to earn God's favor by doing good deeds as a payback (see Chapter 15). Christianity says that payback with God is impossible, though. Think of it like this: Suppose a genie grants you a wish to be transformed into a fish if you want to. Because he asks you in the middle of a heat wave, the idea of being a fish surrounded 24/7 by chilly water sounds really cool, so you take the plunge into the deep blue sea. However, after a long swim and an initial fling with a puffer fish, you decide that the fish's life isn't for you. Your natural response may be to swim upstream to where you initially jumped into the water and hope that somehow that action will reverse the metamorphic process. But no amount of swimming against the current will change you back into a human again. Instead, the genie, by his own initiative, has to change you back.

In the same way, as you see when you read Chapter 3, God had to act on his own initiative to allow some way out of the trap that humans found themselves in. Christianity says that he did this by sending his Son, Jesus Christ (flip to Chapter 5), to take the punishment that is due you and I. In his teaching, Jesus made it clear that the Good News of Christianity is simple: Rather than deal with the bad news of sin, confess your sins and believe in Jesus as Lord and Savior. He wipes your sins clean and gives you eternal life. A single Bible verse sums up his message: "For God so loved the world that he gave his one and only Son, that whoever believes in him shall not perish but have eternal life" (John 3:16).

Understanding how Christians define their faith

If you played a word association game with a sampling of Christians who've been touched by God's gospel and asked them to name a single word or

phrase that sums up Christianity, I suspect you'd get a handful of answers. A few likely candidates are

- ✔ Jesus Christ
- ✔ Grace
- ✔ Truth
- ✔ Life
- ✔ The Bible
- ✔ A transformed life

Each of these words reveals a key aspect of what Christianity's all about. After you begin to paint the terms one on top of another, you begin to see a clearer portrait of the Christian faith.

If you want to understand what true Christianity is, look first and foremost to what the Bible's New Testament says about Jesus. Explore *all* of what Jesus did, said, and taught — not just a couple selected verses. What's more, never look at the actions or words of Christians and conclude that their behavior or attitudes reflect what Christianity is. The Church is often in alignment with Jesus, but as Chapter 15 covers, Christians aren't perfect and make mistakes as well.

Definition #1: Jesus Christ

Christianity is a faith based on the life, teachings, and resurrection of Jesus, a man who lived in Palestine some 2,000 years ago. Jesus claimed to be the Son of God, sent by his Father in heaven to die on the cross for the sins of all humans.

People of other faiths often consider Jesus a good moral teacher, one who preached such memorable principles as "Love your enemies" and "Turn the other cheek." To Christians, however, Jesus isn't just a good teacher. He either was who he said he was — God in human form — or else he was someone who's not trustworthy. Chapter 5 discusses Jesus and the reasons why Christians believe that being merely a good teacher is the one thing that Jesus could never have been.

Definition #2: Grace

You see the word *grace* sprinkled all around the Christian Church — in the song, "Amazing Grace," in church names, such as Grace Baptist Church, and when Christians say "grace" before a meal, to name a few. *Grace* is everywhere. In fact, the New Testament mentions it 123 times.

Christians define *grace* as God's undeserved love shown toward humans. They believe that God's grace is what saves humans through Jesus Christ (see Chapter 3) and enables believers to live a Christian life (see Chapter 14).

Definition #3: Truth

Christians say that their faith isn't just a fairy tale that gives them comfort in times of trouble or blind hope in the midst of tragedy. Rather, they say that Christianity is factual, explaining the way events actually happened in the past, why today is like it is, and what's going to happen in the future. See Chapters 2 and 16 and the "Christianity isn't just a touchy-feely thing" section later in this chapter for more on this subject.

Definition #4: Life

A central teaching of Christianity has always been that life is more than school, marriage, kids, work, 401k's, Florida retirements, and hearing aids. Instead, Christianity claims that every person has an eternal soul that will exist even after his or her earthly body dies. Therefore, those who believe in God's grace through Jesus Christ will have eternal life in heaven and eventually on a new earth, while those who don't will be separated from God forever in hell. As Jesus said, he came so that humans may have life that has meaning, purpose, and joy. See Chapter 9 for more on these life and death matters.

Definition #5: The Bible

Christianity says that God revealed who he is and what his plans are through the written words of the Bible. Christians have historically believed that the Old and New Testaments are the inspired Word of God, are without error in the original writings, and serve as the final authority for the Christian faith. In fact, Christians have traditionally believed that their religion is intricately interwoven with the Bible, so much so that you can't separate them from each other without destroying the fabric of both. See Chapters 2 and 6 for more on the Bible.

Definition #6: A transformed life

When you know a lot about a subject, it's easy to get lost in the details. I can ask a chef about his prize soufflé, and he may bury me with the details of its preparation rather than what I care about — that its taste is to die for! I can ask a Web site developer about her Web site, and she may talk at length about technical aspects of HTML when all I care about is how I can use the site to order books. Or I can ask a theologian about what Christianity is, and he may go off on the particulars of the Nicean Creed, when all I want to know is whether the faith brings peace and joy to life. When the chef, Web site developer, and theologian responded, they were telling me the truth, but I was hoping for something more relevant and tangible.

So, although you explore many aspects of Christian belief throughout this book, don't forget that, for the average Christian, the Good News of Christianity on a practical, everyday level means a *transformed life,* from a life that was empty to a life that has meaning and hope, even when tragedies happen.

Check out Chapters 3, 5, and 13 to discover how Christ changed the lives of people in Bible times as well as those living today in the 21st century.

Being forewarned of stereotypes: What Christianity is not

You get a glimpse of what Christianity is in the preceding sections, but this section helps you take note of several misconceptions about Christianity that permeate popular thought. Some come from people who aren't Christians, while some are from Christians themselves who take Christianity a la carte, emphasizing one part of Christian teaching rather than the entire Christian message.

Consider the following misconceptions that are popular today:

- Christianity is harsh and legalistic.
- Christianity is just about love.
- Christians can't have any fun.
- Christianity is just a European religion.
- Christianity is one of many paths to the same end.
- Christianity is a one-hour-a-week obligation.
- Christianity is a feel-good kick.

I discuss these in the sections that follow.

Christianity isn't just about judgment and condemnation

Because Christianity seeks to change, even kill, the sinful nature, many people have come to think of it as a faith that's based on meeting a certain behavioral standard. And if you don't measure up, then you're going to be judged and condemned.

Movies and TV shows often portray the Church as legalistic and judgmental. Take, for example, the film *Chocolat.* It tells the story of a wandering single mother, Vianne, and her daughter who come to a French village that's

dominated by the Comte de Reynaud, the mayor who has a firm hand on all that goes on in the village and its church. When the mayor learns that Vianne had her child out of wedlock, has no interest in coming to church, and plans to open a chocolate shop during *Lent* (the religious season when Christians traditionally abstain from eating something, such as chocolate), he resolves to run her out of town. The film portrays a stark contrast between the Comte's strict legalism and Vianne's loving grace throughout the movie.

Many undoubtedly identify with *Chocolat*'s depiction of the Church. Perhaps you even grew up in a church like that. Yet, the irony is that, in watching the film, Jesus would be one to identify with the character of Vianne, *not* the mayor. After all, in many ways, the religious leaders of his day looked upon Jesus in the exact same way as the Comte looked upon Vianne.

Throughout history, strands of the Church have had this tendency to slip into legalism. However, this attitude isn't unique to Christianity. When you look at any religion, you find a similar portion of its followers stressing regulation and conformity to an expected standard, looking down on or being suspicious of those who don't live up to the rules. Ironically, even those who profess no religion at all sometimes fall into this legalism trap, criticizing those who believe differently than they do.

Jesus often battled with the *Pharisees*, the Jewish leaders of his day, over these very issues. Time and time again, Jesus made the point that the Pharisees cared more about rules than people and were preoccupied with obeying legal principles rather than loving others.

As you discover in Chapters 3 and 9, Christianity doesn't ignore judgment of sins, but biblical Christianity is a faith for the Viannes of the world, not the Comtes and the Pharisees (although they can be forgiven, too).

Christianity isn't just about love

Another extreme is the tendency to think of Christianity as being all about love — period. End of Story. Using 1 John 4:8 ("God is love") as the mantra, some people proclaim that because God is love, any talk of judgment, punishment, or hell is bogus.

Certainly one of Jesus' key teachings was to love others. And he backed up what he preached by loving the outcasts and the down-and-out of his day. At the same time, love isn't all he spoke about. He also talked a lot about sin and holiness, as I discuss in Chapter 5.

The God of Christianity is a God of love *and* holiness (see Chapter 7). People have always had a hard time trying to grasp the balance between the two, which is why some people tend to focus on holiness and justice and forget about love. Others dwell on love and forget about God's holy nature. But, as Chapter 5 discusses, Jesus walked the tightrope between these two extremes.

Christianity doesn't mean "no fun"

Christians are often portrayed as being "sticks in the mud," or people who want to suck all the fun and happiness out of life. However, biblical Christianity says the opposite — that God is the one who created fun, a sense of humor, wonderful food and drink, sex, and adventure.

Popular culture today says that excess — food, alcohol, sex, or whatever — means fun. In contrast, Christianity says that "more" initially seems liberating, but it ultimately ensnares and dehumanizes you, making you a slave to physical desire rather than allowing you to maintain control over yourself through your mind and will. Or to quote from the popular film *Sabrina*, "More isn't always better; sometimes it's just more."

Christianity insists that in order for these activities to be fun for you now *and* in the long run, you must do them in the right context and with the right amount. Consider, for example, the yeast that goes into a loaf of bread. Because yeast is the active ingredient, thinking that the more yeast you put into the batter, the better the bread will be is only natural. But, as any cook can tell you, you only spoil the loaf by doubling the yeast. Tasty bread features just the right amount of yeast put into the batter at the appropriate time.

Christianity isn't just a white man's religion

Some people think of Christianity as a European or "white man's" religion. Although Europe has played a key role in the history of the Christian Church over the past two thousand years, don't confuse Europe's role as catalyst with being the original source. Jesus was a Jewish carpenter, a Middle Easterner who never set foot in Europe or the United States. The early Church consisted of people from across the Mediterranean region — Palestine, North Africa, Asia, and Italy. As you discover in Chapter 10, it was only a couple hundred years later that Europe started to play a dominant role in leading the Church. Obviously, Europe was a torchbearer of the Christian faith for more than 1,500 years, but the winds of change continue as the 21st century unfolds. As I discuss in the "Putting It into Perspective: Christianity in the World Today" section of this chapter, the majority of Christians are now from the developing nations of Africa, Latin America, and Asia.

Christianity's not a religion?

An expression that has become popular over the past 30 years is "Christianity is a relationship, not a religion." The notion that Christianity is *not* a religion may seem perplexing or even ridiculous to many. If you think of *religion* as referring to a belief system about God and the world around you, then Christianity most certainly does match that definition. But Christians who speak this phrase are referring to a popular understanding of *religion* that means a set of rules that one has to follow to gain approval from God. In this sense, people may consider Christianity an anti-religion, because by its nature, Christianity affirms that humans can't do anything to be approved by God. Instead, it's only by his grace that people are saved.

Jesus spoke against this notion of an earn-your-way religion to the people of his day. Instead, he talked of faith as an intimate relationship with him and his Father in heaven.

Christianity isn't just one of many paths to the same end

Many people treat religions as essentially being the same — as different paths to the same destination. However, each of the major world religions holds fundamentally different, mutually exclusive claims about who God is and what's true. However, they can't all be true without "dumbing down" God into some kind of being who constantly bends to meet the fancies of any human belief.

What's more, from a Christian perspective, the Jesus of the Bible didn't allow for that "all roads lead to heaven" belief. On many occasions, he made it clear that the only way to God is through him and him alone. Most notably, in John 14:6, he said, "I am the way, the truth, and the life. No one comes to the Father, except through me." See Chapter 15 for more on this hot potato topic.

Christianity isn't just an hour-long obligation

To some, Christianity means going to church for an hour once a week. Although the Bible does call Christians to come together and worship God once a week, Christianity is more than just an obligation or an idea that affects life only on weekends. Instead, biblical Christianity is meant to be lived out 24/7 and should impact the way Christians think about every part of their lives and the world around them. Jesus didn't water down his message at all to his would-be followers. He didn't say, "Give me your spare change and a couple hours during the week." Instead, he said, "If any man would come after me, let him deny himself, and take up his cross, and follow me" (Mark 8:34). See Chapter 13 for what his call means on a practical level.

Christianity isn't just a touchy-feely thing

Many people think of Christianity, or any religious faith for that matter, as an emotional tool, which Christians turn to in times of trouble. The thought is: "Hey, if it helps you, great." However, Christianity claims that it's not that kind of religion. Instead, Christianity claims to be a historical faith, directly tied to real space-and-time history. Given that, it's either literally true and far more than a feel-good kick, or false and therefore not worth investing your emotions in. (See Chapters 2 and 16 for more on this subject.)

Making Sense of Christian Paradoxes

The film *Catch Me If You Can* tells the real-life story of Frank Abagnale, Jr., a teenager who impersonates an airline pilot, a doctor, and a lawyer and extorts more than $4 million — all before his 20th birthday. If I were to write a movie with such a plot line, I'd be laughed out of Hollywood for coming up with such an unrealistic story. Indeed, truth is often stranger than fiction.

The Christian faith is strange like this, because so many of its teachings are so contrary to human expectations. It's true: Christianity is filled with paradoxes that go against the grain of your natural line of thinking — you expect one thing, but get blindsided by another. Consider the following examples:

- ✔ **God is love, but he requires justice.** The Christian God is all-loving, but he still will punish those who don't come to him.

- ✔ **God is one God, but three "persons."** Talk about confusing — the idea of the Trinity is surely the most difficult concept to grasp in all of Christianity. God is one God, but reveals himself in three "persons" — the Father, Son, and Holy Spirit. Chapter 7 explores this mind-bending topic.

- ✔ **God is fully in control, but humans have free choice.** The Bible makes it clear that God is all-powerful and is actively engaged in this world, but at the same time, allows people to have the freedom to make their own decisions and be responsible for the decisions they make.

- ✔ **Jesus was fully God and fully man.** Core to the Christian belief is that Jesus was a man who walked on the earth and who was both fully God and fully man. Confused? Flip to Chapter 5.

- ✔ **God is all-powerful, but he died for humans.** Because Jesus was fully God, it follows then that God — in the person of Jesus Christ — literally died for humanity. How can an infinite, eternal God die? And why did he do it? See Chapter 3 for more on this paradox.

✔ **Humans can't earn their way to heaven by being good.** A key Christian belief goes against the rugged individualistic fabric of culture today. It says that you can't pull yourself up by your own bootstraps (go on over to Chapter 15 for more). In other words, being a good person or keeping the Ten Commandments (see Exodus 34) won't help you earn God's favor and get you into heaven. Instead, it's God's grace alone that saves you, not yourself (go to Chapter 3 for the lowdown on grace).

✔ **The Church is full of sinners.** To some, the fact that Christians can't seem to live out their faith consistently is grounds for dismissing the truth of the Christian faith. Yet, ironically, the sin in a Christian's life only serves to underscore a core part of Christian teaching — that all people have and will continue to sin as long as they live on this earth. See Chapter 15 for a full discussion on this subject.

Ironically, these paradoxes of the Christian faith serve to underscore its truth. As C.S. Lewis once said, "Reality, in fact, is usually something you could not have guessed. That is one of the reasons why I believe Christianity. It is a religion you could not have guessed" (*Mere Christianity*, Harper San Francisco, 2001).

Understanding How the Branches of the Church Came About

Most every human organization has groupings within it. Corporations have divisions and branches. Pro football divides its teams into two conferences, while professional baseball has two separate leagues. Professional wrestling probably has some kind of division to it as well, but I was too scared to ask.

The Christian Church is no different. Although it started out as a unified entity and remained so for a thousand years, geography and doctrinal differences eventually caused a split in A.D. 1054 between the Western Church (Catholic) centered in Rome and the Eastern Church (Orthodox) centered in Constantinople. Then, nearly five hundred years later, the Protestant Reformation caused a new group, called the Protestants, to emerge from the Catholic Church. These three major divisions of the Church — Catholic, Protestant, and Orthodox — remain to this day.

Protestants further divide into many different denominations; some of the most notable are Lutheran, Baptist, Methodist, Presbyterian, and Anglican. Although these denominations agree on the major issues of the Protestant Reformation, they've tended to divide based on differences in doctrine and perspectives on how churches should be structured and governed.

The Catholic Church is the largest of the three major branches in the world, while the Protestant Church is the largest segment in North America (though it too is dispersed throughout the world). The Orthodox (Eastern) Church is more geographically oriented, being dominant in Greece, Russia, and parts of Eastern Europe and less elsewhere. You find out all about the Catholic and Orthodox Churches in Chapter 10 and about the Protestants in Chapter 11.

Putting It into Perspective: Christianity in the World Today

Binoculars are handy when you want to gaze upon a distant object, but you don't hold them up to your face as you drive a car or walk down the street. If you did, you'd end up hitting a tree or stepping into a mud puddle. Instead, before using a pair of binoculars, it often helps to first stop, scan the landscape, and then use the binoculars to center on what you want to see more clearly. Similarly, before you look closely at the Christian faith in the rest of this book, take a step back and put Christianity into a larger perspective.

Focusing on facts about the faith

Christianity originated with Jesus Christ some 2,000 years ago and remains a growing faith in the world today. To help you understand Christianity's role in the world, consider some of these facts about the faith:

- **Christianity is the largest religion in the world.** In terms of raw numbers, Christianity is the world's largest religion, with more than 1.9 billion people professing faith, or 33 percent of the world's population. Islam is next, with 22 percent, followed by Hinduism (15 percent), non-religious (14 percent), Buddhism (6 percent), and Judaism (0.5 percent) (www.adherents.com, 2002). Check out the section, "Relating Christianity to other world faiths," later in this chapter, to see the major differences among these religions.

- **The developing world, including Africa, Latin America, and Asia, has more Christians than North America and Europe do.** As I discuss in the section, "Being forewarned of stereotypes: What Christianity is not," earlier in the chapter, people sometimes consider Christianity a European religion. But, more and more, Christianity has truly become a world religion, spread out fairly evenly over all the continents: Europe holds 29 percent of all Christians, followed by Latin America (23 percent), Africa (18 percent), Asia (16 percent), North America (13 percent), and

Oceania (1 percent) (www.zpub.com, 1995). Although many people think of North America as the major hotbed for Christian activity over the past 150 years, it's interesting to note that Africa now has more Christians than the United States and Canada combined.

✔ **More than 8 out of 10 Americans classify themselves as Christians.** According to Barna Research, in 2002, 85 percent of Americans identified themselves as Christians. Further, 40 percent of Americans label themselves "evangelical" or "born-again" Christians.

✔ **Not all Christians live biblical Christian lives.** Being from Massachusetts, if I were asked what baseball team I support, I'd respond that I'm a Boston Red Sox fan. However, because baseball is one of my least favorite sports, I've never been to a Red Sox game nor do I even follow the team in the newspapers. At best, I try to act like I know what I'm talking about when my buddies discuss the Red Sox's chances of winning the World Series.

Truth be told, many of the 85 percent of the Americans who identify themselves as Christians do so in the same way I call myself a Red Sox fan. Therefore, in order to prevent being misled by statistics, recognize the distinction between the season ticket holders (firmly committed Christians) and the fair-weather fans (those who make their faith as much a part of their life as the Sox are of mine).

Relating Christianity to other world faiths

An outsider may look at the world's religions and conclude that they're all pretty much the same. But those who profess faith in one of these religions would beg to differ. Keep reading to find out how Christianity relates to the other dominant world faiths:

✔ **Judaism:** Christianity is most closely tied to Judaism. In fact, Christians share a common legacy and heritage with Jews (check out Chapter 10 for the lowdown). Moreover, Jesus — the very reason the Christian faith exists — was a Jew.

Both Jews and Christians believe in the Old Testament teachings of the Bible (Jews call this part the Hebrew Bible or the *Tanakh*) and proclaim people like Noah, Abraham, Moses, and David as pillars of their faith. Their paths split, however, with Jesus Christ. Throughout the Old Testament, the authors refer to and prophesy of a coming *Messiah* (meaning Savior) that will save the Jews (and non-Jews as well). Christians believe that Jesus was this Savior, while Jews believe that their Messiah hasn't yet come.

✔ **Islam:** Islam is the other major *monotheistic* (believing in one God) religion in the world. *Muslims* (believers of Islam) say that Allah is the same God as that of Jews and Christians. However, unlike Christians, Muslims don't believe in a Trinity (see Chapter 7). Instead of Jesus being the Son of God like the Christians believe, Muslims say that he was just a prophet and wasn't crucified (Qur'an 4:157). They also believe that the prophet Muhammad, who lived in the seventh century, was the greatest prophet sent by Allah.

Islam says that people gain salvation by observing the Five Pillars of Islam: professing the statement of belief, praying daily while facing *Mecca* (the most holy city of Islam), giving to the poor, fasting during *Ramadan* (the holy month), and making a pilgrimage to Mecca.

✔ **Hinduism and Buddhism:** Chances are that if you encounter someone who claims to be a Hindu or a Buddhist in the West, he or she practices a pantheistic religion. Instead of having the belief in God as Creator and distinct from the world, *pantheistic* religions, while different from each other in their own right, claim that the world is actually identical with God. In Hinduism, for example, God is really *Brahman,* or the ultimate power underlying the universe. Everything comes from Brahman and everything eventually returns to it.

The differences in belief between Christianity and pantheistic religions are great. For example, if God is in everything, then it follows that God is in both good and evil, rather than separate from it. Therefore, "good" and "evil" become relative, even illusionary terms. Additionally, while Judaism, Christianity, and Islam focus on a written Word of God given to man, pantheistic religions tend to focus on private mystical experiences instead.

✔ **Christian-related religions:** A final group of religions is made up of Christian-related faiths that differ from historical and biblical Christianity. These groups include Mormons (the Church of Latter Day Saints), Jehovah's Witnesses, and Christian Scientists. Although non-Christians sometimes consider them part of the Christian Church, most Christians stress the major differences in belief between these groups and traditional historical Christianity.

Table 1-1 shows a summary of beliefs of these various religions.

Table 1-1					
		Summary of Religious Beliefs			
Faith Group	*Who Is Jesus?*	*What Is God's Nature?*	*What Is God's Written Word?*	*Problem of Man*	*How Is One Saved?*
Christianity	Fully human, fully God	Trinity (one God in three persons)	Bible (Old and New Testaments)	Sin	Accepting God's grace
Judaism	Just a man	One God	Hebrew Bible or Tanakh (same as Christianity's Old Testament)	Sin	Observance of the law
Islam	Just a man, a prophet	One God (Allah)	Qur'an	Sin	Following Five Pillars of Islam
Hinduism	Just a man	Brahman (part of the world)	N/A	Ignorance	Goal isn't heaven, but to be absorbed into Brahman
Buddhism	Just a man	No personal God exists	N/A	Suffering	Enlightenment is needed, not salvation
Mormonism	Fully human, fully God	Three Gods and three distinct personalities	Book of Mormon, Doctrine and Covenants, Pearl of Great Price, Bible	Sin	Good works and merit
Jehovah's Witnesses	A man	One God (not a Trinity)	Bible and additional teachings	Sin	144,000 Jehovah's Witnesses are specially anointed in heaven, the rest of Jehovah's Witnesses earn eternal life on earth (no belief in hell for non-members)
Christian Science	God, but not a real man	One God (not a Trinity)	*Science and Health with Key to the Scriptures* by Mary Baker Eddy, miscellaneous writings, Manual of the Mother Church	Sin	Everyone will be saved; no final judgment

Chapter 2

Christianity: But Is It True?

● ●

In This Chapter

▶ Getting a grip on apologetics

▶ Considering whether one ultimate God exists

▶ Seeing how Christianity coexists with "real life"

▶ Digging up the historical roots of the Christian faith

● ●

I'm a PK (a preacher's kid). Growing up, I learned about the Christian faith from my parents and church, and I became a born-again Christian at an early age. The question of whether Christianity was valid didn't enter into my mind at that point; I just accepted it as true because that's what I was taught. When I entered college, however, I started to reevaluate my faith and ask myself, "Is Christianity *really* true?" After all, an awful lot of smart people don't believe in God, much less in Christianity.

Today, as I look back at that time in my life, I realize that the honest questioning I did as a college freshman was the crucial turning point of my life, transforming my squishy lump of unformed beliefs into a solid steel–equipped faith, ready for a lot of stormy weather. When I actually started to look under the hood of Christianity and ask hard questions, I realized that Christianity not only satisfies my spiritual and emotional needs, but also my intellectual needs.

In this chapter, I survey several important claims to truth that Christianity makes and help demonstrate the idea that what the rest of this book covers is more than just fancy or wishful thinking. I explain how Christians respond to questions about the existence of God, the relationship between faith and reason, and the historical reliability of Christianity's claims.

Throughout this book, I address further topics that deal with Christianity's claims of truth. Be sure to check out the following:

✔ For a discussion on the belief that Jesus rose from the dead, see Chapter 5.

✔ To explore why Christianity claims to present the only way to God, see Chapter 15.

     ✔ To assess whether Christian faith and Darwinian evolution are compatible, see Chapter 16.

     ✔ For an exploration of whether absolutes are necessary in a relative world, see Chapter 16.

Defending the Faith Through Apologetics

The term *Christian apologetics* may sound like a description of a very sorry and pathetic-looking group of churchgoers, but it actually refers to the study and practice of demonstrating the truth of Christianity. In this context, the word *apologetic* isn't sorry at all, but originates from the Greek word *apologia,* which means "defense."

Like any religion or belief explaining the world, not everything that's part of Christianity can be proven — it requires faith to believe in the unseen. But don't take that to mean that you should simply throw evidence out the window. On the contrary, although facts and logic don't explain everything, Christians believe they work hand-in-hand to support the faith's claims to truth. That's why Christians work across a spectrum of fields — science, archaeology, philosophy, history, and more — to provide a solid intellectual basis for the Christian faith.

Apologetics often deals with one of the most basic questions of all: Does God exist? I discuss this issue in the next section.

Exploring Whether God Exists

Certainly, one of the most hotly contested issues throughout history is whether a God exists or whether humans are on their own. Although no one can definitively prove or disprove God's existence, Christians consider several aspects in order to make an informed decision. In this section, I provide a snapshot of the many debates that rage in this arena.

If you want to look further into this topic, check out the resources available on my Web site at www.digitalwalk.net.

The world appears to be intelligently designed

On a vacation in Colorado a few years ago, I gazed upon the brilliant sun as it made its slow, swooping descent toward the purple mountain skyline. The

sunset was drop-dead gorgeous, and in my amazement, I remember saying to myself, "Who can deny that a God created this?" Later, when my first child was born, I uttered a similar line as I held my 7-pound, 14-ounce miracle in my arms. I'm certainly not alone in experiencing these thoughts when confronted with the wonders of this world. This kind of intuitive belief or "gut feeling" is enough to convince many that a God who created the earth and its inhabitants really exists.

This intuition-based claim is similar to the *teleological argument,* a theory to prove God's existence that William Paley originally put forth back in the 19th century. Paley argued that if you found a watch when you were on a walk through the woods, you could quickly size up the object and conclude that such a highly engineered piece of equipment didn't just bud on a nearby maple tree. The logical conclusion is that the watch wasn't formed by accident, but was designed and constructed by an intelligent being. After establishing this idea, Paley told his students to back up and look at the universe — like the watch, its engineering is so complex, precise, and ingenious that it screams out evidence for a designer.

Although this argument is logical and can be compelling, it doesn't convince everyone. An atheist looks at the same sunset or the same human birth and sees these incidents as nothing more than evolution in action. Ultimately, the intuitive argument helps confirm suspicions you have toward believing in God, but doesn't often change a diehard skeptic's mind.

However, a second, more compelling argument goes beyond mere intuition and says that not only does the world appear to be designed, but correct science cries out that there *must* be a designer. For example, in his critically-acclaimed book *Darwin's Black Box* (Free Press, 1998), biochemist Michael Behe argues that evolution can't sufficiently explain the complexity of organisms. Darwin insisted that evolution occurred through a series of small steps that transformed simple structures into complex ones. Yet, the more scientists discover about the complexity of cells, the more they realize the practical impossibility of them developing gradually. (See Chapter 16 for more on Behe's arguments against Darwinian evolution.)

People (most, anyway) can think and reason

A second argument that Christians hold up as proof that God exists is what goes on in that noggin of yours and mine. The fact that people have the ability to think in a logical and rational manner is explainable only by claiming the existence of God as designer and creator. Okay, I admit, not all people think rationally, but for the sake of argument, let's keep the discussion using you and me as examples . . . okay, you.

A faith-filled atheist?

A step of faith isn't unique to Christianity. Every religion, theory, or system of belief that attempts to explain the world requires *faith* — believing in something that can't fully be proven. At first glance, you may think an atheist is exempt from this rule, but that's not true. An atheist has faith, all right — not in a divine God, but in the belief that God doesn't exist.

The fact is that people reason — no one can deny that. Therefore, God either created people with the unique ability to think, or else reason developed on its own. But believing that people acquired rational thought in small steps through natural selection reduces people's ability to reason to nothing more than a biological process. In his book *Mere Christianity* (Harper San Francisco, 2001), C.S. Lewis points out the problem in this line of thinking by comparing human reason to human eyesight. Your vision is far more helpful and useful to you than the vision of a single-celled organism that's sensitive to light but doesn't have eyes to see. Now, suppose you give that cute little creature a set of eyes and throw in a pair of eyeglasses to boot. In doing so, you would enable the organism to see better, but you wouldn't bring it any closer to an intellectual understanding of what light is. Remember, it's not scientists with really good eyes who are experts in light. Instead, it's the ones who've specialized in the related sciences. From this perspective, trying to fit human reason into an evolutionary process is like trying to watch a 3-D film without wearing those funny-looking glasses — everything important is lost in the process.

People instinctively sense right and wrong

Regardless of culture, religion, or walk of life, every person has an impression of right and wrong. Whether liberal or conservative, evolutionist or creationist, pro-choice or pro-life, "less filling" or "tastes great," everyone appeals to some sort of standard that he or she expects others to know and follow. In the political realm, for example, liberals uphold tolerance while conservatives focus on personal accountability, but the key is that both groups point to some standard that they believe is right. But step back and ask yourself: Why do people have this sense of right and wrong, a "little voice" inside them that guides them and brings outrage when they see someone violate that standard?

To Christians, Christianity provides a credible answer to the mystery of that little voice inside of you and I. It says that this awareness is from God, whose very nature (ultimate righteousness) sets the standard (see Chapter 7 for more on the Christian understanding of God's nature). When he created people, he gave a conscience to guide humans and let them know when they stray from that end.

A must-read: *Mere Christianity*

In the very act of trying to prove that God did not exist — in other words, that the whole of reality was senseless — I found I was forced to assume that one part of reality — namely my idea of justice — was full of sense. Consequently atheism turns out to be too simple. If the whole universe has no meaning, we should never have found out that it has no meaning: just as, if there were no light in the universe and therefore no creatures with eyes, we should never know it was dark. "Dark" would be without meaning.

—C.S. Lewis, *Mere Christianity* (Harper San Francisco, 2001)

Mere Christianity by C.S. Lewis is a witty, persuasive, common sense–based account of the basics of Christian doctrine and the logic of the faith. Lewis was an atheist and set out to disprove Christianity only to become a Christian in the process. Early in my Christian walk, I often wrestled with intellectual doubts about my faith; more than anything else, *Mere Christianity* was the means that transformed my faith into a rock solid belief system.

This idea of right and wrong poses problems for people who don't believe in God, because they allow nothing apart from the human race to back their standards. They may sincerely believe that morality is based on each individual's personal decision, but this belief is out of step with how people actually live — everyone holds others up to some sort of a standard that they adhere to.

 If you're skeptical, consider a test: Try cutting in line at the supermarket. The first time you do it, politely explain to the person you cut in front of that you're sorry, but you've got a sick child at home and you simply must get cough syrup to her as soon as possible. In this case, most people will be glad to help out and aren't bothered by the inconvenience. However, try cutting in line a second time, but this time be rude and aggressive when you do so, offering a sneer rather than an explanation. I guarantee the person you cut in front of will be outraged, and his anger will run deeper than the inconvenience you're causing. Your rude action crosses a line in his mind over what's acceptable and unacceptable behavior. Yet, without a God who gives us an idea of right and wrong, your belief that line-cutting is okay isn't morally different from his belief that first come should be first served. (See Chapter 16 for more on the shortcomings of the belief that truth is relative.)

Demonstrating Christianity as a Livable Faith

In order to be credible, any belief system that attempts to explain the world must be in line with known historical and scientific facts and provide answers to the big questions of life without contradicting itself. But it must also be

consistent with how life is actually lived out in the real world. Any theory can look good on paper, but if you can't live it out, then it's not worth more than the paper it's written on. Christians say that their faith not only has facts and consistent logic on its side, but is livable as well. Two examples are as follows:

✔ **Christianity gives life meaning.** At some point in life, everyone — atheists, Christians, and Buddhists alike — grapples with the issue of finding meaning in life. Teenagers often go through a time of "soul searching" as they contemplate what they should do with their lives. When middle age looms, people often deal with a mid-life crisis in a desperate attempt to find meaning in a life that is already half spent. Christians believe that God designed people to have an instinctive need to find meaning — to enable humans to ultimately search and find him through this process. Even the most outspoken skeptics in history have struggled with finding meaning in their lives. Although some sincerely believe that people are nothing more than machines, their quest for meaning betrays that claim.

✔ **Christianity meets people's deepest need for grace.** Although other religions focus on people's ability to reach God through their own effort, Christianity is unique in saying that humans can't reach God through their own means, but require God to do the work for us. From a Christian perspective, the quest for salvation by our own doing ultimately proves to be just like Sisyphus, the mythological Greek character who the gods forever condemned to roll a rock to the top of a mountain, only to have the stone always fall back due to its own weight. Because people can never measure up to the standard that their conscience holds them to, people need help, as hard as it is for them to admit it. In this light, Christianity's offer of grace is liberating in a way that nothing else is. Grace, which I discuss fully in Chapter 3, meets people's deepest spiritual needs and frees us from the Sisyphus-like effort of trying to be good when we do bad things most every day.

Is real life like *The Truman Show*?

In the film *The Truman Show*, Jim Carrey stars as Truman Burbank, a thirty-something man who doesn't realize that his whole life is a non-stop television show and has been ever since the day he was born. At one point, an interviewer asked Christoff, the creator and director of the show, why he thought Truman took so long to figure the secret out. Christoff replied, "We accept the reality of the world with which we are presented."

Christoff's remark seems to describe the way most people deal with life's big issues — accepting what's given to them without too much bother. People grow up either believing or rejecting what their parents taught them (for reasons that often have nothing to do with whether they thought the teaching was true or not), go off to school and usually accept what they learn as fact, and then get on with building a career and raising a family.

In this hustle-bustle world that never sleeps, it's easy to remain distracted for decades with work, kids, exercise routines, TV, the Internet, sports, and vacations. Yes, people do experience angst about death and yearn to lead meaningful lives, but most tend to put off dealing with such matters until they're hit smack dab in the face with them. Occasionally, a tragedy like 9/11 comes along, causing people to reprioritize and think of life-and-death matters . . . for a while. But unless the tragedy personally affects you, the normal grind of life gradually steers you back onto autopilot like you were before. Frankly, unless you deliberately work at it, modern life doesn't promote a serious investigation of much of anything.

But when it comes to the big issues, the most important question that people should ask about what they believe is: "But is it true?" Ultimately, when all is said and done, a "yes" answer to that question is all that matters.

Retracing Christianity as a Historical Faith

The Christian faith isn't an obscure belief system with Jesus as a mythological figure. Rather, Christianity is based entirely on real space-time history; in the words of Francis Schaeffer, its central figure is an actual man who "hung on a cross in the sense that, if you were there that day, you could have rubbed your finger on the cross and got a splinter on it" (*The God Who Is There,* InterVarsity Press, 1968). Therefore, when you consider the Christian faith, you also have to examine its historical claims of truth.

Examining artifacts

Archaeologists, historians, and other researchers have closely scrutinized the historical events of Jesus' life and the Bible as a whole and continue to do so. Although some skeptical archaeologists have been quick to discount historical accounts of the Bible, particularly the Old Testament, actual findings have proven that they're credible. In fact, a century of archaeological discoveries underscores the fact that the more evidence that researchers unearth in the Holy Land, the more the biblical record becomes authenticated.

The Dead Sea Scrolls are arguably the most significant discovery in many centuries. This collection of 500 scrolls and scroll fragments was accidentally discovered in 1947 by a shepherd in a series of caves along the Dead Sea.

These scrolls were written in a period between 250 B.C. and A.D. 68 and provide amazing insights into the practices and beliefs of the Qumram Community, a particular group of Jews who lived during this timeframe. The scrolls include a variety of documents, including: a complete manuscript of the Book of Isaiah and parts of Exodus, Leviticus, Numbers, and Deuteronomy; commentaries on several Old Testament books (such as Habakkuk, Job, Isaiah, and Micah); non-canonical books; and a Qumram manual of conduct and other community-related documents. Although the scrolls are Jewish and not Christian, they nonetheless serve to underscore the reliability of the Old Testament scriptures and have helped scholars reconstruct the history of Israel and the Holy Land area between 300 B.C. and A.D. 135.

Perhaps the most sensationalized discovery since the Dead Sea Scrolls is a first-century limestone box designed to hold a deceased person's bones. This bones box (or *ossuary*) has an Aramaic inscription carved on the side that says, "James, son of Joseph, brother of Jesus." (See Matthew 13:55, 1 Corinthians 15:7, and Acts 15 for references to James in the Bible.) The possibility exists that this bones box actually contains the bones of James, the brother of Jesus Christ. Skeptics don't even argue strongly against this, because it would've been unusual to add "brother of [so-and-so]" unless that brother was well-known. So, chances are that this wasn't just any random Jesus, but was indeed Jesus Christ. Experts continue to examine the artifact to determine its authenticity, but if it were proven to be authentic, this box would be the oldest nonbiblical, nonliterary reference to Jesus that has ever been recovered.

Documenting history in the Bible

The Christian faith is based on the life, death, and resurrection of Jesus Christ. But because it's been some 2,000 years since Jesus walked on this earth, Christians face a problem: First-century Palestine didn't have CNN or the *New York Times* to refer to in order to gather archival details on the life and teachings of Jesus. As a result, Christians today are more than a little dependent on the events, eyewitness testimonies, and teachings recorded in the New Testament.

It follows that an essential factor in determining whether Christianity is true is examining the reliability of the New Testament. Although the whole Bible is important to examine, the New Testament is particularly critical to Christianity because it provides the historical accounts of Jesus Christ's death and resurrection as well as the complete written teaching of the early Church. Is the New Testament accurate history, something that would make a good journalist proud? Or is it nothing but a compilation of first-century tabloid tales rejected by the *National Enquirer*?

In order to determine the New Testament's reliability, one must explore two questions:

✔ Are the ancient manuscripts reliable?

✔ Are the New Testament authors' testimonies legit?

I address these questions in the two sections that follow.

Evaluating the reliability of New Testament manuscripts

Christians believe that the apostles and early Church leaders, after several years of sharing with others around them the Good News of Jesus Christ, realized that they had to do more than communicate verbally (see the sidebar, "Before the Internet existed: Communication in the ancient days"). They needed to document a full written account of Jesus' life and his teachings to reach people they couldn't get to because of geographical limitations and to reach those who would live in the future. Two of Jesus' disciples (Matthew and John) and two others (who had direct access to the disciples and other eyewitnesses) wrote individual accounts of Jesus' life (called *Gospels*). During this same era, the apostles also put Christian teachings into writing and distributed them as letters to different churches across the Mediterranean region. These letters, written by Paul, Peter, and other apostles (see the section, "Assessing New Testament authors' credibility," later in this chapter), fill in the cracks on Christian teachings that the Gospels and Acts, a book that records the history of the early Church, don't discuss. All together, 27 books form the New Testament.

Obviously, the writers couldn't just print the books out on their inkjet printers and then run to the nearest copy shop to buy 1,000 collated copies of their work in shiny plastic spiral binders. The New Testament writers had to write the accounts on *papyrus,* a paper-like material that's even more prone to deteriorate than that cheap recycled stuff I buy at a discount at the local office supply store. And in order to preserve and distribute an original manuscript like this, the early Church had to make copies of these originals the old-fashioned way: one copy at a time.

The people who did this work were known as *scribes,* and based on accounts of them, they were a special breed of people. Think of them as accountants on steroids: mind-bogglingly exact in transcribing an original to a duplicate. They made sure that every letter, word, and syllable was kept intact from the original to the copy. And, rumor has it that if a coffee stain or jelly smudge marked the original, they'd purposely spill on the new copy as well. (Okay, I made that part up, but you get the idea.)

The scribes' attention to detail is crucially important to Christians today, because the original manuscripts of the New Testament books no longer exist — at least any that people know about. On first take, that news seems unsettling, because it means that the Christian faith isn't just reliant on the

original testimony of the apostles, but on *copies* of that testimony. However, before you call the Gideons and tell them to stop distributing their Bibles at Motel 6, consider this: To historians, this is standard fare when looking at documents from the ancient world, whether they're parts of the Old Testament (see the section, "Examining artifacts," earlier in this chapter) or New Testament or are the writings of Plato and Homer.

Because the original writings don't exist anymore, you examine the reliability of the manuscripts by looking at

- ✔ The number of copies that exist
- ✔ The time gap between when the original was written and when the first known copy was made

I discuss these factors in this section. For the lowdown on how the Church decided which manuscripts made it into the Bible, check out Chapter 6.

Considering how many New Testament copies exist

Imagine you're mistakenly put on trial for shoplifting at a luxury clothing store in Hollywood. Although you claim innocence, the store manager is intent on setting an example and wants you locked away for good. During the trial, you have a single eyewitness who testifies that the shoplifter wasn't you, but was actually a well-known film actress. The statement may help your case, but reality bites, and a lone witness may not be enough to convince the jury. But suppose your lawyer brings to the stand several thousand witnesses all proclaiming your innocence. In this scenario, you'd have the jury deciding in your favor quicker than you can say "Beetlejuice." Clearly, then, the more witnesses you have testifying on your behalf, the more credible you sound.

This principle carries over when you examine ancient manuscripts. If you have just two copies of an original document that are quite different, then it's hard to know which was transcribed by Mr. Xerox and which was written by a John Grisham wannabe who simply wanted a creative outlet. However, if you have thousands of copies, all of which are consistent with each other, then you have a very strong indicator of what was in the original manuscript. Therefore, the general rule is that the more copies of an ancient manuscript you have, the more you're able to check them against each other to determine their accuracy.

More than 5,600 Greek manuscripts contain parts or all of the New Testament, an amount far beyond that of any other ancient book. In comparison, only 600 copies of Homer's *Iliad* and a mere 7 copies of Plato's writings exist. What's more, when you cross-check these New Testament manuscripts and compare the results with other ancient writings, the accuracy of the New Testament manuscripts is nearly perfect, word for word — much more accurate than the

copies of these other writings. For example, Bible scholar Bruce Metzger compared the New Testament to Homer's *Iliad* and the *Mahabharata,* a Hindu scripture that's sometimes referred to as the Hindu Bible. Check out his findings in Table 2-1. As you see from this investigation, only 40 lines of the entire 20,000-line New Testament are questionable. The only passages in doubt are John 7:53–8:11 and Mark 16:9–20. Therefore, if you leave those two passages out, then all the New Testament manuscripts are in total harmony.

Table 2-1	Comparing the Accuracy of Ancient Manuscripts		
Book	**Total Lines**	**Conflicting Lines**	**Accuracy**
Hindu Mahabharata	Approx. 260,000	26,000	90%
Homer's *Iliad*	15,600	764	95%
New Testament	20,000	40	99.98%

Source: Bruce Metzger, Chapters in New Testament Textual Criticism (E. J. Brill, 1963)

Measuring the gap between original manuscripts and copies

A second critical issue when exploring the reliability of the New Testament is the time gap between when a document was originally written and when the first known copy was made. Obviously, the shorter the gap, the more reliable a manuscript is.

Before the Internet existed: Communication in the ancient days

I'm admittedly spoiled by the wealth of information that's available all around me. I've got a library of books in my study, the Internet at my fingertips, an MP3 player on my belt, and a television and DVD player in the next room. If you need any type of written, visual, or audio information, give me a sec and I'll get it for you. Consequently, it's hard for me to fully appreciate the struggles that people had for nearly all of history over the seemingly trivial matter of recording and distributing information.

For much of the ancient past, people communicated history primarily by word of mouth, passed down through generations. Oral history may sound haphazard, but when you don't have a laptop to store information, you'd be surprised at how much stuff your brain can retain when it has to. Still, although oral history is a valid form of sharing information and was ideal for master storytellers, people soon found that the written word proved to be more reliable and more convenient should the storyteller get laryngitis or get hit by a speeding donkey.

By historical standards, the New Testament time gap is relatively small — all first copies of the books date within 250 years, nearly all within 200 years, many within 100 years. And one fragment of the Gospel of John was written around A.D. 95 — a mere 15 to 30 years before the first copy was dated between A.D. 110 and A.D. 125.

As Table 2-2 shows, the New Testament time gap is much more favorable compared to the gap in the writings of Homer (500 years), Plato (1,200 years), and Aristotle (1,400 years).

Table 2-2	Comparing the Time Gap of Ancient Manuscripts		
Author	*Date Written*	*Earliest Copy*	*Time Gap*
Aristotle	384–322 B.C.	A.D. 1100	1,400 years
Plato	427–347 B.C.	A.D. 900	1,200 years
Homer	900 B.C.	400 B.C.	500 years
New Testament	A.D. 50–100	A.D. 100–300	30–250 years

Source: Based on Norman Geisler's Christian Apologetics (Baker Book House, 1976).

Overall, more manuscript evidence supports the reliability of the New Testament writings than it does for any other ancient book. Therefore, if one wants to throw out the New Testament on grounds of the manuscripts themselves, then you'd first have to throw out *every* other ancient historical document, from Plato to Caesar.

Verifying New Testament details with non-biblical sources

The history of the New Testament and the apostles' claims are all consistent with external non-biblical sources. Josephus, a first-century Jewish historian, mentions Jesus in a passage in *Antiquities* (published today in *The Works of Josephus*, Hendrickson, 1987) and, in a passage that's disputed for its authenticity in the same book, discusses the details of Christ's life, death, and resurrection claims. Other references to Jesus Christ are in the writings of two Roman historians (Cornelius Tacitus and Suetonius), a Greek writer (Lucian), a Samarian-born historian (Thallus), and the Jewish Talmud. Each of these secular sources help confirm the basic historical details of the New Testament authors.

Assessing New Testament authors' credibility

A second issue concerning the New Testament's reliability is the trustworthiness of the accounts of the original writers. After all, the precise words of the original manuscripts look certain to have survived intact (see the section, "Considering how many New Testament copies exist," earlier in this chapter), but that doesn't account for the idea that the original writers could've been mistaken or misleading with what they wrote.

Several factors strongly indicate the trustworthiness of the New Testament authors, including

- ✔ Authors personally knew Jesus or were in direct contact with the apostles.

- ✔ Authors wrote within the lifetimes of eyewitnesses.

- ✔ All known non-biblical historical sources are consistent with the claims and accounts of the New Testament.

- ✔ The nature of the authentic New Testament books is far different from fake gospels that occasionally surfaced in later centuries.

- ✔ Minor inconsistencies in the accounts actually help confirm the trustworthiness of the writings.

I discuss each of these in the sections that follow.

Authors were qualified to write

Christians believe that the New Testament authors were qualified to write the books based on two factors:

- ✔ **Proximity to Jesus:** Each of the writers of the New Testament books either had direct contact with Jesus or else was in close contact with those who did.

- ✔ **Attention to detail:** All the authors (except Luke) were Hebrew. Hebrew writers were renowned for their meticulous nature when writing. For example, if a fact was questionable, they didn't include it. And although Luke, a physician by education, wasn't Hebrew, he was the most precise of all the New Testament authors in the details he provided in his Gospel and the Book of Acts, which makes it easy to cross-check his facts with non-biblical sources.

Authors wrote shortly after New Testament events occurred

Authors wrote nearly all the New Testament writings within 40 years of Jesus' crucifixion, and all within 65 years. Although it was essential that contemporaries of Jesus wrote all the books, 40 years still seems like an awful long time to remember details. After all, I can't remember many details about my second grade math class, and I'm not even 40 yet! Yet, several important differences exist between how the New Testament writers documented events and how I faintly recollect Mrs. Geedy's arithmetic class.

First, the Gospels serve as the written version of the oral history that the disciples and eyewitnesses relayed during the first years of the early Church. As I discuss in the "Before the Internet existed: Communication in the ancient days" sidebar, oral history was much more precise and reliable in those days than it is in today's modern era, where memories need only be exercised for a moment until you can jot the idea down on a yellow sticky note or in your handheld computerized planner.

Second, at the time authors recorded the Gospels, many people were alive who could cross-check accounts to confirm or disprove their authenticity. At the beginning of his Gospel, for example, Luke indicates that he investigated many accounts from eyewitnesses and wrote an orderly account that synthesized these various reports (Luke 1:1–4).

Third, Jesus made it clear that the Holy Spirit would remind his disciples of all that he said to them (John 14:26). Therefore, if Jesus really was who he said he was (see Chapter 5), then it's not that big of a deal for the God of the universe to help the Gospel writers fill in the details.

Authors didn't sensationalize people or events

Some skeptics argue that the authors wrote the Gospel accounts based not on whether the incidents occurred, but on how these stories fit into Christian teaching. Basically, they're saying that the miracle stories were added to boost the claims of Jesus. But this criticism doesn't square away with what's written in the New Testament. The Gospels are notable for their brutal honesty (such as the often less-than-stellar descriptions of the disciples) and their matter-of-fact details. They discuss — but don't overly sensationalize — miracles and often tend to mention them without any fanfare.

If you compare the New Testament Gospels with a few Gospel-wannabes that were written in the second and third centuries, you notice a huge difference between the two sets of books. Although the fake gospels contain amazing childhood miracles and idealized accounts of the apostles, the genuine ones have a down-to-earth quality to them.

Authors were consistent theologically in spite of inconsistencies and discrepancies

One of the most common arguments against the reliability of the Gospels is the fact that some inconsistencies spring up in the accounts of the writers. For example, Matthew says that the two criminals crucified with Jesus curse him, while Luke makes a special point of talking about the repentant heart of one of them. Also, Matthew reports of only one angel at Jesus' tomb, while Luke mentions two. Although these inconsistencies do raise questions in determining the *exact specifics* of what happened, Christians believe that they shouldn't call into question the *reliability* of the writings. First, the inconsistencies that appear are relatively minor details in the grand scheme of things and never create theological differences between accounts. Second, ironically, these discrepancies actually show the authors' integrity, as they wrote what they believed to be true instead of trying to put on a united front on all matters. If Christianity was a conspiracy among the apostles, then they could easily have gotten their story straight on such matters.

Chapter 3

That Amazing Stuff Called Grace

If you were to ask a random sampling of people on the street to name a Christian song or hymn, chances are that many of these folks — whether they are Christians or not — would respond with "Amazing Grace." This song is amazin', not only because it's one of the most popular and beloved Christian songs of all time, but also because it so perfectly captures the heart of what Christianity is all about.

"Amazing Grace" was written a few hundred years ago but has certainly stood the test of time. I think it's rather fortunate that the song wasn't written in this day and age when superlatives go in and out of fashion at a moment's notice. If the song were written today as a teeny bopper tune, I can just imagine it would be entitled something like "Wicked Cool Grace." Or, if some marketing folks got ahold of it, you'd surely have "Super-Sized Grace" or "Turbo-Powered Grace."

When you actually start to think about God's grace, a legitimate question to ask is, Is it really worthy of the "amazing" label? Or is this song title just another example of superlatives gone amuck? In this chapter, you find out about the core teaching of Christianity — the grace-filled message of Jesus Christ dying for the sins of the world — and explore what the grace of God is all about. You can then make up your own mind on what superlative to use.

Defining Grace

If Christianity is all about how mere mortals like you and I can have an intimate, eternal relationship with God, grace is what makes such a relationship possible. You could say then that grace serves as the underbelly of the Christian faith. But to really understand what grace means, consider three stories that illustrate what this concept is all about. I tell you the accounts in the following three sections and explain them in the fourth, so get a glass of milk and some cookies, because it's story time.

Grace is a costly gift

Les Miserables is the classic Victor Hugo novel that has been made into a musical and several films. It tells the story of Jean Valjean, a man imprisoned for 17 years in France simply because he steals a loaf of bread to feed his hungry family. Valjean starts off as a well-meaning guy, but by the time he is released from prison, he's transformed into a hardened, embittered man with no hope for the future. After being refused by an innkeeper on a rainy evening, Valjean knocks on the door of a church's parsonage and asks for a night's lodging. In true Motel 6 fashion, a bishop "leaves the light on" for Valjean, opening up his home, giving him a warm meal, and offering a comfortable bed and pillow.

Valjean, however, isn't of the mindset to feel much gratitude for this display of kindness; he awakens in the middle of the night, steals some silver plates, and runs off toward the edge of town. In the morning, the police catch Valjean with the suspicious goods and bring him back to the bishop for questioning. Valjean's fate now seems sealed — he knows that being found guilty of theft a second time brings a permanent prison sentence.

Yet, when the bishop sees Valjean, he does something completely unexpected. Rather than berating the thief and turning him over to the police, the bishop greets him warmly and asks why he didn't take the candlesticks as well. As the police leave, satisfied that no crime has been committed, Valjean looks at the bishop with an expression of total disbelief: "Is it true that they let me go?"

The bishop then goes home to retrieve two silver candlesticks, the only remaining property of value that he owns, and hands them to Valjean. He challenges Valjean to use the silver to make himself into a new man, finishing with, "Jean Valjean, my brother: you belong no longer to evil, but to good. It is your soul I am buying for you."

A must-read: *What's So Amazing About Grace?*

Phillip Yancey's *What's So Amazing About Grace?* (Zondervan, 1997) is a brilliant, brutally honest, and totally absorbing account of what *grace* means. Sometimes Christians seem to have forgotten about the seemingly simple concept of grace — core to the teachings of Jesus — when you consider the legalistic way many of them live (see Chapter 16) and what preachers speak from the pulpits each Sunday. This book attempts to bridge that chasm. Before reading it, as a long-time Christian, I was skeptical that I had much to learn about grace; I was wrong. I personally found the book to be life transforming, completely altering the way I look at my relationships with God and with others around me.

Grace is undeserved

Jesus' parable of the prodigal (wasteful) son in Luke 15 has proven to be one of the most well-known and loved of all his parables. It tells the story of an ungrateful son who does the unthinkable — asks for his inheritance before his father has even keeled over — and tells of an amazing (there's that word again) father who actually grants the offensive request.

The son cashes in on his inheritance and leaves home for Rio de Janeiro — well, some far-off land, anyway. While there, he goes hog wild with his cash, probably squandering his fortune buying cheap touristy trinkets and a T-shirt to send to his dad that says: *My prodigal son went to Rio and all he got me was this lousy T-shirt*. But after his brief fun in the sun, the prodigal finds both his wallet and his stomach empty. He looks for work but is unable to find it, leaving him as desperate as a homeless man in a deserted soup kitchen. He goes on for awhile, but eventually realizes that his only option is to return home.

A father in any day and age would deal with the prodigal son severely after such an escapade and would have a lifetime of "I told you so's" to share with him. In the Middle Eastern culture of Jesus' day, the treatment would have been even more harsh, because the prodigal's actions were a slap in the face of two key beliefs of that culture — family ties and respect for family authority — both which were valued more than life itself.

Everyone in the village likely expected the prodigal to be forced to work off his debt like a slave and never be fully accepted as a son again. The villagers would certainly never let the prodigal live it down. They'd endlessly humiliate, harass, and taunt any person who's done such an unspeakable deed.

A must-read: *The Cross and the Prodigal*

In this parable we have a father who leaves the comfort and security of his home and exposes himself in a humiliating fashion in the village street. The coming down and going out to his boy hints at [Jesus' coming to earth]. The humiliating spectacle in the village street hints at the meaning of the cross.

—Ken Bailey, *The Cross and the Prodigal* (Concordia Publishing House, 1973)

Ken Bailey's *The Cross and the Prodigal* is perhaps an obscure "must-read" selection because it's hard to find, yet I recommend it because Bailey's look at the prodigal son parable in Luke 15 has been instrumental to my faith. The relatively short 132-page book has deeply impacted my perspective on Christ's sacrifice, the extent of God's love, and the nature of sin.

The purpose of this book is to examine the parable of the prodigal son from the perspective of a Middle Easterner. Postmodern Americans and Europeans are removed from biblical culture in two ways — through 2,000 years of history and the differences between the Eastern and Western cultures. The result is to overlook some of the subtleties of the text and miss some of the underlying assumptions. Only when you look at the parable through Middle Eastern, 2,000-year-old eyes can you understand the father's true sacrificial love and both sons' equal sin, not just that of the prodigal.

Unfortunately, *The Cross and the Prodigal* isn't widely available and takes a bit of searching to find. Visit my Web site at www.digitalwalk.net, where I point you the way.

But the father in Jesus' story responds in an unexpected way. When he sees his son walking back, the father is sick to his stomach with compassion for his son as he realizes the suffering that his child has gone through and will go through by the villagers' taunts. The father knows that the only way to prevent his son's future shame is to take a drastic action himself, taking the focus off of his son and onto himself. Therefore, he sprints out to meet the ungrateful son, much like a track star running a 100-meter dash. Since senior citizens jog for exercise in this day and age, you and I don't think much of his mad dash in public, but to the people of Jesus' day, this sprint would have been a total embarrassment. No older person would ever jog, let alone run; it's a matter of dignity. What's more, in order to run, he'd have to expose his undergarments when he lifted his robe.

But the father's surprising behavior doesn't stop there. When he gets to his son, he puts his arms around him, hugging and repeatedly kissing him. He then calls his servants to kill a fattened calf and put his finest robe on his son, a ring on his finger, and sandals on his feet. Not only does this amazing response show the prodigal the boundless love that the father has, but his action also signifies to everyone that his son is to be welcomed back as a *son*, not as a servant.

Grace is an unexpected surprise

"Babette's Feast" is a short story written by Isak Dinesen that was made into a film and won the Oscar for Best Foreign Film in 1987. "Babette's Feast" tells of a minister's two daughters from a remote village in Denmark called Norre Vosburg who give up love and fame to remain in service to their tiny, strict Lutheran church. In spite of the women's intentions, the years take their toll on the people of the church, which begins to deteriorate — consumed with rules and regulations and plagued by bitter feuds among the congregation members.

Out of pity, the two sisters reluctantly take in a woman refugee from Paris who knocks on their door one rainy night. She has an accompanying note with her that concludes with the simple statement, "Babette can cook." Babette settles in and obediently cooks for the two sisters, fixing only what their pleasure-denying palettes would allow — bland cod and gruel.

Twelve years go by, and one day Babette receives surprising news in the mail that she holds the winning French lottery ticket, redeemable for 10,000 francs. Upon hearing this news, the two sisters, who've grown attached to and dependent upon Babette over the years, realize that Babette will leave them soon.

Around this time, the tiny church holds an anniversary celebration in honor of its founder, so Babette asks the sisters if she can prepare a special French meal for this event. To the sisters, the thought of a French meal seems worldly and self-indulgent, perhaps even originating from Satan himself. However, Babette has never asked for anything before, so the two sisters feel compelled to agree to her request in spite of their fears. After Babette receives her prize money, she begins to purchase supplies for the meal, and the sisters watch in horror as Babette brings in champagne, chocolate, turtles, pheasants, and even a cow's head. The duo meet secretly with the other members of the congregation, and they all conspire to eat the meal out of duty, but won't enjoy it or even speak of the meal to each other.

The night of the celebration comes, and the congregation sits down to dinner. A church member's nephew, a high-ranking, cosmopolitan general, joins them; as the meal starts, the congregation eats and drinks without comment, but the general is amazed — he is drinking the finest Amontillado he's ever had and eating real turtle soup, a delicacy never found in remote Denmark. Later, when he tastes the main course, the general announces that the only place he'd ever had this one-of-a-kind dish was at Café Anglais, a famous Parisian restaurant that was once well-known for its female chef. Throughout much of the meal, the general's unbridled enthusiasm stands out against the stark silence of the rest of the dinner guests.

Grace versus mercy: Knowing the difference

Although the terms *grace* and *mercy* are often used interchangeably, there's a subtle difference in meaning between the two: *Grace* is receiving something that's undeserved, while *mercy* isn't receiving punishment that's deserved. For example, in *Les Miserables*, the bishop's mercy saves Valjean from life imprisonment, and his grace gives Valjean a new life. In the same way, God shows humans grace by giving the gift of salvation through Jesus Christ, and he shows mercy by not punishing for their sin those who accept his gift.

As the meal continues, the feast has a transforming effect, and the church members gradually loosen up and begin to enjoy the meal. They begin to laugh and talk of good times in the past. Feuds that had gone on for years are dealt with and buried. Finally, at the evening's conclusion, they go outside together, form a circle under the stars, and sing a hymn together. What was, hours before, a decaying, feuding congregation is now a unified, joyful one, transformed by Babette's feast.

The story ends with two bombshells. Babette first tells the two sisters that she was, in fact, the famous chef at Café Anglais (which the general had spoken of earlier in the evening). She then adds that she'll be staying with the two in Norre Vosburg permanently. When the sisters ask about the prize money, Babette reveals that she spent the entire sum on the celebration meal. After all, that's what a dinner for twelve costs at Café Anglais!

Grace in a nutshell

The stories in the previous sections underscore two realities of what grace is all about:

- ✔ **Grace is costly.** Grace is a gift that costs everything for the one who gives it. The bishop in *Les Miserables* gives Jean Valjean his silver dishes and candlesticks, the only belongings he possesses that have any value. In the parable of the prodigal son, the father gives a costly gift, too: he takes on the humiliation due his son when he sprints out to him. In "Babette's Feast," Babette's gift to the church congregation costs her everything — the 10,000 francs that she's won.

✔ **Grace is undeserved by the recipient.** In each of these three stories, none of the recipients of grace had any claim to the gift they received. They didn't deserve the gift, nor could they have earned it in any way. Valjean is given the candlesticks in addition to the silver dishes he's already stolen. The prodigal son deserves shame, punishment, and servitude — not the gift the father gives him on the road home. In Norre Vosburg, the church members, in judgment and skepticism, do their utmost to resist the delicious spread that Babette prepares — so obviously, they don't deserve to partake of something that cost her everything.

Grace, then, is the idea behind a gift that costs the giver everything and is wholly undeserved by the recipient. All that the receiver has to do with grace is receive it. Or, as the general in "Babette's Feast" says, "Grace demands nothing from us but that we shall await it with confidence and acknowledge it in gratitude."

Receiving God's Gift of Grace: Salvation

From a Christian perspective, grace is what God shows to humans by offering *salvation* — freedom from the punishment of sin and the promise of eternal life — through the death and resurrection of Jesus Christ. God's grace is costly because it cost Jesus Christ his life. God's grace is also undeserved — humans have sinned against him from the Fall of Adam and Eve and have done nothing — and *can* do nothing — to earn it.

In order to understand why Christians believe all people need such a gift in the first place, take a moment to explore Salvation 101, or the four basic principles of salvation. When you understand these, the necessity of God's grace starts to make sense. The four principles are

✔ God loves and wants a relationship with each person.

✔ Everyone has sinned. And this sin, whether large or small, separates people from God. (See Chapter 4 to find out more about a Christian's beliefs about sin.)

✔ God came to earth as Jesus Christ (flip to Chapter 5) and paid the costly penalty for this sin.

✔ Anyone who accepts this gift of grace receives salvation.

I discuss each one of these ideas in this section.

God's motivation for grace

Not only does the prodigal son story (see the section, "Grace is undeserved" in this chapter) offer a vivid picture of grace, but the parable also hints at the reason God offers grace — his amazing love for his people. You can see this by the father's reaction when he finishes his run and gets to his child. He doesn't just shake his son's hand or give him a high-five. Instead, Jesus gives a much more intimate description — the father excitedly hugs and kisses the prodigal repeatedly. Charles Spurgeon, an evangelical preacher who lived in the 19th century, spoke of the love this parable portrays in his sermon, "Prodigal Love for the Prodigal Son" (www.spurgeon.org/sermons/2236.htm):

> God on the neck of a sinner! What a wonderful picture! Can you conceive it? I do not think you can; but if you cannot imagine it, I hope that you will realize it. When God's arm is about our neck, and his lips are on our cheek, kissing us much, then we understand more than preachers or books can ever tell us of his . . . love.

Principle #1: God loves

God desires all people to be saved and come to full knowledge of the truth.

—1 Timothy 2:4

Christians believe that, from the very beginning, God created people because he loves them and wants a relationship with them (John 3:16). And he designed humans in such a way that they would naturally seek him, desire a relationship with him, and have a hunger for what he offers — long life, hope, peace, and joy. Yet, as discussed fully in Chapter 1, God also gave humans a wild card — the free choice of whether to follow him or to go their own separate ways. As a result, while God loves each person and has his arms outstretched, he's a "gentleman" and never forces anyone to do what he or she doesn't want to do.

Principle #2: People sin

All people have sinned and fallen short of God's glory.

—Romans 3:23

If you read the Bible through cover to cover, two truths about God become very clear: God loves people, and he hates sin. The problem is that everyone is born with a sin nature (see Chapter 4) and sins (Romans 3:23). And this sin, whether it's a little or a lot, separates everyone equally from God.

God's not simply being a meanie by making a big deal out of sin. Rather, sin isn't something he can just sweep under the table or pretend isn't there. Christians believe that he doesn't ignore it for three major reasons:

- ✔ **Sin breaks God's heart.** Imagine the reaction of parents whose only child, on her 16th birthday, stole their life savings and ran off to Fiji. Yes, they'd be upset that she broke the rules, but that anger pales in comparison to the hurt they'd feel at the betrayal and selfishness of their own flesh and blood. Similarly, when you sin against God, you're not violating an arbitrary list of do's and don'ts that God wants you to obey; instead, you're hurting God. As you explore in Chapter 4, thinking of sin as simply breaking rules is overly simplistic and even downright misleading. No, sin is all about breaking God's heart.

- ✔ **A holy God can't turn a blind eye to sin.** Even if God, in spite of his hurt, wants to overlook sin, he can't. Ignoring sin is the one option that isn't open to God, because he's perfectly holy and completely pure. In fact, if he tried to close his eyes to it, he'd no longer be who he is. In the same way, an ice cube can't simply ignore a pot of boiling water. If the cube doesn't take reality into account and jumps into the steamy liquid, it ceases to be an ice cube. So, although the common belief is "Nothing is impossible with God," that statement is only partially true. Yes, he's all-powerful and in control, but God can't do anything that goes contrary to his nature.

- ✔ **God established the law of cause and effect in the beginning.** When God introduced choice to the world, a natural side effect of that decision was the introduction of consequences: Every decision you and I make has an outcome that we can't reverse. In other words, every cause has an effect.

    This earth is a beautiful place, but it's also, quite frankly, dangerous and treacherous. Sometimes actions have painful consequences, no matter how harsh or seemingly unfair the result. For example, getting into a pizza-eating contest with your 300-pound cousin may leave you with a stomachache. But wishful thinking or denial doesn't change the cold hard fact that your poor decision has indigestion-inducing consequences. Reality wins in the end, whether you like it or not. In the same way, after you sin, you can't simply wash away its effects.

    The cost of freedom also plays a major factor in why Christians believe God allows bad things to happen in this world. See Chapter 16 for more on that topic.

Are you yearning for a few examples? Consider a couple of parallels to fully grasp why God can't ignore sin:

- ✔ Imagine that someone dear to you jumps into a pit of slimy, poisonous goo. When that person gets out of the pit, a gooey substance coats the individual and reeks of the sulphur-smelling poison. When you get near the person, the poison gas spewing from the slime burns your lungs and makes it impossible for you to breathe. You may still love that person, but you can't carry on a normal relationship with him or her as long as the slime remains.

- ✔ Suppose a wife has an affair and shamelessly brings her lover home to her husband. With another man hanging all over his wife, the husband can't simply carry on as usual with her, ignoring the reality that's in front of him. He may still deeply love her and hope their relationship can be rekindled, but he can't act on those desires while the other man has his arms around the wife. The other man not only blocks the husband from interacting with his spouse, but he also prevents the wife from being intimate with her husband.

Sin is much like that gooey slime or that underhanded lover. It causes a gigantic rift and has divided people from God ever since Adam and Eve. God made it clear that the penalty for sin is death and eternal separation from God (Romans 6:23). As a result, people find themselves in deep doo-doo: They're in a bad situation and can't get out of it by being good. They're between a rock and a hard place; they're up a creek without a paddle; they've fallen and they can't get up. Well, you get the idea.

People throughout the ages have tried some ingenious tricks to bridge that vast canyon of sin, but no one has been successful (although rumor has it that stuntman Evel Knievel came awfully close in the 1970s). As history has proven, humans simply don't have the goods to pull it off by themselves. See Chapters 4 and 15 on why that's the case.

Principle #3: God responds

God demonstrates his own love toward us, in that while we were yet sinners, Christ died for us.

—Romans 5:8

Because of sin (Principle #2), God had a choice to make — either forget about the lot of us or take the initiative and do something himself to bridge the gap. God's love for humans (Principle #1) drove him to respond to the sin, but that solution came at a great cost to himself.

Because the penalty for sin is death and separation from God, a price had to be paid. But a person couldn't just pay it, because as you've seen, humans can't pull themselves up to God. Therefore, in order for the gap to be closed, God had to take the initiative and pay the price himself. He had to come to earth as a man, Jesus Christ, and die for the sins of the world (1 Peter 3:18).

Therefore, Christians believe God's gift of grace is the work that Jesus Christ did by dying on the cross for the sins of the world and coming back to life again three days later.

Principle #4: People must choose

If you will confess with your mouth that "Jesus is Lord," and believe in your heart that God raised him from the dead, you will be saved.

—Romans 10:9

Why did Jesus have to die for your sins?

Buried in the Old Testament is an obscure Israelite custom that helps makes sense of why Jesus' sacrificial death on the cross redeems (saves) people from their sins. Ancient Israel had a concept of a *kinsmen redeemer,* which was someone who protected members of his or her extended family if they got into trouble. For example, suppose a person got deep into debt and couldn't repay it. By law, that person could be sold into slavery until the debt was paid. However, if the person sold into servitude had a relative who could act as a kinsmen redeemer, then that individual could be freed as the kinsmen redeemer would pay off the debt. The qualifications for a kinsmen redeemer were threefold: you had to be a blood relative, be free, and be willing and able to redeem.

Christians think of Jesus as being the kinsmen redeemer for humanity. People have gotten themselves into a debt of sin that they can never, not in a million years, repay themselves. However, only one person in all history is qualified to serve as humanity's kinsmen redeemer — Jesus Christ. He alone meets the threefold requirements:

- Jesus is God (see Chapters 5 and 7), but he's also a "relative," because he was born into the world as a man.

- Jesus is free, being the only person to have led a sinless life.

- Jesus voluntarily went to the cross on behalf of everyone.

Although a kinsmen redeemer in ancient Israel would pay a financial debt to release a relative from slavery, the penalty for sin isn't financial, but a matter of life and death. Therefore, the price that Jesus had to pay was his own life for the lives of all humans.

Through the work of Jesus Christ, God built a bridge over the gorge of sin that eliminates the consequences of Principle #2 (people sin) and enables Principle #1 (God loves) to happen. Christians believe that one doesn't have to buy a ticket or do anything to earn his way across the bridge, but he does have to decidedly walk across it in order to take up God on his offer. In *Les Miserables,* the candlesticks wouldn't have meant anything to Valjean if he hadn't taken them with his hands from the bishop and carried them away. In the story of the prodigal son, the father's love wouldn't have mattered had the son not accepted it. And in "Babette's Feast," the dinner wouldn't have done its transforming work on the church members if they didn't lift their forks and partake of the food.

In the same way, it's not enough for people to simply nod their heads toward God and the work of Jesus Christ. They must do something about it. Salvation, then, is God's gift, but it requires a *deliberate* act of one's will in response. Christians believe a proper response to God's gift of grace is as easy as A-B-C:

✔ **A**cknowledge your sinful position to God.

✔ **B**elieve that Jesus Christ died in your place for your sins.

✔ **C**onfess that Jesus Christ is Lord and allow him to be lord of your life.

It's important to note that God doesn't treat humans as a group, but as individuals. Although grasping it seems impossible, Christians believe he desires a relationship with every single person who walks the face of the earth. So, given that he singles every person out for love, he also holds every individual accountable for the choices that he or she makes. Christians believe that God gives freedom, but he demands accountability.

Understanding Salvation by Faith

The notion that salvation is totally of God and is the result of nothing that you or I do is hard to grasp. To many, this solution is too easy. Human nature almost demands us to tack something onto the end. And many through the ages have felt compelled to add onto the central message of Christianity. But the Bible makes it clear that salvation is *sola gratia* — by grace alone. As Ephesians 2:8–9 says, "For it is by grace you have been saved through faith. It is not from yourself or anything you've done, but the gift of God." Salvation, therefore, is a free gift of grace from God.

When a person accepts the gift of salvation, he or she is said to be *justified* — made acceptable before (or made right with) God. The process of being declared righteous is called *justification*.

A prayer of salvation

Over the years, you may have seen a Billy Graham crusade on television, during which Mr. Graham speaks to a stadium filled with thousands of people. If you watched the program all the way through, you'd see that Graham always invites people to come down to the front after his talk in order to make a commitment to become a Christian. What Graham is doing here is emphasizing the fact that God's gift of salvation is a deliberate act of the will and so requires an explicit response from an individual. The actual step of becoming a Christian is typically done through a simple prayer that goes something like this:

Dear Jesus, I understand that I'm a sinner and need your forgiveness. I want to turn away from my sins, and I believe that you died for them. I invite you to come into my heart and begin transforming me. I commit myself to trusting and following you as my Lord and my Savior. Amen.

Although all Christians agree that God's grace is what saves people, they disagree considerably over what a person's role is in this whole process. Obviously, a Christian needs to believe in Jesus Christ, but a sticky issue has always been whether faith *by itself* is sufficient for salvation. The Christian Church is split on this issue.

Catholics believe that God's gift of grace is received through faith *and* by partaking of the sacraments (such as being baptized, taking Communion, being confirmed in the church, and confessing sins to a priest). Baptism is particularly important and Catholics consider it a key requirement for being saved. If you read *Catholicism For Dummies,* by Rev. John Trigilio, Jr. and Rev. Kenneth Brighenti (Wiley) for example, you see this viewpoint.

Most Orthodox Christians believe salvation is more of a gradual process in which humans become more and more like God as they participate with him in the work of salvation. Protestants see the act of praying the sinner's prayer (see the sidebar, "A prayer of salvation," earlier in this chapter) as the trigger that brings salvation into a person's life. In contrast, Orthodox Christians typically place far less emphasis on a specific "salvation event" that starts the Christian's life, focusing instead on what must be done over the course of a person's life to continue on in the faith. In other words, while Protestants ask, "What can I do to be saved?", Orthodox Christians ask, "What can I do to be *most* saved?"

Protestants believe in justification *sola fide* (by faith alone). In other words, faith in Jesus Christ is all that is needed to actually save a person. "Faith" or "belief" in this context isn't simply an intellectual belief in God, but rather

something far deeper and life changing than head knowledge. Protestants point to several verses in Acts and Romans to back up their claim:

- ✔ "Believe in the Lord Jesus Christ, and you will be saved." (Acts 16:31)

- ✔ "This righteousness from God comes through faith in Jesus Christ to all who believe." (Romans 3:22)

- ✔ "For we maintain that a man is justified by faith apart from observing the law." (Romans 3:28)

- ✔ "To the man who does not work but trusts God who justifies the wicked, his faith is credited as righteousness." (Romans 4:5)

Protestants are very leery of the *W* word that Paul speaks so loudly against in the Book of Romans — *works*. That's why they disagree with the Catholic link between the sacraments and salvation and the tie that Orthodox Christians place on living a Christian life with one's salvation. Protestants consider these efforts to be works, plain and simple, since they are actions that one takes apart from belief. Although Protestants agree with Catholics and Orthodox Christians that a Christian must live out her faith (Philippians 2:12), they see the practice of "living out" as something that is separate from salvation itself — an effect *of* receiving salvation, rather than a necessity *to* receive salvation.

Is all of this discussion making your head spin yet? Okay, let me put aside all of these debates and nuances and drill down on two key truths about salvation and faith that all Christians agree on:

- ✔ **Faith in Jesus Christ is essential to be saved and justified.** See Ephesians 2:8–9.

- ✔ **True faith has a backbone.** The Book of James makes it abundantly clear that a declaration of faith by itself doesn't amount to a hill of beans if it isn't backed up by action (James 2:14–26). In other words, if you're gonna talk the talk, you've gotta walk the walk. Therefore, if someone is truly a Christian, his or her life is going to be characterized by a growing faith and, over the long haul, he or she will live in accordance with that faith. However, recognize that this is a *consequence* of faith, not a *condition*. See Chapter 13 to find out what it means to live a Christian life.

Being "Born Again"

"Born again" is one of those stereotyped expressions that means different things to different people. To some, the phrase is a perfect summary of what

being a Christian is. To others, the expression sounds like a label that is associated with wacky televangelists. But truth be told, "born again" is a phrase that was first used by none other than Jesus himself.

Born again means to be spiritually reborn by committing your life to Jesus and entering into a personal relationship with him. Jesus said in John 3:3 that unless a person is "born again," he won't see the Kingdom of God. In other words, Jesus is saying that when a person accepts the gift of grace from God and believes in Jesus Christ, a very real change happens, brought about by the Holy Spirit — a second birth, if you will. In that respect, every earnest Christian is "born again" whether he or she ascribes to that label or not.

The New Testament is filled with the idea that something's different in people who've committed their lives to Jesus. Paul says that a Christian is a "new creation," meaning the old things of that person's life in effect die, and all things become new (2 Corinthians 5:17). He adds in Ephesians 4:24 that the Christian "puts on the 'new self,' who in the likeness of God has been created in righteousness and holiness of truth."

Dealing with Hopeless Cases

A common response that many people have when they hear about God's gift of grace is: "But you don't know what I've done!" In other words, God may forgive some people, but the sin in that individual's life is soooooooo bad that God can't possibly forgive him or her.

If you read Chapter 1, you know that Christianity includes a number of beliefs that are contrary to natural train of thought. Well, add this one to that list, because one of the key teachings of Christianity is that no sin is *ever* too great, and no sinner is *ever* disqualified from God's grace — even someone as evil as Adolf Hitler or Saddam Hussein. So long as people confess their sin and believe in Jesus, God forgives them. That may be offensive to one's notion of fair play and the belief that what-comes-around-goes-around, but that's what Christianity is all about.

An amazing truth of Christianity is the way that God treats even the worst of sinners. Consider the following three "hopeless cases" and their unique encounters with Jesus Christ.

Last gasps for a thief

The Romans crucified Jesus between two criminals on a hill outside of Jerusalem. The Gospel of Luke (23:39-43) says that one of the criminals started to taunt Jesus, saying, "Aren't you the Christ? If so, save yourself and us!" But the other criminal was angry at the taunter, responding that they were being punished justly for the crimes they committed, while Jesus was fully innocent. This second criminal then turned his head toward Jesus and said, "Jesus, remember me when you come into your kingdom." Jesus looked back at him and responded with some amazing (the word that keeps popping up) words, "Today, you'll be with me in paradise."

The thief may not have said the words of the "sinner's prayer" (see the sidebar, "A prayer of salvation"), but Jesus knew his heart. The thief acknowledged his sin and believed in Jesus Christ. Jesus then wiped out everything bad that the thief ever did before being nailed to that cross and welcomed him into heaven.

The thief proves that as long as you've got one more breath, you're never too late, and your deeds are never to despicable for you to receive God's grace.

Within a stone's throw of judgment

A group of Jewish teachers brought a woman caught in the act of adultery to Jesus and wanted to stone her, based on the laws of Moses in the Old Testament. When they questioned Jesus about this, his response startled everyone: "If any one of you is without sin, let him be the first to throw a stone at her" (John 8:7). One by one, the leaders slowly left as Jesus wiped away their grounds for punishment with his bold statement.

Jesus turned to the woman and said, "Who are your accusers now?" The woman responded, "No one, sir," to which Jesus replied, "Then neither do I condemn you. Go now and leave your life of sin."

This woman had received a death sentence from the what-comes-around-goes-around crowd. But Jesus forgave her and gave her a chance to turn from her sin-infested life into a life of belief in him.

The original "wretch like me"

John Newton was a captain of a slave ship in the 18th century and had a heart that was as wicked and cruel as you'd expect a slave trader to have. For many years, Newton rebelled against God and would have nothing to do with him. That is, until a violent storm occurred one night during a voyage. The storm was so bad that it seemed like certain death for all aboard. During the

worst of the storm, he cried out for the Lord to have mercy on them. God rescued the ship that night, and Newton, who was certain he'd narrowly escaped death's door, now saw his life in a different light.

Newton committed his life to Christ and began a slow process of changing his life of sin into a life fully dedicated to the Lord. After several years, he even felt called by God to become a minister and spent the remaining decades of his life preaching the good news he discovered on that slave ship years before. As a preacher, Newton often wrote hymns for weekly church services and prayer meetings. He penned hundreds of them, but one stands apart from the rest. You guessed it — "Amazing Grace"!

On first take, it's perhaps natural to think that a traditional hymn like "Amazing Grace" must have been written by a goody-two-shoes whose worst offense was fighting with his kid sister. But when you grasp that someone as despicable and slimy as a slave trader wrote the song, you realize that God's gift of grace does indeed live up to that "amazing" label.

Unplugging "Amazing Grace"

John Newton's "Amazing Grace" captures so well the gift of grace that I've explained throughout this chapter. Check out Newton's original lyrics:

Amazing grace! (how sweet the sound)
That sav'd a wretch like me!
I once was lost, but now am found,
Was blind, but now I see.

'Twas grace that taught my heart to fear,
And grace my fears reliev'd;
How precious did that grace appear,
The hour I first believ'd!

Thro' many dangers, toils and snares,
I have already come;
'Tis grace has brought me safe thus far,
And grace will lead me home.

The Lord has promis'd good to me,
His word my hope secures;
He will my shield and portion be,
As long as life endures.

Yes, when this flesh and heart shall fail,
And mortal life shall cease;

I shall possess, within the veil,
A life of joy and peace.

The earth shall soon dissolve like snow,
The sun forbear to shine;
But God, who call'd me here below,
Will be forever mine.

In this song, Newton shows how grace saved and transformed his wretched life. A stark contrast — "I was lost, but now am found, was blind, but now I see" — is made between his dead-end life of sin and his new one found with Jesus Christ. The song also perfectly depicts the protagonists in the three stories told in the section, "Defining Grace." Valjean was a thief ready for permanent imprisonment, but he received a new life, paid for by the bishop's candlesticks. The prodigal son prepared for a life of payback, but his father wiped the slate clean. The people of Norre Vosburg were wasting away until Babette's feast filled them with peace, joy, and a newfound freedom.

Part II

Exploring the Basic Principles of the Christian Faith

The 5th Wave   By Rich Tennant

"This is our family bible. It's truly a lamp to my feet, a light for my path, and a balance unto our bookshelf."

In this part . . .

A nytime you dive into unfamiliar territory, you need gear to help make the most of your effort. This part equips you for the long haul as you discover the core messages and beliefs of Christianity. You begin by looking through Christian goggles at that nasty business of sin. From there, you take out your compass and follow the trail that leads to Christianity's answer to sin — Jesus Christ, who Christians believe came to earth as God in human flesh and died for all the sins of the world. Next, you check out the Christian's sword — known as the Bible — which is where Christians after Jesus' day found out about sin and the Savior in the first place. Further, you don your pith helmet as you run head-on into who Christians believe God is (known as the Trinity), how Christians express their faith through sacraments (or ordinances), and what God's plans are for humans after this earthly life.

Chapter 4

Sin: Why "Do's and Don'ts" Miss the Bigger Picture

● ●

In This Chapter

▶ Considering the origin of sin

▶ Defining sin

▶ Getting a grip on the Christian idea of God's perception of sin

▶ Viewing life thousands of years after the Fall

▶ Deconstructing Satan

▶ Discovering the tactics of temptation and responses to it

▶ Seeing how sin affects Christians

● ●

Sin sells. In years gone by, *sin* was considered a dirty word, something to avoid like the plague. But these days, more often than not, sin is thought of as cool. If you watch any TV ads, you see this in action; a popular advertising trick used on products ranging from chocolate pudding to sandwiches to automobiles is tying the product to sin. Slogans like "Sinfully delicious," "Wonderfully decadent," "Indulge yourself," and "Join the fun in Sin City" all associate sinning with fun and pleasure.

Consider whether sin is like these ads say: Is it just another word for "having a good time"? Or is the pleasure of sin like a Trojan horse — fun on the outside, but insidious danger lurking within? In this chapter, you explore what sin is, where and how it originated, and what Christians believe about people's general understanding of sin and temptation compared to how God sees it.

Desiring to Be Different: The Original Ego Trip

When I used to live in Silicon Valley, I often drove along Highway 101 and came upon a prominently displayed series of black-and-white billboard ads

by Apple Computer. These ads featured such people as Albert Einstein and John Lennon with a simple slogan at the bottom: *Think different.* These Apple ads have been one of the company's most popular campaigns; they're effective because they appeal to something deep inside of people — a desire to not conform and a perceived need to go against the flow to be successful.

Although the desire to "think different" can be positive for entrepreneurial and creative activity, oftentimes people twist and manipulate this motto. They tend to see rebelling or going against anything — even good things — as "hip" or "cool." This idea is exactly what Satan, the prime enemy of God, used to confuse humans a long time ago — see the section, "Warring with Satan (And Knowing Who You're Fighting Against)," later in this chapter. Satan didn't use a Macintosh computer as part of his manipulation, but he did feature an apple (well, some sort of fruit, anyway) as part of his scheme.

Revisiting the Fall

In the Book of Genesis, the Bible traces the origin of sin all the way back to the original dynamic duo, Adam and Eve. Adam and Eve were the first flesh-and-blood humans that God created and lived for a while as perfect humans, without a blemish. Think about that — no diet plans, no bald spots, and no eyeglasses or contact lenses. But then they had to go and screw everything up.

The Bible says that God gave Adam and Eve free reign to everything on earth with a single exception: They were not to eat, not even touch, fruit that hung from a particular tree in the middle of the Garden of Eden, a garden paradise that God had created for his new creatures. If they did, God made it clear that the consequence would be death.

Satan makes his grand entrance into the biblical account in Genesis 3, and you can easily guess exactly what he harps on: the lone "Do Not Touch" placard in the midst of a world of "Do As You Wish" signs.

When Eve is alone, Satan, in the form of a serpent, begins to question God's restriction, making it out to be some cockamamie scheme God crafted to make sure that Adam and Eve don't become like God himself. Satan urges Eve to eat the fruit so that her eyes will be opened, so to speak, and she'll see the world as God sees it. In a nutshell, Satan's challenge to Eve was: *Think different.* Think different from the way God designed you. Be your own master. Don't take limits from anyone else.

Eve gave in to the temptation and took the fruit and ate it, but didn't stop there. She got Adam to eat it too. This original disobedience by Adam and Eve is often referred to as the *Fall of man.* Satan got his way that day, and the world has been forever changed since then.

Think different: The sequel

Satan used the same *Think Different* strategy when he tempted Jesus in the desert. Check out the account in Matthew 4:1–11:

Then Jesus was led up by the Spirit into the wilderness to be tempted by the devil. When he had fasted forty days and forty nights, he was hungry afterward. The tempter came and said to him, "If you are the Son of God, command that these stones become bread." But he answered, "It is written, 'Man shall not live by bread alone, but by every word that proceeds out of the mouth of God.'" Then the devil took him into the holy city. He set him on the pinnacle of the temple and said to him, "If you are the Son of God, throw yourself down, for it is written, 'He will give his angels charge concerning you,' and, 'On their hands they will bear you up, so that you don't dash your foot against a stone.'" Jesus said to him, "Again, it is written, 'You shall not test the Lord, your God.'" Again, the devil took him to an exceedingly high mountain, and showed him all the kingdoms of the world and their glory. He said to him, "I will give you all of these things if you will fall down and worship me." Then Jesus said to him, "Get behind me, Satan! For it is written, 'You shall worship the Lord your God, and him only shall you serve.'" Then the devil left him, and behold, angels came and served him.

Satan, in effect, told Jesus to "think outside the box" — be a king without the cross. The first temptation was to misuse his miraculous power by changing the stones into bread; the second was to use sensational means to win the world (resulting in pride), and the third was to escape crucifixion (the Bible says Jesus' death and resurrection is the *only* way we can be reconciled to him; see 1 Timothy 2:5–6, Acts 4:12) and worship him instead. Unlike Adam and Eve, Jesus didn't fall prey to Satan's temptation.

Considering how the Fall changed everything

In *Raiders of the Lost Ark,* Indiana Jones discovers a long-lost statue that's hidden in a cavern filled with booby traps. When he finally arrives at his destination, he faces a huge obstacle — the weight-sensitive stand on which the treasure lies. If the exact weight doesn't remain on the stand, a booby trap goes off. Jones attempts to replace the artifact on the mount with a bag of sand weighing roughly the same amount. When he does so, everything seems okay for an instant, but then the fact that his measurements are off becomes quite obvious as the stand sinks and all heck breaks loose. The cave begins to collapse, boulders fly everywhere, and poison darts fly in every direction, shooting at Jones as he runs away.

When I think about the Fall of man, that scene comes to mind. Perhaps for a brief moment after they sinned, Adam and Eve thought everything was fine, but soon after, all heck began to break loose. First, they both realized they were naked as a jaybird and had to flee to the nearest Gap store for the latest

button-fly fig leaves. Second, they tried to hide from God (though, as Jonah later testified, running from God is a lost cause). Third, in speculation, perhaps it was at this time that Tony, their pet tiger, started to look upon them as lunch. In short, everything had changed in their perfect world.

When Adam and Eve disobeyed God, sin was introduced into the world and has been a problem ever since. Several fundamental changes happened as a result of their disobedience, and they affect us today:

- ✔ **Sin tore relationships among humans.** An immediate effect of the Fall was a psychological barrier between Adam and Eve. Not only did they want to clothe themselves and hide their bodies from each other out of embarrassment, but also when God questioned Adam later, Adam immediately blamed Eve for their sin, further dividing the couple. Not many years later, the ultimate expression of a severed relationship occurred when one of their sons (Cain) murdered the other (Abel). Check out Genesis 4 for details on this saga.

- ✔ **Sin severed humanity's intimate relationship with God.** Genesis paints a picture of a very intimate father/child relationship between God and Adam and Eve before the Fall. Amazingly, he is even depicted as walking in the garden with them. But after the Fall, God's garden strolls are noticeably absent from the rest of the Bible. Adam and Eve were both fearful of God and ran from him, terrified of his holiness in light of their sin. Clearly, a brick wall was put up between humans and God that ultimately had to be broken down by God himself, when he sent Jesus to earth (for that story, see Chapters 3 and 5).

- ✔ **Sin brought humans into bondage.** Although Satan fooled Eve into thinking that disobedience would free her from God's rule, the reality was that she and Adam just exchanged masters. When they obeyed God, he was their master. But through disobedience, sin became a master for Adam, Eve, and everyone else who followed after them. Paul wrote in Romans that humans, without the help of Jesus, are slaves to sin (Romans 6:17).

- ✔ **Sin introduced decay and deterioration into the world.** The Bible is very clear that sin not only had a spiritual significance, but also had physical ramifications. Before the Fall, death didn't exist. But after that, sin's effect was as if a deadly virus was injected into the world's bloodstream, bringing death, decay, and disorder.

- ✔ **Sin is inherited by every generation.** Take a glance at any world history book, and you'll quickly realize that every chapter of human history has been marked by sin: wars, persecutions, slavery, conquest, pollution, colonialism, and terrorism, to name a few. Through the years, people have developed a variety of schemes to deal with the effects of these sins, but the reality is that a lot of really bad stuff has and continues to happen in this world, regardless of how well educated, well fed, or comfortable people are. No one seems to be able to shake loose of it.

Grappling with the Definition of Sin

Sin is any deliberate action, attitude, or thought that goes against God. You and I often think of sin as an obvious act, such as murder, adultery, or theft. Although that's true, sin is also wrongdoing that's far subtler and even unnoticeable at times, such as pride, envy, or even worry. Sin includes both things one shouldn't have done, but did *(sins of commission)* and things one should've done, but didn't *(sins of omission)*.

The two-word description I once heard from a former pastor that, to me, best captures the essence of sin is "deliberate disobedience."

No matter the kind of sin, I see evidence of sin's reality in the world around me. I just can't seem to get away from it. Sin infects me and everyone around me. Each of my kids wants to be the first one to get a plate at supper. (I patiently wait until everyone else is served.) My wife and I argue over who cleaned up the dog's mess last. (No matter what she tells you, I did!) My former co-workers loved to gossip about the incompetence of another worker. (I never gossiped, I assure you!) My friend gripes about the feud he's having with another friend of mine. (I wonder what he says about me behind my back!) I could go on, but you get the point. Here's the deal: I live on a nice quiet road, raise a nice little family of nice little boys, and worked for years in a nice quiet office. Yet, even in this nice quiet life of mine, sin engulfs me at every turn.

When I read the Bible, however, I realize that this reality shouldn't surprise me. The Bible is pretty outspoken on the yucky stuff that's superglued on the hearts of all people. Check out these verses:

- ✔ "I was sinful at birth, filled with sin from the time my mother conceived me" (Psalm 51:5).

- ✔ "There is no one righteous, not even one . . . there is no one who does good, not even one" (Psalm 14:1–3).

- ✔ "For all have sinned and fall short of the glory of God" (Romans 3:23).

- ✔ "The heart is deceitful above all things and desperately corrupt" (Jeremiah 17:9).

The Bible is positive when it comes to talking about God and his plans, but, as you see, it's continually the bearer of bad news when it comes to the hearts of humans. And, as the next section describes, this bad news surfaces in two ways in people's lives.

Categorizing two types of sin

Though humans can commit thousands of particular sins, you can usually lump them all into one of two camps: sins of impulse and sins of the heart.

Sins of impulse are often what come to mind when you think about sin. The typical scenario is:

1. **I see something.**

2. **I want it.**

3. **So I take it.**

That impulsive desire to own, control, or destroy is what leads to adultery, murder, theft, addictions, or excessive anger or rage. Impulsive sins are usually brought on by emotion, and when you allow it, emotions can control you and take you on an irrational road trip.

Impulsive sins are often considered the worst type of sins, but a second kind of sin, although subtler, is even deadlier — these are called *sins of the heart* (or spiritual sins). Spiritual sins are the sins that don't show up on the outside of a person (such as a blatant action, like theft), but harbor themselves deep inside of the heart. Selfishness, jealousy, envy, bitterness, hypocrisy, and deceit are all sins that can be masked on the outside, but carve a hole into one's soul the longer they're allowed to live inside of a person.

Christians often consider pride the most dangerous sin of them all. Ironically, today's society considers pride a positive trait ("take pride in yourself," "hometown pride," and so on). Although confidence in yourself and appreciation of your hometown aren't bad qualities, *selfish* pride is. It causes you to become consumed with your wants, your needs, your happiness, and your rights and to place them as more important than God and others. Pride also serves as a trigger for sins that seem initially like impulsive sins, such as lust, but are actually motivated by a spiritual condition. You can want something, not for animal-like reasons, but purely out of selfishness. Mine, mine, all mine.

A common saying that helps reinforce that pride is at the root of all sin is that "I" is at the center of "sin."

Jesus spent his entire ministry hovering between these two camps of sin (while remaining sinless himself; see Chapter 5). On one side were the impulsive sinners. The religious leaders labeled all prostitutes, dishonest tax collectors, drunkards, rabble-rousers, and so on as "sinners." On the other side were the spiritual sinners. This group was, ironically enough, composed primarily of the religious leaders of the day, called the *Pharisees* and the *teachers of law.* Although outwardly the Pharisees looked like they had their act together, Jesus referred to them as "whitewashed tombs, beautiful on the outside, but filled with dead man's bones" (Matthew 23:27). In other words, the Pharisees were concerned with *looking* holy rather than *being* holy. Their pride showed up in the legalistic attitude that they had as they scorned the people who were beneath them in the religious hierarchy. Not only did they not love others, but Jesus made it clear that they also didn't love God.

Like the Pharisees, the Church has often been more outspoken against impulsive sins and much less aggressive in dealing effectively with the more invisible, spiritual sins. However, Jesus did quite the opposite; take a read through the four Gospels (Matthew, Mark, Luke, and John) and you see that Jesus always saved his sharp and direct words for the spiritual sinners of his day.

Weighing different sins

Throughout history, humans have always had their own ranking of sins. Certain heinous sins are too awful to talk about, and discussing other seemingly more minor sins may get you only a brief look of consternation or even a shoulder shrug. Some sins are socially acceptable, while others are unacceptable; speeding will get you a smile from a neighbor (unless he's the police chief), but setting fire to your neighbor's car out of spite won't be looked upon with a humorous eye. Parts of the Church have followed suit in categorizing sin, as Catholics classify sin as being either *mortal* (major) or *venial* (minor).

The Bible talks about the consequences of certain sins more than others, but it never gives any kind of ranking to them. Instead, the Bible focuses much of its attention on the fact that all sins, major or minor, stain the soul of a human and come under the same judgment of God. In God's eyes, a little white lie is as big of a stain before God as a mass murder. Anything not 100 percent sin-free is impure — 99.99 percent isn't good enough. According to James 2:10, even one itty bitty sin over the course of a lifetime is too much (but check out Chapter 3 to find out about God's grace and forgiveness).

Are you skeptical that God treats all sin the same? Well, consider the life of King David, the greatest leader in all of Israel. When he was at his peak of popularity and success, he became prideful and self-absorbed, which ultimately led him to commit adultery and murder his mistress's husband. From a human standpoint, this guy was disgraceful and committed unforgivable acts. Yet one of the great ironies of the Bible is that God didn't write off David. In fact, after David repented of his sin, God still called David "a man after God's own heart."

Although the Bible makes it clear that all sin is an offense to God, individual sins impact people differently. The consequences that I must deal with if I'm caught saying a little white lie are much different from the consequences of a mass murder.

Misunderstanding sin

Sin is a confusing subject and is often misunderstood, both inside and outside the Church. I've run into two key misunderstandings of sin, both from completely opposite sides of the tracks, so to speak. I discuss these misunderstandings in the following sections.

The "spring break" mistake

The first common perception people have concerning sin is the belief that sin is fun — more fun, in fact, than not sinning. This idea is what drives those television ads that I mention in the first section of this chapter. Don't get me wrong — sin *is* often fun when you first do it. Yet the fun of sinning is always a limited time offer due to two factors:

- **Spiritual hangover:** After committing a sin, many people experience a *spiritual hangover* — remorse and sorrow over why they allowed themselves to sin. Therefore, a moment of fun often turns into a lifetime of pain and regret.

  Christians believe there are two ways to deal with spiritual hangovers. First, by asking for God's forgiveness through his Son Jesus Christ, which is the only true remedy that will heal the hangover once and for all. Second and alternatively, by continued and persistent sinning (not recommended), as sin can actually sear your conscience and cause you to lose your ability to feel regret. (See the "Sinfested" sidebar for more on this issue.)

- **Law of diminishing returns:** Sin is ruled by the law of diminishing returns. In other words, each time you sin, you receive a decreasing amount of pleasure and fun from the act. So, in order to receive the same amount of fun, you have to escalate the sin or else sin more frequently to achieve the same level of pleasure. People who struggle with addictions are a prime example of this law in action. Many drug addicts start out with "recreational" drugs and progressively move into more and more serious and dangerous drugs. Sin is just like this. In the end, the law of diminishing returns turns what started out as fun into outright slavery. (See the "Considering how the Fall changed everything" section in this chapter.)

Even if you focus on the fun of sin, sin is never the *most fun* you can have. Don't forget that God is the one who invented fun and pleasure. Do you think he'd save the best for those who disobey him? No — the ultimate in fun is free from sin and side effects and never decreases in return the more you do it.

The "Don't drink, smoke, or chew, or go with girls who do" mistake

A second misperception many people have is a preoccupation with *legalism* (following rules, thinking of sin as disobeying a "do's and don'ts" list). On a quick read of the Bible, you may easily conclude that it affirms the idea that Christianity is a system based on rules and regulations. The Ten Commandments are filled with sins a Christian must be on guard for. What's more, start reading through the Book of Leviticus in the Old Testament and you'll see a slew of "do this, but don't do that" commands. Even in the New Testament, Jesus gives a lot of "do's and don'ts" over the course of his ministry. I suppose in a strictly practical sense, sin often comes down to doing and thinking certain things and avoiding other things. But that's not *all* sin is, and it's definitely not how God sees it, as I discuss in the next section.

WARNING!

Sinfested

The Bible talks a lot about the conscience and regret for sin, but what about people who seem to thrive in sin and seem immune to remorse? When you knowingly sin (whether or not you're aware of the definition of *sin*) the first time, you will feel bad about it afterwards. However, the next time, it becomes a little easier to do, and you feel a little less guilty. This cycle continues the more you sin. When you continuously sin, your conscience may become as dry as a bone, so much so that you don't feel bad about it and may actually approve of others who do the same thing. Paul confirms this in Romans when he says that God reaches a point where he gives people over to their sin and sin-infested minds (Romans 1:26–32), which is a hard road to ever come back from.

Empathizing with God's View of Sin

God doesn't look at sin as something you do or think that goes against a list of arbitrary house rules. Instead, as I mention in Chapter 1, God sees sin as a slap in his face and his holy nature. One of the most insightful examples in the Bible that illustrates this point is in the parable of the prodigal son. (For a full refresher on this story told by Jesus, see Chapter 3.) In his book *The Cross and the Prodigal* (Concordia Publishing House, 1973), Ken Bailey gives two insights into this parable that bring home the true nature of sin. First, the story starts off with a son asking his father (who is still very much alive and kicking) for his share of the inheritance. According to Luke 15:11–12, "A certain man had two sons. The younger of them said to his father, 'Father, give me my share of your property.'"

Even in the relaxed culture that you and I live in, this kind of request is a major no-no. But in the more traditional Middle Eastern culture of Jesus' day, this request was unspeakably bad — it's something that was *never* done. However, notice that the reason making such a request was so terrible had nothing to do with rules (the Hebrew Law was silent about such a request), but had everything to do with the relationship between the son and his father. The request was simply understood as impatience on the son's part for his father to die. Through this story, Jesus indicates that the prodigal son's sin wasn't about breaking rules, but about breaking his father's heart.

In addition, the older brother in the story — who's often thought of as the good kid — also sins against the father. When the prodigal returns and his father forgives him, the older brother complains bitterly. Jesus continued:

But the older son was angry, and wouldn't go in. Therefore, his father came out and begged him. But he answered his father, "Behold, these many years I have served you, and I never disobeyed a commandment of yours, but you never gave me a goat, that I might celebrate with my friends. But when this, your son, came, who has devoured your living with prostitutes, you killed the fattened calf for him."

—Luke 15:28–30

Living in the United States, I may overlook the cultural significance of how the older brother behaves, but if you ask a Middle Easterner, you get a much different take on the situation. The older brother's refusal to attend his brother's celebration is a public slap in the face to his dad. What's more, his subsequent heated conversion with his father reveals a deep disrespect and contempt for the man. The older son seems to be the good, hard-working kid who obeys his father, but when push comes to shove, the spiritual sins inside of him hurt his father just as much as the impulsive sin of his younger brother.

When you look at sin in this light, you can see that it's not simply about breaking a "do's and don'ts" list. Sin is all about hurting God's heart. When I sin, I wound God, just like both of the sons in the parable of the prodigal son break their father's heart.

Tying in Humans' Relation to the Fall

I don't think you'll get much of an argument from most anyone that a lot of bad stuff goes on in the world. But you'll get a considerable difference of opinion over how inevitable sin is. Is it something that humans can stomp out with effort? Or are any attempts to remove sin a hopeless cause? Traditionally, Christians express three different opinions on this issue:

- ✔ **Humans are born with a clean slate and can make it to heaven on their own.** This optimistic view says that Adam and Eve's sin didn't directly infect others in later generations. In other words, everyone is born with the same clean slate that Adam and Eve had. Therefore, the logical conclusion is that if people really wanted to, they could go without sinning. As a result, humans can earn their salvation, and God's grace isn't truly essential. This perspective, eliminating the need for Jesus' saving work on the cross (see Chapter 5) is outside of biblical Christian teaching.

People who hold this view believe that people are basically good. In other words, people may sin, but deep inside, they really want to do the right thing most of the time. Therefore, a logical conclusion is that if you and I try really hard and eliminate the conditions that cause people to sin (such as poverty) and educate them, then sin can be stomped out. That sort of optimism was at a fever pitch a hundred years ago, until the two world wars largely shattered the notion of the innate goodness of humans. Mass exterminations, concentration camps, and populations that looked the other way tend to do that sort of thing.

✔ **God needs to give humans a jump-start.** A second perspective drains half of the optimism out. These Christians believe that God's grace is essential to overcome sin and receive salvation, but after an initial infusion of grace (through baptism), people earn their salvation by cooperating with God's grace (by partaking of sacraments). Traditionally, Catholics hold this perspective.

✔ **God needs to do all the work.** The final view, which Protestants (particularly evangelicals) typically hold, sees the state of humanity more pessimistically. Overcoming sin is only possible by salvation by grace, apart from anything humans can do on their own.

From this perspective, Adam and Eve's sin was more than just a prototype of the future. In fact, their sin infected the entire human race. So, they not only transmitted chromosomes to their children, but a *sin nature* (a tendency to sin) as well. As a result, all humans have inherited a sin nature and a stained set of clothes, and they'll never be able to completely get rid of the stains as long as they walk on this earth. Or, to put it in more blunt terms, you've probably seen the bumper sticker that says, "Mean people suck." Well, this perspective says, in effect, "All people suck." Therefore, the good that both Christians and non-Christians do happens only by the grace of God, not from any innate goodness inside of people. (See Chapter 11 for more.)

Warring with Satan (And Knowing Who You're Fighting Against)

Biblical Christianity says that Satan (also called *the devil*) is ultimately the one behind all this temptation and sin. As the sworn enemy of God, Satan seeks to get as many humans as possible to join his team. Satan was originally an *angel* (or spiritual being) in heaven, but because he wanted to have the same "social status" as God, he decided to revolt against God (Isaiah 14:12–15 and Ezekiel 28:11–19 both allude to this event). As a result, God threw him out of heaven, and he persuaded a third of the angels to join him (Revelation 12:3–4).

A must-read: *The Screwtape Letters*

[God's] a hedonist at heart. All those fasts and vigils and stakes and crosses are only a façade ... He makes no secret of it; at his right hand are "pleasures for evermore." Ugh! ... He's vulgar, Wormwood ... He has filled his world with pleasures. There are things for humans to do all day long without his minding in the least — sleeping, washing, eating, making love, playing, praying, working. Everything has to be twisted before it's any use to us. We fight under cruel disadvantages. Nothing is naturally on our side.

—C.S. Lewis, *The Screwtape Letters* (Harper Collins, 2001)

The Screwtape Letters is the fictional account of a senior demon named Screwtape writing to a junior demon on how to tempt humans. Although the book is fiction, it reads like an enemy's secret plans or an opposing team's playbook. With wit and humor, Lewis gives his unforgettable take on the tactics and strategies that the devil uses to tempt humans.

REMEMBER

People have many different perceptions of Satan and his influence in this world. Therefore, consider the following four ideas about Satan that the Bible plainly reveals:

✔ **Satan is real, not a cosmic metaphor.** Some people today believe that Satan is a symbol of evil rather than a living spiritual being. The Bible, however, indicates that Satan is a real-life enemy, not just some kind of cosmic metaphor. Just a handful of examples include

- When Jesus was tempted in the desert (check out the "Think different: The sequel" sidebar), the Book of Matthew says pretty matter-of-factly that he did more than just battle temptations coming from within himself — he actually dealt head-on with Satan (see Matthew 4:1–11).

- Peter often writes about sin, but goes out of his way to speak specifically of Satan as a real entity to combat. In 1 Peter 5:8, Peter talks about "your enemy the devil" and points out that humans are to resist "him."

- John speaks in his gospel of the devil as a real being when he says, "The evening meal was being served, and the devil had already prompted Judas Iscariot, son of Simon, to betray Jesus" (John 13:2).

- Jesus, in the Gospels, and John, in the Book of Revelation, describe at length what's ultimately going to happen to a being called Satan (see Luke 10:18, John 12:31, and Revelation 12:9 and 20:10).

Ironically, the fact that many people today don't believe in a literal Satan fits exactly into his plan, according to biblical Christianity. One of Satan's most effective schemes is to belittle his own existence. C.S. Lewis talks about this in his classic book *The Screwtape Letters* (Harper Collins, 2001), which is a fictional account of a senior demon named Screwtape writing to a junior demon on how to tempt humans. In it, Screwtape notes:

> *The fact that "devils" are predominately comic figures in the modern imagination will help you. If any faint suspicion of your existence begins to arouse in his mind, suggest to him a picture of something in red tights, and persuade him that since he cannot believe in that . . . he therefore cannot believe in you.*

✔ **Satan is just a God-wannabe.** It's easy to think of Satan as the anti-God — a force equally as powerful as God. In fact, however, Satan is a God-wannabe. He's a frightening spirit, he's a great tempter, and he has some inside knowledge, but he's a limited creature (Job 1:12, Luke 4:6, and 2 Thessalonians 2:7–8). Therefore, he doesn't know all things, can't read your mind, and isn't everywhere at every time like God is (because, by definition, only *God* has these qualities). So, although the Bible makes it clear that Satan is a powerful force to be reckoned with, he's no match for God.

✔ **Satan can't make Christians do anything.** Satan may be powerful, but he can't make Christians sin and he can't control them. Satan tempts, but he can't back it up with any muscle power. Paul emphasizes this when he says in 1 Corinthians 10:13:

> *No temptation has taken you except what is common to man. God is faithful, who will not allow you to be tempted above what you are able, but will with the temptation also make the way of escape, that you may be able to endure it.*

So, God promises that Christians always have an escape plan — if they choose to take it.

✔ **Satan is a born loser.** I hate it when a film or book comes out and the ending is a cliffhanger, forcing me to wait until the sequel to find out what happens. Fortunately, God didn't leave you and I with a cliffhanger in terms of what eventually happens in the battle between him and Satan. He says emphatically in the Bible that his team wins and the "bad" team loses (Revelation 20:10).

Satan's something like the quarterback of a football team that's getting trounced 54-0 in the fourth quarter. The losing team still tries to score as many points as possible, and people on the winning team are still prone to injury, but the end outcome is never in doubt, even if the losing team gets a couple mop-up touchdowns.

✔ **Satan battles in the spiritual realm.** Although some people believe that sin is a personal struggle between an individual and his or her con-science, the Bible paints a different picture. Ephesians 6:12 says:

> *For our wrestling is not against flesh and blood, but against the princi-*
> *palities, against the powers, against the world's rulers of the darkness*
> *of this age, and against the spiritual forces of wickedness in the heav-*
> *enly places.*

In other words, a constant unseen spiritual battle is going on that's every bit as real as the physical world that you and I live in. Sound weird? Perhaps. Sci-fi? Yup. Understandable? Not really. But the Bible says it, so Christians believe it's important to recognize that there's more than meets the eye as you face temptation.

Experiencing Temptation

People struggle with different kinds of temptation. To some, it's all about chocolate and éclairs. Others face the temptation to prioritize their careers and money over everything else. And to still others, gossip and backstabbing are struggles to overcome. No matter what temptation you face, it's important to call a spade a "spade" and know what to do when it comes your way.

Recognizing temptation

Satan is hell-bent — literally! — on getting humans to sin. To do so, he tempts, tantalizes, entices, persuades, coaxes, and lures. But keep in mind that temptation itself isn't a sin. Instead, it's how one responds to this temptation that determines whether, in fact, he or she commits a sin. Christians believe that Satan uses several tactics to turn temptation into deliberate disobedience:

- **Blurs and obscures God's black-and-white commands:** Satan attempts to blur the absolute nature of God's commands. For example, when Satan tempts Eve, he starts off by trying to get Eve to dismiss the black-and-white nature of what God said, saying, "Did God *really* say that?" Then he dismisses the consequences of sin, saying something to the effect of, "Ah, you surely won't die. He's just yanking your chain." Satan loves rationalization and doubt, and I'm often eager to follow suit. When tempted, I often have a running dialogue in my head that goes something like, "Hmmm, is that really a sin? That's a gray area that the Bible isn't very clear on. I bet it's not. In fact, I'm sure of it. I think."

- **Makes sin look harmless and desirable:** When Satan tempts Eve, he makes the sin look risk-free, dismissing the penalty of sin by telling her, "You surely won't die." After planting that seed, he goes further by telling her that not only is this act harmless, but it's also desirable, because she'll be like God if she does it. As I talk about earlier in the chapter, Satan carries a banner around saying "Sin is fun" and hopes you believe his advertising is truthful.

✔ **Makes sin look liberating:** Satan also connects sin with liberation. When he tempts Eve, he implies that sinning will free her from the cage that God's placed her in. But, as noted earlier, sin doesn't unshackle you, but only exchanges one master for another.

✔ **Targets the most vulnerable spot:** Satan loves to maximize temptation when you and I are vulnerable and weak. For example, when Satan tempts Jesus, the Book of Matthew says that he waits until Jesus has *fasted* (gone without food) for forty days in the desert — at the exact point in which he was most vulnerable.

Many people are most susceptible to sins of impulse (refer to the section "Categorizing two types of sin," earlier in this chapter) when they're weak or down about life. Even though sinning only makes a bad situation worse, it's easy to want to run away in a moment of pleasure and fun rather than to deal with the tough issues of life. People's escapes into drugs, alcohol, and sex are often the result of something deeper going on in their lives.

Paradoxically, people who seem to have everything going their way in life are often most vulnerable to spiritual sins. Pride and self-sufficiency begin to take control of their lives just when they think the world's their oyster.

As you see, Satan is an equal opportunity tempter. He uses both peaks and valleys of life to lure people into his fold.

✔ **Values economy of effort:** Satan must've taken an economics course at some point. Knowing that little and big sins both amount to equal separation from God, Satan is perfectly satisfied with using small sins to tempt you. In Lewis's *The Screwtape Letters,* the senior devil writes to a junior devil giving advice:

> *You will say these are very small sins; and doubtless, like all young tempters, you are anxious to be able to report spectacular wickedness. But do remember, the only thing that matters is the extent to which you separate the man from [God] . . . Murder is no better than cards if cards can do the trick. Indeed the safest road to hell is the gradual one — the gentle slope, soft underfoot, without sudden turnings, without milestones, without signposts.*

✔ **Uses guilt to drive you away from God:** When you slip up, Satan loves to use that uneasiness and remorse to tempt you into moving further and further away from God. Again, in *The Screwtape Letters,* Lewis writes about this:

> *[Guilty humans] hate every idea that suggests [God], just as men in financial embarrassment hate the very sight of a [check book]. In this state, [a person] will not omit, but he will increasingly dislike, his religious duties. He will think about them as little as he feels he*

> *decently can beforehand, and forget them as soon as possible when*
> *they are over. A few weeks ago you had to tempt him to unreality and*
> *inattention in his prayers: but now you will find him opening his arms*
> *to you and almost begging you to distract his purpose and benumb his*
> *heart.*

Paul makes a clear distinction between guilt and godly sorrow: Guilt drives people away from God and into their own world of despair, but godly sorrow brings them to repentance and cleansing (2 Corinthians 7:10).

Responding to tempting situations

The responses of Eve (see the "Desiring to Be Different: The Original Ego Trip" section) and Jesus (see the "Think different: The sequel" sidebar) to temptation provide case studies in successful and unsuccessful responses to temptation.

What not to do

Eve (and Adam) could both say no to temptation, but both give in to it. Take Eve, for example. She does the following:

- ✔ **Eve listens to the temptation.** Instead of going away from the temptation, she stays and listens to the serpent. That initial decision is the first in a series of poor choices that ultimately lead to her sin. The Apostle Paul urges people to "flee temptation" (1 Timothy 6:11, 2 Timothy 2:22), to run away from it, because people are often so weak that staying and listening will easily lead to sinning.

- ✔ **Eve talks about it.** Not only does she listen, but she also begins to be an active participant in the conversation. She puts up a slight defense, but it seems weak and half-hearted. She essentially buys into the conversation, allowing Satan to continue his temptation.

  When I read the exchange between Satan and Eve, I think about a typical visit to a car dealership. A car salesman starts off with chitchat when someone enters the lot as a way to get him to buy in to the whole experience, to get his listening ear, and to ultimately convince the shopper to buy a car.

- ✔ **Eve deliberately disobeys.** When she finally buys into Satan's sales pitch, she takes the bait and eats it. She toyed with temptation before, but this is the actual act of deliberate disobedience toward God.

- ✔ **Eve convinces Adam to sin as well.** Although you can only speculate on her exact motivation, the fact is that after sinning, Eve doesn't just realize her mistake and repent of it. Instead, she commits a second sin — getting Adam to sin by giving him fruit and telling him to eat it, too.

What to do

Paul gives the best and surest advise on what to do when tempted: Get the heck outta there (see 1 Corinthians 6:18, 2 Timothy 2:22)! If you run away from the temptation, then you certainly won't be lulled into sin.

However, it's not always possible to get away from a tempting situation. Therefore, your next tactic is to do what Jesus did when he faced temptation in the desert (see the "Think different: The sequel" sidebar earlier in the chapter). Although Jesus couldn't exactly flee in this situation, he was wholly prepared to do battle with Satan when he was tempted. Satan gave his "Think Different" speech three different times in three different ways, but each time Jesus responded with conviction using the Bible, God's truth, as ammunition against Satan's tactics. Satan even tried to twist the meaning of a Bible passage to meet his needs, but Jesus would have none of it. He knew the Bible well enough to counter Satan's attempts to fuzzy things up.

What's more, hearing Christian speakers or reading Christian books is no substitute for knowing what the Bible says. Christian authors, speakers, and preachers aren't perfect, and their teaching may not always line up with God's truth. However, the more you know God's truth, the more you're able to discern teaching that doesn't synch up with it.

Sinning After You're "Saved"

Being a Christian doesn't mean living a sin-free life, but it means living a life that is freed from the power of sin. Christianity holds that without Jesus, you are a slave to sin. However, with Christ, you have been freed of these shackles. As Paul writes:

> *Those who belong to Christ have crucified the sinful nature with its passions and desires.*
>
> —Galatians 5:24

> *For we know that our old self was crucified with him so that the body of sin might be done away with that we should no longer be slaves to sin, because anyone who has died has been freed from sin.*
>
> —Romans 6:6–7

God gives Christians the strength to overcome sin. After all, a Christian is regenerated (Titus 3:6) and receives a new nature (2 Corinthians 5:17, Colossians 3:10), as discussed in Chapter 13. With that backdrop, Jesus' famous statement, "The truth shall set you free" (John 8:32), makes much more sense. What he's saying is that a Christian is transformed on the inside and freed from this bondage of sin.

However, this newfound freedom doesn't mean that Christians no longer sin or no longer have a desire to sin. But it does mean that a process toward perfection has begun in each Christian. To illustrate, consider that when you're born, you start off with a body of sin cells. The moment you become a Christian and surrender more and more of your life to Christ, these sin cells are overridden by the godly nature you acquire. Through the years, as Christians grow in their faith, their sin nature becomes lesser and lesser part of them as the godly nature is implemented in their lives.

When this transformation starts, a Christian begins to become aware of sins that he or she never saw before. God is definitely a patient God, as he allows Christians to deal with what they can handle at a time. Dealing with sin in my life reminds me of peeling an onion — shedding one sin layer at a time.

For a discussion on how God deals with sin in people's lives, check out Chapter 3.

Chapter 5

Jesus Christ: His Life, Ministry, and Radical Claims

*W*hen you start to examine the life of Jesus Christ in the Bible, one truth becomes crystal clear: Christianity is all about Jesus Christ. Although it's easy for Christians to get caught up in following rules and "towing the line," the heart of Christianity is Jesus Christ's simple (yet oh so deep) teaching about himself. Christians believe that Jesus wasn't just a special messenger or a moral teacher pointing people toward God. In fact, they believe he was none other than God in the flesh, pointing people to himself and his way of salvation — what Christians today call the "gospel."

In this chapter, you discover who Jesus is and what his teachings were all about and explore whether Jesus was a spiritual guru, a good teacher, or literally God in the flesh.

In Brief: Introducing Jesus

Almost everyone in the world needs some kind of introduction. I, for one, can't even go home to my parents' house for the holidays without needing to reintroduce myself: "Remember me? . . . Rich . . . your son." People in the public eye often run into the same problem. James Bond is the world's most popular spy, but even he's always telling everyone, "My name is Bond, James Bond." Some

of the most famous people in history don't get a much better shake in this day and age; many recognize Plato as a Greek philosopher, but I suspect others think he was just the inventor of that doughy stuff that kids play with. And take Julius Caesar — was he a Roman ruler or the founder of a pizza chain?

Jesus Christ is one person who never needed much of an introduction when he walked the earth, and he still doesn't need much of one today in the 21st century. His name — whether spoken from the pulpit of a church or used as profanity on a TV sitcom — seems to pop up wherever you go. The symbol of his death, the cross, isn't only the centerpiece of church sanctuaries, but it also seems to be an ever-popular fashion statement on the necks of folks on MTV. What's more, hardly a year goes by without his appearance on the cover of *Time, Newsweek,* or some other major magazine.

His name is almost universally recognized the world over and his life influences modern culture, but who exactly is the real Jesus Christ? A strong case can be made that Jesus is the single most significant person to have ever lived on this earth. In spite of his influence, he wasn't a political revolutionary, a military genius, a brilliant philosopher, or a mesmerizing salesman. Instead, Jesus was a common man with a most uncommon claim — that he was the Son of God.

The following sections, what I call the *CliffsNotes* version of Jesus' life, give you the gist of what he did on earth. But, to Christians, his life is far more compelling than just this simple narrative. Specifically, Christians believe that Jesus wasn't just a man who did great things; he was God in the flesh, who came into the world as a man (well, actually as a baby, like everyone else; read the next section for the details) for the express purpose of dying for the sins of all people (see Chapter 3).

Accounting for the early years

Jesus was a Jewish man from the small town of Nazareth, which was situated in Roman-occupied Palestine (modern-day Israel) some 2,000 years ago. Nearly all of what is known about his life is recorded in the Bible's four Gospel narratives — Matthew, Mark, Luke, and John — although a few non-biblical historical documents talk about Jesus as well (see Chapter 2), but not in great length.

When you read these Gospel accounts of Jesus' life, you get the basics of who he was and what he did, but keep in mind that the Gospel writers took a kind of *For Dummies* approach to writing — they weren't concerned with documenting all events and teachings, just the essential facts of what Jesus' followers needed to know. (Rumor has it that the Gospels were originally called *Jesus Chronicles For Dummies,* but I've not yet been able to substantiate that report.) Along this line, John closes his Gospel by saying that Jesus did many more

things than are written down, and that "if they would all be written, even the world itself wouldn't have room for those books."

Jesus was born in the town of Bethlehem. His parents, Mary and Joseph, were very typical Jews living in first-century Palestine. However, Christians believe their son wasn't conceived in the typical "the birds and the bees" manner. Instead, his conception was miraculous. After a visit from the Archangel Gabriel, Mary became impregnated by the Holy Spirit and gave birth to Jesus, even though she was a virgin (Luke 1:26–38). Like other Jewish boys, Jesus was circumcised as an infant and grew up going to the local synagogue. The Gospels share just one incident of his youth; when Jesus was twelve years old, he got into an in-depth theological discussion with the Jewish teachers at the Jerusalem temple. The leaders were amazed, not only because he was so young, but by the extent of his wisdom and understanding for a person at any age.

Although inquiring minds want to know, exactly what Jesus did between the ages of 12 and 30 is largely unknown. Evidently, that information isn't critical for his followers to know about, because the Bible is largely silent about this period of his life. However, a couple facts can be stitched together. He was a carpenter (see Mark 6:3), learning the trade from his father. Jesus may have taken over his father's shop at some point, because Joseph apparently dies sometime during this period of Jesus' life. Very likely, Jesus spent these years as a carpenter, providing for his family and preparing for his ministry to come.

In profile: Jesus of Nazareth

Name: Jesus (translated from the original Aramaic *Yehowshuwa*). Although some people think of *Christ* as being part of his actual name, it's actually a title ascribed to him (meaning "The Anointed"). In fact, Jesus didn't have a last name.

Also known as: Messiah, Christ, Savior, Son of God, Son of Man, Prince of Peace, Alpha and Omega, The Holy One, Emmanuel, The Way, The Truth, The Life, King of Kings, Lord of Lords, The Word, The Lord

Traditional date of birth: The exact year is unknown. The Church in the Middle Ages thought it was 0 B.C., though modern scholars believe it was around 6 B.C. The day of his birth

is also unknown, though Christians traditionally celebrate it on December 25. Traditional birth year (as observed in the Middle Ages) separates B.C. from A.D. in dating systems.

Place of birth: Bethlehem

Place he grew up: Nazareth

Date of death: Was crucified in approximately A.D. 33

Place of death: Golgotha, outside of Jerusalem

Length of ministry: 3.5 years

Claim to fame: Claimed to be God in the flesh, sent to the world to die for the sins of the world. Rose from the dead after three days.

A man of joy

God the Father has set his Son above his companions, anointing him with the oil of joy.

—Hebrews 1:9

One of the stereotypes of Jesus that has persisted over the years is Jesus as a serious, detached person, standing aloof from those around him. I find it hard to relate to such a caricature. But, if you read between the lines of the Gospels, you see that Jesus had to be anything but that wooden stereotype. Instead, Jesus clearly was a man of joy, one who loved life and lived it to the fullest. Anyone who loved people like he did, hung out with "sinners," and was the go-to person for children, prostitutes, and tax collectors had to be someone who radiated infectious joy.

Stepping into the spotlight

When Jesus was around 30 years old, he began his public ministry. It may seem strange that Jesus, the Son of God, would patiently wait around working as a carpenter throughout his twenties before launching his ministry. However, this wasn't unusual in that day and age: Men usually started ministering around the age of 30. In addition, some of the most famous Jewish leaders, such as Joseph (the one with the "Amazing Technicolor Dreamcoat") and David (the guy who toasted Goliath), began their leadership at this age. His public ministry lasted a mere three-and-a-half years (not even the length of a U.S. Presidential term) before he was killed.

Jesus selected 12 common men from various walks of life to be his *disciples* (students and followers). Jesus and his "band of brothers" traveled throughout Palestine preaching and teaching. Jesus spent a lot of time talking to religious leaders who were suspicious of his claims, but he seemed to prefer hanging out with commoners and people who were looked down upon by the religious authorities. His principal message was that he was the *Messiah,* the "anointed one" who the Old Testament predicted was going to come and free Israel and serve as king. He performed many miracles (which Christians believe demonstrated that his authority was from God), showing compassion for the hurting.

Fulfilling his purpose

Jesus may have attracted massive crowds of enthusiastic people wherever he went, but he didn't win any Mr. Popularity awards within the ranks of the

Jewish religious leaders, known as the *Pharisees* and the *Sadducees.* They saw Jesus as a threat. The Jewish people may have been ruled by the Roman Empire, but the religious leaders had a positional standing and degree of local authority, which was something they didn't want to give up. After Jesus started teaching ideas that weren't in line with their perspective and after they saw how powerful he was becoming among the masses, they concluded that they had to get him out of the picture.

Although Christians believe he was innocent of any charges of rebelling against Roman authority, Jesus was tried, found guilty, and sentenced to be *crucified,* a grizzly method of execution used by the Romans in which a condemned man was tied or nailed to a cross. (See the "Questioning Why Jesus Was Crucified" section later in this chapter for more information.) He lay on the cross for several hours before dying, after which he was buried in a tomb. Because leaders heard of his claims that he'd be raised from the dead, they put a huge boulder over the entrance to the tomb and posted Roman guards outside of it 24/7 to ensure that the disciples didn't make any funny business.

Christians believe Jesus was resurrected from the dead on the third day following his death and that he appeared to his followers on several occasions over the next forty days (see the "Peering into an Empty Tomb: Revisiting the Resurrection" section). The Gospel writers make it a point to say that his appearances weren't just some spirit, angel, or hologram like you see in a *Star Wars* film. Instead, they say that his resurrected body, although different from an earthly body, was still every bit as real and physical. Notably, he ate and drank with the disciples as well as touched them. Then, after forty days, he ascended into heaven, where he remains to this day, all the while being actively involved in the lives of all Christians (see Chapter 7). However, he promised that he'll return once more, which you can read all about in Chapter 9.

Looking at How Jesus Lived

"Purpose-driven" is a popular slogan floating around churches these days. That catch phrase is appropriate because Christians serve a purpose-driven Savior. During his brief life, Jesus was motivated by an overriding purpose — to die a sacrificial death, which Christians believe happened so that all may experience salvation (see Chapter 3). Yet, he didn't just wait around to die. Instead, he was bent on accomplishing other objectives while he walked around on this earth. The four Gospels give a detailed look at Jesus' purpose-driven life, but if you have to summarize, you can boil it down to seven major tasks. I discuss these in this section.

Jesus pointed people toward himself

For a man who has a reputation of humility among Christians and non-Christians alike, it's surprising to realize that, more than anything else Jesus may have done, his overriding aim was to talk about himself — who he was and why he came to earth. Jesus made it clear that he and he alone was the route that people can take to be reconciled with God. He said that he was *the* way, *the* truth, and *the* life (see John 14:6).

If you hear someone constantly talking about himself or herself, that person almost always has a "big head," demands to be pampered, and expects privileges. But the way Jesus lived directly contrasts with that behavior. When Jesus spoke of himself, he did so in a way that didn't say, "Look at me!" like you see when you watch a celebrity interview or an awards show. Instead, he uttered the words as if stating a fact. In addition, as I discuss in the sections that follow, his life was characterized by sacrifice, selflessness, and servanthood — terms you don't see floating around on *The Tonight Show* very often.

In spite of the fact that he made bold claims about himself as the Son of God, Jesus made it clear that he wasn't interested in seeking glory. John records two times that Jesus specifically went out of his way to emphasize that point: "I don't want praise from men" (John 5:41) and "I don't seek my own glory" (John 8:50). Therefore, as Christians reflect on who Christ is today, they consider the remarkable paradox of his amazing humility combined with the fact that he's also God in the flesh.

Always ahead of his time

During the time Jesus lived on earth, men dominated culture. Women were considered second-class citizens and weren't often given much respect or attention by men. However, Jesus crossed those social conventions and gave an amazing amount of attention and priority to them. The Gospels say that Jesus treated women as equal to men. A few examples come to mind:

✔ Jesus talked at length with a Samaritan woman, surprising his disciples that he'd associate with a woman, particularly one of a race that Jews looked down upon (John 4:1–26).

✔ When a woman of ill repute anointed Jesus' feet, a Jewish leader who was dining with Jesus became very angry. Yet, rather than sending her away, Jesus praised her devotion and chastised the religious leader (Luke 7:47–50).

✔ Jesus was an equal opportunity healer, healing women as well as men (Matthew 9:18–35, Matthew 15:21–28).

✔ Jesus used a woman as a character in his "Lost Coin" parable (Luke 15:8–10).

✔ Jesus became good friends with Mary and Martha (Luke 10:38–42).

Jesus healed and cared for the down and out

Christians believe that Jesus did far more than preach an hour a day and ride away from the masses on a stretch limo donkey. No, he was constantly rolling up his sleeves and getting his hands dirty. Jesus Christ actively demonstrated his love for people, no matter their race, sex, social status, or walk of life. He spent a lot time caring for others and miraculously healing the sick, lame, and demon-possessed. The Gospels don't aim to account for all his miracles, and sometimes they aren't specific on the exact number of people impacted, but they speak of more than three dozen separate miracles — including healing the sick, giving sight to the blind, feeding thousands of people, and even bringing a couple of people back to life.

Jesus didn't perform all these miracles simply to amaze friends and influence enemies. Instead, he did miraculous works to either show compassion to an individual or to build up a person's faith. For the most part, the Bible indicates that Jesus' miracles were practical, matter-of-fact, and behind-the-scenes. He did some miracles in public, but he was no publicity hound. Jesus seemed to prefer to heal people when he was one-on-one with them, rather than in front of a large crowd.

Just as Christ healed and helped people for the simple reason that he loved them, so too Christians believe they are to live out his example by caring for others, not out of duty or obligation, but purely as an expression of their love.

Jesus taught his followers how to live

Jesus may not have had the domed stadiums available that preachers like Billy Graham speak in today, but he could sure pack the crowds in anywhere he went. During those countless impromptu sermons throughout the countryside, within town squares, and inside city temples, he spent a lot of time talking about how his followers should live.

Jesus was immensely practical in this teaching. He didn't waste time expounding on abstract beliefs of higher learning or want his followers to hang out in ivory towers. Instead, he emphasized how everyday people are to live in a sinful world. I discuss three major themes that rise up from his teaching in this section.

Loving God and one another

Jesus instructed his followers to love one another (Matthew 19:19, John 10:27), love their enemies (Matthew 5:44), and love their God (Matthew 22:37). Over and over again, Jesus drove the point home that if you truly love God and the person next to you more than you love yourself, then you're going to please God.

Living a holy life

Jesus taught his followers to live lives of personal holiness to God. In other words, Christians believe that if you really love the Lord, then you're devoted to pursuing purity and sinlessness. He challenged everyone to be "perfect" (Matthew 5:48) and "righteous" (Matthew 5:20). Though his teachings of love and peace are popular today, Jesus stressed that he also came into this world for judgment in the future (John 9:39), as I discuss in Chapter 9.

When he dealt with people one-on-one, Jesus always showed them love, yet he never once neglected holiness in the process. For example, after he healed a lame man, he warned him, "Stop sinning or something worse could happen to you" (John 5:14). So too, when he saved a woman who was caught in the act of adultery from being stoned to death, he forgave her, but added, "Go now and leave your life of sin" (John 8:11).

People have always had a natural tendency to embrace either extreme — love or holiness. Those in the love camp emphasize freedom and want everyone to "live and let live," but those bent on holiness tend to speak vehemently against sin and to be harsh to the sinner. Jesus said that his followers must be concerned with *both* love and holiness and not neglect either of them.

Being obedient at all costs

Jesus taught that his followers can't be lukewarm in their commitment to him. Instead, Jesus pointed out time and time again that he wanted (and still wants) 100 percent of a believer's devotion. He said to his disciples, "If any man would come after me, let him deny himself, and take up his cross, and follow me" (Mark 8:34). He added to this in Matthew 10:39, "Whoever loses his life for my sake will find it." Jesus showed the literal implications of this teaching in an encounter with a spoiled rich kid. The young man rode his donkey up to Jesus and asked what he must do to receive eternal life. Jesus saw the hold that wealth had on the man's heart, which would get in the way of true loyalty to him. So, Jesus told him first to sell all he had and give it to the poor and then told the man to follow him. As you see, Christians believe that Jesus wants his followers to be loyal to him regardless of the cost — that's the essence of what the Christian phrase *dying to self* means. (See also Chapter 13.)

Not a used car salesman

Jesus attracted followers during his ministry wherever he went, but it wasn't because he was an aggressive salesman. He never persuaded, coaxed, cajoled, or swayed anyone to follow him. He simply taught and let each individual decide how he or she would respond.

What's more, he never made following him sound easy, exciting, or fun. In fact, he said quite the opposite, explaining that following him meant "dying to self" (see the section, "Jesus taught his followers how to live" for more on the Christian life).

Jesus provided the ultimate example of how to live

You may have heard the phrase "What Would Jesus Do?" and seen the WWJD bracelets and T-shirts that were all the craze at the turn of the century. Well, the reason for all the hubbub is that Christians believe they're to live their lives as Jesus did — so many Christians used (and continue to use) this acronym as a sort of reminder. The Bible says that Jesus truly led by example. As the Apostle Peter said years later, "Christ gave you an example, that you should follow in his steps" (1 Peter 2:21). Christians focus on three particular areas:

- **Jesus showed his followers how to live obedient lives.** Jesus spoke of being perfect, but he asked no more from others than what he practiced in his own life. Oh, since he was Son of God, it's natural to think he must have had it easy and wasn't really tempted to sin. But the Bible makes it clear that he did face temptation just like you and I and that he genuinely suffered as he battled it (Hebrews 2:18). Yet, unlike everyone else, when he was "at bat," he never struck out and gave in to temptation. Instead, he batted .1000, living a life without one single sin. Therefore, if a Christian wants to know how to overcome temptation, then he or she needs to look no further than Jesus and observe the ways in which he conquered it (see Chapter 4 for more on overcoming temptation).

- **Jesus demonstrated how to live a balanced life.** Jesus was a man in the middle. On one side, he had holier-than-thou religious leaders who were preoccupied with following rules, yet had no love for their fellow men (and, ironically, for God either — see Matthew 23). On the other, he had the "sinners" — the tax collectors, prostitutes, and other outcasts — who may have been very accepting, but didn't much care about purity.

Time after time, Jesus weaved his way between the legalism of the religious leaders and the permissiveness of the sinners — he was holier than the "holy people" of his day, and yet he loved and accepted sinners as brothers and sisters.

✔ **Jesus showed how to live as a servant.** Christians believe that Jesus called (and still calls) his followers to be servants of others. To show what true servanthood looks like, he performed one of the most humbling and lowly jobs possible — washing his disciples' feet. Jesus said, "If I then, the Lord and the Teacher, have washed your feet, you also ought to wash one another's feet. For I have given you an example, that you also should do as I have done to you" (John 13:14–15). Jesus later provided the ultimate example of being a servant by dying on a cross so that others may experience salvation (see Chapter 3 for more).

Jesus changed the perspective of one's relationship to God

During the Old Testament period, faithful Jews thought of serving a holy and awesome God, but never imagined their relationship as personal with the Lord of the universe. Yet, when Jesus spoke of the relationship that people can have with God, he spoke in terms that were far more intimate than people were used to hearing. For example, when he taught his followers how to pray, he started off with "Our father" (Matthew 6:9). The word *father* (the Greek word *Abba*) is an intimate term that can be translated as *daddy*. On other occasions, such as the prodigal son parable (refer to Chapter 3), Jesus spoke of a warm father who desired a deep relationship with his children. Throughout his teaching, Jesus showed a deep reverence for God the Father, but he replaced formality with the simplicity and intimacy of "my daddy."

What's more, an old hymn, called "What a Friend We Have in Jesus," says the same idea about Jesus Christ. Christians believe that the concept of Jesus as a friend is more than sentimental hogwash; it's really true. Jesus may be the Son of God, but he invites Christians to think of him as a friend as well (John 15:15).

Balancing reverence and intimacy is a tricky act, and different parts of the Christian Church emphasize one part of Jesus' teaching over another. Catholics and Orthodox Christians tend to emphasize reverence, while Protestants (particularly evangelicals) tend to focus on a personal relationship with God.

A must-read: *In His Steps*

I want volunteers from the First Church who will pledge themselves, earnestly and honestly for an entire year, not to do anything without first asking the question, "What would Jesus do?" And after asking that question, each one will follow Jesus as exactly as he knows how, no matter what the result may be.

—Charles Sheldon,
In His Steps (Barbour & Company, 1993)

Over the past few years, the phrase "What would Jesus do?" has become so popular (or overused, depending on your perspective) that it's easy to forget that there's more to the catch phrase than WWJD bracelets and T-shirts. And though "What would Jesus do?" may be a victim of its own success, don't let over-saturation keep you from checking out the book that started the WWJD craze — Charles Sheldon's *In His Steps*. This simple, but powerful novel chronicles the lives of a pastor and several Christians in his church who take up the challenge to live their lives exactly as Jesus would do in their situations, regardless of the consequences.

Sheldon wrote *In His Steps* in 1896, but a contemporary retelling of the story is available under the name *What Would Jesus Do?*, written by Garrett Sheldon (Charles Sheldon's greatgrandson) and Deborah Morris. The newer version is quite well done and is a worthy update to the Christian classic.

Jesus prepared his disciples to be leaders of his Church

During Old Testament times, the people who believed and obeyed God formed an actual nation (Israel) and a particular race of people (Jews). God especially chose the Jews, not because of their goodness, but because of his love. He wanted to have a nation proclaim his truth, live it out, and provide the backdrop for salvation to come to the whole world. However, even in the midst of God's special relationship with the nation of Israel, he made it clear that he'd eventually save the non-Jewish world as well (see 2 Samuel 22:50, Psalm 18:49, Deuteronomy 32:43, Psalm 117:1, and Isaiah 11:10). Therefore, when Jesus came, "God's people" became the Church of faithful believers — whether they were Jews or *Gentiles* (non-Jews).

To transition from nation to Church (see Chapter 10), Jesus handpicked and trained a group of leaders, people who could preach and teach after his death, resurrection, and ascension to heaven. Therefore, when the time for his crucifixion drew near, Jesus spent less time in public and devoted more of his energies to teaching his disciples and preparing them to be future leaders of the Church.

Jesus voluntarily died on the cross

Christians believe that Jesus came to the earth for one main reason — to die on the cross for the sins of the world and to be raised from the dead three days later (see John 12:27). So, although Jesus was tried, convicted, and sentenced to death by others, the Bible says that he knew what was going to happen and that he actually intentionally allowed it: "No one takes my life away from me, but I lay it down by myself" (John 10:18). See the "Saving People: God's Game Plan from the Get-Go" section, later in this chapter, for more.

Considering Who Jesus Claimed to Be

People often think of the President of the United States as one of the most powerful people in the world. Perhaps that idea's due to the fact that he's got so many names, roles, and titles associated with his office. Although President is the official job title, the person holding it also has several other titles: commander-in-chief as head of the U.S. military; head of state as ceremonial leader of the nation; executive branch as the third distinct branch of the U.S. government; and leader of the free world, an informal title that the U.S. President has held since the end of World War II. So, while all these names express different roles, they all point back to the same person.

Similarly, the Bible says that Jesus often described himself by using a lot of different names or roles. At first glance, you may think he comes across as a scatterbrain or a member of the Title-of-the-Month club. But when you start to look at them side by side, you see that all the titles actually fit neatly together to provide what Christians believe is a clear, all-around picture of who he was (and is, as Christians believe he still lives; see the section, "Peering into an Empty Tomb: Revisiting the Resurrection," later in this chapter). Consider the following references to Jesus:

- ✔ **Messiah (or Christ):** The Hebrew word *Messiah* (translated as *Christ* in Greek) means "anointed one," or the one God sent to earth to free people who believe and trust in him. The scriptures of the Hebrews talked much about a coming Messiah, so the Israelites were on the lookout for the "chosen one" for centuries. When Jesus began his ministry, he claimed that he was the Messiah that they were waiting for (check out John 4:25–26).

- ✔ **Son of man:** *Son of man* is a term that the Old Testament book of Daniel uses to refer to the coming Messiah (see Daniel 7:13). It emphasizes the humanity of Jesus (who Christians believe was the Messiah) and his role

as the ultimate, perfectly sinless man. This is the title Jesus seemed to favor over others, as he refers to himself as the Son of man more than 80 times throughout the Gospels. His preference may have been due to the fact that it expressed who he was to people without being as theologically charged as the name Son of God was.

✓ **Son of God:** *Son of man* is a term that emphasizes Jesus' humanity, but the term *Son of God* expresses the Christian belief regarding his divinity as a member of the Trinity (see Chapter 7 for the lowdown on the Trinity). "Son" expresses a distinction from God the Father, but it doesn't imply that he's any less God than the Father.

✓ **God himself:** Although the name *Son of God* implies divinity, the Bible tells that Jesus went even further on occasion and described himself as equal with God — and even outright claimed to *be* God. Jesus said at one point, "I and the Father are one" (John 10:30). In other words, Christians believe that, as the Son of God, Jesus isn't just a super-man or an angel, but that he's literally equal with God the Father. He said that he should receive the same honor that's due the Father (John 5:23). In a conversation with Jewish leaders, Jesus said, "Before Abraham came into being, I AM" (John 8:58). Basically, Jesus was saying that he is eternal, having existed (in heaven) before Abraham — who the Bible calls the "father of the Jews" and who had lived some 1,000 years before. What's more, "I AM" was a likely reference to God's holy name ("I AM WHO I AM" in Exodus 3:14).

✓ **Only True Path to God:** Jesus emphasized that the only way one has access to God the Father is through him. He said flat out, "I am the way, the truth, and the life. No one comes to the Father except through me" (John 14:6). Jesus also used other word pictures to illustrate his primary role in saving the world, including:

  • **Bread of life:** "I am the bread of life. He who comes to me will not be hungry, and he who believes in me will never be thirsty" (John 6:35).

  • **Light of the world:** "I am the light of the world. He who follows me will not walk in the darkness, but will have the light of life" (John 8:12).

  • **Access door:** "I am the door. If anyone enters in by me, he will be saved, and will go in and go out, and will find pasture" (John 10:9).

See Chapter 15 for more on why Jesus is the only pathway to God.

✓ **Good Shepherd:** In the agricultural society of first-century Palestine, shepherding was a common job. Shepherds watched over their flocks of sheep and protected them from wolves, thieves, or stormy weather,

often on a 24/7 basis. The Bible says that Jesus used the analogy of a shepherd to describe his purpose, saying that he is the "good shepherd" (John 10:11), caring, protecting, and sacrificing for his sheep. The Old Testament Book of Ezekiel also shows the shepherd analogy when the Lord says, "I myself will be the shepherd of my sheep" (34:15).

✔ **King:** Jesus accepted the title of king when Pilate asked him during his trial whether he was King of the Jews, meaning the Messiah that the Hebrew scriptures prophesied about. Jesus said, "You are right in saying that I am a king. For this reason I have been born, and for this reason I have come into the world, that I should testify to the truth. Everyone who is of the truth listens to my voice" (John 18:37).

Although Christians believe all these terms appropriately describe Jesus, they also recognize truth in the old saying, "Actions speak louder than words." The Bible says that Jesus undertook certain actions (or promised that he'd perform them in the future) that Christians believe only God has the power to perform, such as forgiving sins (Mark 2:10), raising the dead (John 6:39–40), judging humans in the future (John 5:22), and giving life (John 5:26). Therefore, Christians believe these actions back up Christ's claims, which in turn strengthens their belief that Jesus was (and is) God.

Saving People: God's Game Plan from the Get-Go

When you look at the events that led to Jesus' death on the cross, they appear to be circumstances run amuck or part of an evil scheme crafted by his enemies. However, Christians believe they're but a piece of a larger puzzle that God himself put together.

Christians use ideas from the Old Testament as well as statements that Jesus made (which were recorded in the Gospels) as evidence of God's plan:

✔ Old Testament sacrifices pointed toward Christ's death on the cross.

✔ Old Testament prophecies foretold what Jesus would be like and what he'd do.

✔ Jesus predicted exactly what was going to happen to him.

I discuss these ideas in the sections that follow.

Seeing sacrifices as prototypes of the real deal

Soon after Adam and Eve sinned (find out more about this tragedy in Chapter 4), the idea of a sacrifice required as a payment for sin came into the picture. The earliest recorded practice of this is when Adam and Eve's first child, Abel, offered an animal sacrifice to God (Genesis 4:3). In later years, this practice was formalized as the nation of Israel observed very specific rules, defined in the Hebrew scriptures, concerning what was an acceptable blood animal offering to God.

Christians believe that these sacrifices had no real value in and of them-selves, however, and that they didn't cleanse sin from individuals. The Book of Hebrews says, "It is impossible for the blood of bulls and goats to take away sin." Instead, the sacrificial system instituted by the Hebrews during the Old Testament period was a prototype of Christ's true and final sacrifice that was to come. These sacrifices were beneficial because they were reminders of sin and helped drill into people the true cost of sin and the necessity for a solution.

Uncovering others' prophecies about the Messiah

Christians believe God "tipped his hand" through Old Testament prophecies about a future Messiah who would come and save humans. The consensus among scholars is that at least 109 separate prophecies concerning the Messiah are found in the Old Testament. People who lived hundreds of years before Jesus ever walked the earth wrote these prophecies. And Christians believe that when you match up these prophecies with the events of Jesus' life, you find that Jesus is, like Cinderella's glass slipper, a perfect match. These prophecies provide some amazingly accurate descriptions of the events that occurred in Jesus' life. For example, according to the Old Testament, the Messiah

- Would be born in Bethlehem (Micah 5:2) and born of a virgin (Isaiah 7:14)

- Would be a descendant of King David (Isaiah 9:7)

- Would be preceded by someone (John the Baptist) who would prepare the way for his coming (Isaiah 40:3)

- Would ride into Jerusalem on a donkey (Zechariah 9:9)

- Would be rejected by people and judged and condemned (Isaiah 53:1–8)

✔ Would be betrayed by a trusted friend (Psalm 41:9) for 30 pieces of silver (Zechariah 11:12)

✔ Would die a sacrificial death for sin (Isaiah 53)

✔ Would be crucified on a cross and would have people cast lots for his garments (Psalm 22)

✔ Would have his side pierced (Zechariah 12:10), but his bones wouldn't be broken (Psalm 34:20, Exodus 12:46)

✔ Would be resurrected from the dead (Psalm 16:10)

Christians agree that each of these prophecies (and more) was fulfilled through the life, death, and resurrection of Jesus Christ.

Prophesying about the suffering servant: A look at Isaiah 53

One of the greatest Old Testament prophets, Isaiah served from 740–681 B.C. as prophet to Judah (the southern kingdom that was formed after the nation of Israel split in two). During this time, he wrote the Book of Isaiah. Its purpose was twofold: to call Judah to repentance and to return to the Lord, and to tell how salvation would be achieved through the coming Messiah (for details on the inspiration of the Bible, see Chapter 6). Isaiah's book is chock-full of prophetic passages, but one chapter stands out with its wealth of details covering who Jesus is and what he would do on earth.

Consider some of the following excerpts from Isaiah 53 and the parallels to the real life of Jesus, as recorded in the New Testament Gospels:

He was despised and rejected by men;
a man of suffering, and acquainted with
disease.
He was despised as one from whom men
hide their face;

Jesus, being sentenced to die on a cross, was despised and rejected by humans (Matthew 27:23–24).

But he was pierced for our transgressions.
He was crushed for our iniquities.
The punishment that brought our peace
was on him; and by his wounds we are
healed.

The method of crucifixion required the literal piercing of Jesus' hands and feet with nails (Luke 23:33). What's more, because of his punishment and wounds, people can receive salvation.

He was oppressed, yet when he was
afflicted he didn't open his mouth.
As a lamb that is led to the slaughter,
and as a sheep that before its shearers is
silent, so he didn't open his mouth.
He was taken away by oppression and
judgment;

When Jesus was on trial before the religious leaders, he remained silent (Mark 14:61) and was eventually led away to be crucified.

They made his grave with the wicked,
and with a rich man in his death;

Jesus was crucified next to two criminals, and a rich man named Joseph of Arimathea provided a grave for Jesus (Matthew 27:57–60).

> Yet it was the Lord's will to bruise him.
> He has caused him to suffer.
> When you make his soul an offering for
> sin, he shall see his seed.
> He shall prolong his days,
>
> and the pleasure of the Lord shall prosper
> in his hand.

Ultimately, Jesus' sacrificial death on the cross was a plan by God, designed from the beginning as the way to save people from their sins.

Considering Jesus' prophecies for his own life and death

During his ministry, Jesus talked about his future sacrificial death and his resurrection. On some occasions, the references were subtle, such as when he told some religious leaders that "the Son of man will be three days and three nights in the heart of the earth" (Matthew 12:40), and "Destroy this temple [his body], and in three days I will raise it up" (John 2:19). By saying these things, Jesus prophesied that he would be dead for three days, after which he would rise from the dead. In describing himself as the Good Shepherd, he said, "The good shepherd lays down his life for the sheep" (John 10:11), which prophesied his sacrificial death for humanity.

As time approached his coming death, Jesus started to reveal to his disciples more specific details of what was going to happen to him. On three separate occasions, Jesus told his disciples flat out that he was going to go to Jerusalem and suffer, be killed, and rise from the dead on the third day (Matthew 16:21, 17:22–23, and 20:17–19). And though he couldn't have been much more specific, the disciples still didn't realize until after the fact that he meant exactly what he said.

How'd they miss the hints?

You'd think that Jesus' disciples or religious teachers who'd spent their lifetime studying the scriptures would've picked up on the Old Testament prophecies and predictions that Jesus gave, put 1+1 together, and understood exactly what was going to happen to Jesus. But no one did. This strange truth reminds me of reading an Agatha Christie mystery novel, in which master detective Hercules Poirot solves the mystery. As I read Poirot's wrap-up, where he tells how he figured everything out, I find myself perplexed about why I didn't see the clues like he did. Later, when I read the book a second time, I see the hints leap from the pages, making me wonder, *How could I have missed those the first time around?* I'm sure the disciples scratched their heads after the Resurrection and thought the same thing.

Questioning Why Jesus Was Crucified

Jesus was a controversial figure during his day and remains one today. To understand why he was crucified, understanding the life and times in which Jesus lived is critical.

Though he was crucified in first-century Palestine as a result of all the controversy surrounding his claims to be Messiah, I'm convinced that circumstances would've been far different for him were he to have chosen the 21st century to come to earth. Given his miraculous healing power, he'd surely be offered a job at a hospital — that is, until the administration became concerned about the malpractice implications of miracles. With his amazing teaching capabilities, he'd be a regular on Oprah and Larry King. With his claim to be the Son of God, he'd be on the cover of the *National Enquirer* and receive a multimillion-dollar offer to write a bestseller. Through Christians' eyes, it's clear that in order to die a sacrificial death, Jesus had to enter the world at the right time and place. Modern times just wouldn't have worked — except in the occasional oppressive regime, "different" people with radical ideas just aren't killed today; more often than not, they usually get famous or rich.

First-century Palestine, however, was the perfect choice for a sacrificial death. Much like something you'd see in an Oliver Stone film, it was a powder keg ready to explode. Oppressed Hebrew masses waited anxiously for someone to set them free from Roman authority and had high expectations. Added to that, pompous religious guys jealously fought to keep their authority. And to top it off, the colonial political and military power was deeply resented and feared.

Yet, in spite of the explosive nature of Palestine at the time, why was this nonviolent teacher — who preached about loving others, including enemies, even when it hurts — considered such a menace that he had to be put to death? To answer this question, consider three key factors that Christians believe led to his crucifixion, which I discuss in this section.

Expecting the Messiah to be different

Perhaps the most significant factor that led the Jews to crucify Jesus was that he simply didn't fit the Jewish image of what the Messiah would be. For centuries, Jews read prophecies like Isaiah 9:6 ("For unto us a Child is born, unto us a Son is given, and the government will be upon his shoulders") and concluded that the Messiah would be a political leader, in the mold of the great King David, who would allow the Jews to overthrow the hated Roman Empire

and reestablish the nation of Israel. When Old Testament Messianic prophecies talked about a kingdom, Jews had their minds made up that it was Israel, not the spiritual kingdom that Christians believe God had in mind.

Because of their hope in a true political leader, the Jewish teachers also overlooked the prophecies related to the Messiah being a "suffering servant" (such as Isaiah 53), and most of the Jewish masses weren't knowledgeable enough of the scriptures to decide for themselves. So when Jesus looked like King David Reloaded when he entered Jerusalem, the crowds hailed him. But after it became clear that Jesus wasn't about to play that part, the crowds turned on him quicker than you can say "fickle." In one of the most amazing about-faces in history, people cried out, "Hosanna to the Son of David!" (Matthew 21:9) on Palm Sunday, but just five short days later, they yelled to the Roman authorities, "Crucify him!" (Matthew 27:22).

Feeling threatened by Jesus

Jesus was a thorn in the side of the Pharisees and the Sadducees during his entire ministry; he was someone they didn't know exactly how to deal with. They seemed to collide with Jesus on almost every subject. Take a few examples:

- ✔ The Jewish authorities were focused on obeying the Law, but they became overly concerned with keeping up appearances rather than having a genuine heart for God. In contrast, Jesus said that what's on the outside of a person isn't worth squat; all that matters is what's in your heart.

- ✔ The religious leaders separated themselves from sinners, whereas Jesus ate and socialized with them.

- ✔ The Pharisees had fanatical rules on what someone could and couldn't do on the *Sabbath* (God's ordained "day of rest"). Therefore, when Jesus healed people on the Sabbath, his actions infuriated the Pharisees to no end. (However, the reality was that Jesus never said the Sabbath wasn't significant; rather, he made it clear that demonstrating love to the sick was simply *more* important.)

- ✔ When Jesus claimed equality with God, they called it blasphemy (speech that blatantly dishonors God) and wanted him killed on the spot. Such a claim would indeed have been blasphemy if it were false, but the religious leaders never honestly considered whether his claims might, in fact, be true. Rather than considering the miracles he did as possible proof, the Pharisees dismissed them as being from the devil, even though they had no theological justification in that claim (Deuteronomy 13).

The religious authorities wanted to get rid of Jesus all along. But their concerns escalated as Jesus' grass-roots popularity swelled in his final year. The straw that broke the camel's back was when Jesus raised Lazarus from the dead (John 11:36–44), convincing them that they must do something about him before everyone started to believe in him.

Check out John 11 for the critical discussion, in which the leaders in the *Sanhedrin* (the council of religious authorities) resolve to take Jesus' life. Here's the lowdown on the scene: The chief priests and Pharisees met and said, "What are we doing? For this man does many signs. If we leave him alone like this, everyone will believe in him, and the Romans will come and take away both our place and our nation." Caiaphas (pronounced *ki*-uh-fuss), the high priest, responded, "You know nothing at all. You don't realize that it is better for you that one man die for the people than have the whole nation perish."

Caiaphas and the Sanhedrin wanted to kill Jesus so that they could maintain their power and keep the Roman authorities from fearing any Jewish uprising. However, in a grand irony, the words of Caiaphas were true, though in a way that was quite different from what he expected. Although Caiaphas believed that it was better for one man — Jesus Christ — to be sacrificed to preserve the earthly status quo of the Jews, the reality was that it was God's will that Jesus die rather than having the world perish eternally because of their sins.

Manipulating authority to get rid of the troublemaker

In spite of their differences with Jesus, the religious leaders had no legal authority to execute him. Therefore, they conspired to accuse him of treason against Rome, so that the Romans would do the dirty work for them. Such a solution was the best possible scenario for the religious leaders — they'd be rid of Jesus, and the Romans would be the ones to blame. However, to pull off this plan, they had to get the Roman authorities to see Jesus as a criminal — and one who deserved not just death, but crucifixion, which was a method of death that Jews saw as being a curse from God (Deuteronomy 21:23).

The religious leaders arrested Jesus and performed a rush trial of their own in the middle of the night to convict him. Then, they sent Jesus to Pilate, the Roman governor in Palestine. He found no guilt in Jesus and wanted to free him. In fact, three times he declared Jesus innocent of the charges. However, because Pilate didn't have the courage to follow his convictions and disregard the Sanhedrin's wishes, he tried to do what politicians so often do: weasel his way out of the tight spot! Because it was Roman custom to pardon a Jewish

prisoner during Passover, Pilate decided to use that loophole to free an innocent man without directly opposing the Sanhedrin. But when he asked an
assembled crowd which criminal should be set free, the religious leaders
helped stir the crowd up to demand the release of a notorious criminal called
Barabbas instead and to cry out that Jesus should be crucified (Matthew 27).
After Pilate realized that the crowd had made its choice, he washed his hands
in front of the crowd, symbolically absolving himself of responsibility, and the
Roman soldiers carried out the wishes of the Sanhedrin later that morning.

Peering into an Empty Tomb: Revisiting the Resurrection

Talk is cheap. If you watch sports, you see it all the time — a star athlete
makes a cocky prediction of victory before the big game, and reporters jump
all over it. More often than not, the prediction turns out to be hollow, and the
one who said it just ends up looking silly. Jesus too made a brash prediction
during his ministry — that he'd be raised from the dead after three days. So
it's no wonder why people were skeptical.

When Jesus predicted his resurrection, he put everything else he said and did
on the line. If he stayed six feet under, then all his wonderful words and deeds
wouldn't matter a hill of beans. It would be clear that he wasn't God, didn't
conquer sin through his death, and didn't give any real hope for people. But if
he did rise from the dead, then it would prove to be the crucial turning point
in human history, because according to his claim, the power of sin and death
would finally be conquered once and for all, and the hope he offered (see
Chapter 3) would be verified as being backed by the power of God.

All of Christianity, therefore, rests on whether Jesus was literally raised from
the dead. As the Apostle Paul writes:

> *Now if Christ is preached, that he has been raised from the dead, how do
> some among you say that there is no resurrection of the dead? But if there is
> no resurrection of the dead, neither has Christ been raised. If Christ has not
> been raised, then our preaching is in vain, and your faith also is in vain . . .
> you are still in your sins . . . If we have only hoped in Christ for this earthly
> life, then we are to be pitied above all men.*

—1 Corinthians 15:12–19

As Paul says, the faith of Christians hinges on Jesus actually being raised
from the dead. If the Resurrection is make-believe, then Christianity is just a
huge waste of time and energy.

Reviewing biblical facts

The Bible provides many details of the circumstances that Christians believe happened after Jesus died on the cross. Here's some of what's documented in the Bible concerning his death and resurrection:

- ✔ **Jesus was buried.** Jesus' body was placed in a tomb that was owned by a rich man named Joseph of Arimathea. A huge boulder was placed in front of the tomb to prevent someone from taking the body (Matthew 27:57–61).

- ✔ **Guards stood at the tomb's entrance to prevent theft.** The next day, the Jewish authorities convinced the Romans to put a seal on the boulder and post guards in front of the tomb to prevent the disciples from coming and stealing the body (Matthew 27:62–66).

- ✔ **Jesus' body was missing on the third day.** On the morning of the third day, two women followers of Jesus arrived at the tomb. After a violent earthquake, an angel appeared, rolled the stone back, and sat on it, frightening the guards beyond belief. The angel told the women that Jesus wasn't there, but that he had risen, just like he said he would. He then told the women to tell the disciples what happened (Matthew 28:1–7).

- ✔ **The guards were paid to keep silent.** Upon hearing news from the guards, religious leaders paid them off with a huge amount of money, telling them to say that the disciples came during the night and stole the body (Matthew 28:11–15).

- ✔ **Jesus appeared to his followers.** Jesus made several appearances to his followers over the next 40 days. He appeared to Mary Magdalene, a follower of his (Mark 16:9–11), two followers traveling on the road to Emmaus (Mark 16:12–13), the disciples on several occasions (Luke 24:36–43, John 20:19–25, John 21:1–14, Luke 24:34), and even to a crowd of 500 believers (1 Corinthians 15:6).

- ✔ **Jesus ate.** Jesus made sure his followers knew he wasn't just a ghost or something they were imagining. So, he ate with them to prove that he was still very much a real-live person (Luke 24:40–43).

- ✔ **Jesus ascended into heaven.** Jesus went out with followers to a place near Bethany (a town outside of Jerusalem) and then was taken up into heaven (Luke 24:44–49).

- ✔ **Jesus' disciples were transformed.** Before Jesus died, the disciples wouldn't have impressed anyone with their bravery and valor. When the going got tough, they fled for safety when Jesus was arrested and hid after the crucifixion for fear of persecution. However, something amazing happened when they realized that Jesus was resurrected — they became bold witnesses, testifying the truth of Christianity, and 10 of the 11 even died as martyrs for their faith. Their radically altered behavior — from cowardly betrayal to torture and martyrdom — testifies to the fact that the disciples were certain of the Resurrection.

Explaining it away

Throughout history, there have always been skeptics who have dismissed Jesus' resurrection. After all, one can't make a much more radical claim than saying a person came back to life. Therefore, through the years, various people have come up with alternative theories to explain the events described in the previous section. Here are four of the most common ways skeptics explain what happened (Table 5-1 provides an at-a-glance version of these ideas).

Disciples made the whole thing up

The most common explanation of the Resurrection by skeptics is that the disciples concocted the whole scheme by paying off the guards, stealing the body, and claiming that Jesus rose from the dead. Then, they worked together for the rest of their lives to spread a religion that they knew to be a lie.

Christians disagree with this theory because it flies smack in the face of human nature. Before the Resurrection, the disciples never impressed anyone by being a courageous and zealous group of people. In fact, they were downright cowardly. Therefore, it seems like a weak argument to suggest that this group of 11 men unanimously conspired to make up the whole scheme, preach a lie for many years, be imprisoned and tortured for speaking the lie, and willingly die for something they knew to be false. Many people find it hard to consider dying for a cause that they honestly believe in, but how many people would willingly die for a lie? If it were a lie, one would've expected at least one of the disciple conspirators to try and save his skin just before being executed.

Chuck Colson gives one of the best Christian arguments against this theory by comparing the Resurrection to the Watergate scandal. Colson was the chief legal counsel to former U.S. President Richard Nixon and went to jail because of his involvement in Watergate. One of the reasons that Colson believes in the truth of the Resurrection is the way in which he saw his colleagues and himself react during the Watergate conspiracy. He writes in *Loving God* (Zondervan, 1987):

> With the most powerful office in the world at stake, a small band of hand-picked loyalists, no more than ten of us, could not hold a conspiracy together for more than two weeks . . . Even political zealots at the pinnacle of power will save their own necks in the crunch, though it may be at the expense of the one they profess to serve so zealously.

Another strike against this explanation is that, if the disciples really did make this whole plan up and document the fiction in the Gospels, why are they so often portrayed in less-than-stellar terms? Assuming they had the where-withal to pull off the Resurrection conspiracy, one would think that they would've at least made themselves look good in their made-up stories, rather than so often appearing as a band of bumbling and cowardly nitwits.

Disciples were delusional

Another possibility put forth by skeptics is that the disciples didn't actually see a risen Jesus, they just thought they did. In other words, the disciples saw Jesus either by delusion, hallucination, imagination, or dream. In this scenario, some unknown third party stole the body.

Had Jesus appeared once or twice to individuals, such a case might be more convincing. But given the fact that the Bible says Jesus appeared multiple times to the disciples during a 40-day span (when most or all of them were present at the same time) and to as many as 500 other believers in one setting as well, Christians believe this option also seems to be wishful thinking — it tries to account for the sincerity of the disciples without allowing for the supernatural.

Jesus was "mostly dead"

A third explanation given by skeptics is that Jesus didn't actually rise from the dead, because he was simply unconscious when they put him in the tomb. I call this explanation the Miracle Max theory, because it reminds me of a scene in *The Princess Bride* in which the hero Westley supposedly dies, but is brought back to life by Miracle Max. It turns out that Westley isn't dead, but simply "mostly dead." According to Miracle Max, there's a big difference between the two: "Mostly dead is slightly alive. Now, all dead . . . well, with all dead, there's usually only one thing that you can do. Go through his clothes and look for loose change."

Although the Miracle Max theory may seem more rational because it avoids the supernatural, Christians find it unbelievable for several reasons. First, Jesus hung on the cross for several hours and was presumed dead before he was brought down from it. Second, an essential part of any execution is ensuring that the death actually occurred, so the Roman soldiers would've confirmed the death of a prisoner before releasing the body to the deceased's loved ones for burial. Mark 15:44 even states that Pilate asked that the report be confirmed by one of his men before they released the body. Third, Jesus would've had to somehow revive himself while lying in a dark tomb for three days and receiving no medical treatment. Fourth, in his post-crucified state, Jesus would've required the strength to push the boulder away. Finally, he'd have to change his appearance so that he didn't look like someone who barely escaped death, but instead as someone in a perfect state of health — because that's how the Bible says he appeared to the disciples (see Luke 24:36–42).

Jesus really did rise from the dead

The last option is that a supernatural event did happen and that Jesus really did rise from the dead. This option supports the facts confirmed by the Bible (see the "Rounding up the eyewitnesses" sidebar) and non-biblical sources and is most consistent with the disciples' behavior throughout their post-Resurrection ministries. At the same time, faith plays an important part in accepting this option, because such a belief requires that a supernatural event occurred.

Rounding up the eyewitnesses

The event that many skeptics argue against is Jesus' resurrection (see the section, "Peering into an Empty Tomb: Revisiting the Resurrection," in this chapter). Yet, based on historical standards, the testimonial evidence in support of Jesus' resurrection is compelling. Theologian Norman Geisler notes in *Christian Apologetics* (Baker Book House, 1976), "The number of individual appearances [of Jesus after his resurrection recorded in the scriptures] is more than sufficient to determine the validity of their testimony. No like testimony is possessed for *any* event from ancient times."

In other words, Jesus' resurrection has more eyewitness evidence supporting it than do the military victories of Alexander the Great, the Peloponnesian War, and the ancient Olympic games.

Table 5-1	Explaining the Resurrection
Possible Explanation	*Why It's Hard to Believe*
Disciples made the story up	Goes against how people would normally behave in such a situation
Disciples imagined seeing Jesus	Requires different people to have experienced the same hallucination, because Jesus appeared to multiple people at the same time
Jesus wasn't really dead	Goes against medical science
	Requires gross negligence on part of the Roman authorities
	Requires many believing and non-believing people to be fooled
Jesus really rose from the dead	Requires a supernatural event to occur

Coming to a Conclusion: Was Jesus a Good Teacher or the Son of God?

Even people who aren't Christians usually respect and admire the teachings of Jesus. After all, who would argue against the idea that if people lived according to his moral principles, the world would be a better place? Yet, the

fact is that although many non-Christians readily acknowledge him as a good teacher, they don't accept that he was actually the Son of God.

Limiting Jesus to a teaching role is much like thinking of George Washington as purely a military general or a good husband. Yes, Washington was a successful military leader and a good husband, but his true importance to Americans lies in being the father of our country. If you overlook that fact, then you really miss the gist of who he was. In the same way, relegating Jesus to being just a good teacher ignores much of what Jesus taught and emphasized throughout his ministry.

Christians believe the issue, however, goes beyond just what Jesus emphasized. Because so much of his teaching focused on radical claims about himself, clearly Jesus, by his own deliberate action, painted himself into a corner. Considering that, he must be one of the following:

- ✔ Exactly who he claimed to be — equal with God
- ✔ An ego-driven man who demanded attention at all costs
- ✔ A delusional man who had no grip on reality

Therefore, with Jesus, you either have to accept all his claims as true or else believe that his moral teaching was taught by a notorious self-promoter or by a man who had no grip on reality. Author C.S. Lewis sums up the Christian view best when he writes:

> *I am trying here to prevent anyone saying the really foolish thing that people often say about him: "I'm ready to accept Jesus as a great moral teacher, but I don't accept his claim to be God." That is the one thing we must not say. A man who was merely a man and said the sort of things Jesus said would not be a great moral teacher. He would either be a lunatic — on a level with the man who says he is a poached egg — or else he would be the Devil of Hell. You must make your choice. Either this man was, and is, the Son of God; or else a madman or something worse. You can shut him up for a fool, you can spit at him and kill him as a demon, or you can fall at his feet and call him Lord and God. But let us not come away with any patronizing nonsense about his being a great human teacher. He has not left that open to us. He did not intend to.*

> —*Mere Christianity* (Harper San Francisco, 2001)

Chapter 6

Peeking Inside God's Diary: The Bible

My older sister always kept a diary while she grew up, and, for many years, my overarching goal in life was to sneak into her room and locate it. I figured she must've had deep, dark secrets that, if I could only discover them, I'd make it to Easy Street — she'd wash dinner dishes for life in return for my vow of secrecy. If you looked at my constantly pruned, dishpan hands when I was a boy, however, you'd have realized that I was never able to secure that elusive get-out-of-dishes-for-life promise from her.

As I found out growing up, the thought of discovering another person's diary is alluring; a private journal reveals unique insights into who a person is and what makes him or her tick. Christians believe that amazingly, the infinite Creator of the universe thought it important that you and I should have access to his "diary," which is commonly known today as the *Bible* (or *Word of God*). Although God may not have penned the pages himself, Christians believe the Bible provides a revealing portrayal of who God is and what makes him tick. And by reading the Bible, you discover what's important to him, how he relates to people, and what his future plans are for this world.

To Christians, the Bible is all of this — and more. Yes, it's a book about God and his people, but Christians say it contains real power. In fact, they often refer to the Bible as the "Living Word," because of the way the Holy Spirit works in the hearts of Christians who sincerely read its pages (check out Chapter 7 to find out more on the Holy Spirit).

The Bible: Facts in brief

Name: The word *Bible* comes from the Greek word for "book." Christians consider the Bible the Book of Books.

Original languages: The Old Testament was written in Hebrew. The New Testament was written in Greek.

Number of books: Old Testament (39), New Testament (27), and Apocrypha (11–15)

Also known as: Word of God, scripture, scriptures

Organization: The Bible is divided up into two parts. The Old Testament starts with the Creation story and details the history and revelations for God's special people, the Jews. The New Testament continues what was started in the Old Testament with the accounts and teachings of Jesus and the early Church.

Consistent teaching: Although the emphases of the Old and New Testaments are different, the consistent message throughout is that God's faithful are saved by faith (see Romans 4 and Hebrews 11).

In this chapter, I provide the info you need to know about the Bible to understand Christians and why they put so much faith in what many nonbelievers call an ordinary book. If you find yourself hankering for more, run to the nearest bookstore and check out *The Bible For Dummies* by Jeffrey Geoghegan and Michael Homan (Wiley).

Retracing the Bible's Formation

When I was a young pup of a Christian, I didn't think much about how the Bible came to be what it is today. I figured that God must've hired a team of ghostwriters to record the saga of the "early years," perhaps having it published through his official publishing house (Abraham and Sons). Then, after Jesus Christ came, he cranked out the presses again with a sequel. The reality is that the Bible's formation followed a windier path than what a published book follows today. Not only were the books written over a span of many years (over 1,200!), but each also had to be considered authorized by God among God's faithful and set apart from other religious literature.

Christians believe that during the ancient eras, God set apart certain writings to be treated as *inspired*, or being his very own words (find out more in the section, "Reading the Bible Appropriately," later in this chapter). To Christians,

his purpose in having special inspired writings — commonly called *scripture* or *scriptures* — is to bring people into a relationship with him and to teach people how to live a holy life. Paul says this best in 2 Timothy 3:16:

> *All scripture is God-breathed and is profitable for teaching, for reproof, for correction, and for instruction which is in righteousness, that the man of God may be complete, thoroughly equipped for every good work.*

The Christian Church calls this authorized set of books the *canon,* which stems from a Greek term that means "measuring rod." Therefore, books that are considered part of the canon are the measuring rod or bottom line for the Christian faith.

The selection process — known as *canonization* — was both painstaking and self-evident. With the exception of the apocryphal books (see the "To Be or Not to Be: The Apocrypha" section, later in this chapter), Christians never had any fierce or fiery debates over which books should make it into the Old and New Testaments. In the end, when all the facts were gathered and put out on the table, it was obvious to the Church leaders (the bishops) which books stood out as being from God.

When you look at the Bible's historical development, you see six loosely defined stages that it went through to become the authoritative Word of God that the Christian Church universally recognizes today:

- ✔ **Stage 1:** The Hebrews recognized certain writings (known today as the Old Testament) as sacred.

- ✔ **Stage 2:** Jesus and the apostles treated the Old Testament writings as authoritative.

- ✔ **Stage 3:** Indicating that the Bible wasn't yet complete, Jesus alluded to more scriptures coming from the apostles.

- ✔ **Stage 4:** The apostles understood their New Testament writings as equal to the Hebrew scriptures in their authority.

- ✔ **Stage 5:** The early Church recognized a set of the apostles' writings as New Testament scripture.

- ✔ **Stage 6:** Because apostle leadership was a requirement for any New Testament scripture, the Church closed the book on the canon after the last apostle died.

Figure 6-1 illustrates the progression of these six stages, each of which I discuss in the sections that follow.

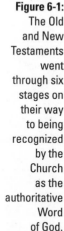

Figure 6-1:
The Old and New Testaments went through six stages on their way to being recognized by the Church as the authoritative Word of God.

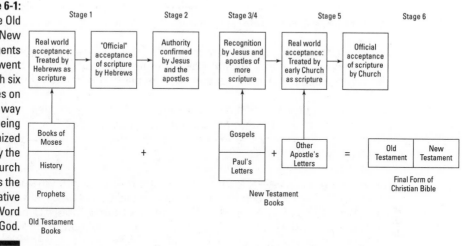

Stage 1: Hebrews first recognized writings as sacred

Oral history was an important part of ancient cultures, but Christians believe that by Moses' day, God had instructed the Israelites (Jews) to begin keeping a written account of history and of his revelations to the Jewish people. God continued to call certain people to write sacred literature throughout the history of the Jewish nation of Israel. This scripture included instructional law, historical narrative, poetry and songs, and words of prophecy.

The authors of these Hebrew (another term meaning Jewish) books (which Christians refer to as the *Old Testament*) often mention God's special role in the writing process. Moses, who is usually attributed as author of the first five books of the Bible, indicates that the Lord communicated to him in some manner as he wrote the accounts (see Exodus 20:1, 24:4). The prophets also frequently mention that their writings came from the Lord (see Hosea 1:1, Joel 1:1, Amos 3:7–8, Ezekiel 2:7).

The Israelites universally recognized the books shown in Table 6-1 as scripture. They regularly worshipped using the Psalms and read the writings of Moses and the prophets. Later, religious leaders made it official by canonizing them, declaring the writings the authentic (sometimes called *authoritative*) Word of God, but they were really only putting their seal of approval on what people already understood to be true.

No one today knows all the precise details concerning this process, but many scholars believe that canonization took place during multiple phases over a period of hundreds of years.

Table 6-1	Books of the Old Testament
Category	*Books*
Historical accounts and Hebrew Law	Genesis, Exodus, Leviticus, Numbers, Deuteronomy (also called the Pentateuch, Torah, and The Five Books of Moses)
History of the Hebrews	Joshua, Judges, Ruth, 1 Samuel, 2 Samuel, 1 Kings, 2 Kings, 1 Chronicles, 2 Chronicles, Ezra, Nehemiah, Esther
Poetry and Wisdom Literature	Job, Psalms, Proverbs, Ecclesiastes, Song of Songs (also known as Song of Solomon)
The Prophets	Isaiah, Jeremiah, Lamentations, Ezekiel, Daniel, Hosea, Joel, Amos, Obadiah, Jonah, Micah, Nahum, Habakkuk, Zephaniah, Haggai, Zechariah, Malachi

Note: This table doesn't include the Catholic deutero-canonical books.

Stage 2: Jesus and the early Church treated Old Testament writings as scripture

Jesus and the apostles consistently demonstrated their acceptance of the Hebrew claim concerning the Old Testament books' sacredness. Throughout his ministry, Jesus considered the Hebrew scriptures to be the authoritative basis for discussions and teaching. Jesus said that he came to fulfill the Old Testament prophecy (Matthew 5:17–18; Luke 24:27, 24:44), adding that scripture can't be broken (John 10:35). Jesus also quoted the Old Testament often, for example in responding to Satan's temptations in the desert, settling disagreements with the religious leaders, and even taking some of his final words on the cross directly from Psalms.

The apostles and New Testament writers also make frequent mention of the authority of the Old Testament books. Paul refers to Genesis and Exodus as "scripture" (Romans 9:17, Galatians 3:8). Luke writes about how the Holy Spirit spoke through Isaiah (Acts 28:25) and David (Acts 4:25). Peter adds that prophecy came through the Holy Spirit, not the will of the writer (1 Peter 1:21, 1:10–12).

Stage 3: Jesus indicated that more scripture would come

Although no indications of Jesus himself writing during his ministry exist, Christians believe that he promised the disciples that the Holy Spirit would guide *them* to reveal more of God's truth. Logically, then, it's easy to conclude that new scriptures are a key component of this revelation. Specifically, Jesus promised that the Holy Spirit would

- Remind the disciples of all that Jesus said and taught (John 14:26)
- Guide the disciples to writing the New Testament (John 16:12–15)
- Reveal prophecy about future events (John 16:12–15)

Why four Gospels?

The Gospels — Matthew, Mark, Luke, and John — all chronicle the life and ministry of Jesus Christ. And, although they all cover similar ground, each is unique, written to slightly different audiences with distinct emphases:

- The Apostle Matthew wrote his Gospel especially for Jews and emphasized the theme of Christ as King.

- John Mark, a close associate of the Apostle Peter, wrote his Gospel for the Christians in Rome and focused on the theme of Christ as Servant.

- Penned by Dr. Luke, the Gospel of Luke primarily addresses Gentiles (non-Jews) and stresses Jesus as the Perfect Man.

- The Gospel of John, written by the Apostle John, addresses a more general audience, depicting Jesus as God in human flesh.

See Chapter 2 for more on the New Testament authors.

Stage 4: New Testament writers recognized their writings as inspired by God

The New Testament writers may not have prefaced each of the books with "Thus sayeth the Lord," but they possessed an unspoken, yet unmistakable awareness that their writings were inspired and on par with the writings of the Old Testament. Consider a few examples of why Christians believe this:

- ✔ **Authors acknowledge divine inspiration.** Paul says that his words aren't his own, but that they come from the Holy Spirit (1 Corinthians 2:13) and the revelation of Jesus Christ (Galatians 1:12). He later expands that statement to include the other apostles' and prophets' writings as well (Ephesians 3:3–5).

- ✔ **Authors cross-reference other New Testament writing.** Paul references Luke 10:7 in his own letter to Timothy (1 Timothy 5:18) and refers to it as "scripture."

- ✔ **Authors put New Testament writings on the same level as the Old Testament.** When Peter refers to Paul's writings in Peter 3:15–16, he equates Paul's writings with Old Testament scripture and indicates that Paul's teaching is perfectly in line with the teachings that Paul heard directly from Jesus.

Stage 5: Early Church recognized New Testament writings as scripture

When the apostles were still living, the early Church relied on this group of individuals to define the teachings and stances of the Church. However, as time passed in the first century, the apostles became fewer and fewer in number. So, the Church had to turn to the apostle's legacy — their writings — in order to guide the young but growing Christian Church.

Although the early Church used many letters and books for teaching, the authenticity of most of the New Testament books set them apart from the pack from the very beginning. In particular, the Gospels and Paul's *epistles* (or formal letters to the churches) were quickly put into wide circulation throughout churches across the Mediterranean region and used as a basis for instruction. In addition, the nonbiblical Christian writings of the second century talked about these writings and referenced them as scripture.

Estrogen and the Bible

The apostles and New Testament authors were all men, but that doesn't mean that the early Christian Church was an "all-male club." In fact, women played a vital role in the life of the early Christian Church. Paul, for example, often speaks of women who played important roles in the Church's ministry. Specifically, in Romans 16, he expressly calls out several women, most notably Phoebe, a deacon in the church who helped many, and Priscilla, who, along with Aquilla, is referred to as Paul's co-worker.

The need arose, however, in the second century to determine an official set of authentic books for the Church. The motivation behind this step was a response to false teaching rather than a perceived need by the churches, considering that they already treated the apostle's writings as authoritative.

To select the writings that make up the New Testament canon, the Church set two criteria that each writing had to meet:

- ✔ **Apostle-driven:** The critical factor that the Church turned to in order to determine the authority of each writing was apostle leadership. The book must have been written by an apostle himself or by an associate who worked intimately with an apostle and who had his writing confirmed by the apostles. John Mark, for example, was the author of the Gospel of Mark. Although he wasn't an original apostle, he worked alongside Peter. Or consider Luke, author of the Gospel of Luke and the Book of Acts. He was a close associate of Paul for a good part of the apostle's ministry.

- ✔ **Consistent with other apostles' teaching:** The second criterion that the Church used to determine whether a writing would be included in the New Testament canon was the writing's consistency with other scripture written by the apostles.

When someone questioned either of these criteria, the recognition process took much longer. For example, the Books of Hebrews, James, 2 Peter, 2 John, 3 John, and Revelation were the last books the Church included in the canon. However, the questions about these books were based more on incomplete information rather than on beliefs that they weren't authentic. Therefore, after the Church fully understood their apostle-driven nature, it readily accepted these books as part of the final New Testament canon (see Table 6-2).

Table 6-2	Books of the New Testament	
Category	*Books*	*Also Called*
Life of Jesus and the early Church	Matthew, Mark, Luke, John, Acts	Matthew, Mark, Luke, and John are known as the Gospels
Letters of the Apostle Paul	Romans, 1 Corinthians, 2 Corinthians, Galatians, Ephesians, Philippians, Colossians, 1 Thessalonians, 2 Thessalonians, 1 Timothy, 2 Timothy, Titus, Philemon	Letters are often called the Epistles; 1 Timothy, 2 Timothy, and Titus are often called *pastoral letters* (because they express Paul's pastoral concern)
Letters from other apostles and prophets	Hebrews, James, 1 Peter, 2 Peter, 1 John, 2 John, 3 John, Jude	
Messages of prophecy	Revelation	

This process of canonization was syrupy slow, lasting from the early second century until A.D. 397, when the Church officially recognized the entire 27-book collection as the New Testament canon. However, like the Hebrew scriptures centuries before, the New Testament writings that were floating around among the churches were, on a practical level, observed as scripture far earlier than that. Therefore, when the powers that be formally defined the canon, this decision only served to rubberstamp what Christians already believed to be true. In fact, one of the early efforts at establishing a canon — referred to as the *Muratorian Canon* — in the late second century is very close to the final adopted canon.

Stage 6: The Church closed the book

When the Church made the New Testament canon official in A.D. 397, it simultaneously closed the book on future newly written additions to the Christian Bible, locking it up and throwing away the key. (The Catholic Church, however, revisited canonization in the 16th century concerning some Old Testament–era Jewish writings, but these were a special case, which I explain

in the "To Be or Not to Be: The Apocrypha" section that follows.) The reason for the permanent closure was twofold:

- ✔ **Jesus was the final piece of the puzzle.** Christians believe that Jesus Christ, in fulfilling the scriptures of the Old Testament, was the full revelation from God. Hebrews 1:1–2 says

  God, having in the past spoken to the fathers through the prophets at many times and in various ways, has at the end of these days spoken to us by his Son, whom he appointed heir of all things, through whom also he made the worlds.

  Therefore, God made it clear that the Bible as you and I know it today is sufficient information (until Jesus returns to the earth again; see Chapter 9) to know who he is and what makes him tick.

- ✔ **No future book could meet the criteria for canonization.** The essential component of each New Testament book was its close ties to the apostles (see the section, "Stage 5: Early Church recognized New Testament writings as scripture," earlier in this chapter). Consequently, after the apostles died, by definition no further writing could be considered part of the New Testament canon. Interestingly, the Apostle John (the last surviving apostle) tacks on a specific warning at the end of Revelation to not add to the book or remove anything from it (Revelation 22:18–19). Given the fact that his book was the last apostle writing, his warning seems a particularly appropriate way to close out the entire New Testament canon, not just his book.

To Be or Not to Be: The Apocrypha

One area of disagreement among Christians concerning the Bible is related to the *apocryphal* (or *deutero-canonical*) books, a set of 15 Jewish writings that were written between 200 B.C. and A.D. 70, after the other books of the Old Testament were canonized (which officially happened in the centuries before 300 B.C.). Collectively, these books are sometimes called the *Apocrypha,* a term that comes from the Greek word for "hidden" (or, as Protestants stress, "questionable").

The debate over the Apocrypha has its origins in the centuries immediately preceding the birth of Jesus. The Jews living in Palestine, the geographical and historical center of the Christian faith, recognized the books of the Hebrew Bible in Table 6-1 (which you find earlier in this chapter). However,

the Jews living in the Greek-dominated areas around Alexandria tended to be more open to recognizing these additional apocryphal books as scripture.

As Greece dominated the Mediterranean region in the centuries before Christ's birth, Greek emerged as the popular spoken and written language of the entire area. Consequently, the Greek-speaking Jews of Alexandria saw the need for translating the Hebrew scriptures from the original Hebrew into Greek. This translation became known as the *Septuagint*. Given the fact that the Jews in Alexandria recognized other writings as scripture in addition to the already set canon, the translators naturally included the apocryphal works along with the core set of scriptures.

However, the early New Testament Church was centered in Jerusalem and Palestine (where Jews acknowledged as scripture only the books of the Hebrew Bible). As a result, the first-century Christians knew of the Apocrypha but didn't regard it as scripture. However, after later Christians used the Septuagint (because of its Greek language) as the key document when they translated the Old Testament into Latin, the apocryphal books took on increased authority within parts of the Christian Church.

More than 1,300 years later, in the 16th century the Catholic Church canonized 11 of these apocryphal books at the Council of Trent and today considers them part of the Old Testament. In contrast, the Protestant Church has always rejected these books as scripture. The Orthodox Church stands in the middle, treating the apocryphal writings as scripture but not with the same weight as the other Old Testament and New Testament writings.

I show you reasons for these differing claims in the sections that follow.

Reasons for including the Apocrypha

Catholics and others who consider the apocryphal books as scripture make the following points in defense of these books:

- ✔ The New Testament refers to the apocryphal books. Specifically, Hebrews 11:35 alludes to the Book of 2 Maccabees, and Jude 14 references the Book of Enoch.
- ✔ Several early Christian leaders quoted the Apocrypha, and a few, most importantly Augustine, explicitly claimed it to be authoritative.
- ✔ Many of the early Greek translations of the Old Testament contained the apocryphal books.

Reasons against including the Apocrypha

Protestants raise the following points against raising the apocryphal books to the level of the Old Testament canon:

- ✔ Jewish writers wrote the apocryphal books, but Jews themselves have never considered the Apocrypha to be part of their canon.

- ✔ Jesus never quotes or alludes to the apocryphal books.

- ✔ New Testament references don't indicate divine authority. Although the New Testament does include a couple references to apocryphal books, it never quotes them as scripture. For that matter, the New Testament also alludes to Greek pagan writings, but these references didn't mean that the apostles believed them to be the Word of God.

- ✔ Although some early Christian leaders referenced the apocryphal books, each of the major Christian "fathers" before Augustine didn't treat them as inspired.

- ✔ No church listing of the Old Testament canon included the apocryphal books until after A.D. 325.

- ✔ Protestants believe that Christians at the Council of Trent, where they officially canonized 11 of the 14 apocryphal books in the 16th century, perhaps had mixed motives in the canonization process. The Council rejected an apocryphal book that supported the Protestant stance against the practice of praying for the dead, but included a book that supported the pro-Catholic position on purgatory. (See Chapter 9 for more on the issue of purgatory.)

In the end, no matter which perspective Christians subscribe to concerning the Apocrypha, they should keep the following points in mind. First, none of the core teachings of Christianity are contained in these debatable books. Christians universally accept the New Testament and core Old Testament books. Second, disputable matters that the Apocrypha causes are perhaps best left as side issues. So Christians should, as the old saying goes, "Major on the majors and minor on the minors."

Reading the Bible Appropriately

If you ask people where in their house they keep a Bible, you get some revealing answers. Some people, who think of their Bible much like a favorite pair of worn slippers, rattle off a response right away. Others have to think about their answer for a minute, but then they tell you which shelf they last put it on. A final group, however, has a different response: They talk about a quest to find their Bible much like Indiana Jones would tell of the trials of excavating a long lost, ancient artifact.

Earlier in this chapter, I talk about that Bible on your bookshelf (or perhaps buried under rubble), but in this section I dust off the cover and open it up. I also show you several issues to keep in mind as you start to read what Christians call the written Word of God. One of the most important ideas to note is that Christians believe it's way more than just a good book — it's God's message to humanity.

Believing the Bible is inspired

Christians who believe in historical and biblical Christianity (refer to the Introduction for an explanation) say that the Bible is the inspired Word of God; in modern times, however, the *inspired* tag often gets a skeptical glance. Many intellectuals say that the Bible is an ordinary human book — its writings have good moral value, but people shouldn't treat them as actually having come from God's mouth. This is the perspective of so-called liberal Christians, who I discuss more in Chapter 11.

But, frankly, the Christian faith is completely dependent on the Bible's divine authority and reliability. That's because *everyone* upon whom the Christian faith is based assumes the scriptures to be true and bases his teachings on this fact. If folks like Jesus, Paul, Peter, Moses, David, and Isaiah were wrong on this issue, then Christianity has no credibility, no legs to stand on. In other words, traditional, historical Christianity puts all its eggs into the inspired basket: If the Bible is inspired, then people must treat its commands and teachings seriously. But if it's just a book of human ideas, then it may have some nice ideas to live by, but it's not something to base your life on.

Inspiration refers to the way that the Holy Spirit supernaturally guided the biblical authors to write, giving them special revelations from God. The Bible never discloses *exactly* how the Holy Spirit inspired the authors, but don't think of it as a mechanical process. The authors didn't simply become zombies and allow the Holy Spirit to take bodily control of them. Instead, by exploring the style of the books, you can see that the Holy Spirit clearly worked through each author's unique writing talents, styles, and experiences.

At the same time, the Bible indicates on several occasions that the words the authors used have significance. On more than one occasion, biblical authors make the point that God is concerned not only with broad concepts, but with the words being written as well. Exodus 24:4 says that Moses wrote down *everything* the Lord said. The prophet Jeremiah reported that God told him, "Do not omit a word." Jesus himself pointed to particular Old Testament words when he said, "It is written" (Matthew 4:4, 7, and 10), a phrase that the New Testament authors reiterate dozens of times.

Most biblical Christians believe that every major spiritual concept taught in the Bible is invariably tied to an actual historical event. Adam and Eve, in the Garden of Eden, introduced sin into the world through a deliberate act. A worldwide flood, survived only by Noah and his family, demonstrated the first major judgment of sin. Jesus' actual death and factual resurrection confirm the message of salvation he taught. And a specific event on Pentecost (described in Acts 2) inaugurated the coming of the Holy Spirit to guide Christians. Other Christians, though claiming that the Bible is inspired and reliable, allow for the possibility that some of the Old Testament stories are allegorical in nature rather than actual history.

Dealing with inconsistencies

If the Bible is the inspired Word of God, biblical Christians believe that the logical follow-up is that the Bible is also *inerrant,* fully true and without error. After all, if God can't make mistakes, then anything he says can't be in error.

However, inerrancy only pertains to the *original* manuscript of the books, not necessarily the copies of the originals that were passed down through the years. The copies of the manuscript are only inspired as much as they faithfully and accurately represent the original. (Chapter 2 explores the reliability of the New Testament manuscript copies that modern-day translations are based upon.)

Critics often charge that the Bible has numerous errors, inconsistencies, and contradictions, but the fact is that not a shred of evidence indicates a single error in the original text of the biblical writings.

You will certainly come across stumbling blocks if you read through the Bible cover to cover. But, as Augustine (see Chapter 18) once said, when you run into a passage you believe to be in error, you either have to assume that the original manuscript wasn't copied accurately or that you've misunderstood the passage. Therefore, when you encounter an apparent stumbling block, keep in mind the following issues:

- ✔ **Researchers are continually discovering historical evidence.** Critics often claim the Bible is suspect when it discusses a historical event that has no evidence outside the Bible to support the claim. However, time and time again, archaeological discoveries have confirmed biblical accounts rather than dismissed them.

- ✔ **Rare errors in copying did happen.** Although the manuscript copies that exist today are very close to the originals (see Chapter 2), they aren't 100 percent accurate. For example, one well-known snafu is found in 2 Chronicles 22:2. This verse indicates that king Ahaziah was 42 years old when he became king, which would have been an astounding feat,

because his father wasn't even that old! In contrast, 2 Kings 8:26 lists the correct age of king Ahaziah at 22. Any copy errors discovered like this one, however, have been associated with issues such as dates or names and have never been critical to actual doctrine.

✔ **Differing accounts don't mean one is wrong.** On certain occasions, the Bible appears to contradict itself when describing certain events. For example, the Gospel of Matthew says that the two criminals crucified by Jesus hurled insults at him, although Luke memorably says that one of them was repentant (see Chapter 3). Matthew and Luke also disagree on the number of angels at Jesus' tomb after his resurrection. Matthew says one, but Luke says two. However, the important fact to keep in mind is that in these situations, the two accounts aren't necessarily mutually exclusive. In each case, Matthew seems to be offering a partial account, while Luke provides a fuller account.

✔ **Interpretation isn't always easy.** Even though some Christians believe the Bible is inerrant, they don't believe that interpreting the meaning of a passage is *easy*. In fact, the idea that many people interpret certain passages differently causes many stumbling blocks and apparent inconsistencies. Sometimes the exact meaning of a passage is hard to figure out due to its particular context or because the exact word choice the author used is hard to define.

Many of the theological splits in Christianity that have occurred throughout history happened as a result of different interpretations of specific passages. For example, Catholics and Protestants differ in lots of ways due to scriptural interpretation, most notably in how they observe sacraments and ordinances (see Chapter 8 for the specifics).

A common adage that Christians use when interpreting the Bible is "The plain things are the main things, and the main things are the plain things." In other words, the important themes of the Christian faith are clear and are usually repeated multiple times in scripture, but the lesser important or questionable details aren't. Therefore, Christians should use restraint when placing great emphasis on debatable passages.

Confronting contextual issues

Imagine you asked spy novelist Tom Clancy, a suddenly revived William Shakespeare, and me to each contribute a chapter for a book you were compiling. Your instructions to the three of us were simple: Write about the assigned topic, but use your own individual writing style. When you got each manuscript back, you'd see that each of us had unique ways of expressing ourselves on the printed page. (My chapter would be the most riveting, of course, but I'm sure the other two authors would have their own cute, though amateurish way of talking about the given subject.)

I don't wanna read Shakespearean English!

The King James Version of the Bible served many good purposes since its introduction in the 17th century and remains popular in some churches even today. But one of the side effects of the King James Version is that some Christians associate scripture only with Shakespearean English and its ever-present *thee*s, *thou*s, and *shalt*s. When this happens, the Bible is often treated as old school, outdated, obsolete, ancient, or — to use a most dreaded label — uncool. Because the Bible was originally written in Hebrew and Greek, it has as much to do with Shakespearean English as it does with the "wicked cool" expressions of teenage slang today.

Fortunately, many English translations of the Bible are available that make for much easier reading than in days gone by. Some of the most popular versions include the New International Version (NIV), New Revised Standard Version (NRSV), New King James Version (NKJV), New English Translation (NET), and the New Living Translation (NLT). The NRSV is noteworthy because it's the one translation that has a broad base of support among Protestants, Catholics, and Orthodox Christians.

Paraphrases are perhaps the most readable of all Bibles. A *paraphrase* is a version of the Bible that not only translates the words into English, but also rewords or explains concepts so that they're easier to understand. The advantage to paraphrase versions is that they are quite easy to read. The disadvantage is that the person who translated the text also interpreted its meaning for you — and people interpret scripture in many different ways, as you see throughout this book. Many Christians find paraphrases useful for devotional reading, but turn to a pure translation when they seriously study the Bible.

Perhaps the most popular paraphrase today is *The Message,* a contemporary rendering of the Bible that can seem like a breath of fresh air. I find it a nice change of pace, although I have to admit that I get weirded out when Jesus and the apostles use modern day slang. The Phillips Bible is a harder to find paraphrase of the New Testament, but I recommend checking it out if you can find a copy. It's my personal favorite of the paraphrased versions.

In a similar manner, under the guidance of the Holy Spirit, the biblical authors were able to use their unique writing styles and human personalities as they wrote scripture. That's why you see so many different literary styles — analogy, metaphor, poetry, prose, historical narrative, and so on — used throughout the pages of the Bible.

For those of you who read through the Bible, you have to keep this variety of textures in mind. You can't simply open up your Bible to a random page, read a verse or two, and expect to fully understand God's truth. When people do this, they often come up with some wacky beliefs. Instead, you

need to consider not just the words of the Bible, but also the overall situation and historical backdrop in which it was written. Therefore, keep the following in mind:

✔ Interpret each verse only within the context of its chapter, and each chapter within the entire book. Never take a passage by itself.

✔ Familiarize yourself with the author and original purpose of the writing. Many modern Bibles have an introduction at the beginning of each book that provides an overview of the chapter and the major themes to watch out for.

✔ Understand the literary style of the book you're reading. Is it historical narrative, instructional teaching, or an obvious metaphor (such as the parables of Jesus)?

✔ Get to know the culture in which the book was written. For example, as I mention in Chapter 4, the parable of the prodigal son in Luke 15 takes on a far deeper significance with a thorough understanding of the Middle Eastern culture of Jesus' day.

✔ Finally, and most importantly, start off by asking the Holy Spirit to guide you as you read the Bible.

Finding No Expiration Date for the Bible

One of the top priorities that the American colonies had after gaining independence from Britain back in the 1780s was the necessity of formulating a constitution, a document by which the newly formed nation would govern. Although the writers of the Constitution allowed for limited flexibility in amending the document, they agreed that the core Bill of Rights was non-negotiable and could never be altered. Although it's not perfect, the U.S. Constitution has withstood the test of time for more than 200 years.

But did you ever consider what would happen to the United States if no standard governed the nation? Suppose the freedom that Americans enjoy depended entirely on the whims of the current officeholder of the President. Without the Constitution, the only way to stop the president from disbanding Congress or outlawing the free press would be to form a brigade of angry, armed congressmen or an alliance of rebel news reporters. Obviously, the very existence of the United States as it is today is based on having a solid, reliable foundation in place for governing.

Similarly, the Bible serves as something like the Constitution of the Christian faith. It provides a nonnegotiable standard by which God's truth can be understood apart from the fashions of the times, the wisdom of the day, and emotions of the moment. Without the Bible, Christianity becomes something much like the United States without a constitution — power, emotion, and what's culturally acceptable dictate belief rather than what the founders agreed is really true.

Yet, because the Bible was written thousands of years ago, many people don't see its relevance to the modern world that you and I live in today. I admit that it does sometimes seem hard to relate to the Israelites back in the Book of Exodus, who wandered through the desert for 40 years looking for the Promised Land. Today, I'd just take a handheld GPS and a 4 x 4 and make their generation-long trek a fun weekend getaway. Or, take the apostles as they started to grow the Church after the ascension of Jesus (see Chapter 5). If they'd have used modern marketing techniques and high tech mass communication, they could've grown the Church even quicker.

It's natural for every generation to look back on people of previous times with a patronizing attitude, writing them off as simpletons and irrelevant to the more sophisticated times of today. Yet, technology and progress don't change the same basic issues that humans have always faced since Day One. The major problems of current society — such as war, injustice, greed, infidelity, and lust — are all scattered throughout the Bible's pages. The major needs of people — such as love, happiness, meaning, truth, and a sense of purpose — are also dealt with throughout the Bible. Therefore, although the technology, culture, and language may be different, the applicability of the biblical message remains timeless.

Perhaps even more important to note is the idea that although society may change through the years, God is the same as he ever was. And Christians believe that because God's character is revealed through his "diary," that same character is as relevant and timely in this century as it was when it was written thousands of years ago.

Chapter 7

The Trinity: How 1+1+1 Equals 1

• •

• •

I just don't get it. My wife is so perplexing to me at times. In the midst of a conversation, she doesn't think twice about throwing in a topic that we talked about days before. (She calls it web thinking.) She frowns when I try to solve all her problems. (She much prefers that I listen.) My wife could also talk on the phone 24/7 (Doesn't her ear ever hurt?), thinks she needs shoes for every occasion (Won't two pairs suffice?), and doesn't even like to play Xbox video games (not even football!). Frankly, some of my wife's behavior is beyond my understanding — it must be that Venus and Mars thing. Yet, in spite of the fact that I find her mystifying on occasion, I don't let that get in the way of our relationship. I deeply love my wife, and we continue to grow closer as the years go by.

As I reflect on who God is, I believe that you can look at him in much the same way. When you concentrate on God as Creator of the universe, infinite in power and greatness, your mind goes numb. Yet, Christians believe he's more than just some unexplainable Being in the sky — he's profoundly personal. To Christians, God is someone whom you'll never fully fathom in your head, but is who you can know intimately in your heart.

In this chapter, you explore who Christians believe God is and what he's like. Christianity says that God is a Trinity — one God expressed in three beings. That's kind of confusing, so I start off by talking about God as a whole. Then, after getting your feet wet, you dive headfirst into the mystery of the Trinity and the distinct roles of the Father, Son, and Holy Spirit, find out why the Trinity is perhaps the most important concept of the Christian faith, and wade through the biblical basis for the whole idea.

Introducing the Trinity

The basic gist of the Trinity is that one God exists, with three distinct identities (or "persons"): God the Father, God the Son, and God the Holy Spirit. Each member of the Trinity has a unique personality and role, but they are all coequal and unified.

The term *trinity* literally means "three-oneness" — combining the terms *tri* (meaning "three") and *unit* (meaning "one"). Although the idea of the Trinity is plainly rooted in the Bible, the word isn't mentioned in scripture. Instead, it's an attempt by the Church to explain, as much as possible in human terms, the mystery of who God is. Check out the section, "Digging Up the Biblical Foundation of the Trinity," later in this chapter, to find out where Christians got this idea.

Think of the Trinity as an equilateral triangle, such as the one shown in Figure 7-1. The triangle consists of three equal, distinct sides that are never separate from each other — the Father, Son, and Holy Spirit. Together these sides form a triangle, the area of which is "one" — God.

Figure 7-1:
An equilateral triangle is a helpful illustration of the Trinity.

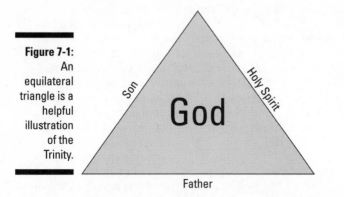

Another way to think of the Trinity involves the three states of water — or, for the science buffs, H_2O. Depending on the temperature, H_2O takes on one of three forms: solid ice, liquid water, or a steamy vapor. In the same way, God is "one," but expresses himself in three distinct manners.

Before I explain more about each member of the Trinity, however, I provide a foundation with the Christian belief on God's very nature. Find out about these qualities in the following section.

Considering God as a Whole

In spite of the fact that Christians believe God's the greatest being in existence, he remains the most elusive personality to grasp. If you ask a passerby who God is, chances are you get some really interesting answers. To some, he's the Man Upstairs. To others, the Eye in the Sky. And to the rest, he's simply "God." Everyone has some way of trying to express the inexpressible.

Although God is and will always remain mysterious, Christians find that he actually provides many insights into who he is inside of the Bible. You can divide these qualities into three groups:

- Qualities that are hard for us to grasp
- Qualities that humans display to a limited degree
- Qualities that show God's intimate relation to humanity

I explain the qualities that fall under these groupings in this section.

Qualities of God that'll make your head spin

My family loves to quiz each other with those "mind-bender" puzzles — you know, those puzzlers that brainiacs can figure out in seconds, but that give folks like me headaches. When my wife reads one to all of us, I sit there staring expressionlessly at the wall, while one of my kids blurts out the answer faster than you can say "Rubik's cube."

When I think about the first set of qualities, known in theological speak as *incommunicable attributes,* my eyes get that same "mind-bender" stare in them. These are the qualities of God that Christians believe humans don't have at all, so they become pretty difficult to grasp:

- **God is eternal.** Although the human race had a Day One of its existence, God never did. He's always existed and always will, being independent of time itself. Refer to Isaiah 57:15, Jude 25, and 1 Kings 8:27.

- **God is independent and exists apart from his creation.** God is totally independent from everything, including his creation. He is self-existent, self-sufficient, and has no causes or needs; he just *is.* Even the name that God identifies himself with in the Old Testament — "I am who I am" — suggests his independence. Check out Isaiah 45. Similarly, God is also *transcendent,* meaning that he exists apart from his creation. Therefore, although the universe that he created is huge, far larger than any human can grasp, God exists apart from it. See Isaiah 40:22.

✔ **God is involved with all of his creation.** Although God does exist apart from the world, he's *immanent,* meaning that he's near to you and I. As a result, God isn't a mere spectator to events on earth, but is an active participant (which is why Christians believe prayer is so important — see Chapter 13 for more). Although he doesn't dictate every little thing that happens, he can and does engineer circumstances in this world. Refer to Isaiah 57:15 and check out Chapter 16 to find out why bad things happen even though God's involved.

✔ **God is everywhere at the same time.** God is also *omnipresent,* not bound to space, enabling him to be everywhere at the same time. The good news is that you're never alone because he's always by your side. The bad news is that, even if you want to, you can't run from him. The prophet Jonah was one guy who testified firsthand about this fact in his self-named Book of the Bible. See Jeremiah 23:23–24 for more on this quality of God.

✔ **God is in control.** If God's all-powerful, then it follows that he's also *sovereign,* that is, in control of everything. Therefore, his will is going to be accomplished. No questions asked. As I discuss in Chapter 16, this doesn't mean that everything that happens is always his deliberate will, but it does mean that he allows it to happen. Check out Psalm 135:6.

✔ **God doesn't change.** God's creation may change constantly, but God never does. He's unchangeable (or *immutable*). Christians take great confidence in that, because it means he'll never go back on his promises or change his mind. See Malachi 3:6.

✔ **God is not understandable.** Although it may be possible to gain some understanding of who God is, humans on this earth will never be able to fully understand him. Refer to Romans 11:33.

Qualities of God that humans resemble

A second group of qualities, often called *communicable attributes* by theology geeks, is more approachable for humans; they are the qualities of God that he allows people to share in. Humans have a slice of the following qualities, and God has the characteristics in their fullest, most perfect forms:

✔ **God is all-knowing.** You can't slip one past God. Because he's *omniscient,* he knows everything. And I mean everything. Remember that cookie you stole from the cookie jar? Busted! Check out Psalm 139:1–6.

✔ **God is all-powerful.** Sure, Superman is more powerful than a locomotive, faster than a speeding bullet, and able to leap tall buildings in a single bound, but he's got a fatal flaw — kryptonite. In contrast, God is all-powerful (or *omnipotent*), with no Achilles' heel. He can do what he wants when he wants. But keep in mind that what he does is always in synch with his other qualities discussed in this section. Refer to Job 42:2.

✔ **God is holy.** The Lord is morally perfect and excellent in every way. God commands his followers to "Be holy as I am holy." Check out Isaiah 6:3.

✔ **God is loving.** God is also all-loving, loving every person with an intense *agape* (or selfless) love. Refer to Romans 5:8 and 1 John 4:8.

✔ **God is righteous and just.** Hating sin and anything impure, the Lord always does the right thing, making it impossible for him to ignore evil and turn a blind eye. His righteousness and justice are displayed in the Old Testament laws regarding sacrifice for sin, the necessity for the sacrificial death of Jesus, and eventual punishment for disobedience on Judgment Day (see Chapter 9). Check out Deuteronomy 32:4 and Psalm 89:14.

✔ **God is merciful.** Because of his enduring love, God is merciful and compassionate. He desires everyone to come to him, so he can shower them with mercy, as I discuss at length in Chapter 3. See Romans 9:14–16.

✔ **God is good.** Although the term *good* seems watered down in modern English, God is the very *definition* of goodness. Check out Romans 11:22.

✔ **God is patient.** The Lord is also patient, having a much slower timetable than I'd often like him to have. He's never in a hurry and always acts at the perfect time. His patience means that he's slow to anger when people blatantly go against him. The reason for God's patience ties back to his mercy — because he desires that everyone come to him, he wants to give people as much time as possible to make that decision before it's too late. See 2 Peter 3:9.

✔ **God is truthful.** Although Satan is defined primarily as being a liar (see Chapter 4), God is always truthful. Therefore, you can take God's promises to the bank, so to speak, because he'll never back out of them. Refer to Titus 1:2.

✔ **God is wise.** Always choosing the best way, God is perfectly wise. He won't take an action that he'll later regret, because he'll always choose the right moves. What's more, because he's all-powerful, all-wise and all-patient, he'll never panic and make a rash decision. Check out Daniel 2:20.

✔ **God is faithful.** As the original promise keeper, the Lord will always back up his words with action. See 2 Timothy 2:13.

The Bible calls Christians to be more and more Christlike in how they live their lives. That doesn't mean taking on the "mind-bender" attributes of God. Instead, it means allowing God to work in the life of each Christian to take on more and more of the above communicable attributes in the Christian's life, such as holiness, truthfulness, wisdom, and faithfulness. These qualities are enhanced in Christians the more they submit to God and avoid sin. In this world, Christians will never fully attain these in perfect form like God does, but the objective is to realize them more as they grow closer in relationship to God.

Qualities of God that express his personal nature

Theologians usually describe God with the traits in the preceding two sections, but if you stop there, God ends up being someone that may be great, but is highly unapproachable. Christians, however, believe in a final set of God's qualities that need to be added to the list — ones that express his deeply personal nature:

- **God is personal.** Christians believe that in spite of being infinite and everywhere at the same time, the Lord is a personal God. He has intelligence, emotions, and a will. Therefore, he's not simply some mindless blob of goo hanging out in space.

- **God is a loving father, a daddy.** Given God's complexity, it's easy to put him on a pedestal and think of him as being aloof from mere mortals. But the picture that Jesus and Paul paint of God in the New Testament is startling in terms of its intimacy. Rather than shower God with endless formal titles when you pray, Paul says to cry out, "Abba! Father!" (Romans 8:15–16). *Abba* is a term that indicates deep affection and intimacy and is a word that Hebrew children call their father, much like "daddy" or "papa" is used in English-speaking countries. Jesus also uses this word when he teaches his followers to pray (Matthew 6:9) and uses it himself when praying to his Father on the night before his crucifixion (Mark 14:36). Further, Jesus paints a vivid portrait of God as a loving father in his parable of the prodigal son in Luke 15. For more on God as a loving father, see Chapter 3.

- **God is a friend.** If you have a best friend, you know how special it is to have someone you can turn to when times are tough and the rest of the world seems to be against you. Jesus, who is fully God and fully man, said that you can think of him in the same way. In fact, he called all of his followers his "friends" in John 15:15.

  When you become friends with someone, that person is always someone you can relate to. If not, the friendship never sticks. The New Testament emphasizes that Jesus is someone you can relate to (see Hebrews 4:15). Because he was a human as well, he understands what you battle on this earth and sympathizes with the tight spots you find yourself in. Or, as former President Clinton might say, Jesus can "feel your pain."

Ultimately, Christians believe that in order to get to know and understand the personal aspects of God, you should get to know Jesus Christ. Read the next section and turn back to Chapter 5 to find out more.

Examining the Three Parts of God Individually

Each of the three members of the Trinity have the incommunicable, communicable, and relational qualities that I discuss in the previous section. In that sense, each part of the Trinity is equal with the others.

Although each of the members of the Trinity are equal, the role that each of them plays is distinct. Ephesians 2:18 provides a good summary when it says, "For through the Son we both have access to the Father by one Spirit." In other words, the Christian has access *to* the Father *through* the Son *by* the Holy Spirit. If all those prepositions have your eyes glazing over, perhaps an illustration will help distinguish among the roles.

Suppose you want to travel to Europe from the United States. Because thousands of miles separate the North American and European continents, you can't just put one foot in front of the other and make it there. An ocean fills the chasm between the continents and connects them together, providing a way to sail a ship to the destination. In this example, you travel *to* Europe *through* the ocean *by* a ship. Similarly, when you approach God the Father, Jesus mediates while the Holy Spirit enables.

Because Christians believe that God the Father plays the leading role, they traditionally call him the "first person" of the Trinity, referring to Jesus as the "second person" and the Holy Spirit as the "third person." (Note that *person* refers to his personality and doesn't imply any idea of humanness.) At the same time, although Father, Son, and Holy Spirit is the most common order, it's not like a law firm where the names are always sequenced in the same way. The Bible has several examples of alternative orders (see 2 Thessalonians 2:13–14, Ephesians 5:18–20, and Jude 20–21).

I explain each of the roles of the Trinity members in the sections that follow.

God the Father

The Father is considered the first person of the Trinity. He's the one who people are usually referring to when they say "God." In fact, in the New Testament, Paul and other apostles often use the term "God the Father."

The Father is fully in control and is the chief planner (Ephesians 1:3–5). He planned salvation through the Son and is the one who actually does the forgiving, not Christ. God the Father is also the one whom Christians normally direct their prayers to. So, he listens to prayers and answers them according to his will.

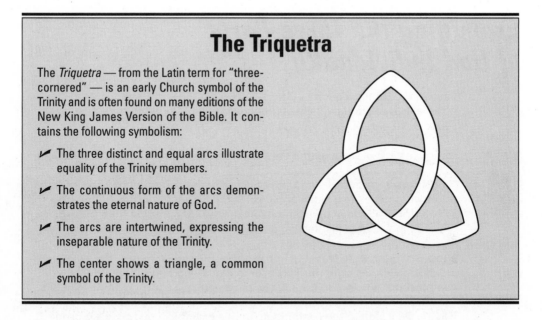

The Triquetra

The *Triquetra* — from the Latin term for "three-cornered" — is an early Church symbol of the Trinity and is often found on many editions of the New King James Version of the Bible. It contains the following symbolism:

✔ The three distinct and equal arcs illustrate equality of the Trinity members.

✔ The continuous form of the arcs demonstrates the eternal nature of God.

✔ The arcs are intertwined, expressing the inseparable nature of the Trinity.

✔ The center shows a triangle, a common symbol of the Trinity.

Many people assume that God the Father is the Creator of the universe, but that's only partially correct. Although all things originated *from* the Father, all things were created *through* the Son (see 1 Corinthians 8:6, John 1:3, Hebrews 1:2). Therefore, even in regard to the actual creation of the world, you see that two members of the Trinity had distinct roles in the process.

God the Son

The second person of the Trinity is the Son, Jesus Christ. He's the one who came to the earth as a man to die for the sins of the world (check out Chapter 5 for an entire chapter devoted to Jesus). The Son always does the will of the Father and sits at his right hand in heaven. He's the go-between, smack in the middle of a perfect Father and a most unholy people. This mediation played out for all people when he died a sacrificial death on the cross, but he also continues to intercede for Christians on a day-in, day-out basis, as they pray to the Father (Hebrew 7:25).

The Bible indicates that Christians should normally direct their prayers to God the Father, but that's not a hard and fast rule. Occasionally, in the New Testament (such as in Acts 7:39), believers prayed directly to Jesus.

Most Christians tend to feel closest to the Son, identifying with him because he came to the earth as a human and was the one who actually died in their place. What's more, as Hebrews 2:17–18 says, Jesus experienced all the temptations that humans have to deal with. So, he's able to help everyone out because he knows what it feels like to deal with the yucky stuff.

God the Holy Spirit

The third person of the Trinity is the Holy Spirit (sometimes referred to as the Holy Ghost). The Holy Spirit is said to do the will of the Father and of the Son (see John 14:26). Of the Trinity members, the Holy Spirit is the one that's hardest to relate to for many people, because "spirit" is such a vague concept. But, in spite of the mystery, the Holy Spirit performs many critical roles in the lives of Christians.

He has been involved throughout history, such as in revelation to the authors of the Bible and in supernaturally impregnating Mary for the virgin conception of Jesus Christ (see Luke 1:35). He also is actively involved in the life of every Christian. First, he participates in the salvation of a person, which is often referred to as the "baptism of the Holy Spirit" (see Chapter 8 for more on baptism). Second, he dwells inside all Christians, filling them with spiritual gifts, giving assurance, convicting them of sins in their lives, helping in worship, and empowering them for service.

The Holy Spirit also plays an important role in a Christian's prayer life. First, the Holy Spirit prompts believers to pray. Second, Christians believe that even when they don't know exactly how to pray for something, the Holy Spirit serves as their translator, so to speak, so that even when they don't know how to express themselves, God the Father understands their needs (Romans 8:26–27).

Understanding the Significance of the Trinity

Because the term "three-oneness" doesn't often roll off most people's tongues these days, you probably wonder what all the fuss is about. After all, is the Trinity just something for theology geeks to discuss, or is it practical for all Christians to think about in their daily lives?

Although the issue is a mind bender, Christians have practical reasons for why the Trinity is fundamental to their faith.

Origins of the doctrine of the Trinity

Although the doctrine itself wasn't fully defined until the fourth century A.D., the common, popular belief of the early Church was in the divine nature and essential unity of the Father, Son, and Holy Spirit. But, just like the finalizing of the biblical canon happened out of a response to false teaching (see Chapter 6), so too the doctrine of the Trinity was not fully developed until the spread of false teaching forced the Church to deal with the matter once and for all.

Sabellius was a Roman teacher who lived in the third century. He said that one God exists, but that he revealed himself in history in three different, temporary ways. His position later came to be known as *modalism*. Next, in the early fourth century, a teacher named Arius again focused on the unity of God, arguing that Jesus was not God, but instead was the first and greatest of created beings, something like a super-angel. (This *Arianism* position is very similar to what Jehovah's Witnesses believe today, which explains why the Christian Church doesn't consider Jehovah's Witnesses as part of it.) The beliefs of Arianism spread rapidly, and soon the Church began to divide over this issue. Although Arianism was popular in some Church circles, the local churches rejected it.

Around this time, Emperor Constantine, who saw Christianity as a way to bring his people together and stop regional in-fighting, took control of the vast Roman empire. But in order to use the religion as a tool, he needed to deal with this split in the Church. As a result, in A.D. 325, Constantine called together a council of Church leaders in the town of Nicaea in order to settle this issue. The council met and reached a consensus that Christ was indeed God, which they wrote down and called the "Nicean Creed," but Arianism still had a foothold for some time. Another council that helped further define the doctrine was held in A.D. 381 at Constantinople. Since that second council, the Nicean Creed has stood for nearly 17 centuries (see the sidebar, "The Nicean Creed," later in this chapter) as a basic, non-negotiable belief of the Christian faith.

A key early defender of the Trinity was Athanasius, who was one of the Church leaders on the Council of Nicaea and devoted his life to upholding the position. Athanasius believed that the Trinity is essential to Christianity and that the Christian understanding of salvation falls apart if Jesus is not God. I explain this idea further in the section "Understanding the Significance of the Trinity."

The Trinity made Jesus' sacrifice worthwhile

The primary reason that the Trinity is essential to Christianity is because of the sacrificial death of Jesus Christ. Christianity says that salvation is possible because Jesus Christ, being fully God and fully man (see Chapter 5 to wrestle with that doozy), was in the unique position of being able to offer the perfect sacrifice on behalf of all people — because *he* was perfect.

If Jesus wasn't God, then his sacrifice would've been illegitimate — meaningless. The Old Testament clearly says that humans can't achieve salvation on their own, picking themselves up to God by their own bootstraps. The Israelites tried that route by following the Law that God, through Moses, gave them. But they failed to keep up their end of the bargain with God, falling into disobedience time and time again. Therefore, if salvation is possible, it must fall on God and God alone to provide it on his own initiative and his own doing, not on anyone else.

Further, Jesus Christ can't simply have been some super-angelic lackey that God sent to the earth to do his dirty work for him. Because God is the one grieved by people's sin, he's the only one in a position to restore the severed relationship between humans and himself. Or, to put it in a catch phrase: He alone can atone.

The Trinity justifies worshiping Jesus

A second reason supporting the practical significance of the Trinity deals with worshiping Jesus. Quite simply, if Jesus isn't God, then it makes no sense to worship him. You wouldn't *worship* any other good person, would you? You may *respect* him, but that's a whole different ballgame.

Christians believe that the Ten Commandments make it clear that humans are to worship one and only God, and no one — or nothing — else. Whenever the Bible says angels appeared, it also says that they told people not to worship them, which reinforces this point.

Yet, Jesus encouraged worship of himself, and the apostles emphasize that throughout the remainder of the New Testament. Because Christians believe that Jesus spoke the ultimate truth (see Chapter 5), they trust his encouragement to worship him and regard him as Lord. And because Jesus is the *only* human the Bible tells us to worship, that instruction helps back up the claim that Jesus is indeed God, in light of the Bible's earlier instruction to worship only the one true God.

Digging Up the Biblical Foundation of the Trinity

It would surely make for a great quiz show question: What is a key component of historical, biblical Christianity, but isn't once mentioned by name in the Bible? The answer: the Trinity. Although the Bible doesn't call it out by name, scripture reveals the Trinity doctrine as an underlying theme in several different ways.

Over the years, some people have objected to the idea of the Trinity because it's not explicitly found in the Bible. But it's important to keep in mind that the Trinity creed is intended only to explain what Christians believe the scriptures imply, not expand on them.

Consider the following parallel which explains how Christians got the idea of the Trinity doctrine. Suppose I come up to you and share with you the following story:

> *I drove to the store today. But before leaving my garage, I put the top down, because it was sunny outside. At the store, I had a flat tire and called AAA to come fix it for me.*

Although I never once mention a convertible car by name, it's obvious that it's the underlying subject of the story. In fact, no other vehicle — a bicycle, semi, or a horse carriage — would provide a logical explanation that takes into account all of the stated details. In much the same way, the Trinity is like the convertible — the lone explanation that is consistent with the characteristics of God that scripture portrays.

Picking up on hints in the Old Testament

Because the Old Testament (discussed in Chapter 6) emphasizes the "oneness" of God, Christians often think of the New Testament as the sole provider of biblical proof of the Trinity. And although the Old Testament doesn't provide any definite evidence, it includes several hints about the Trinity that pave the way for the more explicit teaching that follows in the New Testament:

✔ **Plural pronouns refer to God.** Genesis makes curious use of plural pronouns in two passages:

- God said, "Let us make man in *our* image, after *our* likeness" (Genesis 1:26).

- God said, "Behold, the man has become like one of *us,* knowing good and evil" (Genesis 3:22).

Although the use of a plural pronoun may not conclusively confirm the Trinity, it is quite intriguing and noteworthy. Some argue that it's just a reference to the collective "we," but that seems unlikely because its usage doesn't make sense in the context and because this was unknown as a literary device until modern times and has no equivalent in ancient literature.

✔ **God addresses another being like himself.** Psalm 110:1 seems to reference the Father and Son when it says, "*Yahweh* [God] says to my *Lord,* 'Sit at my right hand, until I make your enemies your footstool for your feet.'"

> Isaiah 48:16 appears to reference the Father and Holy Spirit when it says, "Come you near to me, hear you this; from the beginning I have not spoken in secret; from the time that it was, there am *I:* and now the *Lord God* has sent me, and his *Spirit.*"

In an ancient world that worshiped multiple gods, Judaism and Christianity uniquely served one God. (For a discussion on how Christianity emerged from Judaism, see Chapter 10.) Both the Old Testament (Deuteronomy 6:4) and New Testament (Mark 12:29) reinforce that point continually. But the fact that the Bible hammers on this basic fact over and over again is usually the biggest stumbling block for people in accepting the Trinity — because they often think that the Trinity represents three gods. However, Christians believe that the Trinity *maintains* the unity and oneness of God.

As I show you in the preceding bullets, although the Old Testament emphasizes that one God exists, it also suggests that something deeper and more mysterious lies under the cover when humans consider who God is. It's only later, in the New Testament, that these clues develop more fully.

If God is a Trinity, then you may legitimately ask why the Old Testament isn't more explicit. One possible explanation is that, other than Israel, the cultures of that day were invariably *polytheistic* (worshiped multiple gods). As a result, the Trinity may be easily misunderstood as meaning three gods. Therefore, it was perhaps most important to first hammer the point home about the oneness of God before telling the rest of the story. (See the "An argument of convenience?" sidebar.)

An argument of convenience?

Just because the Old Testament doesn't make the Trinity crystal clear doesn't automatically make attempts to justify this idea mere arguments of convenience. In fact, you see the practice of revealing only part of the full story all the time in the world. Think, for example, of that 1980s neo-classic movie *The Karate Kid*. If you recall, Daniel is a teenager who wants to learn to be a karate expert and eventually talks an old master, Mr. Miyagi, into teaching him. However, when the training begins, Mr. Miyagi doesn't begin in the gym. For two weeks, he makes Daniel wash his cars repeatedly, using the same hand and arm motions. Daniel grumbles, wondering why he's wasting his time washing cars rather than learning karate when the big match is quickly approaching. However, after Daniel gets to the gym, it becomes clear that Mr. Miyagi was teaching him karate all the time — the car-washing technique that had become second nature to Daniel was actually the basic karate move that he used to win the karate match. Similarly, the Old Testament concept of God is true, but it only makes full sense when you look at in the broad context of the entire Bible.

Putting the pieces together in the New Testament

If the Old Testament shines a pen light at the Trinity, then consider the New Testament to flash a super-sized spotlight on the idea of "three-in-oneness." In particular, the New Testament refers to all three members of the Trinity as God, clarifies their roles, considers them unified, and treats them as equals.

New Testament refers to each Trinity member as God

The New Testament scriptures talk much about each of the three members of the Trinity and, at various points, refers to each of them as God.

- **Father as God:** The Father is certainly the most obvious reference to God, because the Bible is littered with statements tying the Heavenly Father with God. Romans 1:7 is one such example: "Grace to you and peace from God our Father and the Lord Jesus Christ."

- **Son as God:** In Chapter 5, you explore the ways that Jesus expresses his divine nature during his earthly ministry. However, in addition to what Jesus himself said, the Bible has a lot of other references to his deity, including:

   - Hebrews 1:8 says, "But of the Son he says, 'Your throne, *O God,* is forever and ever. The scepter of uprightness is the scepter of your Kingdom.'"

   - After seeing the resurrected Jesus for the first time, the disciple Thomas exclaims in John 20:28, "My Lord and *my God."*

   - Paul writes in Philippians 2:5–6, "Jesus, being in very nature [in the form of] *God. . . ."*

   - The Gospel of John starts out immediately stressing the fact that Jesus is God. In 1:1, John writes, "In the beginning was the Word, and the Word was with God, and the *Word was God."* In context, the "Word" is a clear reference to Jesus Christ.

   - Peter opens up his second letter with reference to "our *God* and Savior, Jesus Christ" (2 Peter 1:1), and Paul does the same in Titus (2:13): "Looking for the blessed hope and appearing of the glory of our great *God* and Savior, Jesus Christ."

   It's easy to get hung up on the term "Son" because contemporary society usually thinks of a son as someone junior or unequal. Yet, in biblical times, sonship was thought of as meaning "likeness." John 5:18 also expresses this popular understanding of "sonship" in Jesus' day. In this passage, John indicates that the Jews tried to kill Jesus because he "called God his own Father, making himself equal with God."

✔ **Holy Spirit as God:** The Holy Spirit is often equated with God through many parts of the Bible, but perhaps the most specific reference is in Acts 5. This chapter of the Bible tells the story of Ananias and Sapphira, two dishonest believers in the early Church. Peter says to Ananias, "Why has Satan filled your heart to lie to the Holy Spirit? . . . You haven't lied to men, but to *God"* (Acts 5:3–4).

New Testament distinguishes among Trinity members and their roles

The three names of the Trinity aren't just different names referring to one identity, because the Bible distinguishes each from the others and shows that they all have distinct roles:

✔ When Jesus was baptized, all three members of the Trinity were present and active. Luke 3:21 chronicles the events: "Now it happened, when all the people were baptized, *Jesus* also had been baptized, and was praying. The sky was opened, and the *Holy Spirit* descended in a bodily form as a dove on him; and a *voice* came out of the sky, saying 'You are my beloved Son. In you I am well pleased.'"

✔ Jesus prays to the Father constantly throughout his ministry, making an unmistakable distinction between his Father in heaven and himself on earth.

✔ In John 14, Jesus talks to his disciples about the coming of the Holy Spirit. In several instances, he noticeably refers to each member of the Trinity:

- "*I* will pray to the *Father,* and he will give you another *Counselor,* that he may be with you forever, the Spirit of truth, whom the world can't receive; for it doesn't see him, neither knows him. You know him, for he lives with you, and will be in you."

- "If a man loves *me,* he will keep *my* word. My *Father* will love him, and *we* will come to him, and make *our* home with him. He who doesn't love me doesn't keep my words. The word which you hear isn't mine, but the *Father's* who sent me. I have said these things to you, while still living with you. But the *Counselor,* the *Holy Spirit,* whom the *Father* will send in *my* name, *he* will teach you all things, and will remind you of all that *I* said to you."

New Testament refers to Trinity members as "one"

The essential unity of the Trinity is referenced when Trinity members are called "one." John 10:30–31 calls the Father and Son "one," and Romans 8:9 considers the Spirit and Son "one."

New Testament associates all Trinity members as equal

Several times, the New Testament associates the Trinity members together in ways that wouldn't make sense if they weren't each distinctly God. A few examples follow.

> ✔ Perhaps the best example is in Matthew 28:19–20, when Jesus gave parting words to his disciples just before he ascended into heaven: "Therefore go, and make disciples of all nations, baptizing them in the name of the *Father* and of the *Son* and of the *Holy Spirit,* teaching them to observe all things that I commanded you. Behold, I am with you always, even to the end of the age."
>
> ✔ In his closing, Paul writes in 2 Corinthians 13:14, "The grace of the Lord *Jesus Christ*, the love of *God,* and the communion of the *Holy Spirit* be with you all."

Throughout the Bible, God makes it clear that he doesn't share power with anyone. Therefore, if the Son and Holy Spirit aren't part of the same being as the Father, then these verses are nothing more than heretical, because they treat the three as equals.

The Nicean Creed

The Nicean Creed (referred to by Orthodox Christians as the Nicene-Constantinopolitan Creed) was developed at the Council of Nicaea and refined at subsequent councils in the fourth century. The creed is significant because, for over sixteen hundred years, it has served as the definitive statement on the doctrine of the Trinity and put to rest the question of what the Church considered acceptable teaching on this matter. It's also significant because it's the lone Christian creed that Protestants, Catholics, and Orthodox Christians all accept. Below is the creed in its final form:

> *We believe in one God, the Father, the Almighty, maker of heaven and earth, of all that is, seen and unseen.*
>
> *We believe in one Lord, Jesus Christ, the only Son of God, eternally begotten of the Father, God from God, light from light, true God from true God, begotten, not made, of one Being with the Father; through him all things were made. For us and for our salvation he came down from heaven, was incarnate of the Holy Spirit and the Virgin Mary and became truly human. For our sake he was crucified under Pontius Pilate; he suffered death and was buried. On the third day he rose again in accordance with the Scriptures; he ascended into heaven and is seated at the right hand of the Father. He will come again in glory to judge the living and the dead, and his kingdom will have no end.*
>
> *We believe in the Holy Spirit, the Lord, the giver of life, who proceeds from the Father [and the Son], who with the Father and the Son is worshiped and glorified, who has spoken through the prophets. We believe in one holy catholic and apostolic Church. We acknowledge one baptism for the forgiveness of sins. We look for the resurrection of the dead, and the life of the world to come. Amen.*

Chapter 8

The Rite Stuff: Sacraments, Ordinances, and the Christian Faith

. . . .

In This Chapter

▶ Discovering what sacraments and ordinances are and why they're important

▶ Looking at rites from the Protestant, Catholic, and Orthodox perspectives

▶ Exploring baptism

▶ Revisiting the Lord's Supper

▶ Finding a balance between ceremonies and faith

. . . .

This is a laid-back era. It's not unusual to see people wearing Dockers, blue jeans, or cutoffs to work and church — this was unheard of fifty years ago. As someone who has grown up in these times, I certainly reflect that informal attitude. If I had to decide between wearing a tie and getting a root canal, I'd have a tough time figuring out which was the most unpleasant option. (I'd opt for the root canal — at least you get Novocain to deaden the pain.) Given the relaxed nature of today's society, it's not surprising that ceremonies are less important to people today than they were at perhaps any other time in human history. In days gone by, tradition was revered; today, younger generations often consider rituals uncool. Yet, in spite of the cynicism, ceremonies aren't dead just yet; weddings, funerals, graduations, and the like remain ever-important public events that commemorate and honor the people involved.

Rites, or solemn ceremonies, are important to any religion, and Christianity is no exception. A quick scan of the Bible shows you that rites have played an ever-present role in the lives of the Lord's faithful, both in the Old and New Testaments. Christians believe that God ordained certain rites that all Christians should participate in. At the same time, Christians don't all agree on

the meaning of these rituals to their faith or even on what to call them. Many Christians call these practices *sacraments*. Others, such as Southern Baptists, flatly reject that term, identifying them as *ordinances* instead. Throughout this chapter, I use the terms "sacrament" and "ordinance" interchangeably.

In this chapter, you explore what sacraments are and become acquainted with the wide spectrum of perspectives in the Christian Church concerning their purpose. You then discover the two ordinances that all Christians universally recognize — baptism and the Lord's Supper — and the role that they play in a believer's life.

Before getting started, however, I must offer you a word of warning about the minefield you're about to enter. Sacraments are perhaps the most divisive issue in the Christian Church and are a primary cause for the historical split between the Catholics and Protestants (see Chapter 11). Therefore, although I stress the core beliefs of the ordinances that all Christians affirm, a sizable amount of the discussion focuses on the differences and subtleties of belief on these issues. But before you throw the book out the window or skip to the next chapter, let me urge you to hang in there with me for a while. I guide you through this minefield so you can get to know the rocky terrain without having an explosive detonate near you. Then, as you reach the end of the chapter in one piece, I close with a discussion on the importance of maintaining a balanced perspective, just like Jesus Christ did.

Understanding the Role of Sacraments and Ordinances

Want to socialize? If so, you might call your friends over tonight for a get-together and chat the night away, but you're not likely to hold a ceremony just for that purpose. Although ceremonies are public events, they have an underlying meaning and purpose that goes far beyond mingling and hanging out. For example, no engaged couple I know holds a wedding and reception costing thousands of dollars just so they can play dress up, visit with quirky relatives, and watch gobs of people they barely know dance and eat all the cake they can stuff into their mouths. No, a bride and groom hold a formal wedding to commemorate the life-changing commitment that they're making to each other.

A Christian sacrament follows the same idea: Christians observe it for reasons that go far beyond tradition, ritual, or social stimulation. Instead, a *sacrament* (or *ordinance*) is a public action that one undertakes to express an inner transformation in his or her heart. Or, in the words of St. Augustine, a sacrament is "an outward and visible sign of an inward and invisible grace."

Grasping four keys to understanding the sacraments

Rites, ordinances, and sacraments all sound like foreign words to a society that downplays ceremony. So, if you're still confused about what exactly sacraments are, consider the following four keys to understanding the sacraments.

Key #1: Historical terms for sacraments hint at their meaning

The early Church originally called a sacrament a *mystery,* which emphasized the facts that: (1) God kept these rites hidden until after Jesus came to the earth, and (2) God mysteriously reveals himself in some manner through these rites. As time passed and translators converted more Christian terminology from Greek to Latin, they struggled to find a Latin equivalent to adequately express the concept's meaning. They eventually chose the Latin word *sacramentum,* a term that people of that era could easily identify with. *Sacramentum* referred to the oath that Roman soldiers took when they became officers, swearing allegiance to the Roman gods, resulting in a change of the solder's formal legal status. Each of these two terms — *mystery* and *sacrament* — reveals an idea of what these rites are all about. Although Catholics and some Protestants today use "sacrament," the Orthodox branch often refers to the sacraments as "mysteries."

Key #2: Sacraments are consistent with Old Testament rites

Throughout the Old Testament, ceremonies were an important part of Israel's religious life. Religious leaders circumcised infants as a sign of the covenant between the Israelites and God (see Genesis 17:10–14). A Passover meal commemorated the passing over of faithful Hebrews when God judged Egypt (see Exodus 12:11). Jews regularly sacrificed lambs and other animals as a rite that signified the cost of sin. Therefore, when Jesus told people to be baptized and when he inaugurated the Lord's Supper, his Jewish followers immediately recognized the ceremonial significance of this teaching.

Key #3: Sacraments emphasize the unity of the physical and spiritual realms

Hebrew Christians instinctively understood the significance of rites (see Key #1), but newly converted *Gentile* (non-Jewish) believers didn't. The dominant philosophy of the Mediterranean world in the first century recognized no connection between the physical and spiritual parts of a person. Therefore, people believed that the actions they undertook — be they illicit sex, drunkenness, or betting on donkey races — had no bearing on their spiritual lives. (If you read Paul's letters to the Corinthians in the Bible, you notice he speaks at length against this belief.) Therefore, when the early Church emphasized ordinances, it helped show new Christians how tightly interwoven the physical and spiritual parts of a person are. Sacraments helped illustrate that what you

do with your body has a direct effect on your spiritual life. They serve as instruments that help reinforce the idea that outward action, whether sinful or holy, is inseparable from a person's inner heart condition.

Key #4: Sacramental roles have expanded over the years

Jesus ordained baptism and commanded his followers to participate in the Lord's Supper, so the early Church incorporated these acts as part of their teaching and practices. As time passed, other ordinances evolved; by the sixth century, the Church began considering further how the sacraments fit into the overall life of a Christian, from cradle to grave. The role of the sacraments continued to expand over the next several centuries, and by the 13th century, the seven sacraments that the Catholic Church recognizes today — baptism, confirmation, confession, Eucharist (the Lord's Supper), marriage, holy orders, and anointing of the sick — were in place. At the Council of Trent in 1519, Church leaders declared this set of sacraments to be a key Catholic doctrine, proclaiming that the sacraments are necessary for a person's *salvation,* or being cleansed from sin and receiving eternal life in heaven (see Chapter 3 for more on salvation).

As the role of sacraments grew larger, so too did the role of the Church. Catholic teaching stressed that Christ commissioned the Church to administer the sacraments and its leaders to guide all Christians. Therefore, the sacramental system that was established in the 16th century formalized the Church's role as sole mediator of the sacraments between God and the individual Christian.

However, not everyone agreed with the dominant role of sacraments and the mediator position of the Church in an individual Christian's life. In fact, this debate proved to be a spark that eventually ignited the Protestant Reformation (check out Chapter 11).

No matter whether one holds to the Catholic or Protestant position on ordinances, one point must be underscored: The belief that God gives saving grace through the sacraments as the Church administers them is the product of theological writings from Augustine through the Middle Ages, not from the New Testament or the first-century Church.

Viewing sacraments through different lenses

As the role of sacraments increased in importance through medieval times, different views began to surface concerning what exactly ordinances were and which rites should be considered sacraments. These views tend to be

sharpest between Catholics and Protestants, while the Orthodox branch of the Church has always been less defined on its stance. I discuss three major areas of disagreement below.

How sacraments affect Christians

Most Christians affirm the idea that sacraments are a significant part of the life of a Christian, but the roles of the sacrament itself and the faith of the person taking it differ greatly. Catholics believe that God uses the gift of the sacrament to distribute saving grace to Christians in a very literal, physical sense. They believe that the sacramental act itself has real power packed into it, which God uses to transform a person's heart. In contrast, most Protestants view ordinances as an outward sign of a change that has already happened inside of a person.

A smaller minority of Protestant denominations, such as the Quakers and Salvation Army, dismiss the belief that sacraments play any role in the life of a Christian and therefore don't observe any sacraments at all.

To Catholics, the sacrament *causes* a transformation inside an individual. To Protestants, an individual's inner change is the motivation that prompts him or her to participate in the sacrament. See Figure 8-1.

What role sacraments play in salvation

Considering that Christians debate over whether ordinances are the cause or effect of God's grace, you may expect two different perspectives on the role that sacraments play in salvation. (See Chapter 3 for more on salvation.)

Because Catholics believe that the sacraments are the means that God uses to give his saving grace, they believe that sacraments are *required* in order for a person to receive salvation. They allow for some exceptions, however. For instance, if you were on your way to be baptized and died in a car accident, Catholics believe that you fulfilled your obligation. Similarly, unbaptized babies go to and remain in *limbo* (a location on the outer rim of purgatory where they neither suffer nor enjoy bliss), not hell. Further, for negligence in partaking in sacraments other than baptism, the consequence is more likely additional time in purgatory (see Chapter 9) than the loss of salvation.

From a Protestant perspective, the Catholic Church strays from biblical teaching (see Acts 16:31, Romans 3:28, Ephesians 2:8–10), because it ends up leaving the role of a person's faith in salvation as secondary. Protestants further disagree with Catholics, saying that no matter their significance, ordinances don't put a person's eternal future at stake. From a Catholic perspective, Protestants overlook the traditional role of the Church as administrator of the sacraments and ignore such biblical references as John 3:5 (which I discuss in the section, "Exploring the relationship between baptism and salvation," later in this chapter).

In summary, Catholics believe you receive saving grace *by practicing* the sacraments, but Protestants believe you receive saving grace *through faith alone* in Jesus Christ.

How the Church should select which sacraments to observe

The seven sacraments of the Catholic Church — baptism, confirmation, confession, Eucharist (the Lord's Supper), marriage, holy orders, and anointing of the sick — were selected on the grounds of being (1) based implicitly or explicitly on New Testament teaching and (2) *holistic,* covering each phase of a Christian's life.

In contrast, Protestants generally believe a valid ordinance must meet three criteria. It should: (1) be explicitly authorized by Jesus himself, (2) contain a physical sign, and (3) express grace. As a result, Protestants only recognize the two ordinances that are clearly initiated by Jesus Christ — baptism (Matthew 28:19) and the Lord's Supper (Matthew 26:26–29). Although Protestants practice certain rites like confirmation, marriage, and anointing of the sick, they don't see them as observances that should be on the same level as the two "authorized" ordinances.

Given this criteria, a few small Protestant denominations, such as some groups in the Brethren Church, consider foot-washing an ordinance, because Jesus' act of washing his disciples' feet (see John 13:4–11) seems to meet that same criteria.

Officially, the Orthodox Church has no fully defined position on the sacraments. Some Orthodox churches use the list of seven sacraments of the Catholic Church. Other Orthodox churches reject any sacraments other than baptism and the Lord's Supper.

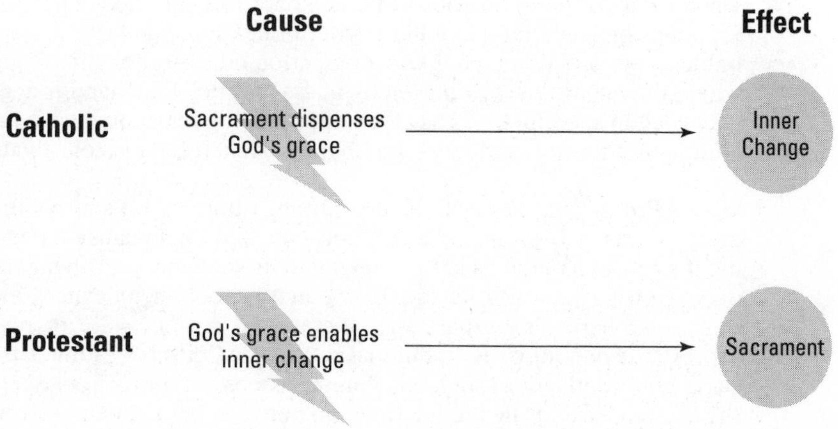

Cause   **Effect**

Figure 8-1:
The Catholic and Protestant views of the cause and effect of sacraments are essentially opposites.

Catholic   Sacrament dispenses God's grace   ⟶   Inner Change

Protestant   God's grace enables inner change   ⟶   Sacrament

The five sacraments Christians disagree on are

- ✔ **Confession (penance):** Allows Christians the opportunity to confess their sins to a clergyperson for assurance of forgiveness. Catholics, Orthodox Christians, and Anglican Protestants (Church of England; see Chapter 11) commonly practice confession.

- ✔ **Confirmation:** Considered by Catholics to be the second half of baptism, which signifies being able to participate in the Eucharist and receive the gift of the Holy Spirit (see Chapter 13 for more on receiving the Holy Spirit). They see confirmation as the spiritual equivalent to adolescence, the point at which one grows up in the Christian faith. In the Catholic Church, a person is normally confirmed after attending a series of religious classes taught by a bishop. Though they don't consider it a sacrament, some Protestant denominations have confirmation as well, in order to prepare them for church membership.

- ✔ **Marriage:** Considered a sacrament by Catholics, some Anglicans, and some Orthodox.

- ✔ **Holy orders:** The rite of setting a person apart to become a member of the Catholic clergy (deacon, priest, or bishop) to serve the spiritual needs of others.

- ✔ **Anointing of the sick:** Based on James 5:14–15; the rite of the church leaders anointing a sick person with oil (by placing oil on the fingertip and touching it to the receiver's forehead) and praying for healing for the person. In biblical times, oil was used both as a medicine and as a symbol of the presence of the Holy Spirit.

Christians don't argue about the other two ordinances; baptism and the Lord's Supper are universally practiced across the entire Christian Church.

Who's allowed to participate in the sacraments

Many parts of the Christian Church have specific conditions on who's allowed to participate in the sacraments. Catholics require you to be a member of the Catholic Church to participate in observing the sacraments. The Orthodox Church has similar limitations. For example, a Protestant or Catholic attending a Greek Orthodox Church wouldn't be able to participate in the Lord's Supper. However, a visiting Serbian Orthodox Christian would be able to. When a church places restrictions on partaking of the Lord's Supper, it is commonly referred to as *closed communion.*

Several Protestant denominations have conditions as well, particularly with respect to the Lord's Supper. Some Baptist churches require you to be a member of that particular church in order to take the Lord's Supper. Other Protestant groups that have some form of closed communion include the Lutherans (Missouri Synod) and Mennonites. In contrast, other Protestant churches, particularly evangelical ones, only require that a person partaking of the sacraments is a professing Christian.

Baptizing Christians into the Faith

Don't you know that all we who were baptized into Christ Jesus were baptized into his death? We were buried therefore with him through baptism to death, that just like Christ was raised from the dead through the glory of the Father, so we also might walk in newness of life.

—Romans 6:3–4

Baptism is the ceremonial act of being cleansed with water — either by being dipped into or sprinkled with water or by having it poured over you — and has the following purposes:

- ✔ Expresses the death of sin in your life (just as Christ died on the cross; see Matthew 27) and your resurrection into a new life in Christ (just as Christ was resurrected; see Matthew 28)
- ✔ Expresses a person's regeneration into a new creature in Christ
- ✔ Publicly identifies an individual with Christ's death and resurrection
- ✔ Serves as the initiation rite of the new covenant

Just as water is a common symbol of cleansing, baptism expresses the purification that happens when a person commits his or her life to Jesus Christ.

Christians have considerable differences in opinion on the role and practice of baptism in response to the following questions:

- ✔ What exactly is the meaning of baptism?
- ✔ Is baptism a requirement for salvation?
- ✔ Who should be baptized?
- ✔ How should people be baptized?

Been there, done that: Baptism before Christ came

Baptism is often considered a specifically Christian ceremony, but it actually has its roots in the Old Testament (which pre-dates Christ's life on earth, and thus Christianity). Israel used baptism as a purification ceremony (Exodus 30:17–21). So, when John the Baptist (the prophet who was born shortly before Jesus was and helped get people ready for what Jesus was going to say) baptized people for repentance, the Hebrews already understood the significance of baptism as a rite.

Considering the nature of baptism

Within the Christian Church, you find three major differences of belief about the nature of baptism. Read on to unravel the different ideas.

Baptism is a turbo-powered act

The *sacramental view,* held by Catholics and Orthodox Christians, says that baptism is the primary means by which God gives grace. Baptism isn't just a symbol; it's a specific act that God uses to release his power to produce salvation. As a result, baptism produces an internal change (known as *regeneration*) in which the person being baptized receives forgiveness of sins, a new godly nature, and a stronger faith. To Catholics, the person's faith as part of the saving and regenerating process is much less important compared to what God himself does through the act of baptism. Lutherans, of the Protestant tradition, hold a sacramental view as well, but emphasize faith of the person being baptized as an essential component to this process.

The key verse that those who hold the sacramental view use to back up their stance is John 3:5:

> *Most certainly I tell you, unless one is born of water and spirit, he can't enter into the Kingdom of God!*

Proponents of this view say that this verse indicates that Jesus is stressing the essential role that baptism plays: Unless a person is literally "born of water" — baptized — he or she can't experience God's salvation.

Baptism is a committed act

The *covenantal view,* held by Presbyterians and other Reformed Protestant denominations (see Chapter 11), says that baptism isn't the *means* of receiving salvation, but it's a *sign* of God's covenant with man and the way that Christians are initiated into that covenant relationship. The covenantal view sees baptism as the new way God ordained to express the covenant, replacing the act of circumcision in the Old Testament (find out about the Old Covenant in Genesis 11:17, Genesis 12:1–3, and Exodus 24:3–8). Christians with this view of baptism claim Colossians 2:11–12 as key verses:

> *In [Christ] you were also circumcised with a circumcision not made with hands, in the putting off of the body of the sins of the flesh, in the circumcision of Christ; having been buried with him in baptism, in which you were also raised with him through faith in the working of God, who raised him from the dead.*

In this passage, holders of the covenantal view point to the close relationship that Paul implies between "old style" circumcision and "new style" baptism.

Baptism is a symbolic act

The *symbolical view,* held by most Protestants (other than those who hold the covenantal view — see the previous section), says that baptism is an act of obedience by a believer so that the person can be publicly identified with Jesus and initiated into the Church (not into the Christian life). Salvation is completely dependent on the person's decision of faith (which happens before he or she is baptized) and has nothing to do with the act of baptism itself.

Believers with this view point to Ephesians 2:8–10, which emphasizes that salvation is by faith, not baptism:

> *For by grace you have been saved through faith, and that not of yourselves; it is the gift of God, not of works, that no one would boast. For we are his workmanship, created in Christ Jesus for good works, which God prepared before that we would walk in them.*

According to proponents of the symbolical view, the fact that this passage doesn't mention baptism is a clear indication of baptism's symbolical role. Faith is the critical element in a Christian's life, and baptism, regardless of its importance, plays a secondary role.

Exploring the relationship between baptism and salvation

Given the wide disagreement on what exactly baptism is and does, as well as on the role of ordinances in general, it's obvious that Christians have a difference of opinion on the relationship between baptism and salvation.

Baptism is absolutely necessary for salvation

Catholics believe baptism is a requirement to receiving salvation, plain and simple. They point to two key passages in the Bible to back up their position:

- In Mark 16:16, Jesus talks about what one must do to be saved:

  > *He who believes and is baptized will be saved; but he who does not believe will be condemned.*

  A Catholic understanding of this verse is that Jesus links both faith and baptism to God's saving grace.

- In John 3:5, Jesus tells a curious Jewish leader named Nicodemus about salvation. Catholics believe his reference to being "born of water" is a direct reference to baptism:

  > *Most certainly I tell you, unless one is born of water and spirit, he can't enter into the Kingdom of God!*

However, Catholics do allow for certain special case exceptions, as I discuss in the section, "What role sacraments play in salvation," earlier in this chapter.

Baptism is important, but is not necessary for salvation

Other Christians, mostly Protestants, believe that baptism is an act of obedience to Jesus because he tells his followers to be baptized. But they disagree with the connection between the act of baptism and a person's salvation. They make three arguments in response:

- **The emphasis in Mark 16:16 is on faith, not on baptism.** Notably, Jesus doesn't say at the tail end of the verse, "He who is not baptized will be condemned." Rather, he says, "He who does not *believe* will be condemned."

- **The primary emphasis of the New Testament, whether spoken by Jesus (John 3:16) or Paul (Romans 3:28 and Ephesians 2:8–9), is that Christians are saved by grace through faith.** Mark 16:16 is the only place in the New Testament that directly alludes to any connection between baptism and salvation. Also, many Protestants aren't convinced that the "born of water" reference in John 3:5 actually refers to baptism (another perspective is that it refers to amniotic fluid). In addition, Protestants say that the rest of the conversation that Jesus had with Nicodemus focuses on the teaching that people who *believe* in him will be saved (John 3:15, 18).

- **The "last gasp" conversion of the thief on the cross in Luke 23:40–43 shows that at least one person entered heaven without having first been baptized.** See Chapter 3 for more on the thief on the cross.

Deciding who should be baptized

All Christians believe that a person "of age" (see the "A Christian's age of accountability" sidebar in this chapter) who believes in Jesus Christ and wants to follow him should be baptized. However, the debate centers on people who are too young to make a deliberate decision for or against Jesus. Should infants and small children receive this sacrament? Or should only people who've already made a decision for Christ take this step? The Bible is unclear on this issue; it doesn't explicitly authorize one way or another. As a result, people on both sides of the fence point to verses that suggest support for their positions.

Baptizing infants

Different Christian groups allow for infants to be baptized, but for a variety of reasons. Some of the more prominent ones are

- **Catholics:** Catholics and others who hold a sacramental view of baptism (see the section, "Considering the nature of baptism," earlier in this

chapter) believe that infants should be baptized because the baptism itself is what gives saving grace. The nature of the parents' faith (or, for that matter, the faith or spiritual condition of the priest) is a non-issue to Catholics.

✔ **Lutherans:** Although Lutherans don't believe that saving grace is present in the act of baptism, they allow for infant baptism on the grounds that they believe the Bible implies that infants have an implicit or natural faith (Mark 10:15), and so their baptism is a outward sign of that faith.

✔ **Covenantal view believers:** People who hold a covenantal view of baptism (see the section, "Considering the nature of baptism," earlier in this chapter) point out that circumcision was a sign of the covenant between the Hebrews and God, and infants were active participants in that covenant, with their parents acting on their behalf. Therefore, because baptism is the New Testament's version of circumcision, infants can and should be baptized, as long as the child has Christian parents. In this view, the key is the child's *potential* faith in Christ, not his or her faith at the specific time of the baptismal act.

Proponents of infant baptism often point to three justifications:

✔ **Households were baptized in the New Testament.** Although the Bible doesn't specifically account for any child being baptized, it does list several occasions in which entire households were baptized at the same time (such as Acts 16:15, 16:33, and 18:8.) And though the ages of the people in the households aren't known, advocates for infant baptism insist that odds are likely that some of them would've been infants or small children.

✔ **Jesus gave special attention to children.** Jesus gave special priority and blessing to children throughout his ministry, so forbidding infants and small children from baptism contradicts his actions.

✔ **Infant baptism has been practiced throughout Church history.** Infant baptism wasn't something that came along late in Church history, but was a practice started as early as the second century, just a few generations from the age of the apostles.

Baptizing believers only

The opposing view held by most Protestants is that only people who have consciously and deliberately made a decision to become a follower of Jesus should be baptized. People who uphold the symbolical view of baptism (see the "Considering the nature of baptism" section, earlier in this chapter) insist on believer's baptism. Proponents of this position use the following grounds for their argument:

✔ **The Bible doesn't explicitly endorse infant baptism.** In every specific instance of baptism in the New Testament in which the person is known, the person is always an adult. Although the Book of Acts mentions whole

> households being baptized, the ages of the members are completely unknown and could've easily been older children, teenagers, or even all adults.

✔ **Baptisms in the Bible exclusively involve adults who've converted.** Where specific examples of baptism are mentioned in the New Testament, the baptisms are always observed after a person has repented and believed. Therefore, because infants don't consciously repent or have faith, it's premature for them to be baptized.

✔ **Infants should be blessed, not baptized.** Jesus *did* bless children and give them priority, but no account exists of him ever baptizing them.

Add one part water (But how?): Choosing a method of baptism

A final area of disagreement is the procedural issue of how exactly to baptize. Everyone agrees that H_2O should be the liquid used, but debate occurs over how exactly to get the person wet. Because using a squirt gun isn't an option, should the minister dunk a person under water, pour water over his or her head, or sprinkle a little on top? The issue seems minor compared to the other great debates of this chapter, but it's deemed quite important by certain segments of the Christian Church. The Church holds two basic positions on this issue.

A Christian's age of accountability

A question that Christians have always wrestled with is the *age of accountability,* or the age at which a person is held accountable by God for his or her actions. Obviously, a one-year-old doesn't have the ability to distinguish between good and evil, but an adult clearly does. Because biblical Christianity claims the existence of original sin, which says that people are born with a sinful nature (see Chapter 4), Christians have historically debated what this means for children who die at a young age.

In spite of their inherited sinful nature, many Protestant Christians believe that until a child reaches an age of accountability, God will grant salvation to the child in the event of his or her premature death. Catholics believe that God sends infants to limbo (see the "What role sacraments play in salvation" section, earlier in this chapter) if they die before that age. However, a minority of Protestants dismiss the idea of an age of accountability completely, stressing the sin-soaked nature of all humans, no matter their age.

The Bible never discusses any age of accountability. Christians have come up with various ages, ranging from as early as 5 years old to as late as 20. Other Christians say that the exact age depends completely on the individual, according to his or her ability to discern between right and wrong and to understand God's truth.

Baptizing by immersion only

Some Christians, such as Baptists, believe that the only valid way to baptize people is to dunk them underwater and lift them back up. People who hold this view argue that the Greek word for baptism is only correctly translated as "to dip." They add that the Bible only explicitly endorses baptism by immersion, supporting their stance with verses such as John 3:23 and Acts 8:36. Researchers agree that baptism by immersion seems to have been the common practice in the New Testament Church, and even by the early second century, the common teaching was to immerse, if at all possible.

Advocates of this method also say that immersion best represents the true meaning of baptism — that the act of dunking underwater signifies the believer's death and burial to sin, and the act of rising up from water depicts the resurrection to a new life.

Baptizing by multiple ways

The alternative position views immersion, pouring, and sprinkling as all valid forms of baptism. This view, held by Catholics and such Protestants as Methodists and Lutherans, claims that, although the Greek word *baptism* is translated as "to dip," it can also mean "to put liquid over or on." Therefore, because the exact Greek translation is vague, proponents argue that it's impossible to make a decision based on language translation alone.

In addition, though immersion seems to be the dominant method recorded in the Bible, it may have been impractical or even impossible for some of the baptismal incidents recorded in the Book of Acts (such as Acts 16:33, Acts 18:8, and Acts 19:5). Moreover, proponents argue that purification ceremonies in the Old Testament often used a variety of methods, including immersion, pouring, and sprinkling.

Finally, holders of this view also typically believe that pouring and sprinkling best represent the meaning of baptism, showing the "pouring of the Holy Spirit" onto a person.

Dedicated babies

People who believe in believer's baptism (see the section, "Deciding who should be baptized," in this chapter) don't baptize their babies, but many have their child *dedicated* (or *christened*) to God in a ceremonial manner during a worship service. During a *dedication* (or *christening*), the parents and the church congregation as a whole dedicate the child's life to God and dedicate themselves in the participation of raising the child in a godly manner.

Exploring the Lord's Supper

The *Lord's Supper* is the sacramental act of eating bread and drinking wine (or grape juice) in the same way that Jesus did with his disciples on his final night before his death. Luke 22:19–20 gives the account:

> Jesus took bread, and when he had given thanks, he broke it, and gave to them, saying, "This is my body which is given for you. Do this in memory of me." Likewise, he took the cup after supper, saying, "This cup is the new covenant in my blood, which is poured out for you."

The purpose of the Lord's Supper is fourfold:

✔ Remembers and expresses gratitude for the death of Jesus Christ, his saving work on the cross, and the future hope that Christians have through his resurrection and coming kingdom (see Chapter 5 for more on the death and resurrection of Christ)

✔ Enables the person taking the bread and wine to receive strength, nourishment, and empowerment from Christ

✔ Reaffirms a commitment to Christ

✔ Highlights the communion of believers with Christ himself and with each other

This sacrament is known by many names throughout the Christian Church (see Table 8-1), each of which signifies different aspects of its meaning.

Table 8-1	Different Names for the Lord's Supper	
Name	**Biblical Reference**	**Meaning**
Lord's Supper	1 Corinthians 11:20	Remembering Christ's Last Supper
Eucharist	1 Corinthians 11:24, Matthew 26:27	From the Greek word for "giving thanks," emphasizing offering thanksgiving to God for Christ's work that is being done in the life of a Christian.
Communion	1 Corinthians 10:16	Emphasizes the intimate bond between the Christian and God, as well as with the entire Body of Christ.
Lord's Table	1 Corinthians 10:21	Remembering Christ's Last Supper
Cup of Blessing	1 Corinthians 10:16	Similar to *Eucharist*
Breaking of Bread	Acts 2:42	Remembering Christ's Last Supper

Wine? Grape juice? Snapple?

The Christian Church has historically varied on whether to use alcoholic wine or non-alcoholic grape juice as part of Communion. Catholics, Episcopalians, and some Lutherans use wine. Methodists, Congregationalists, Baptists, and most evangelical churches prefer to use grape juice. Orthodox Churches allow for either.

Although, throughout history, the Church traditionally used wine for Communion, non-alcoholic grape juice became increasingly popular in Protestant churches in England during the temperance movement and in the U.S. in the 19th and early 20th centuries.

At the same time, the debate is over more than just whether or not to serve alcohol during the Lord's Supper. Much of the issue concerns whether Jesus used fermented or unfermented wine during the Last Supper and whether Matthew 26:29 refers to grape juice or wine when Jesus refers to the "fruit of the vine."

Deciphering Jesus' explanation of the elements

Surprise, surprise. Like they do with almost every other sacrament you've read about in this chapter, Christians debate on what exactly is the nature of the bread and wine, commonly known as the *elements*. Throughout Church history, Christians have speculated over what exactly Jesus' words, "This is my body" and "This is my blood," meant. The Church portrays four diverse interpretations of this statement:

✔ **Elements are transformed into a real presence of Christ.** The first perspective is that Jesus meant that when people participate in the Lord's Supper, the bread and wine *literally* become transformed into the actual body and blood of Christ. The elements may still look, taste, smell, and feel like bread and wine, but their "inner reality" changes.

Catholics hold this view and call it *transubstantiation*. In this case, because God actively transforms the elements into a bodily presence of Christ, the power of the Eucharist is not dependent on a person's faith. Check out *Catholicism For Dummies* by Rev. John Trigilio, Jr. and Rev. Kenneth Brighenti (Wiley) to uncover more on transubstantiation. The Orthodox Church also believes Christ is really present in the Eucharist but tends to treat Christ's presence as a mystery rather than explain it using the full Catholic teaching of transubstantiation. Anglicans (see Chapter 11) similarly believe that Christ is spiritually present in the Eucharist, but his presence is dependent on the faith of the person receiving the Communion. Therefore, from an Anglican perspective, Christ is in the elements if the receiver believes he is.

- ✔ **Elements take on Christ's nature.** Lutherans believe in *consubstantiation,* which means that Christ's body and blood are spiritually present in the Eucharist, but so too is the original nature of the bread and wine. In other words, the elements take on an additional nature, enabling Christ to be present in the elements.

- ✔ **Elements are purely symbols of Christ's body and blood.** The Baptist denomination, along with many other Protestant churches, believes that you shouldn't take Luke 22:19–20 literally because Jesus often used figurative language throughout his ministry to illustrate concepts. Instead, they believe that the elements are symbolic of Christ's body and blood and serve as reminders of Christ's work. This view holds less mystery of God and says that Communion is more of a remembrance than spiritual nourishment.

- ✔ **Elements are symbols of Christ's body and blood, but Christ is present through the Holy Spirit.** Presbyterian, Reformed, and other Protestant Churches also believe that the Lord's Supper is symbolic and that the bread and wine don't change in nature. However, they still account for the belief that the Lord's Supper gives spiritual nourishment to Christians when they receive the elements.

Timing the observance of Communion

As you may expect, Christians have different takes on the frequency of participating in the Lord's Supper.

- ✔ Orthodox Christians have Communion regularly and often make it a central part of their worship services. Although some Orthodox believers have Communion two or three times a year, the Church encourages them to have it more frequently, weekly, if possible.

- ✔ Catholics encourage regular participation in Communion, but only need to partake of it once a year to be considered a "good Catholic" according to the precepts (see Chapter 10).

- ✔ Protestants vary in frequency; most observe the Lord's Supper on a monthly or quarterly basis, although some churches do it more often.

The great Protestant preacher John Wesley, for example, took Communion every four to five days and urged people to do it as often as they could. Wesley believed that the Lord's Supper was an important part of a Christian's spiritual nourishment. He didn't mean that God doesn't empower through means other than the Lord's Supper, but he believed that Christ's presence through the sacrament strengthens Christians.

Being earnest regarding the Eucharist

Paul strongly commands Christians to approach the Lord's Supper seriously and never to take it lightly. Taking it lightly is as much as a slap in the face to Jesus after the work that he did on the cross. Paul writes in 1 Corinthians 11:27–34:

> *Therefore whoever eats this bread or drinks the Lord's cup in a manner unworthy of the Lord will be guilty of the body and the blood of the Lord. But let a man examine himself, and so let him eat of the bread, and drink of the cup. For he who eats and drinks in an unworthy manner eats and drinks judgment to himself, if he doesn't discern the Lord's body. For this cause many among you are weak and sickly, and not a few sleep. For if we discerned ourselves, we wouldn't be judged.*

Paul indicates that some people in the Corinthian church feel sick and some even died as a result of their disrespect for the Eucharist. Therefore, one must take the Lord's Supper in a repentant, earnest, and focused manner.

Maintaining a Christlike Balance

Most Christians believe that ordinances should be a focus in a believer's spiritual life. But after you begin to get more specific on their roles or meanings, you soon discover what the expression "all over the map" means. The differences in belief that exist across the Body of Christ are very real, have been around for centuries, and can't be simply swept under the rug. At the same time, no matter which perspective a Christian holds on the sacraments, it's essential that Protestant, Catholic, and Orthodox Christians seek a Christlike balance in their views.

When you look at the life and ministry of Jesus Christ, you see that he valued rites and ceremonies (see the "Jesus had the rite stuff" sidebar). Not only did he revere and practice the Hebrew observances of his day, but he also authorized baptism and the Lord's Supper for his followers. What's more, Jesus didn't downplay these rites to be side activities but considered them acts that go to the very heart of one's faith.

But Jesus wasn't a man preoccupied with rituals, either. Within a religious culture that was used to observing countless rites, Jesus trimmed the numbers and gave his followers just a couple to observe. Also, Jesus spoke often of the dangers and pitfalls of rituals because they can so easily tempt people to become focused on outer acts and appearances rather than on the heart. Further, when Jesus had a face-to-face encounter with a person — whether a prostitute, a Pharisee, a Roman soldier, or a leper — he was invariably preoccupied with the person's inner spiritual condition, not his or her ritual participation.

This pattern of balance is consistent with the teaching of the apostles in the New Testament. Ceremonies — baptism and the Lord's Supper — are firmly embedded in the life and teaching of the first-century Church. However, the apostles talk much about how grace justifies through faith.

Frankly, I suggest that both Protestants and Catholics have something to learn from Jesus and the apostles. Protestants would do well to remember that when you downplay the ordinances to be purely symbolic acts, you run the risk of treating them casually, dumbing them down, and filtering out any mystery that God may use within them. On the other hand, Catholics would do well to ensure that sacraments don't become more important than a person's faith. For if my eternity is dependent on something I do rather than on my faith, I begin to stray from the most basic teaching of Christianity, found in John 3:16: "For God so loved the world that he gave his one and only Son, that whoever *believes* in him will not perish but have eternal life" (italics mine).

Jesus had the rite stuff

Rites played an ever-present role in the life of Jesus, including the following examples:

✔ His baptism by John the Baptist launched Jesus' ministry.

✔ At the end of his earthly ministry, Jesus commanded his disciples to "Go, and make disciples of all nations, baptizing them in the name of the Father and of the Son and of the Holy Spirit" (Matthew 28:19).

✔ He observed the traditional Hebrew rites and ceremonies of his day, including baptismal purifications, Passover, and the other Jewish holy days.

✔ He instituted the Last Supper and charged his disciples to partake of it until he returns again.

Chapter 9

Heading for Home: The End Game

In This Chapter

▶ Discovering the secrets of heaven

▶ Confronting hell

▶ Debating the idea of purgatory

▶ Predicting the End Times events

*W*hen I co-founded a company several years ago, the legal and marketing experts whom my partner and I talked to asked us, "What's your end game?" Being the savvy entrepreneur that I am, I supposed they were chit-chatting about board games, so I quickly chimed in that I loved Yahtzee, though Parcheesi and Trivial Pursuit were good choices, too. After getting some strange looks, I figured out that the end game they were referring to was the long-term objective for the company. A bop in the head from my partner helped me determine that, in the business world, you have three possible outcomes for your company: Grow your business, sell your business, or go out of business. Given my renowned business expertise, let me help you with these options in case you're uninitiated — the first two scenarios are good; the last one is bad.

Biblical Christianity also has multiple end game scenarios — two desirable (die and go to heaven, or go straight there when Jesus returns to earth) and one quite undesirable (go to hell). Catholics complicate my nice little metaphor by adding purgatory as a fourth and final option.

In this chapter, you explore the Christian teachings of heaven, hell, purgatory, and the whole business of the Second Coming of Jesus. You also find out why Christians believe that the "exit strategy" that each human being makes is the most important decision he or she will ever make in life.

Enjoying Heaven for Eternity

Christians believe that people are designed by God, not just for seventy or so years on planet earth, but for eternity. The Bible calls the future home of all Christians *heaven*.

If one heaven's not enough . . .

Paul speaks of the "third heaven" in 2 Corinthians 12:2. The Bible refers to heaven in different ways. The first heaven is the earth's atmosphere (Acts 1:9–10, Genesis 7:11–12), the second heaven is the entire universe (Genesis 1:14–17), and the third heaven — sometimes called the *heaven of heavens* — is where God lives (1 Peter 3:22). Generally, when people speak of heaven today, they're talking about that "third heaven" that Paul mentions, God's dwelling place (Genesis 28:17, Revelation 12:7–8).

Field of Dreams is among my all-time favorite movies, but I blame it for the bad rap that heaven gets these days about being a boring place to live. You see, in the film, the word "heaven" is often used interchangeably with Iowa. Now, don't get me wrong; I've visited Iowa and think it's pretty good, as far as states go. What's more, all my wife's relatives come from Iowa, so you could practically call me a Hawkeye. Still, I've been to Iowa during the summer when the humidity is thicker than syrup, and it sure did feel far more like another place that's located due south of heaven.

Heaven may not be altogether like Iowa, but exactly what it's like is largely shrouded in mystery. Great Christian thinkers through the ages have long speculated on heaven and have provided some vivid and imaginative perspectives. Yet, in the end, most of these ideas are simply educated guesses. The Bible fills in some details, but not nearly enough to satisfy curious minds who want to know more.

At the same time, as the next section describes, consider what you can glean from the pages of the Bible about what this incredible place called heaven is really like.

Exploring seven ideas about a place called heaven

As I consider what heaven is like, I find myself wishing that God would've simply provided humans with a Picture Bible filled with photos of heaven. It could even be something like those annoying timeshare vacation resort brochures that come in the mail; I wouldn't care. I'd just like to know what it's going to look like! However, when you open the Bible and start to read about heaven, you see that the Bible tends to say much more about the spiritual conditions of heaven than concrete details of its physical qualities. All in all, seven ideas of heaven that you can find in the scriptures are

✔ **Heaven is a real place.** The Christian view of heaven isn't some cosmic ethereal state of bliss, but a real, tangible place that's the dwelling place

of God, angels, and his followers (see John 14:1–4 and Hebrews 11:16). However, it's not likely a part of this universe or a place you could simply fire up the space shuttle or the Millennium Falcon and navigate to in the sky.

✔ **Heaven is anything *but* boring.** With an opinion that must strike God as simply clueless, some non-believers say they don't want to go to heaven because it sounds all so boring: playing harps on clouds, sitting through endless church services, and being goody-two-shoes for all time. In the grandest of ironies, hell is often seen as being the interesting place, where interesting people will go and have a good time.

Yet, Christians believe that the idea that God's plans for his faithful are going to be dull simply shows a misguided outlook compared to the picture that the Bible paints. For example, the fantastic language that John uses in the Book of Revelation expresses, in an allegorical fashion, awesome realities that humans can't fully comprehend. C.S. Lewis, a renowned Christian author, sees this perspective as that of "an ignorant child who wants to go on making mud pies in a slum because he cannot imagine what is meant by the offer of a holiday at the sea" (*Mere Christianity,* Harper San Francisco, 2001).

✔ **Heaven is a social city, but it doesn't have slums or city limits.** The Bible often describes heaven metaphorically as a walled city (see Revelation 21, Hebrews 11:16, and Hebrews 13:14). I'm a country guy at heart, so I've never been all that thrilled about the image of heaven as a vast metropolis in the sky. Yet, the allusions to a city are meant to symbolize *community* rather than some prophetic reference to an angelic city with urban sprawl, congestion, and skyscrapers. In reality, heaven isn't limited to a big city in the sky. In fact, as the "Frolicking around the new heaven and new earth" section describes later in the chapter, the future home of Christians will be a vast new world.

✔ **Life in heaven is a continuation of a person's earthly life.** Christians believe that a person's life on earth is directly connected with his or her life in heaven. They aren't two distinct, separate existences. Instead, Christians believe that the heavenly life is like a graduated or transformed version of each person's life on earth.

People will certainly retain their memory, as the Bible shows many examples of prior knowledge of one's earthly life being dealt with in the next (Luke 16:19–31, Matthew 25:40, Matthew 7:21–23). People will also be able to recognize loved ones (2 Samuel 12:23, 1 Corinthians 13:12, Luke 16:28) and probably even recognize other Christians that they've never met in person (as a parallel, see Matthew 17:1–8).

After all, this is exactly why Christians believe that making the most of this earthly life is so important. The Bible verses you memorize, the music you play, and the books you read — these aren't just knowledge that passes away when you die. Instead, these resources will be wisdom and knowledge you'll find useful and applicable in heaven.

Also, I speculate that it's the Church's collective knowledge of experiences on earth — the terrible reality of sin and disobedience — that will enable believers to successfully live in heaven in a way that Adam and Eve failed to do in the Garden of Eden.

✔ **Heaven will meet people's deepest longings.** Christians believe that heaven is a place that fills the holes and heals the scars that people carry through life on earth. The joy of heaven will wipe out the dream-killers of this life — death, sorrow, and pain (Revelation 21:4) — and will meet humans' need for love, happiness, peace, and security. But that doesn't mean that heaven is a touchy-feely place where all people do is sit around playing harps and giving group hugs all day long. God also created people with an instinctive desire for adventure, discovery, challenge, and risk. In a way that's impossible to grasp, Christians believe that God will meet humans' need for adventure in a way that isn't life-threatening (because they'll be invincible!).

✔ **Heaven is a place where dreams come true.** One of the lines in the film *Field of Dreams* that always makes me want to puke when I hear it is the statement that heaven is the place where dreams come true. But after thinking about it, I realize it's got a good point. On the one hand, that statement sounds like popular culture mumbo-jumbo — a place where you have a round-the-clock genie at your service. However, when you think of heaven from a Christian standpoint, this phrase actually makes sense, though perhaps not in the way you may think. Because Christians will no longer have a selfish perspective in heaven, their dreams will be completely in line with the perfect will of God (see Chapter 16 for more on God's will). Therefore, in this respect, one's dreams *will* come true.

✔ **People won't sin in heaven, but they're not robots, either.** The Bible is clear that sin doesn't exist in heaven. It's an impossibility. However, that fact doesn't mean that people are somehow turned into robots who *can't* sin. In fact, people simply *don't* sin because they see sin's potential for what it is. For example, imagine you're used to eating a five-course meal at a five-star restaurant every day. Suppose you're walking down the street to dinner and happen to step on doggie doo-doo. Even if you're hungry, you're not about to lie down and start licking the sidewalk. The truth is that you would be repelled by the very thought and wouldn't even be tempted to eat it. Instead, you'd simply wipe your feet and continue on toward your dinner. In the same way, people will see sin like the vomitous mess that it really is, not as something that looks and sounds good.

Speculating on heavenly bods

Some people's concept of heaven is something like a giant vacuum in the sky that sucks up people's souls after they die, keeping them forever trapped in limbo in a giant spiritual vacuum bag. A bodiless existence is definitely not Christianity's idea of heaven (check out 1 Corinthians 15:42–49, 1 John 3:2).

After all, the God of heaven also created the universe, so I presume that he happens to think atoms, cells, and physical bodies are all good, not things that people grow out of.

Scripture tells us that, in the long run, Christians will sport new and improved physical bodies (1 Corinthians 15), just like Jesus Christ did after he was resurrected (Philippians 3:21). Similar to life here on earth, Christians will be able to communicate with each other (Luke 24:13–18), touch and be touched (Luke 24:39), and eat and drink food (Luke 24:42–43). Yet, the new resurrected body is something far more special and powerful than the current physical bodies that you and I know so well. The new body won't be bound to the same space and time limitations that humans are defined by today (John 20:19, Luke 24:36), nor will it be susceptible to any disease or sickness. Paralyzed people will be able to walk again, and the blind will be able to see with 20/20 vision. (Think about it — no more HMOs, laser surgery, or even band-aids!)

Do angels have wings?

"Every time a bell rings, an angel gets its wings" — so goes the classic line from the film *It's a Wonderful Life*. Angels are one of the most talked-about but least understood of all God's creatures. According to the Bible, they're real creatures that actually exist. But, unlike the Hollywood variety, real angels aren't those cute human-like figures sporting white robes and wings, although at times they take on a human form.

When God's angels appear to humans in the Bible, they only appear to believers of God, not to unbelievers. They come looking like humans (see Genesis 18:2, Daniel 10:18, and Zechariah 2:1). However, on occasion, they must've looked like something far more spectacular, because their appearances caused people to be awestruck (see Matthew 28:3–4, Luke 24:4, and Judges 13:6), although the Bible talks about them not always appearing like humans.

An angel is a heavenly being who's smarter and more powerful than humans (2 Peter 2:11, Hebrews 2:7) and who God created at the start of the world, even before he created humans (Psalm 148:5, Job 38:7). Angels are with God in heaven, ready to do his work (Revelation 4:6, 1 Kings 22:19, and Psalm 103:21).

Angels appear throughout the Bible, though it mentions only two of them by name. *Gabriel* (Luke 1:19, 26; Daniel 8:16, 9:21) serves as a special messenger to people, and *Michael* (Daniel 12:1, Jude 9, Revelation 12:9) cared for and protected the ancient nation of Israel. In general, angels are meant to serve (Hebrews 1:14), guide (Genesis 24:7), protect (Matthew 26:53), provide (Mark 1:13), and rescue (Acts 12:6–11) humans. Most Christian teachers suggest that angels probably aren't as active in the world today because Christians have the Holy Spirit to guide them (see Chapter 7) whereas the Holy Spirit only came to believers on special occasions during the Old Testament period. However, as Hebrews 13:2 indicates, even today, people may "entertain angels" without even realizing it when they're entertaining strangers.

Sorry, you won't get angel wings

One vintage Hollywood idea is that people who die become angels (complete with a white robe and wings). Although this notion works well for a Frank Capra movie, the Bible has absolutely no evidence for this belief. So, if you were looking forward to getting equipped with angel's wings, I recommend you settle for watching Clarence Oddbody, the angel wannabe in *It's a Wonderful Life,* instead.

The Bible makes it clear that Christians will have their emotional needs fully met in heaven, as well as their physical desires. All the inner longings (see the "Experiencing security and adventure in heaven" sidebar in this chapter) or the emotional baggage that preoccupy people today will be history. Revelation 21:4 tells that Jesus will wipe away all the tears of sorrow from believers' eyes and will eliminate death, mourning, pain, and heartache.

Also, people often wonder about the age that people will be when they're in heaven. Because heavenly bodies will be perfect, it seems certain that people won't show the effects of aging that they struggle with on earth. The logical assumption that Christians usually believe is that, using Christ's resurrected body as the prototype, people will have a fully mature adult body (around the age of 30 or so).

However, Christians disagree over whether believers will receive this resurrected body immediately when they die or whether they have to wait until the Second Coming of Jesus. In 1 Corinthians 15:51–54, Paul seems to indicate that the resurrected body is given to people after the resurrection of the dead (as I discuss in the section, "Awaiting the Second Coming of Jesus Christ," later in this chapter). If this is the case, one must face the open-ended question of what state the believer is in between his or her death and the final Resurrection. Because the Bible is not completely clear on this point, four viewpoints have developed in the Church:

✔ **Being with the Lord while waiting for a new body:** Perhaps the predominant view in the Protestant and Orthodox Churches is that believers will be fully conscious and with the Lord, yet not in the final resurrected body that Christians will be equipped with at the time of the final Resurrection. Catholics believe that though most Christians go to purgatory, martyrs and people who've been perfected on earth immediately go to heaven and are with God in this manner. (See the "Being Purged of Sin in Purgatory" section that follows for a discussion on this topic.)

Proponents of this view add that any references to the dead as "sleeping" are not meant to be taken literally, pointing to 2 Corinthians 5:8, in which Paul says, "Away from the body and at home with the Lord," indicating being immediately with the Lord after death, not in the ground waiting for the big dance.

They also point out that if the dead are in a veggie state, then all of the great pillars of the faith have been in the ground waiting for thousands of years. Yet, they question why God — who created the world for relationships — would want to delay an ongoing relationship with the most faithful of all peoples. And given that two Old Testament greats — Elijah and Moses — visibly appeared and interacted with Jesus during his ministry (called the *Transfiguration* in Matthew 17), one can assume that at least two people aren't turning over in their graves, so to speak.

Christians who hold this view have differences of opinion on the specifics. Some believe that God supplies some sort of temporary body that, although it's not as good as the resurrected body that believers will eventually have, it's still better than your earthly digs. Others believe that this intermediate state is a conscious existence that's apart from any body at all.

✔ **Sleeping until the Second Coming, while the earthly body fades away:** Because the Bible sometimes refers to death as "sleep" (Acts 7:6, John 11:11), Seventh Day Adventists and some other Protestants believe in *soul sleep,* the idea that all who've died are in a kind of deep freeze and are waiting for the Resurrection to occur before springing back to life. Therefore, God lets their earthly bodies fade away, while their souls remain sleeping until the big day when they receive new, resurrected bodies.

✔ **Enjoying a new body immediately, while waiting for the Second Coming:** Other Protestant Christians believe that a Christian's soul immediately receives a resurrected body when he or she dies, which resides with God in heaven. Then, the Christian joins Jesus and is *revealed* to the earth at the time of the Second Coming of Jesus in the final Resurrection (Colossians 3:4).

✔ **Doin' time in purgatory while waiting for the new body:** The final view, held by Catholics, is that after death, most Christian souls go to purgatory. See the "Being Purged of Sin in Purgatory" section that follows for a discussion on this topic.

Experiencing security and adventure in heaven

Different people seem to be naturally wired differently, having deep, God-given longings that they strive to fulfill in this world — but they're never truly satisfied. Some people long for security, while others' deepest desire is for adventure. In fact, many people's lives often revolve around a quest to meet either of those needs. On this earth, Christians believe that none of these searches will ever end up in satisfaction, but heaven will be a place that meets such longings for security and adventure.

Being Purged of Sin in Purgatory

One of the key belief differences between Catholics, Protestants, and Orthodox Christians is the issue of purgatory — Catholics believe it exists, but Protestants and Orthodox believers don't.

The belief in a place called purgatory evolved over many centuries. Although it's not the Christian Church's official teaching, some early Church fathers and writers, including Augustine, believed in an intermediate state that exists after death but before heaven. The Catholic Church made this part of their official doctrine in the 16th century.

In general, *purgatory* serves as an interim place for people who will eventually go to heaven but who aren't yet purified enough to do so. In Catholic teaching, purgatory isn't a place where unsaved people get a second chance to avoid going to hell. Instead, it's a place for eventual heaven-to-be's to wait expectantly for the joys to come.

Catholics: Purgatory is part of God's plan

Catholics believe that a person must be purified before entering heaven. *Martyrs* (Christians who've been killed for their faith) and a few rare Christians who've lived exceptionally holy and pure lives — have already accomplished that purification. So, upon death, they immediately go to heaven. However, most other folks need some more time before they're able to be cleansed of their sin enough to be considered holy for heaven. Catholics believe that purgatory isn't a place where you go to receive forgiveness (because only Christians, who asked for forgiveness during their earthly life, and those who aren't capable of making decisions for Christ go to purgatory), but instead to get rid of the baggage that accompanies sin. Therefore, the grace and love of God scrub away these nasty effects of sin in a person's life.

The exact time that Catholics believe a person stays in purgatory varies. If you were a pretty decent sort of person — didn't rob any banks, helped out your neighbor, and flossed regularly — your time is pretty short. But, if you were a really bad boy or girl, watch out, because you'll have a lot of time to kill before seeing those pearly gates of heaven.

That's why Catholics believe in praying for people who've died. The belief is that the more people who are living on earth pray for you, the quicker the purification process becomes, which in turn shortens your time in purgatory.

Neither the Old Testament nor the New Testament mentions purgatory. However, as Chapter 6 details, Catholic Bibles include an additional set of books called the *Apocrypha*. The ancient Jews didn't accept these books as part of the Old Testament; as such, Jesus and the early Church wouldn't have

recognized them as scripture. It's at one point in one of these disputed writings that we read about praying for people in purgatory: "It was a holy and pious thought to pray for the dead so that they may be freed from sins" (2 Maccabees 12:46).

Catholics believe that all souls in purgatory will be released at the time of Christ's Second Coming, will join Jesus immediately, and will go to heaven.

Protestants and Orthodox Christians: Purgatory is a Colorado destination

The Protestant and Orthodox Churches, on the other hand, say that the only place you're going to find purgatory is with a pair of skis, a lift ticket, and a map to Durango, Colorado. They believe that purgatory is a non-biblical invention, using the following ideas as their reasoning:

- **Jesus Christ already paid for sins in full.** According to 1 Peter 3:18, Jesus Christ paid the price for sins once and for all time on the cross. Protestants believe that if Christ paid for people's sin already, then Christians don't need to go through a cleansing process a second time. What's more, they say that the idea of purgatory cheapens the work that Jesus Christ did on the cross by putting the burden back onto Christians to persevere through a purification process.

- **Purgatory is missing from the teachings of Jesus and the apostles.** Although Jesus talks much about heaven and hell, he never specifically mentions or alludes to a place called purgatory, nor do the apostles or anyone else in the New Testament. Protestants and Orthodox Christians claim as support the idea that any New Testament scriptures that Catholics use for support are speculative and don't provide clear evidence of purgatory's existence.

- **Purgatory isn't mentioned in the Old Testament, either.** The one statement in the Catholic Bible that Catholics bring up as supporting prayer for the dead wasn't a part of the ancient Hebrew Bible or the scriptures of the early Church. (See Chapter 6 for more on the Bible.)

- **Jesus' encounter with the thief on the cross implies immediate entry into heaven.** Protestants look at the words that Jesus said to the thief on the cross (see Chapter 3) at face value and believe they teach against any sort of limbo in between earth and heaven. In Luke 23:43, Jesus tells the thief who had an on-the-cross conversion, "Assuredly I tell you, *today* you will be with me in paradise" (italics mine).

- **The concept of purgatory evolved over time.** The idea of purgatory expanded over time — it's not an idea that has consistently been part of Church doctrine since the beginning. Purgatory didn't get much attention in the Church until the fifth century; the idea of a division between

martyrs and average Christians came first, followed by praying for the dead, and then the idea of purification before entering heaven followed much later.

✔ **When you're forgiven, your sins are forgotten.** Although Catholics distinguish between one's forgiveness and purification, Protestants believe the Bible doesn't make a distinction. They point to Hebrews 10:17–18, which says, "I will remember their sins and their iniquities no more. Now where these sins have been forgiven, there is no longer any sacrifice or offering for sin." They also point to Romans 8:1 where Paul says, "There is therefore now no condemnation for those who are in Christ Jesus." Finally, the Apostle John writes in 1 John 3:3, "Everyone who has this hope set on him purifies himself, even as he is pure."

Going to Hell: Considering the Underworld

"You can just go to hell." "To hell in a handbasket." "Hell, no." People casually say the word "hell" all the time in expressions like these, but the Christian concept of hell is anything but casual. Frankly, it's scary business, though one that people outside of the Church find silly, unfair, or politically incorrect. Hell isn't a very popular topic inside church walls, either. People much prefer more positive messages. Go to a thousand churches on a Sunday morning, and for each of the ministers you hear preach on hell, I'll give you a nickel. I suspect that I won't need much spare change to pay you.

Yet, the belief in hell is closely tied to the Christian faith. After all, if Christ died to save people, it follows logically that he had to save humans *from* something. Without hell, the whole notion of Jesus suffering on the cross for humanity doesn't make sense.

All Christians agree on the broad definition of *hell* as being the state of complete separation from God. And yet the specifics of what that separation means have always been the subject of debate. Ever since the first century, three distinct viewpoints on hell have permeated the Christian Church:

✔ Eternal punishment of the *unsaved* (people who aren't Christians)

✔ Annihilation of the unsaved

✔ No punishment, because all will receive salvation from God

The last perspective — commonly known as *universalism* — may be much more palatable and politically correct than the others, but this view has no biblical legs to stand on and has never been considered a position that's in synch with biblical Christianity. Universalism can't be proven by the Bible, but proponents of the other two perspectives both argue that the Bible supports their hellish claims.

Eternal suffering

The traditional understanding of hell is as a place of never-ending conscious suffering. The Bible seems to support this belief strongly, referring to hell in quite sobering terms:

- ✔ "The unquenchable fire of hell" (Mark 9:43)

- ✔ "The everlasting fire" (Matthew 25:41 and Jude 7)

- ✔ "The smoke of torment rises for ever and ever, and they have no rest day or night" (Revelation 14:11)

- ✔ "The blackness of darkness" (Jude 13)

- ✔ "The lake of fire" (Revelation 20:15)

In addition, one of the parables that Jesus teaches also describes the conditions of hell in terms that fit this same description. In Luke 16:19–31, Jesus tells the story about a rich man and a beggar:

> Now there was a certain rich man, and he was clothed in purple and fine linen, living in luxury every day. A certain beggar, named Lazarus, was laid at his gate, full of sores, and desiring to be fed with the crumbs that fell from the rich man's table. Yes, even the dogs came and licked his sores. It happened that the beggar died, and that he was carried away by the angels to Abraham's bosom. The rich man also died, and was buried. In hell, he lifted up his eyes, being in torment, and saw Abraham far off, and Lazarus at his bosom. He cried and said, "Father Abraham, have mercy on me, and send Lazarus, that he may dip the tip of his finger in water, and cool my tongue! For I am in anguish in this flame."

> But Abraham said, "Son, remember that you, in your lifetime, received your good things, and Lazarus, in like manner, bad things. But now here he is comforted and you are in anguish. Besides all this, between us and you there is a great gulf fixed, that those who want to pass from here to you are not able, and that none may cross over from there to us."

> He said, "I ask you therefore, father, that you would send him to my father's house; for I have five brothers, that he may testify to them, so they won't also come into this place of torment."

> But Abraham said to him, "They have Moses and the prophets. Let them listen to them."

> He said, "No, father Abraham, but if one goes to them from the dead, they will repent."

> He said to him, "If they don't listen to Moses and the prophets, neither will they be persuaded if one rises from the dead."

Based on biblical texts like this one, many Christians believe that hell involves suffering that's both spiritual and physical. Proponents of this idea believe it's hard to read this parable that Jesus told any other way than as a strong warning against a hell that's a scary, uncomfortable place to be.

Other Christians, however, agree with the view that hell involves eternal punishment, but think of the punishment as more spiritual in nature and don't necessarily believe that actual physical torture is involved.

Extinction of the unsaved

The concept of *annihilationism* originated in certain parts of the Protestant Church over the past few centuries. Annihilationists believe that rather than suffer eternal torment, unsaved people simply cease to exist after they die. Supporters often cite four justifications for their belief:

- **God's nature is to be a kind, loving God.** Having nonbelievers suffer endlessly doesn't make sense and just makes God look like a warmonger rather than a God of love. From this standpoint, nonexistence is torture enough. Let justice be served, but swiftly, not strewn out for eternity.

- **Eternal life is itself a gift.** Because eternal life is a gift from God, the idea of an eternally damned life doesn't make sense.

- **Jesus Christ came to conquer and destroy evil.** The Bible speaks of Jesus Christ conquering evil on the cross and eventually destroying evil in the Final Judgment, but if a hell of eternal torment exists, then evil doesn't seem to be totally destroyed, just contained.

- **Hell destroys.** Annihilationists look at the Bible and emphasize that it speaks of hell in terms of "death" and "destruction" — words that don't go with a place that lives on and on and on forever:

  - Jesus speaks of the "soul and body" being destroyed in hell (Matthew 10:28).

  - The Apostle John writes in Revelation 20:14–15 that the unsaved "will be thrown into the lake of fire, which is the second death."

  - The Apostle Paul speaks of hell as "death" in Romans 6:23 and as "destruction" in 1 Corinthians 3:17.

Some Christians put up two strong challenges, however, to annihilationism, based on biblical teaching. First, Jesus Christ spoke quite clearly that people who are confronted more with opportunities to receive grace but refuse it will receive greater punishment. For example, Matthew 11:20–22 says:

> *Then Jesus began to denounce the cities in which most of his mighty works had been done, because they didn't repent. "Woe to you, Chorazin! Woe to you, Bethsaida! For if the mighty works had been done in Tyre and Sidon which were done in you, they would have repented long ago in sackcloth and ashes. But I tell you, it will be more tolerable for Tyre and Sidon on the day of judgment than for you."*

Second, the Bible talks much about hell, using the word "eternal." An annihilationist believes that this speaks of the everlasting consequences of death. Those who disagree point to other Bible verses, including Matthew 25:46: "These will go away into eternal punishment, but the righteous into eternal life." In this context, if "eternal life" is the same as "everlasting life," then it seems to some a stretch to translate "eternal punishment" to mean not "everlasting punishment," but the "everlasting consequences of a one-time punishment."

Awaiting the Second Coming of Jesus Christ

Christians believe that Jesus Christ came to earth some 2,000 years ago and lived as a suffering servant, and, before his ascension (see Chapter 5), he promised to return to earth one final time (John 14:3) — this time as a conquering and triumphant King. Christians believe that only God knows when exactly Jesus will come back to earth, though most every generation since the early Church looks at the events of their day in light of prophecies in scripture and concludes that surely he'll come within their lifetime. (For more, check out the sections "Enduring Tribulation" and "Being taken up in the Rapture" that follow.)

The Bible talks about several events that will take place surrounding the time of Jesus' Second Coming. However, the Christian Church often debates on the exact timeline, sequence, and meaning of these events.

Some Protestants, called *premillennialists,* believe these are literal events that will take place sometime in the future before the Second Coming. Other Protestants, Catholics, and Orthodox Christians hold *amillennialist* or *postmillennialist* positions, saying that the biblical references are metaphoric, and therefore the events actually won't take place prior to Jesus' Second Coming. (I discuss each of the premillennialist, amillennialist, and postmillennialist positions in the section "Enjoying the Millennium: Peace on earth," later in this chapter.)

Enduring Tribulation

The Bible forewarns that before the Second Coming of Jesus, people will endure a time of great trial and suffering, often referred to as the *Great Tribulation* (suffering and pain don't sound so great to me). During this time, Satan's work in the world will become more and more rampant. Matthew 24 speaks of this as a time of great deception, wars, natural disasters, and intense persecution of Christians. On this stage, a person whom the Bible calls the *antichrist* will lead the opposition to God. Christians believe he'll gain power as a leader and even proclaim himself to be God (2 Thessalonians 2:4), demanding power and allegiance (Revelation 13:11–18).

Many Protestants believe that the Tribulation will be a seven-year period, based on the prophecies in Daniel 9:24–27. However, the Book of Revelation, the Bible's fullest account of prophecy relating to Christ's Second Coming, doesn't make any mention of a specific period of time. Instead, it talks about three "woes," or outpourings of wrath from God that will occur in the Tribulation (9:1–12, the first woe; 9:13–21 and 11:1–13, the second woe; and 11:18, the third woe).

Other Protestants, Catholics, and Orthodox Christians believe that the Tribulation has been taking place since the first century and that the Tribulation prophecies spoke of events that have transpired since that time.

Being taken up in the Rapture

The *Rapture* refers to the belief that Christians will be physically removed from the earth at some point during the Second Coming of Jesus. The basic idea is that Christians will be zapped from where they are on earth — something like the effects of those old Star Trek phasers — and will meet Jesus in the sky (1 Thessalonians 4:16–18, 1 Corinthians 15:51–54).

Many Protestants believe in a literal rapture, though other Protestants, Catholics, and Orthodox Christians don't. Instead, they say that Paul is writing symbolically, referring to the unifying of the living and dead believers that will take place at the time of Jesus' Second Coming.

However, the Protestants who agree that the Rapture will occur differ on when this event will happen in relation to the Tribulation. Three main views stand out:

> ✔ **Before the Tribulation:** The *pre-Tribulation* viewpoint says that Christ will return for Christians before a seven-year tribulation. Christians then are spared from going through the ordeal. If you've read or heard of any of the *Left Behind* books by Tim LaHaye and Jerry B. Jenkins (Tyndale House Publishers, 1996) that were all the craze at the turn of the millennium, this is the view presented in that fiction book series.

 ✔ **In the middle of the Tribulation:** Proponents of the *mid-Tribulation* viewpoint believe that the Rapture will occur in the middle of the Tribulation.

 ✔ **At the end of the Tribulation:** The *post-Tribulation* view argues that the Rapture and the Second Coming of Jesus are two parts of a single simultaneous event, occurring after the Tribulation.

From the pre-Tribulation perspective, the Rapture can occur at any time, as no prophecy needs to be fulfilled prior to the event happening. Mid- and post-Tribulation proponents naturally believe that the Tribulation must start first. At the same time, some Christians who hold the post-Tribulation position believe that you can't necessarily pin down the start of the Tribulation, making Christ's Second Coming still unpredictable.

Celebrating Jesus' triumphant return

The Bible says that Jesus came to earth the first time in a most humble manner — as a helpless infant born in a barn. It also says that the second time he comes, he will come down from the sky with visible power and glory (Matthew 24:29, Luke 1:11, 1 Thessalonians 4:16).

When movies are released or new products are announced, marketing folks like to publicize the event to achieve maximum impact. Christians believe that Jesus could care less about publicizing his return. He isn't going to send out an advance team to appear on Larry King Live, put a press release on the wire, or host a sneak preview Web site — he already foretold his return. Instead, the Bible says that he's going to come like a thief in the night (1 Thessalonians 5:2, Matthew 24:42–44), when people least expect it.

Exactly when Christians believe this will occur is anyone's guess. Every year or so, you hear about some so-called expert who looks at current events with an eye on the Bible and predicts the date of Jesus' return. And yet, these dates come and go, leaving the one who predicted the date with nothing more than egg on his or her face. The simple fact is that no Christian knows when Jesus will return, and the Bible says that only the Father does (Matthew 24:36), so guessing is pointless.

Resurrecting the dead

The Resurrection of the dead will also occur at the time of the Second Coming. The Bible says that all Christians who've died before Jesus comes to

earth again will be resurrected first, and then the living Christians will join them (1 Thessalonians 4:14–18). However, the Gospel of John tells that not only will believers be resurrected, but nonbelievers will, as well (John 5:28–29). The believers will rise to go on to eternal life, and the nonbelievers will rise to be condemned (see the section "Going to Hell: Considering the Underworld," earlier in this chapter). Whether the resurrection of believers and nonbelievers will occur at the same time is a subject of debate.

Enjoying the Millennium: Peace on earth

The Apostle John writes in Revelation 20 about a period of 1,000 years during which Jesus Christ will temporarily harness Satan (find out about Satan in Chapter 4), prevent him from tempting people, and rule the earth in peace and justice. Yet, at the end of the period, John says that Satan will be released and evil will finally be disposed of. Christians, however, have different perspectives on what will actually happen during the millennium:

- ✔ Held by many Protestants, the *premillennialist* view is that what is written in Revelation 20 is exactly what is going to happen: Christ will come, martyrs will join him to help rule the earth, and in the end, Satan will be released and tempt the peoples of the world once again, calling them to rise up together against God. But Satan and his forces will be quickly defeated by Jesus Christ and thrown into the lake of fire (often associated with hell).

  Premillennialists see the purpose of the millennium as showing non-Christians what God's rule is like apart from Satan's tempting influence. And, in spite of Satan being removed, they continue to rebel against God due to their sinful nature (see Chapter 4), leaving them without excuse when the final judgment occurs.

- ✔ The *amillennialist* viewpoint, held by Catholics, Orthodox Christians, and many Anglican, Lutheran, and Reformed Protestants, says that John wasn't speaking of a literal millennium in Revelation, but rather of the time period between the first and second coming of Jesus. So, when John speaks of Satan being bound, what he means is that Satan is prevented by God from working in the lives of Christians. Also, amillennialists see the reign of Christ that Paul talks about as a symbol of the work Jesus Christ is presently doing in the lives of Christians living on earth.

- ✔ The *postmillennialist* view, held by a smaller number of Protestants, claims that the situation described by John will be accomplished by a gradual transformation of the world by Christians. Through the process of evangelism, the entire world will eventually turn to Christ.

Facing final judgment

The final event that Christians believe will occur and close out history as this earth knows it is the final judgment. The purpose of the final judgment (also called Judgment Day) will be to reveal an individual's character and hand out his fate: heaven or hell (Matthew 25:31–46, Revelation 20:11–15). God will judge each nonbeliever according to what he or she knew about right and wrong (Romans 2:15). The Lord will reveal nonbelievers' guilt and will sentence those who didn't accept his grace to condemnation.

The Bible says that Christians are saved from punishment, but they will undergo a separate judgment, as well. Eternal life isn't at stake in their judgment, but rather Christians will give individual accounts of what they did with the time that God gave them on earth (Matthew 6:20, 2 Corinthians 5:9–10). Did they use it by serving others, bringing glory to God, and living lives of eternal significance? Or did they live self-serving lives that had no impact whatsoever on eternity? God will use the accounts to determine the extent of the reward he'll grant each person in heaven (Ephesians 6:8).

Frolicking around the new heaven and new earth

Christians believe their ultimate habitat will be a new heaven and new earth that will be created by God, replacing the old, sin-laced world that God originally created. Revelation 21:1–3 describes it:

> *I saw a new heaven and a new earth: for the first heaven and the first earth have passed away, and the sea is no more. I saw the holy city, New Jerusalem, coming down out of heaven from God, made ready like a bride adorned for her husband. I heard a loud voice out of heaven saying, "Behold, God's dwelling is with people, and he will dwell with them, and they will be his people, and God himself will be with them as their God. He will wipe away from them every tear from their eyes. Death will be no more; neither will there be mourning, nor crying, nor pain, any more. The first things have passed away."*

Isaiah 65:17–19 adds to the picture:

> *For, behold, I create new heavens and a new earth; and the former things shall not be remembered, nor come into mind. But be you glad and rejoice forever in that which I create; for, behold, I create Jerusalem a rejoicing, and her people a joy. I will rejoice in Jerusalem, and joy in my people; and there shall be heard in her no more the voice of weeping and the voice of crying.*

Both passages describe this new creation as a place that's completely new and wonderful and that will have a never-ending balance of love, peace, security, and adventure. See the section "Enjoying Heaven for Eternity," earlier in this chapter, for more.

Many Christians believe that a literal new heaven and earth will be created at that time. (*Heaven,* in this case, refers to the earth's atmosphere.) In other words, God is going to destroy the old earth and create a new one that may be similar to the existing earth that we inhabit today, but with a huge difference — it will be without sin and its harmful effects. This new earth might be very much like what it was before Adam and Eve sinned in the Garden of Eden (see Chapter 4).

Other Christians say that the concept of a new heaven and earth is figurative and refers to a new order of things to come. This new order refers to the righteous being in a literal heaven with God and the unrighteous being condemned in hell. They point to the fact that Christians are supposed to be strangers to the earth (1 Peter 2:11) and citizens of heaven (Philippians 3:20).

Part III

Here's the Church, Here's the Steeple: Peeking into the Christian Church

The 5th Wave   By Rich Tennant

"When did we stop giving an 'amen' and start giving the 'wave'?"

In this part . . .

Although the Church is nicknamed the "Body of Christ," it's made up of a bunch of imperfect people. Given the wide spectrum of tradition and doctrine across the Christian Church, many big differences — and occasional loud arguments — have surfaced since the very beginning of Christianity.

In the chapters that follow, I show you key highlights of Church history from its humble origins in a stable to 21st-century megachurches. You then go on a whirlwind tour through the major branches of the Church today, including Catholic, Orthodox, and Protestant Churches, exploring their beliefs and worship traditions. You also consider how modern society has impacted the Church and look at changes that have developed over the past century.

Chapter 10

Tradition, Tradition: The Catholic and Orthodox Churches

*I*n the well-known musical *Fiddler on the Roof,* Tevye is a Russian peasant in pre-revolutionary Russia who belts out the memorable song "Tradition," emphasizing the importance of tradition as a guide for his family's life. Although tradition means something far different for them, Catholic and Orthodox Christians may as easily join alongside Tevye and sing the same tune. That's because tradition is all-important to Catholicism and Orthodoxy; it's a defining characteristic of these two parts of the Christian Church. In fact, they hold tradition so dearly that they place it on the same lofty plane as the Bible in terms of divine authority.

In this chapter, you explore the Catholic and Orthodox Churches and discover how tradition plays out in their beliefs. You also find out what's unique about Catholics and unique about Orthodox Christians and how they distinguish themselves from each other and others within the Christian faith.

Transferring from a Nation to a Church

During Old Testament times, Judaism was something like a state religion — it was a religion of the Jews, by the Jews, and for the Jews. Occasionally, non-Jewish people converted to the faith, but the vast majority of worshipers of the One True God, whom they called "Yahweh," were born and bred Hebrews. The Old Testament itself backs up this Jewish orientation with its emphasis

on Israel's history, on prophecy directly related to the nation of Israel, and on talk of a coming Jewish messiah to save the nation. Yet, in spite of the priority it places on "God's chosen people," the Old Testament provides hints that God's future plans involved reaching out to the *Gentiles* (non-Jews), as well.

Although Jesus died for the sins of both Jews and Gentiles, his ministry focused primarily on the Jews. Jesus made it clear that he came first for the Jews, then for the Gentiles. He wasn't saying that the Jews deserved salvation more than the Gentiles. Instead, God, in his mercy, gave his chosen people the first focus, so that they could branch and share the news of the coming Messiah. Quite naturally, then, all the twelve disciples that he selected were Jewish, and their early activities concentrated on getting Jews to believe in Jesus as the fulfillment of Jewish prophecy. During these early years, the Christian Church was still centered geographically in Jerusalem and had almost exclusively Jewish leadership. So it probably doesn't surprise you to hear that Romans saw the Christian faith as an offshoot version of Judaism. And, in reality, that's exactly what Christianity was — a branching of Judaism; the first Christians were Jews who saw Jesus as the fulfillment of their faith, while the rest of the Jews rejected Jesus as Messiah and maintained their Jewish faith.

The close connection between the two faiths began to change, however, around A.D. 70. In what's known as the Fall of Jerusalem, Rome cracked down on Jewish rebels who were trying to throw the Romans out of the Holy Land and, in the process, burnt the entire city of Jerusalem to the ground. Not only did this event cause major changes in Jewish religious life, but it also impacted the Christian Church. Because Jerusalem could no longer be the Church's home base, the Body of Christ began spreading throughout the Mediterranean region in Italy and parts of Asia Minor. Gentile leadership became increasingly important as Christianity stretched out geographically and increased in size during this time. As a result, even by the early second century, Christianity took on its own distinct identity apart from Judaism.

Following the deaths of the apostles: The apostolic Church

In this day and age, start-up companies follow a common pattern as they move from small enterprises in back lots to major corporations on Wall Street. A common scenario goes something like this: A start-up begins humbly with a small team of workers working around the clock in an old factory building. The founders, besides running the company, get their hands dirty and contribute like everyone else. The company is small enough that it has little organizational structure. The sole objective of everyone in the company is identical — get the product to market and start getting customers. Yet, after the start-up company has success and begins to grow, change is inevitable. The founders begin to play a less hands-on role, and they form an organizational chart.

In many ways, the Christian Church experienced a similar phenomenon during its early years. People usually call the first sixty years of the Church's life the *apostolic Church,* indicating the key leadership that the apostles held during their lifetimes. The apostles headed up the teaching and missionary activities of the Church and were the ultimate authority in Church matters, given their direct relationship with Jesus Christ. However, as the original apostles passed away one by one, Church leaders knew that in order to keep growing and remain viable, they needed to put certain building blocks in place to ensure consistency and stability going forward. These included

- ✔ **Bishop leadership:** The Church's organizational structure during the first century was dynamic and practical. Apostles led the Church as a whole, while leaders in the local churches were known as *bishops* (overseers or shepherds of the Church), *elders* (spiritual leaders, particularly strong in teaching the Word of God), or *deacons* (responsible for supporting the ministry of elders and other spiritual leaders). However, over the years, a more formal bishop-led structure of the Church as a whole started to develop that was quite different from the way the early Church and Jewish synagogues were organized. A handful of bishops provided leadership as the Church grew throughout the Mediterranean region, each one providing overall leadership for a given geographical area.

- ✔ **Creeds:** In order to emphasize correct and unified teaching for all Christians during this era, Church leaders developed *creeds* — simple statements of belief — as important elements of Church worship. Creeds proved to be a stabilizing factor, ensuring the integrity of what the Church and its local congregations believed.

  One of the most popular creeds for Catholics and Protestants is the Apostle's Creed (see the sidebar "The Apostle's Creed" in this chapter), which has its roots in the first-century Church. However, the one universally accepted creed for Catholic, Protestant, and Orthodox Christians is the Nicean Creed (usually referred to by Orthodox believers as the Nicene-Constantinopolitan Creed).

- ✔ **New Testament canon:** The apostolic Church based its teaching and doctrine on the spoken testimony of the apostles themselves. However, as Chapter 6 discusses, it became clear that someone needed to write down this oral doctrine, both to reach other Christians outside of Palestine and to speak to future generations. Therefore, various Christians transferred the apostles' spoken words to a written account that people today call the New Testament. As the written Word of God, the New Testament enabled the Church to have a solid foundation on which to base its principles. Although much of the canon was set as early as the second century, it took until A.D. 397 for a concrete list of New Testament books to be officially approved.

As a result of all these developments throughout the critical early days, the Church was able to keep *heresy* (false teaching that seriously undermines all of Christianity) out of official doctrine and keep congregations spreading throughout the region, united in one faith.

The Apostle's Creed

I believe in God, the Father Almighty, Maker of heaven and earth;

And in Jesus Christ, his only Son, our Lord: who was conceived by the Holy Spirit, born of the Virgin Mary, suffered under Pontius Pilate, was crucified, dead, and buried. He descended into hell; the third day he rose again from the dead.

He ascended into heaven, and sits at the right hand of God the Father Almighty; from there, he will come to judge the living and the dead.

I believe in the Holy Spirit, the holy catholic Church, the communion of saints, the forgiveness of sins, the resurrection of the body, and the life everlasting. Amen.

Expanding and governing as a single Christian Church

The Church grew explosively during the first hundred years after Christ's ascension into heaven. One factor that proved extremely helpful for the budding Christian Church was the political and economic stability of the Roman Empire. Although persecutions were pretty common, this environment nonetheless enabled Christian missionaries, such as the Apostle Paul and his mates, to easily move throughout the region and spread the gospel (except for those inconvenient times when they were in jail). They spoke the Good News of Jesus Christ to a Gentile population that was sick of the dead-end pagan gods of the Roman Empire and was eager to follow a religion of hope, joy, and salvation. The Church's rapid growth was also due in part to the fact that the early Christians practiced what they preached. They didn't wear WWJD bracelets or put *Got Jesus?* bumper stickers on their donkeys, but they lived out their faith by caring for the poor and helpless, sharing material resources with each other, and reaching out to their neighbors. The early second-century Church scholar Tertullian wrote that the pagan neighbors remarked in amazement, "See how they love one another."

However, Christianity's rapid growth proved unsettling to Roman authorities, who saw Christianity as a much different religion compared to Judaism. On one hand, Judaism was a self-contained body of believers. The Jews didn't reach out to others much, so Rome was content to let them be so long as they didn't rebel against Roman authority. Christians, on the other hand, were a bothersome bunch of folks. They were always seeking to evangelize others throughout Rome, refusing to honor Caesar as Lord and to worship the Roman gods. Seen as a thorn in the mighty empire's side, Christians during the first three centuries after Christ's ascension periodically fell under intense persecution by the Roman emperors.

Martyrs: Dying for their faith

Throughout history, Christians have been persecuted, tortured, and executed for their faith. A Christian who goes through this persecution on behalf of Jesus Christ is known as a *martyr* (derived from the Greek word meaning "witness"). The Book of Acts (Chapter 7) records a man named Stephen as the first Christian martyr — he was stoned to death by religious leaders because of his testimony about Jesus as the Messiah. Although most martyrs aren't mentioned in the Bible, Church tradition says that all the original apostles (except John) died martyr's deaths:

✔ Andrew was crucified in Archaia in A.D. 80.

✔ Bartholomew was whipped, crucified, and beheaded in Armenia.

✔ James the Son of Alphaeus was either beaten to death or was crucified.

✔ As recorded in Acts 12:2, James the Son of Zebedee was beheaded by King Herod Agrippa in A.D. 43.

✔ Judas (not Iscariot, who was the one who betrayed Jesus) was either clubbed to death or crucified.

✔ Matthew was speared to death in Nadabah, Ethiopia in A.D. 60.

✔ Philip was stoned and crucified in Phrygia.

✔ According to early Church fathers Tertullian and Origen, Simon Peter was crucified upside down at his request, feeling unworthy of being crucified in the same way as Jesus was.

✔ Simon Zelotes was crucified in Britain in A.D. 74.

✔ Thomas was speared to death in Calamina, India.

✔ Matthias was stoned to death and beheaded by the Jews in Jerusalem.

Martyrdom continued in the early Church during the first three centuries of its existence as Christians were persecuted intensely by the Roman Empire (see the "Expanding and governing as a single Christian Church" section). Christian persecution has occurred off-and-on throughout history and occurs even in this day and age. The best-known book available on Christian martyrs is the classic *Foxe's Christian Martyrs of the World* (Barbour and Company, 1989), written by a 16th-century man named John Foxe. The book is a compilation of the stories of Christian martyrs, from the apostles through Foxe's lifetime.

While Christians in the West enjoy religious liberty, an estimated 200 million Christians living in non-Western countries — such as China, Vietnam, Indonesia, and Iran — face the threat of persecution (prison, torture, or even death) because of their faith. Groups within the Church have set aside a specific day of prayer, called the International Day of Prayer for the Persecuted Church, to pray for persecuted Christians. For more information, check out www.idop.org.

All of this changed in the early fourth century, when the Emperor Constantine came to power. Constantine saw Christianity as a potentially unifying force that could bring together and stabilize his empire, which was rapidly decaying and becoming increasingly fragmented. Because of Constantine, the Christian Church, for better or worse, moved from being persecuted to being prestigious. The Church gradually became more

involved in the state and with politics, an idea that was a fundamental part of the Church for more than a millennium until the idea of the separation of Church and state started taking shape. This dominance of Christianity throughout Europe and the marriage between Church and state is commonly known as *Christendom*.

Throughout the first thousand years of the Christian Church, the Body of Christ was one entity, often referred to as the *catholic* (meaning "universal") Church.

The Great Separation: Western and Eastern Churches go their own ways

Although the Church was united during the first centuries of its existence, geography defined two distinct parts. The Western Church was centered in Rome and in the surrounding Mediterranean region. The Eastern Church gravitated around Greece and Asia Minor. Although they worked under the umbrella of a universal Church, strains between Western and Eastern Christianity came to a boil in the 11th century.

In 1054, a representative of the bishop of Rome traveled to Constantinople to deliver an official document from the leader of the Western Church (Pope Leo IX) to the leadership of the Eastern Church. The message was plain and simple — the Eastern Church was *excommunicated* (excluded from the Church because of conduct judged as offensive to God) from the Western Church. He placed the paper on the altar of the main church in Constantinople and walked out. Seeing what was occurring, a deacon ran out to catch the pope's representative and pleaded for him to take back the document. He refused, the decree dropped, and the document was left as litter in the street. This event was the starting point of what has become known as the *Great Schism of 1054* in which the Western and Eastern parts of the unified Church split up (see Figure 10-1). The Western Church assumed the name "Roman Catholic" (conveying their belief that they were the "universal" Church), while the Eastern Church named themselves the "Orthodox" Church (depicting their belief that they're the Christian Church providing the "right teaching").

The huffy events that took place in 1054 were really only the final straw that broke the camel's back. In fact, the Christian Church throughout the centuries struggled with differences between the Western and Eastern divisions. I explain these differences in this section.

Western Christians are from Mars; Eastern Christians are from Venus

Western Christians (Catholics, Protestants) and Eastern Christians (Orthodox) don't just disagree on certain issues — they have a different way of thinking. For example, Catholics and Protestants may go head-to-head on issues, but the two groups think the same way; they just disagree on the answers. In contrast, Orthodox Christians often sound like they're on a totally different page from Catholics and Protestants.

To illustrate, suppose you have two roommates in college — Pi Guy, a computer science geek, and Aris Totle, a philosophy major. Pi always looks at issues logically, while Aris always takes discussions to an abstract level. So, when you talk about whether or not to order a pizza at 12 a.m., Pi calculates the exact cost and exact minute that the delivery guy will knock on the door. In contrast, Aris speculates on whether the desire for a midnight pizza is really a metaphor for the call for help that the three of you sense in the darkness of the world. Pi and Aris think differently from each other, which can lead to problems unless they're very careful.

As a result, Orthodox believers sometimes look upon Catholicism or Protestantism as being too simplistic, while Catholics and Protestants look at the beliefs of the Orthodox Church with glazed-over eyes.

Cultural and philosophical differences

When North American companies first started going to Japan after World War II to sell their products, they faced many cultural barriers that they hadn't expected. A business practice or custom that was acceptable in America or Europe was simply unheard of in Japan, and vice versa. Businesspeople learned many painful lessons, and companies finally began to experience success when people on both American and Japanese sides understood each other's cultural nuances and worked together in spite of the differences.

A similar culture clash has always existed between the Western and Eastern Churches, from the early centuries of the Church to the present day. (See also the "Western Christians are from Mars; Eastern Christians are from Venus" sidebar, in this chapter.) The Western Church spoke Latin and was greatly influenced by Rome and its Latin culture. The Eastern Church spoke Greek and was largely influenced by Greece and its culture. While the Western Church valued thinking logically and practically, the Eastern Church embraced mystery and the exercise of exploring abstract issues of the faith. For example, the Western Church saw creeds as the way to end arguments and explicitly define the Christian faith. In contrast, the Eastern Church tended to think of creeds as launching points for diving even deeper into these theological areas and starting further discussion.

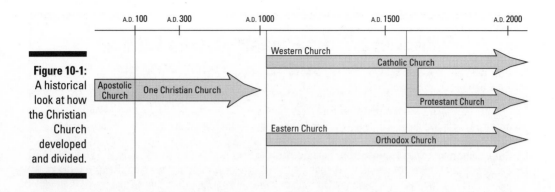

Figure 10-1:
A historical look at how the Christian Church developed and divided.

Theological differences

Subtle theological differences also developed between both parts of the Church, but two issues in particular proved touchy for centuries and were principal factors that led to the Great Schism of 1054:

- **Wording of the Nicean Creed:** In A.D. 589, a Church council added the Latin word *filioque* (meaning "and from the Son") to the Nicean Creed (see Chapter 7 for the full text) so that the creed now said that "the Holy Spirit . . . who proceeds from the Father *and from the Son.* . . ." The Western Church rapidly accepted this change, while the Eastern Church vehemently protested its inclusion, viewing the tweak as invalid and reckless. As you see in the section "Divine Revelation through Tradition," later in this chapter, the Eastern Church considers creeds as much the Word of God as the Bible itself, so any changes they make to the creeds are a huge deal.

- **Authority of the pope:** For centuries, a group of bishops led the Church, heading up geographical areas such as Rome, Antioch, Alexandria, and Constantinople. From the very beginning, Christians displayed a general willingness to give preference to the bishop of Rome (the *pope*) in terms of leadership, calling him *Primus inter Pares,* or "first among equals." Over the years, however, the bishop of Rome assumed stronger leadership as the Western Church paid less attention to the "among equals" part. The East became frustrated when the bishop of Rome began acting as sole authority, making decisions without discussion with the Eastern bishops. Ultimately, the Eastern Church refused to accept the bishop of Rome's claim to be the supreme authority of the Church.

Decision-making differences

Christians in the East and West even differed in how they reached decisions. In the Eastern churches, decision making was a collaborative process, involving participation by the *laity* (the non-clergy congregation). Western churches reached decisions through the *clergy* (ordained ministers) alone and through those in higher positions of the Church hierarchy.

"Yo ho, yo ho, the monastic life's for me"

Both the Catholic and Orthodox Churches have a *monastic* tradition, meaning some of these Christians take a vow to forsake the world and live solely for God. (Monasticism comes from the Greek word *monachos*, meaning "to live alone.") Men who take this vow are *monks,* and women who do so are *nuns*. Catholic monasticism focuses on communal life, in which a group of monks (or nuns) live, pray, and work together. Although Orthodox monks (and nuns) live together in monasteries, Orthodox monasticism embraces the ideal of living alone with God as one's only companion. Both Catholic and Orthodox monks and nuns often return to secular communities for Christian service as a way to demonstrate Christian perfection.

Catholics also have a tradition of *religious brothers* (or *friars*) and *religious sisters*. Religious brothers and sisters are members of one of the *mendicant orders*, which means they live on the voluntary offerings of faithful Catholics. They take vows of poverty, chastity, and obedience within a religious community. Brothers live in friaries and sisters live in convents, and traditionally they work in humility and poverty among poor people in cities. They also have governing rules and guidelines that are quite distinct from those of monks and nuns. Check out *Catholicism For Dummies,* by Rev. John Trigilio, Jr. and Rev. Kenneth Brighenti (Wiley), for more.

Political and geographical differences

Although the West and East were parts of the same Roman Empire during the early centuries, the political environment became more and more splintered as time went on, making geographical differences harder to deal with. What's more, after Islam spread into places geographically in-between where the Eastern and Western Churches dwelled in the seventh and eighth centuries, travel and communication became more challenging due to the hostile Muslim territory. As a result, the Western and Eastern Churches found it harder and harder to resolve theological disputes.

Viewing the split today

After the split in 1054, the Churches made some initial attempts to reunify, but these were always unpopular in the Eastern churches and didn't go anywhere. Then, when the Western-led *Crusades* (medieval military campaigns that the Western Church undertook to reclaim the Holy Land from Muslims) occurred years following the split, these campaigns only served to reinforce the separation, as Eastern churches viewed the Western Crusaders as aggressors.

After a certain point, both sides gave up trying to restore a single unified Church and went their separate ways. The Eastern Church remained largely

isolated from the rest of the Christian Church for nearly a thousand years. While the Eastern Church expanded into Russia and parts of Eastern Europe, Western Christianity, mainly through the work of Catholic and Protestant missionaries, spread throughout all the continents of the world and emerged as mainstream Christianity.

Because of its isolation, the Orthodox Church is the one arm of Christianity that remains most mysterious to many Catholics and Protestants today, particularly Protestants. However, recently, Catholics and Orthodox Christians have made attempts to resolve their historical problems through an ongoing dialogue that started in the 1960s and continued during the period of Pope John Paul II's reign.

The Catholic Church: From Rome to a Parish Near You

The Catholic Church, or Roman Catholic Church, is the single largest branch of the Christian faith in the world, with over one billion members. The Catholic Church has churches spread throughout the continents, all of which fall under the authority of the pope, who resides in the Vatican, in the heart of Rome, Italy.

One of the foundations of the Catholic Church is what it calls the Four Marks of the Church: *unity* within the diversity of its members; *holiness* as the visible Body of Christ; *universality* as a worldwide Church; and *apostolic continuity* to connect today's Church with the original apostles. Together, these principles form the nucleus of the Catholic Church. However, within this broad foundation, there are specific identifiable beliefs that make a Catholic distinct from other Christian believers. I tell you about these in the next section.

Understanding what it means to be Catholic

All Christians believe that the Bible is God's revelation to humans, but, unlike Protestant Christians, Catholic Christians believe that God revealed his ultimate and sovereign Word in *more* ways than just the Bible.

Catholics believe that God reveals his truth through

- The Bible, or the written Word of God
- Sacred Tradition, or the unwritten (or spoken) Word of God

Catholics define *Sacred Tradition* as a set of beliefs that, although the Bible doesn't mention them, Christians have consistently believed for centuries, and Catholics therefore consider them to be authoritative. The Catholic Church says that Sacred Tradition fills the practical purpose of knowing what to believe and how to act in a changing world. Because the Bible doesn't speak to every issue that comes up, Catholics say that Sacred Tradition helps fill in the cracks to clarify God's Word on all matters.

Both Catholics and Orthodox Christians differentiate between Tradition with a capital "T" and tradition with a lowercase "t." Human traditions are customs or practices that aren't directly revealed by God, so they can be changed over time. Examples include the practice of priests not marrying, specific fasting days, or the procedures in electing a pope.

Catholics consider creeds, such as the Apostle's Creed and the Nicean Creed, the most important part of Sacred Tradition. Other parts of Sacred Tradition include

- **Beliefs surrounding the Virgin Mary:** Catholic tradition says that Mary was always a virgin, had no other earthly children, and went directly to heaven when she died. (To find out how Catholics believe her after-death situation differed from most Christians, read about purgatory in Chapter 9.)

- **Role of the sacraments in salvation:** The sacraments are the vehicle that God uses to dispense his saving grace. As a result, sacraments are required in order for a person to receive salvation (though not all seven sacraments, such as marriage, are required). Turn back to Chapter 8 for more on sacraments.

- **Changing nature of the Eucharist:** During the Eucharist, the elements are transformed into the literal body and blood of Christ (known as *transubstantiation*). The bread and wine still appear physically the same, but their nature changes.

These are examples of a type of belief called a *dogma,* a revealed truth that the Catholic Church formally defined either through the *Vincentian canon* (what has always been believed by Christians at all times) or when the pope speaks *ex cathedra* (see the "Revering the pope as supreme leader" section later in this chapter).

Although Catholics hold to the foundational Christian beliefs discussed throughout this book, in this section, I discuss a core set of dogmas that are uniquely Catholic. These include

- Leadership of the pope
- Apostolic succession
- Nature of the sacraments
- Adoration of Mary

- ✔ Praying to Mary and the saints
- ✔ Purgatory
- ✔ Apocrypha as scripture
- ✔ Precepts to live by

For a complete discussion on the beliefs and practices of the Catholic Church, check out *Catholicism For Dummies*, by Rev. John Trigilio, Jr. and Rev. Kenneth Brighenti (Wiley).

Revering the pope as supreme leader

The Orthodox Church has a group of bishops that provide shared leadership, and the Protestant Church has more leaders than you can shake a stick at. However, the Catholic Church distinctively has a single leader in charge — the pope. (Check out Chapter 11 for a discussion on why the pope and other Catholic leaders are always men.)

The pope is technically the bishop of Rome, but he has authority over all of the Catholic Church. He resides in Vatican City, which is an independent nation located in the heart of Rome, Italy. Since the early days of the Church, Rome has always played a special role in Church leadership. During that time, Rome was the political and economic center of the world, much like New York, Washington D.C., and Tokyo are today. Added to that, the Roman church was large, vibrant, and faithful to the apostles' teaching. As a result of all these factors, the Roman church exerted an enormous amount of respect and influence within the Church as a whole. Other regions recognized this special role and considered the bishop of Rome "first among equals" (see the "Theological differences" section earlier in this chapter).

The bishop of Rome was influential in the early centuries, but he didn't show authority until the fifth century, when Leo held the office. Leo was the first bishop of Rome to call himself "pope," though at the time, the Greek word *papas* and the Latin word *papa* were both used for many different church leaders. Over the years, however, Christians used the term more and more exclusively for the bishop of Rome, especially after the Great Schism in 1054 (refer to the section, "The Great Separation: Western and Eastern Churches go their own ways," earlier in this chapter).

Catholics believe Jesus himself established the *papacy* — the Church's supreme authority — with the apostle Peter when he said, "On this rock I will build my church" (Matthew 16:18). In other words, Jesus is foreshadowing that Peter would take a leadership role in establishing the Church after Jesus ascended into heaven. However, Catholics interpret this verse to mean not Peter personally, but the *office* of Peter, because he was head of the apostles. Because of this interpretation and because, by the second century, the Church considered Peter a father of the church in Rome, Catholics declared that all future officeholders of the bishop of Rome share that same leadership role.

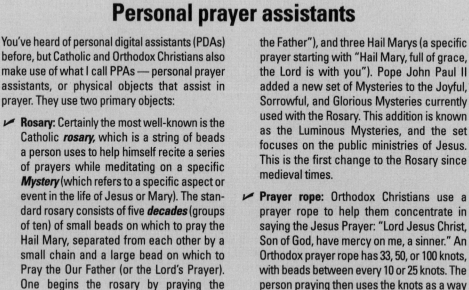

Personal prayer assistants

You've heard of personal digital assistants (PDAs) before, but Catholic and Orthodox Christians also make use of what I call PPAs — personal prayer assistants, or physical objects that assist in prayer. They use two primary objects:

✔ **Rosary:** Certainly the most well-known is the Catholic *rosary,* which is a string of beads a person uses to help himself recite a series of prayers while meditating on a specific *Mystery* (which refers to a specific aspect or event in the life of Jesus or Mary). The standard rosary consists of five *decades* (groups of ten) of small beads on which to pray the Hail Mary, separated from each other by a small chain and a large bead on which to Pray the Our Father (or the Lord's Prayer). One begins the rosary by praying the Apostle's Creed on the cross at the end of the Rosary, followed by an Our Father, Glory Be (a specific prayer beginning with "Glory be to the Father"), and three Hail Marys (a specific prayer starting with "Hail Mary, full of grace, the Lord is with you"). Pope John Paul II added a new set of Mysteries to the Joyful, Sorrowful, and Glorious Mysteries currently used with the Rosary. This addition is known as the Luminous Mysteries, and the set focuses on the public ministries of Jesus. This is the first change to the Rosary since medieval times.

✔ **Prayer rope:** Orthodox Christians use a prayer rope to help them concentrate in saying the Jesus Prayer: "Lord Jesus Christ, Son of God, have mercy on me, a sinner." An Orthodox prayer rope has 33, 50, or 100 knots, with beads between every 10 or 25 knots. The person praying then uses the knots as a way to measure the number of times they've repeated the prayer in a sitting.

Sacred Tradition in the Catholic Church also says that when the pope teaches *ex cathedra* (Latin meaning "from the chair"), he's *infallible,* or incapable of error. Catholics believe that the Holy Spirit prevents a pope from making a mistake when he speaks officially on matters of the Church. They make it clear that this doesn't mean that a pope is infallible in private matters. But when he teaches in an official capacity, he's guaranteed to be free from making a mistake. As a result, a pope can expand on a preceding pope's official teaching, clarify it, or add to it, but never contradict it.

Certain conditions must be fulfilled for the pronouncement to be ex cathedra; not all papal pronouncements reach this level.

A second type of pronouncement is known as a *papal encyclical* (coming from the Latin word for "circular"), in which papal letters that define or clarify the Catholic Church's position on contemporary issues, such as *Humanae Vitae* on abortion and birth control, circulate around the world.

Succeeding the apostles with bishops

All Christians believe that the apostles founded the Church. However, they disagree considerably over how that apostleship carried on after the original apostles left the scene. Catholics believe in *apostolic succession,* the idea that

bishops are the *anointed* (authorized) successors of the original apostles and are set apart to lead the Church. This belief helps justify the Catholic claim that Sacred Tradition carries equal weight to the words written by the original apostles in the New Testament because successive bishops maintain that direct connection to the original apostles.

Seeing the sacraments as necessary for salvation

The formal definition and nature of the sacraments are distinguishing characteristics of Catholicism. As I discuss in Chapter 8, a *sacrament* is a physical act that expresses an inner transformation. While Protestants believe that sacraments are the outward expression that you do after you've changed on the inside, Catholics believe that sacraments are the "change agents" in a Christian's life and the way that God uses to hand out his saving grace. As a result, sacraments aren't just recommended or important to a Catholic, they're an integral part of receiving God's saving grace. This view is often called the *high view* of sacraments.

Catholics believe that the seven sacraments represent the major stages of spiritual development in a normal Christian's life. These include

- **Baptism:** The sacrament of birth
- **Confirmation:** The "sequel" to baptism; the sacrament of coming of age
- **Holy Eucharist:** The sacrament for spiritual nourishment
- **Penance:** The sacrament for the confession of sins
- **Marriage:** The sacrament for establishing a family (not essential)
- **Holy Orders:** The sacrament for becoming a member of the clergy (not essential)
- **Anointing of the Sick:** The sacrament for the sick or dying

Orthodoxy has a high view of sacraments as well, but the Orthodox Church doesn't define the exact set of sacraments or their role in salvation as precisely as Catholics do.

The sacramental system developed gradually during medieval times. Catholicism says that Jesus Christ ordained the Church to serve as mediator for the sacraments, thus becoming a crucial part of a Christian's spiritual life. Check out Chapter 8 for a full discussion on sacraments and Chapter 13 for more on the integral role of the Church in a Christian's life.

Adoring Mary, the mother of Jesus

Jesus' mother holds a special place in the hearts of Catholics. Although Catholics insist that they don't worship Mary, they do express affection and adoration (often called *veneration*) to her. Given the intimate relationship between a mother and child, the Catholic Church believes that the same relationship can and should be expressed between the mother of Jesus Christ and each Christian.

Taking cue from Luke 1:48 ("All generations will call me blessed"), Catholics refer to the mother of Jesus as the Blessed Virgin Mary. Since the fifth century, Christians have referred to Mary as the Mother of God. Catholics explain that this term doesn't mean that she's actually the mom of the Triune God (Father, Son, and Holy Spirit — see Chapter 7), but instead is a reference to the divine nature of Jesus as God in the flesh. Catholics also refer to her as the Mother of the Church.

In conjunction with adoration for Mary, Catholic Sacred Tradition says that she was always a virgin, both before and after the birth of Jesus. In fact, although the Bible speaks of Jesus having a brother James (Matthew 13:55), Catholics say that the word for *brother* actually means "relative" or "cousin." Sacred Tradition also claims that Mary didn't die a physical death, but went directly to heaven as an encouragement to the rest of humanity, a preview of what's to come for other Christians.

Praying to the Virgin Mary and the saints

Catholics embrace the idea of praying to Mary and saints in heaven. When they do so, they're asking Mary and the saints to pray *with* them and *for* them. (In contrast, Protestants don't see Mary and saints as intermediaries between humans and God; they see Jesus as the only true mediator.) Roman Catholics believe that Mary, in particular, is a special intercessor, having a special, unique relationship with Jesus Christ.

Stopping in purgatory on the way to heaven

Catholics believe that most Christians don't immediately go to heaven when they die. Although people who die for their faith (called *martyrs*) are exempt, they believe every other Christian goes to purgatory, an intermediate place where a soul goes for purification before entering heaven.

Catholics believe that God uses purgatory to cleanse the after-effects of sin from a person's soul. After that person is cleansed, he or she is able to enter heaven. Each person stays in purgatory based on how moral and holy he or she was while on earth. Catholics also believe in praying for people in purgatory to shorten their stay there and speed up the cleansing process.

Chapter 9 dives fully into the issue of purgatory and provides a discussion from both the Catholic and Protestant views.

Including the Apocrypha as scripture

Although all Christians agree on the books that compose the Bible's New Testament, Catholics say that a group of Jewish books called the *Apocrypha* (or *deutero-canonical* books) is also the written Word of God. As a result, they add these books to the Old Testament.

Crossing your heart

The Sign of the Cross is closely associated with Catholics, but the practice actually has its roots in the second-century Church before it divided. Christians developed the sign as a practical way to identify with each other during times of intense Roman persecution and as a spiritual reminder of the power of what Jesus Christ did on the cross. The sign starts by touching your forehead with the fingers of your right hand, bringing the hand down to your heart, touching the left shoulder and then bringing the hand across the chest to the right shoulder. This action depicts the image of the cross. Christians often say, "In the name of the Father, the Son, and the Holy Spirit" as they make the sign. Catholics often use the Sign of the Cross during various parts of the liturgy and when they partake of the sacraments. Orthodox Christians also use a Sign of the Cross, but it goes from right shoulder to left shoulder.

Although the Catholic Church didn't officially recognize the Apocrypha until the 16th century (after the Protestant Reformation), this section of the Bible is an important part of Catholic theology. In particular, 2 Maccabees 12:43–46 is the backup verse the Church uses to support the doctrine of purgatory.

See Chapter 6 for more discussion on the Apocrypha, including the Catholic reasons for and the Protestant reasons against its inclusion in the Bible.

Following a code of conduct

The Catholic Church places a great emphasis on following the *eternal law of God*, which it divides into three categories:

- **Divine positive:** Explicitly defined by God, namely the Ten Commandments
- **Natural moral:** Unwritten laws known by all people through reason and conscience
- **Human positive:** Coming from either the government (laws of one's country) or Church (the Canon law)

The *Canon law* is considered the supreme law of the Church and provides detailed rules covering all aspects of Church life. In fact, in the latest revision, the 1983 *Code of Canon Law* contains 1,752 laws. Because not every Catholic (except for lawyers, perhaps) can remember all those laws, the Catholic Church narrowed down the practical applications of Canon law into six precepts. Along with obeying the Ten Commandments, Catholics must follow the following six rules in order to be considered a "good" Catholic:

- Attend Mass every Sunday and on holy days of obligation, such as Christmas (December 25), Assumption of the Blessed Virgin Mary (August 15), and All Saints Day (November 1)

✔ Confess your sins to a priest when needed (sometimes weekly, but at least once annually)

✔ Partake of the Eucharist (the Lord's Supper) regularly, at least during Easter in observance of Jesus Christ's death and resurrection

✔ Fast on designated days — abstain from eating one meal on Ash Wednesday and Good Friday and from eating meat on Fridays during Lent (see Chapter 19)

✔ Follow the marriage laws of the Catholic Church, as defined in the Code of Canon Law. For example, Catholics must be married in a Catholic Church before two witnesses by a clergyman (unless special circumstances apply), marry someone who's never been married before or who has an annulled marriage, and prepare for their marriage 9–12 months in advance by meeting with a priest or a deacon

✔ Support the Church, both with your finances and work

The fact that the Catholic Church has its own specific set of rules helps you distinguish between Catholicism and other expressions of the Christian faith. Protestants view these requirements as legalism, while the Orthodox Church stays away from defining a specific list of requirements one must meet in order to be a "good" Christian.

Vatican II: Catholicism in the modern era

During Vatican II, or the Second Vatican Council, the Catholic congress of bishops convened periodically from 1962–65. Pope John XXIII opened the council, and Pope Paul VI closed it. The council developed 16 documents that restate traditional Catholic teaching and offer extensive teaching on contemporary social issues. Earlier Catholic councils dealt primarily with doctrinal issues, but Vatican II was unique in that it focused its attention on pastoral issues to spark the spiritual life and growth of the Church.

Vatican II initiated several practical changes within the Church. For example:

✔ Mass could now be celebrated in the local language (or *vernacular*) of the particular church rather than in Latin to encourage the laity to participate fully in the Mass.

✔ Many Catholics now have the option to periodically receive both the consecrated bread and wine, whereas before Vatican II, they only received the consecrated bread (commonly called the *host*).

✔ Prior to Vatican II, Catholics were required to abstain from eating meat, eggs, cheese, or other dairy products during Lent. Vatican II relaxed this obligation so that Catholics instead abstain from eating meat on Ash Wednesday and every Friday of Lent and fast on Ash Wednesday and Good Friday.

✔ The laity were encouraged to increase their participation in church life, including in Bible studies and social action groups.

Examining the Catholic Church structure

Unlike the more distributed authority of the Protestant and Orthodox Churches, the worldwide Catholic Church — from the smallest parish to the largest cathedral — is under a single authority: the pope (see the "Revering the pope as supreme leader" section earlier in this chapter). That arguably makes the Catholic Church the single most widespread and distributed "top-down" organizational structure on the planet. In order to make sure this huge organization maintains unity, a hierarchy exists.

Catholics are divided into three overlapping groups:

- **Clergy:** *Ordained* (consecrated or officially dedicated) and authorized to say Mass and carry out the sacraments. Priests and bishops, for example, are part of the clergy.

- **Laity:** Not ordained or authorized to carry out the sacraments. Normal, everyday Catholics are considered part of the laity.

- **Religious:** A special group consisting of monks, nuns, and friars. The consecrated religious can be either clergy or laity, depending on the particular *order* (a special group of clergy within the Church). The Jesuits, for example, require monks to be clergy.

Second, the members of the clergy are the primary people involved in the governing of the Church. The Church has several layers of clergy:

- The *pope* is the bishop of Rome and supreme head of the entire Catholic Church.

- *Cardinals* (a group of 137 worldwide) are responsible for electing the pope. Some cardinals serve in the Roman Curia and work closely with the pope to govern the Church. Other cardinals run *archdioceses* (large regions of parishes). Cardinals are chosen by the pope, who selects a candidate from the College of Bishops (which includes all Catholic bishops, who I discuss in the next bullet).

- *Bishops* are responsible for running local *dioceses* (administrative regions of the Catholic Church that contain local parishes). Because the Catholic Church considers him a successor to the original apostles, a bishop has considerable autonomy in governing. However, the bishop regularly reports to the pope. Catholics also have a special category of bishops called *archbishops*, bishops who are responsible for *archdioceses*, which are larger dioceses that incorporate more territory or population.

- *Vicar generals* are priests who can perhaps be considered the "vice bishops," or those second in responsibility in a diocese who often perform

certain tasks in support of the bishop. These priests are sometimes given the honorary title of *monsignor*.

✔ *Parish priests* are responsible for local *parishes*, which are communities of believers living in a group of neighborhoods or some other small geographical area. The parish priest is called a *pastor*.

The Orthodox Church: Restoring the Image of God in People

The Orthodox Church has some 140 million followers worldwide, with half of them in Russia and the Ukraine. However, this division of the Church (also called the Eastern Church) is the least known to people living in North America and other parts of the world, such as Africa and Latin America. Much of that is due to the historical fact of their isolation from mainstream Christianity for almost a millennium (refer to the section, "The Great Separation: Western and Eastern Churches go their own ways," earlier in this chapter). However, don't think that Orthodox Christians ever had an inferiority complex as a result. Instead, they refer to themselves as the "Mother Church of Christendom" and see Orthodoxy as uniquely preserving the true Christian faith. After the Great Schism of 1054, Eastern Christians began to refer to themselves as *Orthodox*, meaning "right teaching."

Through the years, Orthodox Christians have maintained their own unique identity and have several distinguishing beliefs that set them apart from other Christians. Keep reading in this section if you want to know more.

Understanding what it means to be Orthodox

Like Catholics, Orthodox Christians believe that God speaks his truth through Sacred Tradition (sometimes referred to as *Holy Tradition*), but they believe that Sacred Tradition includes the Bible. (Catholics believe that God reveals his truth through the Bible and through Sacred Tradition separately; see the section "Discovering basic Catholic beliefs," earlier in this chapter.) From the Orthodox perspective, the Bible is an *epiphenomenon* (an "outward form") of Christian Tradition. In contrast to Protestants, Orthodox Christians believe that the Bible doesn't contain all of God's truth. Therefore, the Orthodox Church doesn't submit exclusively to the Bible, even if it's the most authoritative Tradition, but submits to Sacred Tradition as a whole.

Orthodox Christians see a direct link between the apostles and the Church today. Because of this permanent connection, the Traditions that have developed in the Church throughout the ages are always in synch with the apostles' teachings. *Tradition,* from the Orthodox perspective, is the life of the Church through the work of the Holy Spirit. It includes verbal and written teachings of apostles and *fathers* (important leaders) of the Church, sacraments, the *Divine Liturgy* (the liturgy used in an Orthodox worship service), creeds and conclusions of early Church councils, and even church architecture and iconography (see the "Icons: a sneak preview of heaven" section below for more on icons).

Although Eastern Orthodoxy has the same core beliefs as Catholics and Protestants concerning the Trinity, the divine nature of Jesus Christ, the inspiration of the Bible, and other beliefs that I discuss in Part II, it retains its own peculiar flavor, particularly in the following areas:

- ✔ Nature of salvation
- ✔ Icons
- ✔ Worship

Keep reading in this section for a taste.

Contemplating the nature of salvation

The Orthodox Church views the nature of sin and restoration from a different perspective than Catholics and Protestants do. Instead of seeing it in legalistic terms, they view sin as a tarnishing of the image of God inside a person. Jesus Christ's purpose in coming to the earth, then, was to restore the "image of God" in humans. He was able to pull this off because he was the perfect image of God (since he was God) and his death and resurrection enables Christians to restore this likeness of God within themselves.

In contrast to the salvation event in Protestantism, salvation is the lifelong process of restoring that image of God inside a person, recreating him or her. Salvation starts with baptism and is a continual process through the Christian's life. Orthodox Christians refer to this process as *theosis* (or divinization), which they believe ultimately produces a union with God. While Protestants believe that all saving work in a Christian's life is performed by God alone (the idea of *Sola Deo Gloria;* which you can read about in Chapter 11), Orthodox Christians believe that they'll reach a union with God as they participate in the life of the Church and as they seek to become more and more like Christ. As a result, the believer takes on qualities that God has (see Chapter 7), grows more aware of who God is, and, as a result, experiences more of his fellowship.

The Orthodox Church teaches that salvation isn't so much an individual act as it is a corporate act. A person can't be saved unless he or she is part of the Church. Orthodox Christians believe that the whole Church will be saved

together, and not simply as individuals. (Not that a disobedient person attending church can take others down; instead, that person wouldn't be considered to be truly part of the Body of Christ.) The Divine Liturgy, discussed in the "Worshiping with the five senses" section, is the chief vehicle the Orthodox Church uses to collectively restore the image of God inside of the Body of Christ.

Focusing on icons: Getting a sneak preview of heaven

Icons are a unique part of Orthodox worship that has no real Catholic or Protestant counterpart. *Icons* are the Byzantine-style paintings that represent a person or story from the Bible. To the Orthodox Christian, they're far more than just works of art, but are instead like windows looking into heaven and are an integral part of their faith. When you consider the Orthodox perspective on salvation (see the "Contemplating the nature of salvation" section, earlier in this chapter), you see that the icon paintings are the means by which they further come into union with God.

Icons are hung in the *iconostasis,* a wall of paintings outside of the sanctuary. Orthodox believers kiss the icons before going into a service. When Orthodox Christians focus on (or *witness*) an icon, they're not just viewing a picture, they're expressing their faith. They believe that the icon becomes a real presence (or essence) of the person or story portrayed — so much so that they believe an icon is equivalent to the Bible as a source of revelation.

Orthodox Christians considered icons the "books for the illiterate" and began to use them back in the Middle Ages to teach the Bible and experience God's truth in a way that everyone could understand, whether they could read or not.

By definition, an icon can't be realistic. To Orthodox Christians, realism is the depiction of sinful humanity. Instead, an icon must be true to what's known as a "transfigured reality" and faithful to the iconographic traditions of the Church (the same Byzantine style as they've always had). The Orthodox Church says that composing an icon according to your own personal preference invalidates it, much in the same way that twisting the meaning of a Bible verse to meet your whim eliminates the true revelation of God in that passage.

Orthodox Christians don't consider icons as painted, but rather written, each stroke of the paintbrush representing a prayer by the artist. Also, an artist never signs (or takes personal credit for) an icon because it's supposed to represent the Word of God.

Worshiping with the five senses

Celebrated each Sunday morning and on holy days, an Orthodox worship service isn't just an event you go to; it's an *experience.* In fact, when participating in an Orthodox service for the first time, a Russian prince supposedly said, "We knew not whether we were in heaven or on earth, for on earth there is no such splendor or beauty, and we are at a loss to describe it. We know

only that God dwells there among men." To the Orthodox Church, the Divine Liturgy (or Holy Eucharist) is more than just part of the worship service — it's the very centerpiece of what it means to be an Orthodox Christian.

The Divine Liturgy is a sensory experience, including singing and chanting, burning incense, observing ritual movements of the priests and acolytes (assistants), and witnessing iconic images throughout the church. Even the architecture of an Orthodox church reinforces this experience (see the "Form follows symbolism" sidebar in this chapter). This focus on the senses isn't just a nice touch or a pleasantry; it goes to the very heart of Orthodox beliefs — Christ's work on the cross redeems more than just a person's spiritual soul. Instead, the physical is also good and is in the process of being restored as well, because God manifested himself as a physical person (Jesus Christ) through the incarnation.

The order of the Divine Liturgy used in Orthodox churches today goes back to the early second century. One of the most well-known and widely used is the Divine Liturgy of St. Chrysostom. It consists of the following order:

- ✔ **Beginning:** The priest begins with a blessing of the Kingdom of God.

- ✔ **Prayers of Petition:** The priest prays a series of small prayers for peace, while the people respond to him in turn, "Lord, have mercy" (or *Kyrie eleison*).

- ✔ **Antiphons:** The Priest, deacon, and congregation participate in Old Testament readings, with refrains that call out the Christian meaning of the text.

- ✔ **The Entrance:** The priest enters the sanctuary with the Gospel scriptures, symbolizing the early Church practice of a priest who took the Gospel scriptures by torchlight from an underground hideaway to protect them from pagans and brought it up to the church.

- ✔ **Trisagion Hymn:** The priest speaks a prayer emphasizing God's holiness. Deacon and congregation respond in turn with a refrain.

- ✔ **Readings from the New Testament:** A reader reads a section from an Epistle or the Book of Acts. Next, the priest reads a passage from the Gospels. The Orthodox Church decides which scripture should be read, and they keep these same scriptural references year after year.

- ✔ **Homily:** The priest shares a sermon related to the gospel of Jesus Christ.

- ✔ **Cherubic Hymn and Entry with the Holy Gifts:** Procession of the unsanctified bread and wine (referred to as *Species*) taken from the Table of Preparation and brought to the Altar. During this proceeding, the congregation sings the Cherubic hymn, which says, "Let us put away all worldly care so that we may receive the King of all."

✔ **Ectenia of the Oblation Prayers:** The priest offers prayers of *supplication* (request), to which the congregation responds, "Grant this, O Lord."

✔ **Creed:** The congregation chants a short creed proclaiming the Trinity, then recites the Nicene-Constantinopolitan Creed (see Chapter 7).

✔ **Prayer of Sanctification:** The priest prays a prayer of sanctification, which is the heart of the Divine Liturgy. The priest begins with the offering of the *Oblation* (unconsecrated bread and wine), in which he speaks the words of Christ ("This is my body; This is my blood") and prays for the sanctification of the *Species* (consecrated bread and wine). After the priest lifts the bread and wine, the congregation kneels.

✔ **Prayers of Petition:** The priest prays for the spiritual health of the people, both inside and outside the church.

✔ **Lord's Prayer:** The congregation recites the Lord's Prayer.

✔ **Breaking the Lamb:** The priest raises up the newly consecrated bread (called the *Lamb*) and breaks it to symbolize the actual sacrifice of Jesus. The priest then pours warm water (called *zeon*) into the *chalice* (the cup used in the Eucharist) of consecrated wine. The water symbolizes the water that flowed from Jesus' side while he was on the cross (John 19:31–34).

✔ **Prayers before Holy Communion and Partaking of the Holy Gifts:** The doors of the altar are closed, and then the priest partakes of the bread and wine.

✔ **Holy Communion (Eucharist):** The congregation partakes of the bread and then wine. The Orthodox Christians consider the Eucharist the very means by which they're able to reach unity with Jesus Christ and with other Christians. See Chapter 8 for more on the Eucharist (the Lord's Supper).

✔ **Prayers of Thanksgiving:** The priest offers up prayers of thanksgiving and gratitude to God.

✔ **Dismissal Hymn:** The priest prays and blesses the congregation.

Form follows symbolism

The distinctive architecture of an Orthodox church is designed symbolically. The main part of the church is called a **nave** (sanctuary) that symbolizes God's dwelling place. The focal point in the nave is the **altar**. Separated from the rest of the church by the **iconostasis** (meaning icon screen), the altar contains the altar table (representing the throne of God) where the Reserved Sacrament (consecrated bread and wine) and the Book of the Gospels sit. Outside of the nave is the **narthex** (or vestibule) which serves as the entryway into the church. It symbolizes preparation for entering heaven. A dome is situated on top of the church and is meant to represent heaven.

Examining the Orthodox Church structure

The Catholic Church is one huge monolithic organization, while the Protestant Church is divided into completely autonomous denominations with no overarching organized activity. The Orthodox Church has its own distinct flavor. About 15 different self-governing Orthodox Churches exist, but they're all held together by a shared history and doctrine.

These separate Orthodox Churches are historically ethnically-driven, including the Greek Orthodox Church, the Russian Orthodox Church, the Serbian Orthodox Church, and so on. Each of these Churches are headed by a *patriarch* (a bishop that presides over other bishops). However, most Orthodox Churches today are governed by a *synod* (a council of bishops and laypeople), of which the patriarch is the synod moderator.

The Patriarch of Constantinople governs the Greek Orthodox Church, and the Patriarch of Moscow heads the Russian Orthodox Church. They're equal with the other Eastern patriarchs in Alexandria, Antioch, and Jerusalem, although special reverence ("first among equals") is given to the Patriarch of Constantinople, given Constantinople's leadership role in Eastern Church history. In contrast to the Catholic Church's view of the pope, the Orthodox Church doesn't consider patriarchs to be infallible on doctrinal issues.

Recently, in the U.S., the Orthodox Church has made attempts to move beyond ethnic-centered Orthodox groups, producing the Orthodox Church of America, the Antiochean Orthodox Church, and the Evangelical Orthodox Church (which was established by former evangelical Protestants who sought the restoration of the one holy catholic and apostolic Church and a faith that was more closely tied to the early Church than they believed Protestantism was).

Chapter 11

Back to the Basics: The Protestant Church

In This Chapter

▶ Considering why Protestants split from the Catholic Church

▶ Exploring what all Protestants believe

▶ Shedding some light on all those denominations

▶ Discovering what different labels, such as evangelical, mean

▶ Seeing how modernism affected Protestant churches

▶ Identifying contemporary trends in Protestantism

*T*he film *Back to the Future* tells the story of Marty McFly, a typical 1980s teenager who accidentally travels back in time to the 1950s in a rigged up DeLorean automobile. After he's there, Marty has to make sure that his presence doesn't prevent his parents-to-be from meeting and falling in love, and then he has to figure out how he can get back to the future and life as he knows it.

Back in the early 16th century, another Marty — Martin Luther — found himself going back in time, figuratively anyway, when he rediscovered the core teachings of the first-century apostles. What he found was far different from the Christianity he'd always known. From Luther's perspective, over the years, the Catholic Church had gotten away from the heart of the gospel that Jesus and the apostles taught. His remedy: Go back to the central teachings of the Bible that he believed the Church had lost, in order to move on to the future. Luther's radical beliefs got him into such a pickle that I'm sure he'd have liked to hop into a DeLorean and escape in time travel. But he made it through the sticky spots and, in the process, kicked off the Protestant Reformation.

In this chapter, you start off by traveling through time and exploring the key factors of the Reformation and chronicling the rapid growth of Protestantism. You then explore how Protestantism exists today by looking at denominations and notable trends as the 21st century unfolds.

Exploring the Protestant Reformation

Most significant moments in history — whether they're battles, revolutions, or discoveries — have a single individual behind them who spearheaded events and got them rolling. The Protestant Reformation is no different; although the Reformation was expansive and went beyond a single person, Martin Luther nonetheless was the catalyst that set the wheels in motion for a movement to forever change the Christian Church. In the next section, you get to know more about Luther and what caused the Reformation in the first place. Then, you explore how Protestantism expanded into four distinct strands.

Urging the Church to reform

Martin Luther was a German monk born in the late 15th century who became preoccupied with his own utter sinfulness (refer to Chapter 4) and God's awesome holiness. The more he studied who God is, the more he became terrified, petrified, mortified, and stupefied about what God's holiness meant for him personally; he wanted to experience salvation and go to heaven, but he believed that he was utterly destined for hell, given his sin. He tried *penance* (confessing his sins to a priest), *self-flagellation* (whipping oneself), and *mysticism* (which distrusted the Christian Church and said that a person achieves salvation by entering his or her "innermost being"). Performing the Eucharist (see Chapter 8) terrified him all the more, because he believed he was doing so unworthily. Martin's superiors urged him to simply love God, yet he found himself resenting and despising the Lord because of the hopeless situation.

Reexamining the Bible

Luther found the hope that he'd been desperately searching for in the pages of the Bible. After he took on a new position heading up biblical studies at Wittenburg University, he began to study the Bible like he'd never done before. He found himself drawn into the Book of Romans and was amazed by what he was reading. He discovered a common theme of the Apostle Paul throughout the book — that God justifies humans by grace through faith, and faith alone. As Luther read, he saw Paul paint a far different picture of the Christian faith than what he'd known. His eternal soul wasn't dependent on his personal worthiness or on the penance he performed. Salvation wasn't something that could be earned. The angst and despair that he felt inside gave way to hope and joy in the idea that people are saved not by anything that they do, but only by accepting in faith the work of Jesus on the cross (see Chapter 5).

Condemning indulgences and corruption

When Luther glanced at the Book of Romans and then looked up at the Christian Church around him, he did a double take. The two didn't seem to synch up, leaving Luther frustrated over what to do about it. He didn't agree

with some of the Church's teachings and had long been dismayed at the spiritual state of the Church, but he certainly didn't see himself as a rebel or revolutionary.

What ultimately set him into action was what he saw as widespread corruption regarding the Church's sale of indulgences. An *indulgence* is time off from purgatory (see Chapter 9) that Catholics believe they receive by performing certain acts, such as reading the Bible daily. They believe that these acts help them receive greater sanctification in their earthly lives and thus spend less time in purgatory.

The Catholic Church believed it could dispense indulgences to people because Catholics believed that, as Christ's representative on earth, the Church possessed a storehouse of merit for such purposes. This practice had started centuries earlier to help fund the *Crusades,* which were medieval military campaigns that the Western Church undertook to reclaim the Holy Land from Muslims. Whatever the original intent, by this time, indulgences became as common and as simple as a pill that everyone wanted in order to take care of sins quickly and easily. A person's spiritual state became a non-factor in his or her forgiveness.

While Luther was at Wittenburg, a church spokesman came to Germany to raise financial support for the completion of St. Peter's Basilica in Rome. Like a used car salesman, the spokesman offered not just forgiveness of one's own sins through indulgences, but he went even further — he offered a sort of Get-out-of-Purgatory-for-Free card that people could cash in for their dead loved ones. Luther was horrified by the theology of this teaching. In response, he posted a list of 95 calls for debate on indulgences (known as the *Ninety-five Theses*) on the outside of a church door in Wittenberg, Germany in 1517.

Going to trial

Church leaders denounced Luther for his rebellious act and brought him to trial in 1521 at the Diet of Worms (a name that sounds more like a radical new weight-loss fad than an imperial heresy hearing in the city of Worms). He demanded that the Church provide biblical evidence that his ideas were a *heresy* (false teaching that seriously undermines Christianity) and argued that the Bible is the authority for these kinds of matters, not the pope or anyone else in the Church. In his memorable words, Luther said, "I am bound by the scriptures . . . and my conscience is captive to the Word of God."

The Church declared Luther guilty of heresy at the Diet of Worms and placed him under the emperor's ban, a severe sentence because he was fair game to be killed by anyone at any time. However, Luther was able to escape any sentencing and gain protection from a sympathetic prince in Germany, in whose castle he hid out for many years, spending some of this time translating the Bible from the original Hebrew and Greek to German.

From reformation to separation

Martin Luther didn't set out to separate from the Catholic Church. Even after the Diet of Worms, he and some of the original reformers of his day hoped that their calls to reform would bring about change within the Church. Yet, as the years passed, they slowly began to give up on that idea and increasingly developed their own churches apart from the Catholic Church.

Martin Luther was the first of what the Catholic Church came to call *Protestants,* a term that comes from the Latin word meaning "one who protests." Over the next fifty years, four initial strands of Protestantism developed: Lutheran, Reformed, Anabaptist, and Anglican. This section discusses each of these strands.

Following Luther: The Lutherans

By the late 16th century, the effects of the Reformation were having a significant impact on much of Europe. Christians who supported Luther's reforms were given the name *Lutheran,* a term that they eventually coined for themselves. Lutheran churches sprang up in Germany, Scandinavia, and other parts of Northern Europe.

Lutheran churches focused on the "saved by grace through faith alone" beliefs that Martin Luther had been fighting for, but they still had many similarities to the Catholic Church. Lutheran churches remained intertwined with the state leaders and politics around them. And although Luther rejected all the Catholic sacraments that he believed didn't have biblical justification, he still was closely aligned with Catholic theology on the nature of the Lord's Supper and baptism (see Chapter 8).

Developing five-point Calvinism: The Reformed Church

The second major Protestant movement brought about the Reformed Church, which the Frenchman John Calvin started. Calvin had a reputation as a stern, somber sort of guy who had a liking for tough moral discipline and a strict work ethic. He became famous for his book *Institutes of the Christian Religion* in 1535, roughly 14 years after the Diet of Worms (see the section, "Going to trial," earlier in this chapter). His book became perhaps the most influential piece of writing to describe Protestantism.

Calvin soon moved to Geneva, Switzerland, and was the church leader in that city. During his time there, Geneva became the hip place to be for Protestants. Persecuted Protestants found a welcome mat for them in Geneva. The Swiss city had everything — a missionary training school, a model community for Christian living, and all the cheese fondue you could eat.

Although Calvin was fully in line with Luther on core Protestant beliefs (see the section, "Examining Core Protestant Beliefs," later in this chapter), he disagreed with him on other issues, such as the nature of the Lord's Supper

(Calvin didn't agree with Luther that the body and blood of Christ are spiritually present in the bread and wine. Flip back to Chapter 8 for more on this belief, called *consubstantiation*). The churches that followed Calvin began to stress that if people are saved by God's grace alone, then God must be the one who takes the initiative for salvation. That is to say, no one can choose God unless God chooses him or her first. This belief came to be popularly known as *Calvinism* and is often summarized with five points:

- **Total depravity:** Sinful humans are totally unable to save themselves. (see Romans 6:20, Mark 7:21–23).

- **Unconditional election:** God's purpose for saving people isn't based on anything that people have done, but solely on his will (see Romans 9:11,15).

- **Limited atonement:** Christ's death was sufficient to save all people, but only actually saves the *elect* (or the people who will be saved; see Matthew 25:32–33). Check out the "Debating on predestination" sidebar in this chapter for more.

- **Irresistible grace:** Those who are elected by God will also choose him with their own human wills (see Romans 9:16).

- **Perseverance of the saints:** Those people who are chosen by God will never opt out, but will persevere in their faith and receive salvation (see John 10:27–28).

Observant readers will notice that these five points spell out TULIP as an acronym. In fact, five-point Calvinism is often referred to using that acronym.

The influence of Calvin's teaching spread throughout various parts of Europe, notably in regions of France, the Netherlands, and even Scotland. In fact, by the 17th century, the Calvinist movement even surpassed Lutheranism in terms of its influence in the Protestant Church.

Furthering reform: The Anabaptists

As radical as Luther and Calvin appeared to the Catholic Church, they didn't go far enough for other Protestants. Another group, which became known as the *Anabaptists* (a term that means "rebaptizers," given to this group by its opponents), argued that in order to truly seek reform, one must separate the Church from the state altogether. Anabaptists looked at the New Testament Church and saw no intermingling with government authority, no stories of Paul and Peter hobnobbing with Emperor Nero. Instead, the Anabaptists focused on reaching the world with the Good News of Christ. From their perspective, anything else was just a distraction.

Debating on predestination

An age-old mystery for Christians has always been how human free will balances with God's *sovereignty,* his ability to do anything he wants and accomplish anything he wants. The Bible offers considerable proof for both of these truths, making them seem hard to reconcile. One man who grappled with this and came to a conclusion that many churches today accept was John Calvin. Coining the doctrine of *predestination,* Calvin believed that God, in his sovereignty, chooses exactly who's going to believe in him and who's not. This doctrine, central to the TULIP beliefs (see the section, "Developing five-point Calvinism: The Reformed Church" in this chapter), became a fundamental teaching in Reformed churches.

An opposing position, known as *Arminianism* (named after a 16th-century Dutch pastor, Jacobus Arminius), sprang up and said that humans do the choosing, because God gives people the gift of free will. This perspective says that because God knows the future, he knows in advance who's going to come to him. But they emphasize that this foreknowledge doesn't *determine* a person's salvation, but instead it's purely an act of the human will responding to Christ's work on the cross.

Reformed churches still hold the Calvinist position, while Methodists and a variety of other Protestants are Arminian.

Here's a comparison of the Calvinist and Arminian perspectives based on the Five Points of Calvinism.

Calvinism	*Arminianism*
Because of sin, humans never seek God.	Some Arminians say that even though sin made it impossible for human beings to save themselves, God left their wills intact so that they can choose him at the right opportunity.
God chooses the believer. No matter if he has to come kicking and screaming, he'll come around.	The believer chooses God, but God — being all-knowing — knows beforehand which people will come to him.
Jesus died only for the elect.	Jesus died for the whole world. You still have to believe in order to receive the atoning power of his sacrifice, but his sacrifice was for all.
God's grace is irresistible.	God opens the door for salvation. People are free to choose whether or not to walk through it.
Once a person is saved, she's always saved.	A person can lose her salvation through unrepentant sinning over the whole of her life.

Anabaptists had issues that went beyond how the Church relates to state and society. They actually got their nickname because of their stand on baptism. Unlike the infant baptism of the Catholic and Lutheran churches, Anabaptists

believed that only adult believers who openly confess Jesus Christ as their savior can be baptized. (See Chapter 8 for more on infant versus adult baptism.) Because they didn't see infant baptism as legitimate, many of the Anabaptists were baptized again as adults. Their enemies saw this practice as rebaptism, an idea that they considered heretical and punishable by death. Anabaptists countered by saying that it's not rebaptism at all. They believed that baptism at birth isn't really baptism, because baptism implies a conscious faith.

Anabaptists had some extreme fringe groups whose radicalism gave them a bad name throughout parts of Europe during this era. However, some Anabaptists were ahead of their time on several issues that are commonplace today (separation of Church and state, religious diversity, believer's baptism). But like so many mavericks throughout history, they were persecuted, not only by Catholics, but also by other Protestants.

Some Anabaptists were also ahead of their time on the issue of freedom of religious expression. Many believed that a person should be able to worship where he or she wanted to. To Lutherans and Calvinists in the 16th century who still held to the idea that a single church dominated a geographical area, this smacked of radicalism.

Today, the Mennonites and the Amish are two groups originating from the Anabaptist tradition. The Baptists, a major Protestant denomination, are unrelated to this group, as most Baptists come from a Reformed background.

Taking a Middle Ground: The Anglican Church

The fourth and final original Protestant movement brought about the Anglican Church. Unlike the previous three, this split from the Catholic Church didn't come about initially due to theological differences, but instead because of that nasty, unseemly business of politics.

Not too long after the Reformation began, England's King Henry VIII wanted to get a divorce, but in order for the divorce to be valid, he needed the pope's approval. Try as he might, he couldn't get it. So, if you're a spoiled king who always gets what he wants, what do you do? Why, of course, you simply tell the Catholic Church to take a hike, form your own national Church (the Church of England), and then get a divorce approved by the head of that Church. And that's exactly what the king did. However, when he took this action, the Church of England didn't immediately become Protestant in orientation, but instead kept a doctrine in line with Catholic teaching.

In time, the Church of England moved closer to the Protestant position, believing that the Bible, not tradition, was the final authority and that the only two legitimate sacraments were baptism and the Lord's Supper (see Chapter 8). At the same time, the Anglican Church didn't move as far away from the Catholic Church as the other Protestant groups, retaining a "high church" liturgy (see Chapter 12), among other ideas.

Examining Core Protestant Beliefs

The original goal of Protestantism was to provide new answers to age-old questions concerning Christianity for which some people felt the Catholic Church gave unsatisfactory answers. These questions included

- How is a person saved?
- Where does religious authority lie?
- What is the Church?
- What's the essence of Christian living?

Protestants share common answers to each of these questions. They summarize these beliefs as a set of *solas,* a word derived from the plural Latin word meaning "only." These are

- *Sola Scriptura:* The Bible is the only authority for Christians to determine God's truth.
- *Solus Chrisus:* Jesus Christ is the only mediator between God and man.
- *Sola Gratia, Sola Fide:* Salvation is by grace alone through faith alone.
- *Sola Deo Gloria:* Only God gets the credit for offering the solution of salvation, not people.

A final core belief, *priesthood of the saints* (all people are considered equals before God) doesn't begin with *sola,* but all Protestants hold it closely.

Together, these core beliefs served as the foundation for Protestantism centuries ago and remain valid to biblical Protestants today. I discuss each of them in this section.

Yielding to the Bible as the one and only authority

Protestants believe that the Bible is the sole and final authority as the written Word of God. They believe that Church tradition (referring to the historical beliefs and practices of the Church that I discuss in Chapter 10) is good and helpful, but that it doesn't carry the authority of scripture. The Holy Spirit works through the Bible, never presents truths independent of it, and isn't going to speak new extra-biblical revelations to people today.

In addition, Protestants believe that biblical interpretation shouldn't be reserved for the lofty domains of the clergy and theologians. Instead, they say that each person can interpret the Bible, not simply the Church. But at the

same time, the original reformers never believed that this meant a "to each his own" freedom of interpretation. Although one shouldn't ignore the clergy's education and special insight into understanding the Bible, the reformers' initial vision was that the clergy and congregation would work together to reach a consensus on understanding the Word of God. In other words, a Christian shouldn't interpret the Bible outside of the instruction and teaching of the Church. However, as the "Breaking It Down into Denominations" section (later in this chapter) discusses, the belief that all Christians are called to interpret the Bible for themselves had the unintended side effect of creating a multitude of denominations.

Luther's belief regarding the authority of the Bible differed from his more radical contemporaries. Luther believed that although the Bible was the only authority, extra-biblical traditions were legitimate so long as they didn't go against the Bible. On the other hand, the Anabaptists and other radicals claimed that if the Bible didn't specifically command something, it was wrong to practice it. By the 18th century, most Protestants came to emphasize the belief that "only scripture" meant that no authority *except* the Bible could determine God's truth.

Seeing Christ as the one and only mediator

Protestants believe that the sacramental system of the Catholic Church incorrectly puts the clergy as the mediators between God and man. In a Catholic's eyes, the individual Christian is dependent on the Church for matters pertaining to salvation (such as baptism) and the Christian life (such as confession and the Eucharist). But this practice prevents the average Christian from being able to go directly to God without mediation by priests.

In contrast, Protestants hold 1 Timothy 2:5 up as their slogan: "For there is one God, and one mediator between God and men, Christ Jesus." Christians believe that Jesus was the one who lived a sin-free life and sacrificed himself so that people can be justified before God the Father (check out Chapter 5 for more). Therefore, to Protestants, "only Christ" means that Christianity is about Christ and what he's done in order to make salvation possible, not something individuals or the Church can do.

Being saved by grace alone and faith alone

Although all Christians believe that salvation is made possible only by God's grace, they disagree on how he gives that grace. Protestants say that Christians receive grace simply by accepting and believing it, but Catholics

believe they receive grace by accepting it in faith and by participating in the sacraments. Orthodox Christians believe that Christians receive grace as they participate with God in the work of salvation through living a life of holiness and worship.

See Chapter 3 for a complete discussion of the issue of grace, including an exploration of the Protestant, Catholic, and Orthodox positions.

Giving kudos to God alone

The idea behind *Soli Deo Gloria* ("To God Be the Glory") is that humans didn't pick themselves up by their own bootstraps and find God, but instead, God did all the work, leaving nothing for the Christian to do but accept the offer of salvation.

The opposite perspective that Luther noted is what he termed the *theology of glory,* in which humans trust in their own efforts to bring about salvation rather than trust in God alone. This theology of glory also leads people to rely on their own wisdom and understanding rather than be humble before the Lord and trust his wisdom as chronicled in the Bible. Instead, Luther argued for a *theology of the cross,* which states that all humans are miserably sinful and can't ever escape sin, and it's only the saving work of Christ on the cross that can give real hope to people.

Because of what God has done for humans, *Soli Deo Gloria* is the reason and basis for Christian worship. God has done everything, so the natural Christian response is to worship God in gratitude and humility. (Check out Chapter 12 for more on Christian worship.)

Considering all Christians as equal in God's eyes

A final classic belief of Protestants is the belief in the priesthood of all believers (Revelation 5:10). That doesn't mean that every Protestant has to go to seminary and wear a collar around his or her neck. Instead, what Protestants mean by the phrase is that all Christians are the same before God. They don't fit into a holiness hierarchy, and God doesn't make a distinction between those who work in the Church and those who work in the secular world. Relying on the Holy Spirit to guide them, Protestants believe that God uses them as his ambassadors in either of these vocations.

Where are all the Protestants?

Catholic Christians identify closely with the term "Catholic," and Orthodox Christians embrace the term "Orthodox." In contrast, many Protestants only marginally relate to the term "Protestant." Not that they don't have Protestant beliefs, but the term itself is so generic that it often holds little meaning to Protestants today. One reason is that no Protestant is just a Protestant, but is instead identified with either a denomination (Methodist, Congregationalist, and so on) or a particular expression of Protestantism (evangelical, fundamentalist, charismatic).

Answering the core questions

Protestants answer the questions raised at the beginning of this section as follows:

✔ **How is a person saved?**

A person is saved by his or her faith in Jesus, not by simply doing good deeds or by being a good person.

✔ **Where does religious authority lie?**

Authority lies solely in the inspired Word of God, not in the pope or in the Church.

✔ **What is the Church?**

The Church is an entire community of believers, each of whom is called to go directly to God through Christ as the sole mediator. All Christians, not just the clergy, are called to reach out as Christ's ambassadors in the world. See the section, "Considering all Christians as equal in God's eyes," earlier in this chapter, for more on this idea of the priesthood of all believers.

✔ **What's the essence of Christian living?**

The essence of Christian living is serving God in a calling, whether it's inside or outside of the Church. (See also Chapter 14.)

Breaking It Down into Denominations

Protestants and rabbits seem to have something in common, and it's not floppy ears or a love for carrots. Since the beginning of the movement, Protestants have had a knack for multiplying churches. Or, as a cynic might say: Put two Protestants in a room and you'll soon have another denomination being formed.

Denominations rose up within the Protestant Church nearly a hundred years after the deaths of Luther and Calvin. Luther, Calvin, and their predecessors were tied to the medieval concept of *Christendom* (a marriage of Church and state) and a single Church for a geographical area. So, they were strict in combating dissention within these areas. But, over time, an openness to denominations began to develop.

Denominations are different from sects. Although the term has many meanings and connotations in contemporary society, a *sect* is much more exclusive and tends to distance itself from other Christians, believing that it alone knows God's truth, and everyone else is either outside the Body of Christ or at least on very shaky ground. One might liken a sect to a cult. In contrast, a *denomination* is often more inclusive, believing that different groups can express their faith in different organizational and worshipful ways, but all are part of a larger Body of Christ. In other words, a person in a sect points to the True Church with one finger. Persons in a denomination, although they may believe that their particular brand of Christianity is best, nonetheless use all their fingers and toes (and then some) to point to all the churches of the True Church. Refer to Figure 11-1 to see some of the Protestant denominations that spun off of the original four strands through the years.

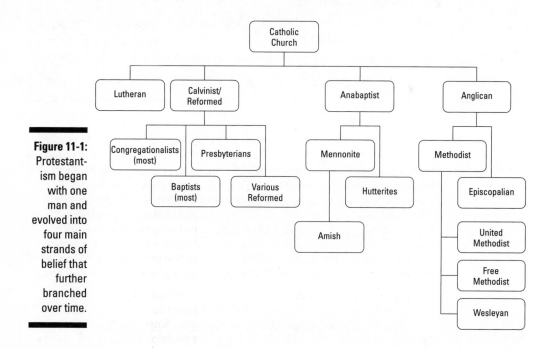

Figure 11-1:
Protestant-
ism began
with one
man and
evolved into
four main
strands of
belief that
further
branched
over time.

Prototype of the 21st-century evangelical

John Wesley (see Chapter 18) was an Anglican pastor in the 18th century who started the Methodist church. He'd been a very devoted minister and had even spent some lengthy time in America as a missionary. But, like Luther, he wrestled with his own personal salvation in light of his sin. Due to close contact with some Moravian Christians (a Protestant denomination) and his reading of Luther's commentary on Romans, Wesley eventually discovered what Luther had seen years before: the doctrine of salvation by grace through faith and personal certainty of salvation.

Wesley didn't set out to move away from the Anglican Church, but it gradually happened. He felt called to preach outside to reach coal miners and other common folk who wouldn't think of going into formal churches. Given the Billy Graham crusades that are commonplace today, that kind of open-air preaching doesn't sound unusual, but it was radical for an Anglican pastor during his day. Undeterred, Wesley was a tireless preacher who, over the course of decades of ministry, traveled an estimated 250,000 miles around Britain to preach the gospel, mostly by horseback!

Wesley emphasized a revitalized faith and a biblical Christianity that the original reformers talked about. He contrasted true Christian faith (a life of faith and discipleship) with the lukewarm faith that seemed to be part of the Church of England of his day.

As he traveled throughout Britain, Wesley helped organize Christians into Methodist societies, which were groups of Christians that met together outside of formal church, but eventually formalized into a denomination. He also worked diligently to reform society, fighting against slavery and drunkenness, fighting for child education, and caring for the poor. Further, he was active in overseas missionary work, establishing the Methodist church in America.

The reasons that denominations came about are wide ranging. For example:

- ✔ **Some denominations formed based on the government of the church.** Congregationalists believe that independent churches should govern themselves by the congregation apart from a higher authority. Congregationalist pastors, then, are ultimately subject to the congregation. Presbyterians (from *presbyter,* the Greek word for "elder") believe that *elders* (leaders) should govern the church alongside the pastor. Episcopalians, closer to the Catholic model, say that the government should be a hierarchy of regional *bishops* (overseers) over pastors in local churches.

- ✔ **Denominations were established due to doctrinal differences**. The Baptist denomination was originally established in the early 17th century by an Anglican pastor named John Smyth. Smyth believed that the Church of England was unbiblical due to its position on *apostolic succession* (the belief that bishops are the anointed successors of the original apostles to lead the Church). In addition, the holiness movement rose up from the Methodist Church in the 1890s based on the belief that the Church should be primarily dedicated to promoting holiness-based living and teaching.

✔ **Other denominations developed almost organically, springing out of ongoing church activities.** The best example of this is the Methodist denomination, which was started by John Wesley (see the "Prototype of the 21st-century evangelical" sidebar in this chapter), an Anglican pastor whose missionary activities eventually created a group of Christians that met together outside of the Church of England.

✔ **Other denominations formed not due to doctrinal differences, but due to geographical considerations.** These include the Dutch Reformed Church in the Netherlands or the north and south churches of the U.S. during the civil war era (Northern Methodists and Southern Methodists). Over the years, some of these geographically-split churches merged together with others (the United Methodist Church).

✔ **Denominations also sprung up due to ethnic and cultural realities.** The African-American churches that emerged during the 19th century are most notable.

An adage among Christians is, "Major on the majors and minor on the minors." Biblically-minded Protestants are characterized by agreement on the majors (see the section "Examining Core Protestant Beliefs," earlier in this chapter), but by splitting along the minors. Issues such as how Christians should express their faith outwardly are less important than the major issues pertaining to salvation, but they're not insignificant and trivial and can't be simply brushed aside.

Protestants believe that individual Christians should follow what they believe the Bible says and find a church that's in synch with those beliefs. At the same time, they believe that no one church body has a monopoly on God's truth. The result is that the Church inevitably consists of multiple church bodies, not a single one. Still, these separate church bodies can be unified by majoring on the majors while allowing for differences on the minors.

To name or be named

Some Christian groups have been stuck with names that people who disagreed with them coined. *Christians* is a label that the Romans first used to condescendingly refer to followers of Christ. *Protestants* is a term that the Catholic Church used when referring to the protestors within the Church. *Anabaptists* got their name too from their enemies, who scathingly were calling them "rebaptizers." But other groups, such as the Catholics, Orthodox, and Presbyterians were more proactive (or had better marketing departments) and got to choose their own names.

Looking at More Protestant Labels

If you talk politics, labels are a given. Conservative or liberal, moderate or extremist, left-wing, right-wing, center-wing, or chicken-wing. Although labels like these are helpful in identifying an individual's political tendencies, they also can be misleading and cause you to stereotype a person rather than understand his or her true position.

Labels are popular in Protestantism, as well, in part because a denominational affiliation doesn't mean much these days. Because some denominations aren't strict on following their confessions of faith (see the sidebar "Confessing a church's beliefs" in this chapter), the denomination name can mean squat. For example, depending on the particular local church they belong to, two Methodists may have wildly diverging beliefs on the cores of Christianity, due primarily to the issue of modernism (see the "Confronting the Challenge of Modernism" section that follows).

Therefore, in spite of the risk of stereotyping, understanding these labels is helpful to better understand how Protestants identify themselves (though some people categorize themselves under more than one of these groups). These include the following:

- **Evangelical:** The term *evangelical* comes from the Greek word *evangel,* meaning "gospel." Back in the 16th century, early Protestants used the term to identify their core beliefs about the gospel and to differentiate between the Catholics and the "out in left field" Protestant sects. Traditionally, an evangelical is someone who believes in the five solas that I discuss in the section "Examining Core Protestant Beliefs" earlier in this chapter. John Wesley (see Chapter 18) is a good example of what evangelicalism entails.

  However, the term has also taken on a more specific meaning among American Protestants, so that not every Protestant is an evangelical. The more uniquely American usage is often closely associated with Christians who place emphasis on seeking to share the gospel with the world through evangelistic crusades and missions, being born again (which I discuss in Chapter 3), and prioritizing the issue of biblical inerrancy (see Chapter 6).

- **Fundamentalist:** Started in the early 1900s, fundamentalism was a reaction against modernism, the secularization of society and the Church. Fundamentalists believed that modernists (or liberals, see the next bullet) were compromising on key components of the faith, including the nature of sin, the need for salvation through Jesus Christ, and the authority of the Bible. However, although the movement initially focused

on "getting back to the fundamentals," fundamentalists took on the stereotype of Bible-belting, narrow-minded anti-intellectuals, a stereotype that still exists to a large extent today, particularly in the media.

✔ **Liberal:** Within the church context, a liberal is someone who embraces many of the contemporary views of the world (postmodernism, relativism, evolution, and naturalism) and looks at Christian faith through these viewpoints. As a result, liberals question the reliability of the Bible and don't consider it to be the authoritative Word of God in the modern world (see Chapter 6 for more on the Bible as being authoritative). They're also more optimistic about the ability of individuals to overcome sin, and they discount the possibility of miracles.

✔ **Charismatic:** Charismatics (which comes from *charisma,* meaning "gift") are Christians who "speak in tongues" — an intense spiritual experience that prompts a person to start talking in non-human speech (see Chapter 12). Charismatics also emphasize other spiritual gifts, including the ability to *prophesy* (highlighting biblical truths for a specific context), see visions, and heal people physically and emotionally. Although they once made up a small minority of Christians, charismatics have grown significantly since the 1960s.

In the past, speaking in tongues was deemed a fringe activity in a few Pentecostal churches, but it's widely practiced today by a growing number of non-Pentecostal Protestants, Catholics, and even Orthodox Christians.

A must-read: *Through the Gates of Splendor*

He is no fool who gives up what he cannot keep to gain what he cannot lose.

—Jim Elliot

In the 1950s, Jim Elliot and four other "twenty-something" evangelical missionaries felt that God called them to go to Ecuador with their young families to share Christianity with a tribe of hostile Indians. Up to that point, no outsider had ever been able to talk peacefully with this remote, jungle-dwelling tribe known as the Aucas. Over a span of months, Jim and his friends established basic communication with the Aucas; during flyovers in an airplane, they gestured to the Aucas using hand signals and performed airdrops of boxed goods for them. When the timing seemed right, they landed their small plane on a sandy beach, prepared to meet with the natives face-to-face. But instead of smiles, the Auca Indians greeted the young missionaries with spears and slaughtered (without resistance) each of them on a chilly morning in 1956. *Through the Gates of Splendor,* written by Jim's widow, Elizabeth, gives a biographical account of Jim's decision to go to Ecuador and the events leading up to that fateful morning. Not only is the story riveting, but the book also taps into the heart and mind of a Christian who was willing to risk all for the cause of Christ.

Confessing a church's beliefs

A confessional church sounds like a church that just did something bad and is very sorry about it. But a *confessional church* is actually one that bases its worship, teaching, and preaching on a confession of faith or *catechism*. Many of the early denominations have a confession of faith that Christians formulated at the time they formed the denomination. In practice, some churches pay close attention to the confession, but others (including many mainline churches) tend to ignore it in modern times.

Confronting the Challenge of Modernism

The original reformers may have intended for the Protestant Reformation to be a religious revolution, but it had ripple effects that eventually impacted all of society and helped bring the end to *Christendom* (the close relationship between the Church and the government in a particular geographical area). The Reformation was a challenge by God-seeking Christians to the dominant Church authority. However, it also paved the way for people with no religious interests to rebel against a Church authority that they didn't want. This anti-authority attitude against the Church showed itself most significantly during the French Revolution, when the revolutionaries publicly dispensed of God and the Church in ways that would've been unheard of just a couple hundred years before that time. Perhaps the defining moment came when they changed the name of the Cathedral of Notre Dame to the Temple of Reason.

As a result, *modernism* (the idea of abandoning tradition in favor of new progressive ideas) was born and spread throughout society in the 19th century and eventually into the churches, as well. Modernism in the Church (or *theological liberalism*) embraced the principles of the 18th-century Enlightenment, holding a much more optimistic view of human nature than biblical Christians did. The idea of original sin became passé. Through education, humans could become good and create a heaven-on-earth society. When Darwinian evolution came in vogue, some churches accepted naturalism and began discounting the possibilities of miracles. Instead of the authoritative Word of God, modernist churches looked at the Bible merely as an account of humanity's evolving spiritual understanding and sought to demythologize the scriptures.

Liberal-minded people tended to embrace this secular modernism and moved to change the Church based on that worldview. Fundamentalists fled from modernity, but evangelicals aimed to balance modern thinking without compromising the core beliefs of the Christian faith.

Ordaining women

Although the original apostles were all men, women still played a vital role in the development of the early Church. Women served in various leadership roles in the Church, but they didn't serve as ordained clergy because of biblical teaching against that practice. Specifically, Paul instructed in 1 Timothy 2:12: "I don't permit a woman to teach, nor to exercise authority over a man."

Christians who don't support female pastors say that the issue is straightforward: The Bible teaches against it. They say that Paul's command still applies to the Church today, in spite of whatever's going on in society outside the Church. They're quick to point out that they believe that men and women are equal before God and that women can and should play many

key leadership roles in the Church. However, they hold that God has specifically ordained men for public pastoral preaching.

On the other end of the spectrum, Christians in support of female clergy insist that Paul's words were specific to the Ephesian Church and point out other examples of Paul allowing women to teach (see Acts 18:24–26).

The Catholic and Orthodox Churches don't permit female clergy, but Protestant denominations remain divided on this issue. Most mainline denominations — such as Episcopalian, United Methodist, Congregational, and some Lutheran — allow women in pastoral positions. Other more conservative denominations and nondenominational churches don't.

Modernism became the dominant view in several of the larger denominations during the 19th and 20th centuries. These *mainline* denominations include the Methodists, Presbyterians, Episcopalians, American Baptists, and United Church of Christ (Congregationalists). However, a minority of people within these denominations held more conservative views in line with the original reformers. Sometimes denominations, such as the Presbyterians, formally divided between conservative (Presbyterian Church in America) and liberal (Presbyterian Church USA) groups. Others, such as the Methodists and Episcopalians, housed both conservative and liberal groups within the same denomination, albeit with periodic tensions surfacing as issues arise, such as ordaining homosexual clergy and dealing with women's rights and social activism issues.

Looking to the Future: Trends in Contemporary Protestantism

As the Protestant Church heads into the 21st century, it displays some notable trends. These include

> ✔ **Shrinking mainline denominations:** Although mainline denominations remain dominant in overall numbers of people, they don't carry the same influence within Protestantism that they did a century ago and

before. As a response to the impact of modernism in mainline denominations, many evangelical and other biblical Christians moved on to more biblically-minded denominations or to nondenominational churches.

✔ **Independent, nondenominational churches:** More and more new churches that are springing up have no denominational ties to them whatsoever. A combination of the congregation and church leadership govern these independent, nondenominational churches, and they tend to emphasize the core teachings of Protestantism. These churches are usually evangelical.

✔ **Seeker-sensitive churches:** Seeker-sensitive churches try to reduce the traditional barriers that non-Christians face in coming to a church and actively becoming a part of it. They focus on the needs of the "seekers," ensuring that the church offers ministries and a worship experience that's relevant to them. See Chapter 12 for more on seeker-sensitive churches.

✔ **Cell group churches:** As churches get larger and larger in number, Christians often struggle with feeling a connection to the Body of Christ. If left unchecked, church simply becomes a place you go to for an hour a week and worship with hundreds or thousands of others you don't know. The *cell group* concept developed as a response to this problem. In the biological world, an organism consists of many, many cells. In the same way, a church is a single local Body of Christ and meets together as a church body to worship, but it should also be divided up into small cell groups to meet people's needs outside of worship. Cell groups may be Bible studies, grief counseling groups, divorce support groups, or even as specific as classic movie cell groups (which serves to give Christians a chance to fellowship with each other and enjoy a common activity). Supporters of cell groups say that this concept enables larger churches to remain in line with the concept of the New Testament group of believers meeting together and loving one another.

✔ **Megachurches:** In some of the larger population areas of the U.S. and other countries, large churches are springing up. And I'm talking large — with sometimes tens of thousands of members. In America, a *megachurch* is typically nondenominational, provides contemporary worship (see Chapter 12) in a large auditorium, and usually has a professional feel to the worship experience — a high caliber worship music team, first class actors in dramas and skits, the incorporation of multimedia, and a preacher with plenty of charm and personality. Willow Creek in suburban Chicago, Saddle Back Community Church in southern California, and Crenshaw Christian Center in Los Angeles (one of the largest African American congregations) are three of the best-known megachurches in the U.S. Many U.S. megachurches are also seeker-sensitive and use cell group techniques for their congregations.

Although most megachurches are located in the U.S., the world's largest megachurch, Yoida Full Gospel Church, resides in Seoul, South Korea, with 800,000 members.

Chapter 12

Making Sense of Worship

My wife and I are happily married, but I have to confess that we're in an all-out coffee war. To me, true coffee means either fresh ground coffee with cream or else espresso with non-fat milk, chocolate, and extra whip cream. However, my wife recently felt compelled to get back to the basics and discover how coffee was originally experienced: black coffee, French press, or a double shot of pure espresso. Sayonara creamsville! My wife and I may need counseling for our coffee incompatibility, but at least we stand united against our woefully mistaken friend who has the nerve to speak against the coffee shop we love so much. Too commercial, she says. Not an authentic bean experience. "Bah, humbug!" we say, knowing she's out of touch!

In these coffee wars, my wife, friend, and I are all striving for a common goal — enjoying coffee the way it was meant to be. But each of us has a different idea on how that's achieved.

Worship is an infinitely more sacred issue than coffee, of course, and it's a fundamental part of Christianity — but the myriad of perspectives on Christian worship is remarkably similar to the percolating debates among the three of us. To some Christians, worship is only pure when you do what the original New Testament Church did. To others, worship should combine the best of the ancient world and our modern world — sound biblical principles mixed with modern creativity and artistry. Still others want to ensure that, regardless of the worship style, they maintain a balance, avoiding the extremes of stuffy and emotionless or emotional and shallow.

This chapter takes a close look at the issue of worship, explaining what worship is, why Christians worship, and how different people express devotion to God — from somber, cathedral-style services to contemporary services with upbeat music played on guitars and drums to charismatic services in which people dance in the aisles.

I Worship, You Worship, We All Worship: Defining the Christian Tradition

Compared to people in earlier societies, most modern people have a hard time understanding exactly what worship is. In the past, showing reverence and awe was a normal part of life, whether it was to a king or to a god of one sort or another. Today's highly individualistic society stands in contrast to this lifestyle, tending to view any kind of authority with either skepticism or as irrelevant. As a result, the word *worship* conjures up images of prehistoric folks bowing down before golden statues and revering them like gods. To a society that prides itself on being sophisticated and savvy, the whole worship idea ends up sounding silly.

Although bowing to a golden calf is outdated, the concept of worship is not. Worship is hardwired into the fabric of humanity; all people worship something, whether they realize it or not. Some people worship God, while others worship more earthly gods. The ancients often opted for golden idols, but today people revere money, power, fame, sex, celebrities, sports, and so on. In short, people worship whatever captivates their hearts.

Christianity says that a believer's all-consuming focus needs to be the Lord and the Lord alone. In this light, *worship* is the act of showing God that you're in awe of and devoted to him. Christians do this through a variety of practices, including singing, reading the Bible or creeds of the Church, praying, sharing in the Lord's Supper, preaching, and enjoying fellowship with other Christians. Christians believe that worship not only honors God but also empowers the worshiper. Some Christians even believe that the Holy Spirit fills up the spiritual gas tank of the individual who's worshiping, enabling him or her to be a disciple who's ready to go out into the world and share the gospel.

The New Testament doesn't provide much specific instruction on what worship should consist of, so the perspectives that developed are based on what the apostles and the early Church did, rather than on the specific teachings of the Bible.

No matter how they do so, Christians agree that they must approach worship with the right attitudes for true worship to occur. These include

✔ **Being reverent:** Both the Old and New Testaments make it clear that God's faithful must always worship in reverence — they're never to approach worship in a light-hearted or an unwilling manner. After all, the Lord said to Moses, "Don't come close. Take your sandals off of your feet, for the place you are standing on is holy ground" (Exodus 3:5).

✔ **Being genuine:** Jesus indicated that true worship means doing so in spirit and in truth (John 4:23–24). By *worshiping in spirit,* Jesus meant that the worship originates deep inside of a person rather than through external activity. *Worshiping in truth* indicates being focused on the Word of God and being genuine in what you do, not going through the motions.

✔ **Being attentive to the Holy Spirit:** Paul tells believers to worship "in the Spirit" (Philippians 3:3). True Christian worship is always inspired by the Holy Spirit, and Christians should acknowledge the Holy Spirit's role as they worship.

✔ **Being humble and surrendering your heart to God:** The story of the three wise men in Matthew 2:11 reminds believers that true worship means giving:

> *The wise men came into the house and saw the young child with Mary, his mother, and they fell down and worshiped him. Opening their treasures, they offered to him gifts: gold, frankincense, and myrrh.*

In the same way, when you worship with abandon, you become completely focused on God, not holding back or sitting on the sidelines. Sometimes that involves giving gifts, like the wise men did, and other times, it means giving one's whole self to participate in the service.

✔ **Being intentional while allowing room for emotion:** Some churches have a tendency to treat worship as a purely outward emotional experience, while others think it's a cerebral activity and much prefer to leave emotion out altogether. But most Christians agree that the Bible points to a balance between these opposing positions.

The Bible indicates that God wants emotion to play a part in worship. Note the word "shout" in Psalm 81: "Sing aloud to God, our strength! Make a joyful shout to the God of Jacob!" In fact, the Old Testament uses "shout" over 20 times and often uses the term interchangeably with "sing" in the original Hebrew.

At the same time, the Bible makes it clear that Christians must not get carried away and let mindless emotion dominate. Paul dealt with this problem in his first letter to the Corinthian church. Their worship services got crazy and out of control, making it impossible for some people in the congregation to worship. As a result, Paul responds in 1 Corinthians 14 about the importance of worshiping in an orderly manner, one that produces a worshipful attitude in everyone, not just a few. As Paul says, God is not a God of confusion, but of peace.

✔ **Being committed to worship as a lifestyle:** The Apostle Paul reminds Christians in Romans 12:1 that true worship is a 24/7 deal, not something you only do for an hour on Sunday or Saturday:

> *I urge you, brothers, by the mercies of God, to present your bodies a living sacrifice, holy, acceptable to God, which is your spiritual act of worship.*

Not that Christians feel that worshiping with others isn't important, because they do, but Paul says that the Christian *life* is, by definition, worship.

Examining the Worship Service as a Whole

Christians worship God in a variety of manners, performing a variety of practices. But, as author Robert Webber notes in *Planning Blended Worship: The Creative Mixture of Old and New* (Abingdon Press, 1998), you can dissect worship into three distinct parts:

- ✔ **Content:** Christian worship proclaims and celebrates God's nature and the gospel of Jesus Christ. It can also serve as a response to what God has done in one's life. This involves all aspects of the service, including singing, Bible reading, participating in sacraments/ordinances, praying, and listening to sermons.

- ✔ **Structure:** Church leaders organize worship services in a particular way. Some churches are highly structured and maintain the same order at every service, while others are more loosely structured and often vary the order of a service.

- ✔ **Style:** Because Christians don't worship in a vacuum, worship always takes on a cultural style. Some Christians believe that churches today should stick to the style of the early Church's worship services, while others think that style is a far more flexible issue.

Worship through the eyes of the early Church

Justin Martyr, one of the second century Church fathers, played an important leadership role in the Church when it was working hard to transition from a faith led by the original apostles to an organized Church that would soon spread throughout the world. As Christians in the 21st century deal with the issue of worship, it's helpful to get a perspective from someone who lived just a few decades after the apostles and well before the modern-day divisions of Catholicism, Protestantism, and Orthodoxy. The following comments are taken from Martyr's *First Apology*, a book he wrote concerning worship.

Who should worship together?

On the day called Sunday, all who live in cities or in the country gather together to one place.

On what day should the Church worship?

Sunday is the day on which we all hold our common assembly because it is the first day on which God, having wrought a change in the darkness and matter, made the world; and Jesus Christ our Savior on the same day rose from the dead.

What should a worship service include?

The memoirs of the apostles [the Gospels] or the writings of the prophets are read, as long as time permits; then, when the reader has ceased, the president [preacher/priest] verbally instructs, and exhorts to the imitation of these good things. Then we all rise together and pray, and, as we before said, when our prayer is ended, bread and wine and water are brought, and the president in like manner offers prayers and thanksgivings, according to his ability, and the people assent, saying Amen; and there is a distribution to each, and a participation of that over which thanks have been given, and to those who are absent a portion is sent by the deacons.

How should believers serve others as part of worship?

They who are well to do, and willing, give what each thinks fit; and what is collected is deposited with the president, who helps the orphans and widows and those who, through sickness or any other cause, are in want, and those who are in bonds and the strangers sojourning among us, and in a word takes care of all who are in need.

Worshiping together: Why Christians believe it's essential

Worship can be an individual or corporate act, but the Church — clearly based on New Testament teaching — has always emphasized the importance of worshiping with other believers (often called *corporate worship*). Christians are called to worship corporately as a reminder that the Church is a family of God and because God is glorified when a group of believers gather in unity to worship him. Jesus promised in Matthew 18:20 that when two or more Christians are gathered together in his name, he'll be in their midst. That doesn't mean that Jesus isn't with an individual Christian who's praying and worshiping, but clearly Jesus was emphasizing that there's something special about worshiping together.

During the New Testament times, worship was usually held in homes and occasionally in Jewish synagogues. However, after the Church grew and became more organized, local communities began constructing church buildings for group worship. That same practice continued on through the centuries to the present day. Some Protestant groups now gather in places outside of church buildings (homes, school gyms, and so on), but the focus remains the same — worshiping together as the Body of Christ.

Deciding when to worship

Protestants commonly call the time when Christians get together to worship a *worship service,* while Catholics refer to it as *Sunday Mass.* Although Jews worshiped on the last day of the week, Saturday (also called the *Sabbath*), the early Christians decided to set aside the first day of the week (Sunday) for worship, instead, because Jesus was resurrected on that day. This tradition has carried on through the ages, although rare exceptions exist where believers still observe the Jewish Sabbath as the proper day to worship God.

For Catholics, Sunday Mass can actually occur on either Saturday evening or Sunday morning. The reasoning is that they follow the old Hebrew practice of recognizing a new day at sundown rather than at sunrise.

Many Protestant churches offer Saturday evening services as well. Sometimes, the service helps accommodate people's busy weekend schedules. Other times, the motivation is to appeal to teen or young adult age groups.

The secret to successful worship: Preparation

Sunday mornings are hectic for many Christians; just getting to church in one piece is often an accomplishment! Consider the following typical scenario: The alarm clock doesn't work (Hmmm. . . .), causing you to oversleep. You rush out of bed, jump in the shower, and then hop in the car — if you're lucky, grabbing a change of clothes and a cup of java in between. Next, you dash off to church, outrunning the local sheriff who tries to chase you down for speeding. Then, just before the service begins and as you're looking out the window for flashing sirens, the kid sitting behind you starts repeatedly kicking your pew, giving you a pounding headache. As a result, by the time the service begins, your mindset is nowhere near being focused on worship. What ends up happening is that your racing mind constantly replays your frustrating and hectic morning before you can finally put on the mental brakes and get focused. But, by then, the worship service is over and you've missed your chance.

Preparation is, therefore, the real secret to being in a proper frame of mind to worship. Consider the following tips:

- ✔ If you attend church in the morning, plan ahead to get up early to avoid the morning rush.

- ✔ Spend time reading the Bible, praying, and listening to worship music *before* you leave for church.

- ✔ Be early or, at least, on time. Coming in late not only makes it hard for you to worship, but it also has an impact on others around you.

- ✔ After you take your seat in church, use the moments before the worship service begins to clear your mind and prepare your spirit for worship.

Overall, a Christian's goal is to have an attitude of worship by the time the worship service begins.

Exploring Ways to Worship: Liturgical Versus Free Worship

Although Christians tend to agree on what worship is, exactly *how* to worship is a matter of much discussion and debate. The Church has had different perspectives on this issue for centuries, but these differences seem to have peaked within the past forty years.

Christians hold two basic viewpoints on how the Church should conduct worship:

✔ **Liturgical worship:** Embracing tradition, the liturgical (or *high church*) view looks at the early Church model and aims to duplicate it. Not only do proponents of *liturgy* (rituals and ceremony) say that it's the most biblical approach, they also say that only through the liturgy can you worship God in awe and reverence. These Christians believe that repeating liturgy from the early Church strengthens Christians today by providing a link to the past.

✔ **Free worship:** The free worship (or *low church*) view embraces the adaptability of the gospel in a contemporary setting, saying that modern worship should pull from the practices of the early Church, but not clone them. Free worship advocates believe that their worship approach is in line with Jesus' ministry because he spoke against the empty traditions that the religious leaders of his day performed. They see free worship as being flexible to the needs of the congregation and allow for a more informal environment that they believe makes people feel more comfortable opening their hearts.

I discuss these two perspectives more in the sections that follow.

It's important to note that, although both sides of this debate make important points about what *can* go wrong using the other worship style, neither side produces an airtight biblical argument in support of its style or against the other. It's important to remember that God didn't use a cookie cutter when he created people. Christians have likes and dislikes that aren't always the same as those of other Christians — a point that they always seem to have a hard time remembering. By and large, Christianity says that so long as worship expression is within the boundaries of biblical teaching, it glorifies God. Ultimately, Christian worship, no matter the style, should emphasize both reverence toward God and a closer personal relationship with the Lord.

Taking the high road with liturgy

A *liturgical church* provides a rigid structure to the order of the worship service and uses liturgy as a key part of the worship experience. Copying the worship patterns of the early Christian Church, they have a set structure for their normal services, often emphasizing written prayers and creeds and a repeated set of music. In general, all churches of the same type (Catholic, Orthodox, and so on) use this structure consistently year after year — see Chapter 10 for more on the Catholic and Orthodox traditions. Liturgical churches also have an organized structure for special services, such as for baptism, Christmas, Easter, and Palm Sunday. In terms of music, liturgical churches sing traditional hymns, either accompanied by an organ or *a cappella*, without musical accompaniment (see the section, "Incorporating Music: A Call to Musical Arms," later in this chapter).

Liturgical churches place a high degree of priority on creating a worship environment that displays grandeur, mystery, and reverence toward God, paying attention to every detail, including the structure of the church buildings themselves. The medieval cathedrals and the traditional American stained-glass-clad churches all reveal this emphasis in the intricacy of their design. Liturgical churches focus their services on expressing reverence and awe to God through these physical surroundings along with the tried-and-true order and ceremonies of worship.

The sacraments play a central role in a liturgical church. Catholic and Orthodox churches, both liturgical, place greater emphasis on the role of the sacraments in salvation than do Protestants (check out Chapter 8 for the skinny on the sacraments). Naturally, then, Catholics and Orthodox Christians believe that the purpose of liturgy is to enable Christ to be present through worship in order to produce a saving encounter with God. Many Protestant denominations, however, such as Episcopalian, Lutheran, and United Methodist, have a liturgical style of worship, but see worship as an expression of a Christian's inward saving faith, not as an activity directly related to salvation itself.

Of all the strands of Christianity, the Orthodox Church undoubtedly places the highest value on liturgy. That's because it sees liturgy as a primary way in which one experiences true Christianity. As Chapter 10 explains, worship becomes something that involves all the senses — sight (icons, architecture), hearing (music), smell (incense), touch (baptism), and taste (Communion) — to awaken the hearts of believers and wipe away the stains of a sinful soul. The Orthodox Church has performed the same liturgical practices for centuries and is resistant to any change in those practices. Because these practices are the main method of the Church's expression, they see changing the liturgy as equivalent to tweaking the core tenets of the Christian faith.

Worshiping freely along the low road

A *free worship church* is more flexible in the order and style of worship and doesn't feel bound to the age-old traditions that liturgical churches do. Services usually follow a general order, but the structure is tweaked as needs arise. Therefore, the focus or structure of a service may change based on what's happening that day — either within the church or in the secular world.

Although in liturgical churches a member of the clergy often reads prayers from a book, free worship emphasizes a scheduled time of off-the-cuff (or unprepared) prayer, which the pastor or even a member of the congregation says aloud.

Free worship services are more informal, relaxed, and even conversational than liturgical services, as these churches believe that Christians can be reverent in an informal setting because true worship is a matter of the heart. This relaxed atmosphere often, but not always, is reflected in the style of dress worn by church attendees. Most free worship churches welcome khakis or even T-shirts, though some hold to a more traditional dress code.

Many free worship churches also believe that the external surroundings are insignificant to worshiping God. That's why they don't have a problem meeting in school gyms if they don't have their own digs or in a multi-purpose sanctuary that they also use for sports. Free worship churches focus on being practical and relevant, all with the aim of reaching out to the world for Jesus Christ and equipping the congregation to be disciples.

This same principle carries over to musical styles and other parts of worship. In light of the fact that the Bible doesn't give specifics on music, many (though not all) free worship churches believe they have the freedom and license to use contemporary music in the services, rather than traditional church music. (See the "Incorporating Music: A Call to Musical Arms" section, later in this chapter.) So too, many free worship churches believe in including skits, plays, and occasionally even interpretive dances as a way to enrich the worship experience.

Free worship churches are predominately Protestant and evangelical and include both *denominations* (groups within the larger Church that express their faith in different ways) that support free worship and many independent *nondenominational* churches (churches that aren't tied to any denomination). Increasingly, some individual churches that are part of a larger liturgical denomination have broken from this tradition and have adopted a more free worship style. To find out more about all this denomination jargon and to see how the different segments of the Protestant Church work together, flip back to Chapter 11.

Understanding when Christians babble in a language you don't recognize

Charismatic churches, which are part of the free worship tradition, are those that emphasize worshiping by using spiritual gifts, especially the gift of speaking in tongues. Christians who practice this believe that *speaking in tongues* is an emotional, spiritual experience that prompts a person to start speaking in non-human speech. The people speaking in tongues understand the words they say to be angelic languages that the Holy Spirit gives to them so that they can pray spontaneously as directed by God.

Charismatic churches have rapidly increased in popularity over the past forty years. Today, a growing number of Catholics, non-Pentecostal Protestants, and even some in the Orthodox Church widely practice the charismatic gift of tongues-speaking, which was once considered a fringe activity in Pentecostal churches, as a form of worship.

Charismatics see speaking in tongues as being an important component of true worship. Non-charismatics disagree, believing tongues-speaking to either be a minor gift or something that is not biblical in this day and age.

If you'd like to find out more about charismatics and speaking in tongues, check out another of my books, *Christian Prayer For Dummies* (Wiley).

One of the free worship trends over the past twenty years is the idea of a *seeker-sensitive church.* The goal of a seeker-sensitive church is to reach out to non-believers by focusing on their needs and making worship services more relevant to them. These churches often use savvy marketing techniques to attract people to church, worship in auditorium style sanctuaries, and integrate multimedia and entertainment as part of the worship service experience. Most people consider Willow Creek, the *mega church* (a fancy way of saying it has thousands of members) located in suburban Chicago, the granddaddy of the seeker-sensitive movement. Proponents see this as a way to effectively present Christianity to the 21st-century person. Critics, both from liturgical and free worship traditions, say that this emphasis on attracting people waters down the true Christian message by telling people what they want to hear rather than dealing with the full written Word of God.

Incorporating Music: A Call to Musical Arms

Musical worship has become ground zero in the debate over traditional versus contemporary worship styles. Perhaps the reason that this discussion gets touchy is because music is so deeply personal and often impacts a person's spirit more than any other act of worship does.

Adding to that reality, every person who walks into a church carries with him or her certain musical preferences and experiences. A person's age is an influence on his or her likes and dislikes; at least since the 1950s, generations have been identified by their music. Individual preferences of one genre over another — such as country, rock, or classical — are a second major influence. As a result, before someone even plays the first note on an organ, electric guitar, or tambourine, the churchgoer has a natural tendency to like or dislike the music he or she is about to hear. As such, musical worship becomes much more of a subjective activity than other forms of worship.

Perhaps the greatest disagreement among churches involves musical style and the types of instruments allowed. Read on to uncover the three main stances Christians take on this issue.

Leaving out the band

Back in the days of the early Church, individual churches didn't use musical instruments — they sang everything a cappella. These Christians avoided instruments for two reasons. First, because other religions commonly used instruments for their worship, the early Christians felt that their worship should be clearly distinct from any other religious worship of their day and age. Instruments were guilty by association, so to speak. Second, these Christians considered instruments less glorifying to God than the voices of the congregation because they believed that only the human voice can adequately express the worship of one's spirit. Even to this day, most Orthodox churches and a handful of Protestant churches continue this tradition of banning instruments during worship.

Tooting a few horns

Through the centuries, as the reasons why the early Church forbid instruments seemed less relevant, Western churches gradually introduced instruments into their services, while the Orthodox churches continued without instruments. The Western Church's rationale was twofold: The Old Testament shows support for praising God through instruments, and nothing in the New Testament forbids them. As a result, people began playing the organ in medieval Catholic cathedrals, and by the 15th century, the Catholic Church widely accepted organ music as part of the service. However, instrumental music at that time was for performance (a singer singing to the congregation) and didn't involve the congregation joining in and singing along with it.

Although the Catholic Church permitted limited instrumental music during this era, the Protestant Reformation (see Chapter 11) brought about considerable change in terms of congregational singing. The "Golden Age of Hymns" began soon after the Reformation, as Protestant songwriters combined theologically rich words with organ or piano accompaniments. They wrote many

of the classic Protestant *hymns* (traditional songs of praise to God), such as *Amazing Grace* (see Chapter 3) and *Holy, Holy, Holy,* within this era. At least within the Protestant community, both liturgical and free worship churches used similar hymn-based music as part of the service.

Different Protestant groups held a growing variety of perspectives on music. Lutherans welcomed instruments (such as organs and pianos) and congregational participation, while Calvinists, like those in the early Church, avoided instruments but encouraged everyone to sing. Over time, nearly all Protestant churches began to allow instrumental music in the church, seeing it as a legitimate way to worship the Lord. And, as time went on, the Catholic Church, too, began to allow more congregational participation in musical worship.

Revolutionizing praise and worship music

During the tumultuous cultural changes of the 1960s and 1970s in North America and Europe, people in free worship churches began bringing music styles that originated outside of the Church into the sanctuary, particularly in the United States. Advocates saw this as a way to draw people into focusing on Christ without getting hung up on the barriers of tradition and "old-fashioned" music. As time went on, churches started to display song lyrics on giant screens using overhead projectors rather than using the now passé hymnals.

A musical genre known as *praise and worship music* (or simply *praise music*) was borne as a result during the late 1960s. Praise and worship music combines contemporary musical arrangements, often including guitars — even electric ones — and drums with words that express praise to the Lord. The meteoric rise of praise and worship music's popularity within Protestant churches in North America since its birth has been nothing short of spectacular. Even individual churches within liturgical denominations are moving to a more contemporary worship style using praise songs. In many evangelical churches across North America, the debate is already over — praise music rules. In fact, walk into almost any evangelical church service, and chances are high that you hear at least some praise music accompanied by a guitar, drums, and keyboards.

One of the criticisms that people often have about praise songs is that the theology the words express is weak, dumbed-down, or self-oriented (rather than God-oriented). However, praise music lovers say that plenty of contemporary songs have as much "meaty" theology packed into them as the average hymn does.

In order to cover both musical grounds, some churches provide blended worship by mixing older, traditional hymns with newer, contemporary praise songs. Their aim is to give the congregation the best of both worlds and be relevant to people of all ages and musical preferences.

Crossing Cultures with Worship

Although Christianity originated in the Mediterranean region and spread initially throughout Europe, it's a world faith that transcends cultures and ethnic groups. And while Christian worship is *transcultural,* it also makes a home in churches that are part of a given culture. Some Christians believe that Christian worship shouldn't conform to the world around it, but should retain its own distinct flavor. Many other Christians disagree; they believe that as long as the culture doesn't conflict with Christianity, Christians can use the culture to better express the purpose and meaning of worship to the people in that culture.

Take, for example, the African American church. As Protestant Christianity spread through the African American slave culture in the 19th century, African American Christians began to form their own unique form of Christian worship — combining Christian teaching with African rhythms, chanting, and *cadenced preaching* (rhythmic preaching in which the congregation frequently repeats the preacher's words). A cappella songs were an important part of African American worship as they created and sung *spirituals,* songs that had a twofold message of hope in God's salvation and their future freedom from slavery. Becoming popular within these churches, the ring shout was a West African group dance performed by shuffling around in a circle while answering a preacher's shouts with corresponding shouts from the congregation. Although many changes took place among African Americans after the Civil War, many African American churches have been able to retain a strong flavor of that unique form of Christian worship to this day.

African Americans aren't alone, of course, because other non-European cultures have also faced the tension between cultural music and values and the Christian Church's Mediterranean/European heritage. Caribbean, African, Latin, and Asian Christians have all struggled with how to best combine indigenous expression with true worship that honors God.

Some early Christian missionaries to these regions viewed local culture with suspicion and had a tendency to westernize new believers and develop indigenous churches using a western mold. Through the years, however, local churches in these areas and expatriate missionaries have done a much better job balancing indigenous cultural expression and Christian teaching to create a worship experience that's meaningful in these local churches.

See Chapter 14 for more on how Christians debate about how they should relate to the cultures around them.

Part IV

Christian Living in a Postmodern World

The 5th Wave   By Rich Tennant

"You know how you're always saying we can learn a spiritual lesson when bad things happen to us? Well, you're about to get a spiritual lesson from Herb's Towing and Collision and the Able Auto Insurance Company."

In this part . . .

In Part IV, you discover what it means to live a Christian life in this busy, ultra-modern, wireless world that you and I live in. You find out what transformation a person experiences after deciding to become a Christian. You also examine how a Christian's faith should go beyond Sunday morning and impact how he or she views life and lives from day to day.

Part IV also helps you navigate through some of the prickly issues that people bring up when considering Christianity, so put on some gloves! Building upon what I discuss in previous sections, I tell you why Christians believe God allows bad things to happen in a world he created, why "being good" isn't good enough, why some Christians seem to be hypocrites, why Christians believe that Jesus' salvation is the only way to heaven, and why Christianity isn't anti-science.

Chapter 13

I'm a Christian — Now What?

My middle son is a Tennessee Titans fan, in spite of the fact that I'm a diehard Denver Broncos nut and that we live in the heart of New England Patriots territory. Because he's vastly outnumbered on this side of the United States, my son decided last year to sign up with the Tennessee Titans Kids Club, so he could team up with like-minded youth. With the membership, he receives his official membership card, a few player posters, a calendar, and, on his birthday, a card in the mail from the team. This year, however, when he received the nonpersonalized birthday card, my son took a look and said, "Dad, that's the exact same one that I received from them last year." But, ever the optimist, he spun it into a positive, smiling, "Oh well, at least they thought of me."

Some people think that when you become a Christian, you're joining a glorified fan club. Say you go to a Christian crusade or a local church rally, hear the gospel message, and make a sincere decision to follow Jesus Christ. When you go home that night, your life looks pretty much the same as you left it, and so you carry on business as usual. Oh, to signify the change, you may add one of those fish emblems to the back of your car and buy a new Bible, but your level of commitment remains at the fan club level, because you're not sure what to do from there. Perhaps someone tries to contact you from the church or ministry, but because you're never home, you end up just getting occasional letters — and perhaps even a birthday card — from them.

A genuine decision to follow Jesus Christ, however, is much different from joining the Titans Kids Club. In fact, it's a life-changing experience! This chapter explores what exactly this transformation is and what it means to live out the Christian faith.

Experiencing Spiritual Transformation

You become a Christian when you accept God's gift of grace and make a conscious and deliberate choice to believe in Jesus Christ. (See Chapter 3 to find out how all this works.)

When you become a Christian, something changes inside of you. It's not like signing up with a guild or having an intellectual change of perspective, but it's something far deeper and significant. This transformation that a new Christian experiences occurs on two levels:

✔ **New spiritual genetics:** As I discuss in Chapter 4, Christians believe that sin ruins the spiritual DNA of everyone who walks on the face of the earth. Therefore, when you become a Christian, God gets rid of that old sin-laden DNA crapola and gives you new spiritual genetics, so to speak. Your spiritual heritage is forever changed as you're now considered born of God (John 1:13) through your rebirth by the Holy Spirit (Titus 3:5). Paul even calls a Christian a "new creation" (2 Corinthians 5:17) and a "new self" (Ephesians 4:23).

This new spiritual heritage isn't based on how good or bad a person is before he chooses to become a Christian. In fact, it doesn't matter whether the person seemed like a saint or a devil before making the decision. God wipes *all* sins away — few or many — as part of his free gift of grace.

✔ **Indwelling of the Holy Spirit:** Not only are you a new creation, but in some mysterious and unexplainable way, the Holy Spirit lives inside of you as well (Galatians 2:20, Colossians 1:27, John 14:16–17). You still have a sin nature (Romans 7:18), but you've also acquired something new — the indwelling of the Lord. Therefore, because the Spirit is living inside of you, you now have the power to not allow your sin nature to control you anymore (Romans 8:9). The reality of Christ's presence in the lives of Christians is what prompted Paul to write, "I have been crucified with Christ and I no longer live, but Christ lives in me" (Galatians 2:20).

This spiritual transformation that occurs in the life of a new Christian isn't just mere symbolism or a feel-good metaphor. On the contrary, Christians believe it's real — as literal as a heart transplant is to a child with a deformed heart.

For many people, the decision to become a Christian is an emotional one and leaves them on a spiritual high for days or even weeks. But don't confuse the real changes that occur inside of a Christian with the passing emotions. The inner change of a new believer may or may not be a touchy-feely experience; every person is different. The danger is when a person links emotional feelings with his newfound Christian faith and comes to think of the Christian life as one big emotional high. If so, when the high goes away, he questions whether anything really happened to him at all. When this happens, he may think of his conversion experience as nothing more than a passing phase.

Fellowshipping with a Church

I recently came across an interview of a Hollywood star who said that, although he was a Christian, he never went to church. Because faith is a private matter, he reasoned, he doesn't believe that a Christian needs to be involved with other believers. Within a society that celebrates self and promotes individual expression, it's not surprising that this belief is quite commonplace.

Considering why biblical Christianity says church is necessary

This individualistic thinking is the norm today, but it's not authentic biblical Christianity. St. Augustine wrote, "He cannot have God for his father who does not have the Church for his mother." Many Christian thinkers agree, saying that Christianity doesn't even *exist* apart from the Church. This perspective isn't surprising coming from the Catholic and Orthodox Churches, given the relatively strong role the Church plays in Catholic and Orthodox Christians' lives (see Chapters 8 and 10). Yet, Protestants, who reject any role that the Church as an institution plays in personal salvation, agree as well. For though salvation is between an individual and God, a key part of living out the Christian faith is being involved in a church home.

If you're skeptical, take a read through the Bible — church involvement is a given. Jesus certainly worshiped regularly with others (see Luke 4:16), and Hebrews 10:24–25 emphasizes the importance of participating in a church:

> *Let us consider how to spur one another to love and good works, not giving up on our meetings together, as the custom of some is, but exhorting and encouraging one another.*

In fact, when you take the New Testament as a whole, you easily see that neither Jesus nor any of the apostles envisioned a stand-alone faith, much less spoke about it.

Consider the following parallel, which sheds some light on the importance of the Church in a Christian's life. Imagine, for example, you're an orphan who's adopted into a new family. Your primary relationship is with your new parents, but because you live in a family environment, you still live day-in, day-out with your new siblings. (That is, unless you're part of some twisted new reality TV series.) You won't set up shop in private rooms and live completely apart from each other. No, you develop your relationship with your parents at the same time you develop them with your brothers and sisters. In the same way, although Christianity centers on a personal relationship with God, it involves more than that. When someone becomes a new Christian, he's immediately part of a new community, the Family of God. As such, a vital part of a Christian's life is getting hooked up in that community.

Although Christians believe that worshiping together regularly is important (see Chapter 12 to find out why), the New Testament model of a church is more than a group of people meeting together for an hour on Saturday night or Sunday morning in which they file in quietly, stand up, sit down, stand up, sit down, stand up, and then head for the exits. Instead, the biblical concept of a church involves *koinonia,* a Greek word that literally means "communion together in God's grace" or simply "fellowship." Biblical Christianity says that God designed Christians with the need for fellowship to be able to grow in their faith. Therefore, when Christians meet together, they are to

- ✔ Love one another, being bound in unity (Colossians 3:14)
- ✔ Provide opportunities to serve one another (John 13:14)
- ✔ Bear one another's burdens (Colossians 3:13)
- ✔ Encourage each other (Hebrews 3:13, 1 Thessalonians 4:18)
- ✔ Be accountable to each other (Proverbs 27:17)
- ✔ Challenge each other (2 Timothy 2:42)

Obviously, if you go to a large church, it's not possible to talk with every person in your congregation. That's why meeting together in small groups with other Christians is so critical, whether that interaction is in a Bible study, a home group, Sunday school, or an accountability group.

See Chapters 10 and 11 for more on the differences among the various Christian churches. Chapter 10 deals with Catholic and Orthodox beliefs, and Chapter 11 focuses on Protestant beliefs.

Finding a church that you can call home

Although you may understand the need to go to church, you may run into barriers to actually finding a church that you want to join. Perhaps the church you attend is so large that it's hard to feel accepted or needed. Maybe the service is so dry that you feel like you get a windburn every time you enter the church doors. Or perhaps your hypocritical neighbor goes there and speaks about how godly his life is, making you want to have one of those bags handy that you find in the backs of plane seats.

On the one hand, it's important to remember that no church is perfect. Although the Church is the Body of Christ, it also is filled with sinners. So you're always going to come up with an excuse as to why you shouldn't go to a particular church (except the church I attend, of course, which may be the only perfect church out there). In spite of that, it's important to find a good church that you feel at home in.

Some tips to keep in mind as you look for a church home are

✔ **Know where you stand.** As you read through this book, you see that Christians have many differences of opinion on certain aspects of the faith. The most obvious ones are those differences between Protestant, Catholic, and Orthodox Christians. Therefore, as you begin to better understand these issues, you need to come to a personal decision on which strand of the Christian faith best expresses what you believe is true.

✔ **Be wary of labels.** If you read the Introduction to this book, you know that Christian churches have an amazing number of different names. And if you try to understand all the subtle differences among them, your mind will quickly turn to mush. For example, do you think the average church-goer knows the differences between the Christian Reformed Church, the Orthodox Christian Reformed Church, the United Reformed Church, and the Reformed Church of the United States? No way, Hosea. In fact, I think you'd have to go to "reformed" school just to figure that out!

Moreover, even if you got a PhD in Christian Labelology, sometimes the label of an individual church is quite misleading. For example, the beliefs of a United Methodist church in Indiana may be altogether different from the beliefs of a United Methodist church in Massachusetts. Or, take Catholic churches — most are traditional Catholic, but some are more evangelical in nature, and some are even charismatic. Further, Vineyard churches vary wildly in their worship approach. Some are heavy-duty charismatic churches, yet others are mainstream evangelical. (For more on what the terms *charismatic* and *evangelical* mean, see Chapter 11.)

Therefore, although a label is often a good guideline, never assume. Make sure you check out the particular church in question.

✔ **Dive into the doctrine of the church.** Although it's easy to assume that all Christian churches are basically the same, just as with worship styles, that's unfortunately not the case. As you decide on a church to attend, be sure to check into the church's doctrine (what the church actually teaches and believes apart from any denominational label they may have outside the door). Ask a church leader for the church's confession of faith (also called a *catechism* or statement of faith), which is usually available in printed form, and inquire as to how much the church pays attention to it. You can also check out the church's Web site, as more and more churches are providing a listing of core beliefs easily accessible via the Internet.

If you're concerned about finding a church that adheres to "mere Christianity," two of the most important ideas to pay attention to are

• **View of the Bible:** Does the church consider the Bible to be the inspired, authoritative Word of God? Some churches hold to the inspiration and inerrancy of the Bible, but others don't consider the Bible to be God's perfect truth (see Chapter 6).

- **View of Jesus Christ:** Does the church believe Jesus was simply a good moral teacher or does it say he was literally God in the flesh? Although Jesus' divinity is a basic foundation of biblical Christianity, a few churches consider themselves Christian that don't hold to that perspective. (See Chapters 5 and 7 for more on Jesus Christ.)

If you seek a biblical, historical Christian faith, then these two issues are key factors in your overall decision-making process. In other words, make sure the church that you attend considers the Bible the complete, final, and authoritative written Word of God and considers Jesus both fully God and fully man. Biblical Christianity falls apart at the seams when these doctrines are compromised.

✔ **Be in synch with the worship style.** As I discuss in Chapter 12, churches today have a wide variety of worship and music styles. Some churches are throwbacks to the first-century Church, others are very ceremonial, a growing number of churches are contemporary, and a few have services that resemble a professional performance — complete with a rock band with electric guitars, drums, and a synthesizer. Make sure that you can worship and give honor to the Lord with whatever worship style that the church features.

✔ **Make sure you're challenged.** I've been in churches where the preaching was as bland as leftover white bread or a "feel good" message pumped up the congregation. However, neither of these, on a consistent basis, satisfies the desire in a person's heart to be fed spiritually. Therefore, make sure that you believe you're challenged by the teaching at the church, whether that's during the main weekly service, a Bible study, or Sunday school. When other Christians regularly challenge you and push you to dive deeper, you grow in your faith.

✔ **Get a sense of the church's spirit.** When you walk through the doors of a church, you often get a good feel for whether the congregation as a whole is earnestly seeking to love God and to serve him. Regardless of whether a church has a liturgical or contemporary worship style, you should sense whether the church is "alive" or whether it's simply going through the motions. You can usually get a strong sense of the church's spirit just by observing how people are worshiping or listening to the minister. Also, when you enter and exit the church, pay attention to whether the church has a spirit of outgoing friendliness or whether people keep to themselves. Finally, look at whether or not the church has a strong missions and outreach program to live out Christ's command of the Great Commission (see Chapter 19).

✔ **Visit multiple times.** Unless you discover a major red flag in the church's beliefs or teachings, don't try to make your decision in one or two visits. You should generally attend at least six times to get a good understanding of what the church is like.

Going One-on-One with the Lord

The other essential component to the Christian life is a growing one-on-one relationship with the Lord. Developing an intimate relationship with God doesn't involve science. Just as in a marriage, you don't assemble it with a do-it-yourself kit.

A common ingredient in the lives of mature Christians is a private, daily encounter with God, often called a *quiet time* (or *devotional time*). Quiet time consists of anywhere from a few minutes to an hour of Bible reading and prayer. These two activities help you develop your relationship with the Lord:

✔ **Reading the Bible:** As I discuss in Chapter 6, there's no better way to get to know God and his will than by diving into the Bible. With a solid grounding in what the Bible says, you can use its teaching as a foundation in your life that you can turn to in times of temptation and trouble.

In addition to the Bible, many Christians read *devotional* books, which have daily readings that Christians often use as a supplement to their Bible reading, enabling them to meditate and reflect on some aspect of God's truth and apply it to their own lives. One popular devotional is *My Utmost for His Highest.* (See the corresponding sidebar in this chapter.) You can find it and others in a Christian bookstore or online at www.gospelcom.net/rbc/utmost.

✔ **Praying:** Praying is simply communicating with God, talking with him one-on-one, just like you do with a spouse or best friend. Through prayer, you worship God, surrender to him, and ask for his help and provision for your life and for others' lives.

Paul calls Christians to 24/7 prayer, or "praying without ceasing," as he talks about in 1 Thessalonians 5:17. This doesn't mean that you lock up your house and pray in your closet around the clock. But what it does mean is that you have dedicated prayer time at some point of the day (for many, morning works best, because it sets the tone for the day) and then pray little sound bites throughout the day, keeping the lines of communication constantly open with God. In this way, prayer is similar to a healthy marital relationship, which has a good balance between in-depth heart-felt discussion as well as chitchat on the practical matters of the day.

If you want to explore more about what prayer is, how you do it, and how it transforms your Christian walk, I recommend checking out another book I've written, called *Christian Prayer For Dummies* (Wiley).

How do I pray?

If you don't know how to pray, just do it in your own way — go somewhere quiet and begin talking to God, out loud or inside your head. Jesus never laid out specific techniques or rules for praying; he left that up to you. As he talked about in the Lord's Prayer (see Chapter 19), the most important idea is that your prayer is from the heart.

However, prayer is more than just reading off a wish list to Santa Claus. Prayer should involve worshiping and thanking him, confessing your sins, and asking for God's help to meet your needs and others' needs. Sometimes, all those parts are hard to remember, so one of the popular techniques that helps you organize your prayers is the ACTS method. *ACTS* stands for adoration, confession, thanksgiving, and *supplication* (a term that simply means praying for your needs and for others around you). The basic gist of this method is to do the following in order:

✔ **Adoration:** Start off by adoring God and worshiping him.

✔ **Confession:** Prepare your heart by confessing your sins.

✔ **Thanksgiving:** Thank the Lord for all that he's done in your life.

✔ **Supplication:** Ask God for his help in meeting the needs and concerns of those in your family, church, friends, leaders, any others you may think of, and yourself.

Keep in mind, however, that prayer is more than just a one-way conversation with God in which you do all the talking and he does all the listening. Prayer also involves simply being still and listening for God — not that he's going to speak to you audibly, but through prayerful stillness and silence, the Holy Spirit does "speak" to a Christian's spirit in unmistakable ways.

A must-read: *My Utmost for His Highest*

Written by Scottish pastor and missionary Oswald Chambers, *My Utmost for His Highest* (Barbour and Co., 2003) is a timeless Christian devotional first published in 1935 and remains a continual Christian bestseller with millions of copies in print. Hundreds of devotionals are available, but what separates Chamber's work from the pack, though, is its uncanny ability to mix deep, thought-provoking teaching with a practical message — all in a single page devotion. It's direct and to-the-point, but it's always challenging.

Incidentally, if you ever want to learn more about the man behind *My Utmost for His Highest,* check out David McCasland's *Oswald Chambers: Abandoned to God* (Barbour and Co., 1999). This biography illustrates how Chambers truly practiced what he preached. In my opinion, Chambers is one of the best models of the Christian life that I've ever seen.

Being a Disciple

The decision to become a Christian — to accept Jesus as your savior (see Chapter 3) — is a key milestone. But this step is really the beginning of a lifetime journey, not the end point. A second step is to make Christ the Lord of your life, surrendering everything in your life to him. A Christian who takes this step of obedience is often called a *disciple*, which means a follower of Christ. Disciples understand that they've been "crucified with Christ," so to speak. As a result, they no longer live for their own selfish wants and needs, but live in obedience to Christ instead (Galatians 2:20).

The original 12 disciples provide a great model of what a modern-day disciple should be. They weren't perfect people by any stretch of the imagination, but each of them gave up creature comforts, his vocation, and personal safety to follow Jesus. They took these bold actions simply because Jesus called them to follow him. What's more, they persevered in their faith as the years went by, reaching out to the world and sharing the Good News of Jesus Christ.

When Christians today follow their example, some of them feel called by God to become ministers or missionaries (see the "Sending out missionaries to evangelize the world" sidebar), while other disciples believe they're called to do God's work and be Christ's servants through their normal, everyday jobs.

How much do I have to give?

Tithing is the Old Testament practice of giving ten percent of one's income or possessions to God as an offering to him. The Old Testament discusses it several times, including in Genesis 14:17–20, Leviticus 27:30–32, and Numbers 18:21–32. This offering was also supposed to be the "first fruits" (see Ezekiel 44:29–30) of one's income or possessions, not just the leftovers.

Many Christians today continue the practice of tithing ten percent of their income, even though the New Testament never specifically commands them to tithe a specific amount or percentage. Instead, Paul gives more general instructions to live by:

✔ "Let each man give according as he has determined in his heart; not grudgingly, or under compulsion; for God loves a cheerful giver" (2 Corinthians 9:7).

✔ "On the first day of the week, let each one of you save, as he may prosper . . ." (1 Corinthians 16:2).

Although the New Testament doesn't specify a fixed percentage, that fact doesn't mean that Christians get off easy and can give peanuts. Instead, consider Jesus' response in Mark 8:34, when he says that those who follow him will give up everything for him, not just part of themselves. Therefore, when it comes to finances, Christians should consider *all* their money and property to be God's, not just ten percent of it. Christians are, therefore, called to be stewards of all that God has provided (see Romans 14:12; 1 Corinthians 16:1–3; 2 Corinthians 8:1–9:15) and to give God what he leads them to give, whether it's a little or a lot.

Still, the fact is that many people make honest, deliberate decisions to be Christians, but hold out on wanting Christ to be Lord of their lives. But when Christians do this, they end up being lukewarm believers with one foot in heaven and one foot in the world, so to speak. John Stuart Mill, a 19th-century political philosopher and skeptic, sums up well the sad state of lukewarm Christians:

> *All Christians believe that the blessed are the poor and humble; that it is easier for a camel to pass through the eye of a needle than for a rich man to enter the kingdom of heaven; that they shouldn't judge, or else they'll be judged; that they shouldn't swear; that they should love their neighbors as themselves . . . that they should focus on today and not worry about tomorrow . . . They are not insincere when they say that they believe these things. They do believe them, as people believe what they have always heard lauded and never discussed. **But in the sense of that living belief which regulates conduct, they believe these doctrines just up to the point to which it is usual to act upon them.***

> —William Ebenstein, *Great Political Thinkers,*
> (Holt, Rinehart, and Winston, 1951)

As convenient as the lukewarm plan might be, Jesus didn't hold this out as an option. He made it clear that everyone who follows him must first take his or her personal agenda and selfish wants and get rid of them. Or, as Jesus said, "If any man would come after me, let him deny himself, and take up his cross, and follow me" (Mark 8:34). He added, "Whoever loses his life for my sake will find it" (Matthew 10:39).

Sending out missionaries to evangelize the world

Before he ascended into heaven, Christ's last words told his followers to go and make disciples of all nations, baptizing them in the name of the Father and of the Son and of the Holy Spirit, and teaching people to obey everything he commanded (see Matthew 28:19; flip to Chapter 19 for more on this *Great Commission*). The apostles responded to this charge by spreading out over the entire Mediterranean region, proclaiming the gospel of Jesus Christ and establishing the Christian Church. Following their lead, the Church, through the centuries, has carried on the Great Commission by sharing the Christian message with people both locally and far away (a process known as *evangelization*) and by meeting people's physical and emotional needs in the process.

People usually think of a missionary as a person who travels to a far-off land to talk to people about Jesus Christ who've never heard of him. Although that's true, the term *missionary* refers more generally to any Christian, no matter where she lives, who simply shares the Christian gospel with others and helps those in need. In that sense, all Christians are called to be missionaries.

A must-read: *The Cost of Discipleship*

Apart from the Bible, I think that no book is as meaty or as significant for Christians as Dietrich Bonhoeffer's *The Cost of Discipleship*. As a pastor in Nazi Germany during the 1930s, Bonhoeffer wrote his greatest work in the midst of the German Church's giving in to Hitler. In this book, the German pastor shows the difference between cheap grace and costly grace. Common in his day and ours, *cheap grace* is all talk, no action. On the other hand, *costly grace* is costly because it calls us to follow Jesus Christ, and it is costly because it cost a man (Jesus) his life.

The Cost of Discipleship is a must-read for those who live comfortable lives and aren't forced to make any big sacrifices (such as their lives) to be Christians in this 21st century. If you want to more deeply understand the true nature of biblical Christianity and what it means to follow Jesus, read Bonhoeffer's book.

That's heavy stuff. When you read these statements, it's very easy to want to water down the commands or dismiss them as being ideals that are reserved for true saints, such as Billy Graham or Mother Teresa. The last thing you and I often want to do is to actually take these commands literally. But Dietrich Bonhoeffer, a martyred pastor in Nazi Germany (see Chapter 18), once put Jesus' call in terms that you can't simply ignore: "When Christ calls a man, he bids him, 'Come and die.'" (See the sidebar, "A must-read: *The Cost of Discipleship*," in this chapter.) "Dying to self" then means gathering up every part of you — relationships, finances, career, ambitions, and hobbies — and giving it to Christ. (See the "How much do I have to give?" sidebar in this chapter.)

Jesus isn't just being a meanie when he asks Christians to take this step. His reasoning is actually very practical — you're only able to follow Christ and do his will if you're dead to yours, because humans' tendency to sin (see Chapter 4) directly contradicts God's will. If you try to keep your own agenda and follow Christ, you constantly have mixed agendas, resulting in lukewarmness.

Living Out Your Faith

As you discover in Chapter 3, Christians believe that faith in Jesus Christ is an essential component in an individual's salvation. However, Christians express their faith in two ways: *Saving faith* is the belief that accompanies repentance and salvation, and *living faith* is the process of living out that belief. They aren't two separate types of faith, but the latter is a progression or a maturity of saving faith. Said differently, saving faith gives birth to living faith.

Unfortunately, *faith* is one of those overused terms in the English language, meaning a variety of ideas. A person is said to have faith in himself or herself. A team down by five touchdowns isn't supposed to ever lose faith during its comeback attempt. My wife has faith that I'll help out with the laundry.

In some people's eyes then, faith is nothing more than a positive mental state. Or, as one skeptic put it, faith is the "illogical belief in the occurrence of the impossible."

Authentic Christian faith, however, should *not* be confused with

- **Head-in-the-sand optimism:** Ignoring reality and simply hoping everything will be alright.

- **A forced "I hope so":** Muttering some positive-sounding words but being pessimistic inside.

- **A psyched-out feeling:** Pumping oneself up to get an emotional high.

- **Superstition:** Believing something that's contrary to all the evidence.

- **Intellectual acknowledgement:** Thinking that faith is simply a matter of brainpower. (At the same time, reason does play a role in coming to faith, as I discuss in Chapter 2.)

On the contrary, Christian faith is a confident obedience to God, no matter the circumstances or consequences. True faith isn't blind or without merit, but it's a natural response to what God has revealed in the Bible — that he is who he says he is and will do what he promised to do (Romans 10:17). Ultimately, faith requires trusting in what you can't see in front of you; if you could see it and hold it in your hands, it wouldn't very well be faith, now would it?

Seeing why faith is fundamental for a Christian

Christians believe that God's primary purpose in their lives is for them to live by faith. When Christians live by faith, they focus on doing what God wants — fulfilling the Great Commission, worshiping him, and staying away from sin.

Living by faith is easy when times are going good, but it's much harder when circumstances are uncertain. And, unfortunately, God doesn't always tell all of the answers as much as you and I would often like him to. The reason for that isn't because he overlooks them or because he's trying to make life hard. Rather, Christians believe that he does this because he wants people to trust in and rely on him more and more, which happens when they live by faith.

Living lives of faith must somehow produce the sort of people whom God wants to be with for eternity. If being a Christian required no faith, the Church would be a bunch of smug know-it-alls who made their decisions much like they solve math problems. But such a rationalization doesn't involve a change of character or inner transformation. Instead, living by faith forces Christians to rely on God, forget about themselves, serve others, and ultimately become more and more like Christ in how they live their lives. In other words, faith is the foundation for the Christian walk.

Clutching four keys to living out your faith

Hebrews 11 is a chapter that focuses entirely on faith and offers insights on how exactly to live out your faith. (Mosey on over to Chapter 19 for more on this key passage of scripture.) This chapter is often called the Hall of Faith, because of its focus on highlighting the faith of some of the great Old Testament believers. When you read through the chapter, you discover the many ways that its subjects expressed their faith and you further get a grasp on what living by faith means. The chapter starts with a simple definition: "Now faith is the assurance of things hoped for, the evidence of things not seen."

You can discover four keys to living out the Christian faith from this single verse. I discuss these in the sections that follow.

Cling to what the Bible says is true about God

According to Hebrews 1:1, faith is the *assurance* of things hoped for. The Greek word for *assurance* is the same as *foundation*, much like the foundation of a house. Therefore, this assurance is at the base of the Christian life, centered on who they believe God is. Perhaps nowhere does the Bible express this assurance more clearly than in the account of the Roman centurion (a military commander) in Matthew 8:5–13:

> When Jesus came into Capernaum, a centurion came to him, asking him, and saying, "Lord, my servant lies in the house paralyzed, grievously tormented." Jesus said to him, "I will come and heal him."

> The centurion answered, "Lord, I'm not worthy for you to come under my roof. Just say the word, and my servant will be healed. For I am also a man under authority, having under myself soldiers. I tell this one, 'Go,' and he goes; and tell another, 'Come,' and he comes; and tell my servant, 'Do this,' and he does it."

> When Jesus heard it, he marveled, and said to those who followed, "Most certainly I tell you, I haven't found so great a faith, not even in Israel. . . ." Jesus said to the centurion, "Go your way. Let it be done for you as you have believed." His servant was healed in that hour.

The centurion's matter-of-fact nature reveals his inner assurance. He knew that all Christ had to do was say the words and the disease would obey him — in the same way that the centurion's soldiers obeyed the centurion.

Christians believe that Jesus calls each of them to have that same faith in him. But the reality is that although most Christians do a reasonable job of trusting God for all that life-after-death business, they act no different from nonbelievers on matters that hit closer to home during times of crises.

Focus your attention completely on God

According to Hebrews 11:1, *faith* is certainty in things hoped for and things not seen. By definition, then, these things are those you don't see, touch, or feel — the spiritual world, future events, and God's sovereignty and control. Hebrews also implies that they will happen in the future. In spite of this, Christians believe that they're every bit as real as the physical world in front of you.

The way that you stay focused on these future hopes is by wearing blinders. Blinders are those funny-looking black contraptions that you see on the heads of some horses; they prevent the horses from being distracted or scared or from drifting off their paths. In the same way, when you wear blinders, you focus your attention on God and don't become distracted with the possibilities, consequences, and circumstances around you.

Don't confuse this faith with head-in-the-sand thinking. Blinders don't *cover* the eyes of the horses but *focus* their eyes on the destination. Therefore, true biblical faith isn't blind faith, but faith that's focused entirely on God.

Noah was a man who demonstrated this type of faith. Imagine being called by God to spend decades building a single boat. It takes a lot of faith to spend years and years doing the same thing before seeing how it all works out. But Noah's situation was even harder than that. You see, prior to the Flood, the Bible says that it never rained on earth. Therefore, Noah built a boat on dry land in a world that never had any rain. Obviously, his neighbors probably teased him for thousands of days over this folly. Yet, through it all, Noah held firm and did what God told him to do. Hebrews 11:7 says:

> By faith, Noah, being warned about things not yet seen, moved with godly fear, prepared an ark for the saving of his house, through which he condemned the world, and became heir of the righteousness which is according to faith.

Noah required no evidence of what was to come. It was a matter of simple trust and obedience. (For the whole story, check out Genesis 6–9.)

Abraham was another man in the Old Testament who lived his life with spiritual blinders on. He left his home without knowing where he was going

(Genesis 12:1–4, Hebrews 11:8), giving up security for insecurity. But he also lived like a nomad by faith, relying on God on an ongoing basis for his needs (Genesis 12, Hebrews 11:9). In addition, God challenged Abraham's faithfulness by testing his willingness to sacrifice his son, Isaac, his only link to God's promise that Abraham would be the father of many nations (Genesis 15, Hebrews 11:17–19). Abraham passed that test with flying colors, because he was certain that God would keep his promise, even if that meant bringing Isaac back to life.

Check out Table 13-1 to find out more about these heroes of the faith, as well as others.

Never ever stop walking

When you're walking in faith, you shouldn't be like a kid on a car trip — always saying, "Are we there yet?" God calls Christians to persevere whether they see him working or not. Shadrach, Meshach, and Abednego are three examples of people who were faithful regardless of circumstances. King Nebuchadnezzar was about to throw the trio into a fiery furnace for refusing to bow down to the gods he worshiped when they said to him:

> *If we are thrown into the blazing furnace, the God we serve is able to save us from it, and he will rescue us from your hand, O king. But even if he does not, we want you to know, O king, that we will not serve your gods or worship the image of gold you have set up.*

> —Daniel 3:17–18

Job set another prime example of faithfulness. When literally everything was going wrong in his life, he didn't whine and say, "Why me?" Instead, he said, "Though he slay me, yet will I hope in him" (Job 13:15). Not that God was actually out to get Job, but Job was saying that regardless of what happened, he would hope in the Lord.

Leave foot tracks of your Christian walk

Hebrews 11:1 talks about faith as having evidence of things not seen. But consider a different spin on the word *evidence*. When you look at the lives of people who have great faith, you always see evidence of their faith in their lives. Both Noah and Abraham, for example, left foot tracks showing their walks of faith. Noah's ark was tangible evidence of his assurance. Abraham's risky life of adventure served as proof of what he knew to be true.

Therefore, in your Christian walk, look to see what evidence you're leaving that practically demonstrates what you believe to be true. Take stock of where you are by asking yourself:

✔ Would someone around me find any proof of my faith in how I make decisions or in how I act?

✔ Have I ever gone out on a limb to follow God in regard to any specific decisions or situations in my life, without knowing how it would all turn out?

✔ Do I trust God even when it seems like he's not nearby?

After you've assessed where you are, prayerfully consider how you can show more evidence of your faith in your Christian walk.

Table 13-1	How Old Testament Believers Lived Out Their Faith	
Hall of Faith Member	**How That Person Expressed His or Her Faith**	**In This Example, Living by Faith Means . . .**
Abel	Offered a sacrifice by faith	Bringing honor to God
Enoch	Pleased God	Producing righteousness
Noah	Built an ark	Consistently following God's call no matter what the odds are
Abraham	Left his home without knowing where he was going	Giving up security and doing whatever God asks
	Lived like a nomad by faith	
	Prepared to sacrifice his son	
	Relied on God continually	
Sarah	Had a child when barren	Knowing God is faithful and trustworthy
Moses' parents	Hid Moses from authorities	Having certainty of God's hand in the events of this world
Moses	Refused to be known as the son of the Pharaoh	Risking a life of ease and comfort for a life of hardship
Israelites	Passed through the Red Sea as if it were dry land	Knowing God can perform miracles in the world
Faithful ones	Faithful without seeing the promises that God gave them	Persevering no matter what the results are

Boosting your faith in three (kind of) easy steps

If you want to strengthen your faith and be practical about it, consider the following three steps:

1. **Determine whether God and the Bible are trustworthy.**

   Your first step is to get your head in the game by ensuring that you trust God's Word as the Bible expresses it. If you don't trust the Bible as the authentic, authoritative Word of God, then you'll never truly be able to walk in assurance.

   But don't just act as if you think it's true. *Know* it's true. Put the Bible to the test. Investigate the reasons why Christians claim the Bible is inspired, reliable, and inerrant. Does it stand up to scrutiny? If not, then assurance is pointless. But if so, then God is trustworthy, and he is who he says he is.

   For more on the reliability of the Bible, see Chapters 2 and 6.

2. **Look at what God did in the past.**

   Even after you believe in your head that God is trustworthy, it takes a while before you have that inner assurance in your heart. Therefore, to jump-start your heart, write stuff down as you see God working in your life — be the situation big or small. Put it in your journal, blog it on the Web, or write it in the freshly poured cement of your neighbor's driveway. Just do something to remember it.

   Remembering is a critical step in growing in your faith, because Christians so easily get spiritual amnesia in times of crisis. If you record them, you can fall back on your past experiences when you have times of doubt and use them to reinforce your assurance and trust in God.

   The importance of remembering is a common theme of the Old Testament. In order to strengthen their faith, the Lord kept drilling into the Israelites what he did for them in days past. Consider a sampling of verses from the Book of Deuteronomy:

   • "Remember that you were slaves in Egypt and that the Lord your God brought you out of there with a mighty hand and an outstretched arm" (5:15).

   • "But do not be afraid of them; remember well what the Lord your God did to Pharaoh and to all Egypt" (7:18).

   • "Remember how the Lord your God led you all the way in the desert these forty years" (8:2).

   • "Remember that you were slaves in Egypt and the Lord your God redeemed you" (15:15).

- "Remember what the Lord your God did to Miriam along the way after you came out of Egypt" (24:9).

- "Remember the days of old; consider the generations long past" (32:7).

3. **Consider God's character and trust him.**

   Remembering past experiences of God's work is something like spiritual milk for newbies. But at some point in their lives, Christians should mature to spiritual solid foods and be able to walk in confidence, not so much because of what they see God doing, but purely because of their assurance in his character.

Taking on a Christian Worldview

My boys love cannonballs. Not the round spheres that you fire from a cannon, but the kind you do in a swimming pool — jumping into the water curled up like a ball to make a big splash. On a recent vacation, my boys and I were having a cannonball contest in a hotel pool that we had all to ourselves. However, after a few minutes of splashing sensations, a mother and her toddler came into the pool as well. I assumed my boys would've taken the cue and suspended the contest, but I was wrong. My youngest son saw the others but was somehow oblivious to the fact that his splashing might get bystanders wet. He proceeded to do yet another prize-winning cannonball splash within the general proximity of the now freshly soaked duo. In his zeal, my son didn't realize the ripple effect that his splash would have on people surrounding him.

Much like the splash from my son's cannonball, a Christian worldview has a ripple effect that reaches out and affects all areas of a Christian's life.

Viewing the ripple effect of worldviews

Think of a worldview as a series of three concentric circles, such as the one shown in Figure 13-1. Each of the circles are interrelated:

- ✔ **Inner circle (authority):** In the center of your life is some sort of authority, the one you hand the keys over to to make the calls on everything. This authority is God, society, another person, you, or some combination of these. People who believe in some concept of God give some or all of the control to that God. People who don't believe in any supernatural being (called *naturalists*) take it all on themselves or, as is more often the case, split the duties between society and themselves.

- ✔ **Middle circle (facts and values):** The decision maker(s) from the inner circle determines *facts* (what's fact and what's fiction) and *values* (what's right and what's wrong). A Christian believes that God is the authority of

both facts (based on the reality that he started everything in the first place) and values (as he revealed in the Bible). On the other hand, a naturalist often defers questions of fact to science, but when it comes to values, the decisions are personal or are based on what's good for society as a whole.

✔ **Outer circle (world around you):** The two inner circles tend to be assumptions that you actually put into practice in the outer circle. Think of this layer as the place that you actually live. You interact with nature and other people and live with your problems and dreams. But again, the assumptions that you make in the inner circles dictate your understanding of reality in the world around you. A naturalist, believing that no higher power exists, makes decisions and value judgments that are very different from someone who believes in a Creator God who's involved with his creation.

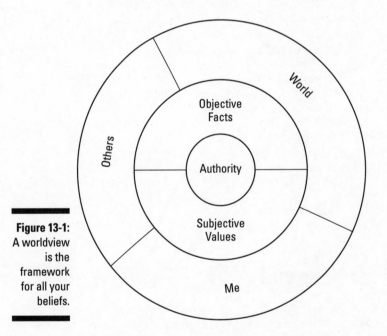

Figure 13-1:
A worldview
is the
framework
for all your
beliefs.

A worldview also provides a framework that enables you to ask the key questions of life. As shown in Figure 13-2, the answers to the questions in each of the circles affect the answers in the layers outside of it.

Finally, a worldview encompasses all fields and disciplines of study, as shown in Figure 13-3. The reason is that when you look at disciplines in the outer circle, you see that you can't consider them apart from the innermost circles; the core has the most authority in your life and affects the angle at which you approach all the other disciplines. Take the following examples:

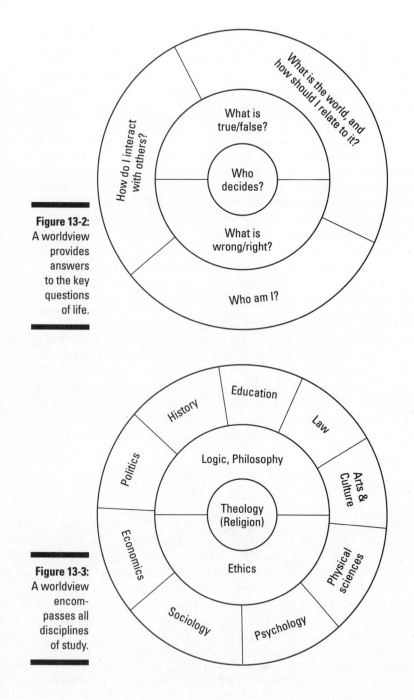

Figure 13-2:
A worldview
provides
answers
to the key
questions
of life.

Figure 13-3:
A worldview
encom-
passes all
disciplines
of study.

✔ **Education:** When you look at education from a worldview perspective, the very idea of a "value-free" education doesn't make sense. All education is influenced in some shape or form by values. These values may be based on a naturalist, Christian, or Hindu worldview, but they're values nonetheless. Education is a field that you can't pursue in a vacuum, because you always have an underlying authority that helps you make education decisions and determine the ethics of education.

✔ **Science:** Scientists often tout their discipline as being separate from religion, but even scientific theories have underlying religious assumptions. If, for example, a scientist is a naturalist, then she has already made the call that God doesn't exist (which is, by definition, a religious, not a scientific, question). This assumption then impacts her science, forcing her to come up with theories, such as evolution, that explain how a godless world came into existence. (Turn to Chapter 16 for more on Christianity and science.)

✔ **Entertainment:** Even the entertainment you watch has an underlying worldview, whether you realize it or not. Consider the underlying assumptions of three recent blockbuster films. Although *X-Men* is fantasy fare, the film has an underlying worldview that assumes evolution as fact. *Castaway* doesn't deal with evolution, but it does have an unstated worldview that ignores God, treating him as a non-factor during times of trouble. As a result, the shipwrecked main character, played by Tom Hanks, must solve his own problem and not turn to God for help. In contrast, *Signs* has a worldview that suggests that nothing is an accident and that a God does exist who engineers circumstances in this world.

Although not every song, TV show, or film has an explicitly stated worldview, look for the unspoken assumptions that undergird the story or song.

Looking at the Christian worldview

When his cosmic battle came to an end, the heavens shook, the stars were near to falling, the sun was darkened for a time, stones were split open, and the world might well have perished, but Christ gave up His soul — Father, into thy hands I commend my spirit. And then, when He ascended, His divine spirit gave life and strength to the tottering world, and the whole universe became stable once more, as if the stretching out, the agony of the Cross, had in some way gotten into everything.

—St. Hippolytus, martyr and saint

A Christian worldview puts God at the center of everything as the ultimate and sole authority. He's the foundation of all facts (because he created reason) and value judgments (because right always lines up with his nature, and wrong always goes against it). Because a worldview impacts every part of life, the Christian's understanding of God proceeds to have a ripple effect through each and every field:

✔ **Theology:** God is the Father, Son, and Holy Spirit as expressed in the Bible (see Chapter 7).

✔ **Logic and philosophy:** A supernatural God created reason and fact.

✔ **Ethics:** Absolute values based on his nature and independent of circumstances do exist.

✔ **Physical sciences:** God created the world and the systems that keep it running.

✔ **Psychology:** People are created with a need for God but are also sinful. Positive and negative emotional and mental issues arise based on how people handle their built-in needs and deal with the side effects of sin.

✔ **Arts:** God created humans with imagination and creativity.

✔ **Politics and government:** God ordained government for order and justice (see Chapter 14).

✔ **Economics:** Personal and national economics should be based on stewardship and justice.

✔ **Sociology:** God created humans as social creatures and instituted basic structures, including the family, the nation, and the Church.

Figure 13-4 illustrates the Christian worldview.

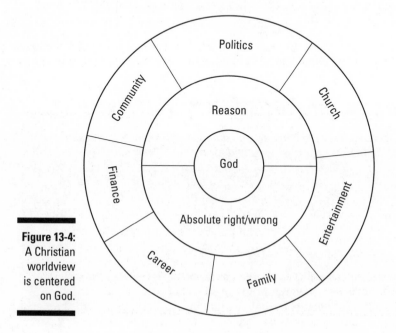

Figure 13-4: A Christian worldview is centered on God.

Because the concept of a worldview is so all-encompassing, it's not surprising that Christians wrestle with the idea of their faith as something this broad. As a result, unless a Christian explicitly surrenders all aspects of her life to the Lord (see the "Being a Disciple" section, earlier in this chapter), she consciously or unconsciously tries to skirt the all-or-nothing nature of biblical Christian faith. Christians who do this are in danger of two pitfalls:

✔ **Compartmentalizing life:** Christians who do this don't consider their worldview as a whole as they live their lives. Instead of trying to make sense out of life, they simply work with each piece in isolation. But because each piece is on its own, they have no broader perspective on how everything fits together. Remember, a Christian isn't born with a Christian worldview. It's something that one gains as he matures in the Christian faith and continually submits to it.

✔ **Trying to maintain control:** Christians in this category prefer to mix and match worldviews, because they want to put God *and* themselves in the center position. They much prefer the idea of renting out the inner circle as a timeshare with God, letting him take the Sundays so long as they get the rest of the week. But authentic Christianity doesn't have a timeshare option.

When Christians fall into one of these pitfalls, they become confused and wonder why God doesn't seem to make a difference to them and why their lives don't make any sense, because they have conflicting values across the various areas of their lives.

In the end, a Christian must embrace the Christian worldview so that all compartments of life are in synch with his or her faith. Authentic Christianity, as it turns out, is a 24/7 gig.

A must-read: *How Now Shall We Live?*

The inconsistent Christian suffers even more than the consistent atheist. The most miserable person of all is the one who knows the truth yet doesn't obey it.

—Chuck Colson, *How Now Shall We Live?* (Tyndale House, 1999)

One of the best-known contemporary Christian authors, Chuck Colson describes *How Now Shall We Live?* as his legacy work. In it, Colson discusses why Christian belief must go beyond personal faith and instead be a complete framework for understanding your world, impacting what you believe about the origin of humans, sin, science, politics, art, music, and more. Colson does a great job making the subject matter readable and relevant to today's readers.

Bringing the Christian binoculars everywhere you go

The modern-day world is a place that someone like Leonardo Da Vinci would find alien: It's become a world of specialists. In higher education, students are becoming more specialized as they orient their careers in narrow fields of discipline. Similarly, in the field of medicine, doctors aren't just doctors anymore; they are general practitioners, pediatricians, brain surgeons, ENTs (ears, nose, and throat specialists), ophthalmologists, or sports medicine doctors, to name a few. In the United States, television is now far greater than the "Big Three" networks; instead, hundreds of cable channels exist, each of which has a narrow area of interest. You don't, for example, have a single sports station, but a slew of them, all having a slightly different focus — such as ESPN (general sports), ESPN News (sports news), ESPN2 (youth-oriented sports), ESPN Classic (sports stories from the past), and the Outdoor Life Network (adventure sports).

As society splinters itself into more and more compartments, it's not surprising that people follow suit and do the same, partitioning their lives and treating each part independently. Christians are as susceptible to this same compartmentalization as everyone else, divorcing their faith from the rest of their lives. It's so commonplace that people who put their faith in a box have a nickname: Sunday Christians.

Take, for example, Daniel (a guy I've made up for the sake of illustration); he's the Sunday Christian poster child. Daniel attends church each and every Sunday morning, worshiping in the service and teaching junior high Sunday School. Daniel and his wife even go the extra mile by attending a Bible study on Sunday evenings. Yet, on Sunday night, Daniel either consciously or unconsciously says to himself, "Tomorrow, I'll get on with the rest of my life." He gets up for work at 5:30 a.m. the next morning and fights with thousands of other commuters for the quickest lane into the city and the best parking spot in the parking garage. At work, he was recently promoted and is now in charge of pursuing an acquisition of another company. At lunch, Daniel flirts with his secretary and then kids around with his fellow co-workers over the saga of the latest hit reality TV show. He leaves work early at 4 p.m. to attend a marital counseling session with his wife, because they're battling communication and anger problems due to their rebellious 16-year-old daughter. Daniel then leaves the counseling session to go straight to a political rally. The rest of the week is similar for Daniel — that is, until the next Sunday morning, when he puts on his Sunday best and heads to church again.

What makes Daniel a model Sunday Christian aren't necessarily his activities during the rest of the week. Instead, it's that *he doesn't see any relationship between these activities and his Christian faith.* Daniel never even considers that his personal Christian faith might impact his morning commute behavior, career goals, the ethical issues surrounding the potential acquisition, his

rapport with others in his office, the TV shows he watches, his priorities as a husband and father, and his politics. As a result, although he may appear to be a Super Christian to fellow churchgoers, Daniel's behavior is far different in the real world that he inhabits.

Many Christians lead fragmented lives like Daniel, with their faith having no bearing on the rest of their lives. To them, Christianity is nothing more than a Sunday morning obligation; the rest of life is their own personal business. Divorce rates, for example, speak to this problem. In spite of the specific teachings against divorce in the Bible, the sobering fact is that faith appears to make little difference on this important issue — various studies have shown that the divorce rate among people who call themselves Christians is identical to that of non-Christians.

To avoid living a disjointed life and dealing with all its shortcomings, Christians should take two steps:

- ✔ Recognize the central role that God plays in all compartments of their lives.
- ✔ Submit to the Lord in each of these areas.

In addition, the more Christians spend time with the Lord daily through prayer and Bible reading, live like a disciple, and lead a life of faith, they can be assured that their worldview is transformed as the Holy Spirit works in their hearts. (Check out the other sections in this chapter for the details on these aspects of Christian life.)

Chapter 14

Being in the World but Not of It

*H*ave you ever bitten into a bay leaf that was mistakenly left in spaghetti sauce or soup? If you have, you know it's not a very pleasant sensation. Bay leaves are a great seasoning to add to a recipe, but they're sure not made for eatin'. Clearly, bay leaves are meant to be *in* the sauce when you cook it, but not part *of* the sauce when you eat it.

Jesus Christ prayed for his followers, asking his Father to help them become something like those bay leaves when it comes to living in the Great Spaghetti Pot of Society:

> *I pray not that you would take my followers from the world, but that you would keep them from the evil one. They are not of the world even as I am not of the world . . . As you sent me into the world, even so I have sent them into the world.*

—John 17:15–16,18

You may wonder, What exactly does it mean to be in the world, but not of it? Should Christians work to create heaven on earth? Should they hide in caves and wait for the Lord to return? Or should they take a balanced position in between?

Although the Bible provides guidelines for how Christians should carry out Christ's mandate to live *in the world* (a common Christian phrase referring to the sinful earth), the Church has struggled for centuries over how to put those principles into practice on Main Street, Wall Street, Pennsylvania Avenue, and Hollywood Boulevard. In this chapter, you discover how Christians wrestle with their role in society and politics and how they deal with a world that has values quite different from those of biblical Christianity.

Being Salt and Light for the World

Jesus Christ tells his followers that they're to live in society alongside non-believers because he has a specific objective for them to focus on: being *salt* and *light* to the rest of the world. Jesus wasn't telling people to become condiments or bulbs that plug into lamps. Instead, as the next sections describe, Jesus wants Christians to impact the world around them.

Adding zest with salt

First, Jesus tells his followers that they're the salt of the earth. He says in Matthew 5:13–14:

> *You are the salt of the earth, but if the salt has lost its flavor, with what will it be salted? It is then good for nothing, but to be cast out and trodden under the feet of men.*

On first take, the "salt of the earth" imagery doesn't mean much to me. Salt is that white stuff that I sprinkle on French fries, so the metaphor ends up sounding to me much the same as "You are the ketchup of the earth." But when you understand how people used salt back in the first century, you begin to see why Jesus used this saline-laden illustration.

Salt was a valuable commodity before the days of refrigerators and picnic coolers, because it preserves food from decay. It was also handy for cleansing boo-boos on Johnny's knee, and, much like today, for seasoning and flavoring food. Therefore, Jesus was saying that Christians are like salt as they

- ✔ **Preserve a decaying world** by seeking God's justice and righteousness in the world to fight off evil and counter its harmful effects.

- ✔ **Cleanse wounds of broken hearts** by showing grace and compassion to others, particularly those who are hurting, in need, or in despair.

- ✔ **Flavor the world with the hope of the Good News of Jesus** by telling the world about the Christian gospel.

Salt's not effective when you simply place it alongside food or a wound. In order for salt to do its thing, you must apply it: Salt works as a preservative when you rub it onto meat, as a cleanser when you apply it to a wound, and as a flavoring when you add it on top of food. Similarly, a Christian can't preserve, cleanse, or flavor the world if he or she doesn't interact with others.

At the same time, Jesus balances this message by warning Christians about diving headfirst into the world and, as a result, being no different from anyone else around them. In the first century, salt was easy to ruin if not

handled properly, and after it was ruined, salt was useless. In the same way, when Christians forget about being obedient to Christ and begin conforming to the world, they lose their effectiveness.

Shining truth with light

Second, Jesus continued in Matthew 5:15–16 by telling his followers:

> *You are the light of the world. A city located on a hill can't be hidden. Neither do you light a lamp, and put it under a measuring basket, but on a stand; and it shines to all who are in the house. Even so, let your light shine before men; that they may see your good works, and glorify your Father who is in heaven.*

Jesus' illustration of light is usually easier for the modern reader to grasp than the salt illustration is. Much like turning on a flashlight in a dark, musty room, Christians are to

- ✔ *Shine* **God's truth onto an unknowing world both through their words and actions:** In other words, live out their faith so that people see God working in their lives.

- ✔ *Expose* **the ugliness and decay of the world for what it is:** Essentially, call sin as they see it, without excusing it or looking the other way.

Notice that Christ's word choice is significant. He doesn't say that believers can aspire to become salt and light after they mature into Super Christians; no, he says that his followers are *already* salt and light. Therefore, that means that all Christians, no matter how young or old they are in their faith, are called to the same purpose.

Living Out Christ's Calling in Different Ways

Although Christians throughout the centuries have tried to follow Jesus' instructions to "live in the world, but not of it" and "be salt and light," they haven't always seen eye-to-eye on what those statements mean from a practical standpoint. In fact, when you look at the approaches Christians have taken from the first century up until the current one, you see various perspectives appearing and reappearing even as societies and cultures change and progress. In his classic book *Christ and Culture* (Harper San Francisco, 1975), H. Richard Niebuhr categorizes these perspectives into five different patterns of thought:

 ✔ Running from the world

 ✔ Hugging the world

 ✔ Working for the greater good

 ✔ Walking a tightrope

 ✔ Transforming the world

The first model separates Christians from the world, while the second shows Christians clinging to it; the remaining three offer various responses between those two extremes. Not all these perspectives are necessarily in line with biblical Christianity, most obviously the "Hugging the world" pattern, because it compromises the need for Christ's salvation as it strives to build a better world. However, concerning the rest of the perspectives, many earnest, biblical Christians have argued that their position most closely resembles the teaching of the New Testament.

As you read through this section, keep in mind that all attempts to lump people together are always imperfect; some people just don't neatly fit into a box. Nonetheless, in spite of this limitation, Niebuhr's matrix remains a helpful tool to understand how Christians attempt to live out Christ's calling in the world around them.

Perhaps you find it strange that Christians have so many contrasting perspectives on living out Christ's calling. But, as you read through each of these, you begin to understand why some Christians keep to themselves and stay out of the limelight, why others volunteer at soup kitchens and help the homeless, and why still others feel called by God to run for a political office and create a more Christian nation.

Running from the world

The *Road Runner* approach that some Christians take is to separate themselves completely from the world. This view (referred to by Niebuhr as *Christ against culture*) sees the world as sinful and wrecked beyond repair, so the only obedient Christian response is to keep pure by quarantining off the world; otherwise, this Christian fears inevitably becoming polluted as well.

The necessity of not being "of the world" overrides any duty or responsibility for the Christian to be involved in the world's doings. This Christian avoids all politics, community involvement, and civic duty. In addition, TV, movies, and modern music are all major no-nos. All in all, these Christians believe they are faithful examples only if they remain apart from the world.

Groups like the Amish, Quakers, Mennonites, and Brethren have responded in this manner, and to a lesser extent, so have some Baptists and Pentecostals.

Hugging the world

In stark contrast, the *World Hugger* approach shows Christians running toward the world, not away from it, and doesn't stop until it embraces the world and slops a big, fat, juicy kiss on its cheek. Popularized during the rise of theological liberalism during the 20th century (see Chapter 11), this view (which Niebuhr called *Christ of culture*) transforms Christianity into a social religion, always in support of society's goals. The sin problem isn't so much with individuals as it is with institutional evils, such as poverty, homelessness, and pollution. Therefore, those who subscribe to this perspective believe that if people only accept the ideals of love, peace, and social justice that Jesus taught, then heaven is attainable on this earth. Salvation through the cross of Christ, therefore, is nonessential.

When you look at the implications of this viewpoint, you see a sharp tension between the world-hugger perspective and biblical Christianity. People who hold this view often mold Christ into the image they want rather than how the Bible describes him and interpret Christ's teaching primarily through the lens of contemporary society and culture. They emphasize Christ's talk of love and social justice but gloss over his calls for holiness and his warnings of judgment.

You see this point of view proclaimed in some parts of the mainline Protestant denominations, such as United Methodist, Congregational, and Presbyterian.

Working for the greater good

The *Brothers-in-Arms* approach to living as a Christian recognizes that good in society — such as peace, love, order, and justice — does exist and comes as a gift from God. However, these Christians believe that only Christ can complete that good work. This view (which Niebuhr termed *Christ above culture*) is perhaps the most difficult to understand of these five models. It sees Christians working together with people from a variety of religious and non-religious backgrounds to bring good to society, as long as society's good is in line with God's greater good of justice, mercy, and compassion.

Christians with this perspective see life as a hierarchy, with the world on bottom and Christ on top, superseding the world as needed. Or, think of this approach as Christian truth as the big brother and society as the little brother. They walk arm-in-arm working together, though the big brother may occasionally need to bop the little brother on the head when he gets out of place.

Given this hierarchy, there's a big difference between "God's work" by the clergy and *secular* (worldly) work by other Christians (often called *laypersons*) working in society. A person can work in the world without being stained by it, but the clergy have the higher calling. Or, to use an everyday illustration,

consider the different levels of credit cards. A regular card is as usable as a gold card, but the gold card has a special standing with the bank that offers it. In the same way, think of priests as being those privileged gold card holders compared to the ordinary credit card holders of the laypersons: Their standing before God is higher.

The great medieval thinker Thomas Aquinas (see Chapter 18) was the original proponent of this idea, and most Catholics still believe this view.

Walking a tightrope

The *Tightrope Walker* approach performs a balancing act between obeying Jesus Christ and dealing with the realities of living in the world. The "Brothers-in-Arms" approach is relatively optimistic in comparison, because this view (which Niebuhr refers to as *Christ and culture in paradox)* sees a constant tension between Christians and the sinful world all around them. Christians can't run from culture or else they'll be neglecting Christ's commandment to be salt and light. At the same time, the Christian will never be at ease within this world because its sins and temptations are at odds with God. Christians are, therefore, called to live out their faith and have as much of an impact on the world as possible without compromising their integrity in the process. The goal isn't to change society so much as to bring individuals within society to Jesus Christ.

This viewpoint is what the Protestant leader Martin Luther (see Chapter 18) believed, and Christians generally consider it as the most in line — if you had to pick any one of the five approaches — with the teachings of the Apostle Paul. It's also the perspective that many Protestants have.

Transforming the world

Although the "World Hugger" model seeks to reshape Jesus Christ based on society's values, the *Transformer* approach strives to change the world based on Jesus' teachings in the Bible. This view (which Niebuhr describes as *Christ transforming culture*) says that the world is sinful, but that Christians are called to work to restore it to its original pre-fallen state. From this perspective, making a difference isn't just an option, but it's something Christians have a mandate to do.

More optimistic than the "Tightrope Walker" approach, this view says that the gospel is intended to transform both individuals and culture. Therefore, these Christians work to convert individuals through personal evangelism and the world as a whole by reforming culture, entertainment, arts, education, and government.

From this perspective, people working in business, politics, and the Church are all equally working together for the Lord. The clergyperson isn't on a higher spiritual plain than the godly small business owner who's serving God through plain old-fashioned hard work at his shop.

Another Protestant reformer, John Calvin, supported this approach. Many Protestants, particularly politically active ones, hold this view.

Delving into the Messy World of Politics and Governing

Remember the old adage that two issues are off-limits at dinner conversations — religion and politics? Well, because that's the case, I advise you not to read this section aloud at supper tonight or you risk being pelted with an olive. In this section, you explore how Christians believe they're called to relate to politics and government.

Looking at what the Bible says about government

The Bible may not be a book about politics, but a distinct political subplot running throughout the Old and New Testaments is quite obvious. That's because God's faithful have never lived in apolitical ivory towers, but rather in the midst of a world filled with political intrigue, scandal, tyranny, and social reform. In the Old Testament, the Israelites were slaves in Egypt and faced the dilemma of rebellion against an unjust ruler. Later, after the Israelites were freed and formed their own nation, they had to deal with politics of a monarchy and issues concerning how to govern justly. In the New Testament, Jesus and the apostles operated their entire ministries within a society that was dominated by a foreign occupier. Therefore, after you explore the Bible's pages, you discover principles God gave concerning how his followers should interact and be involved with politics and the government.

Although many ideas stem from the Bible's teachings, four of the most significant are as follows:

> ✔ **God ordained government.** The need for government doesn't seem to be something God thought of as an afterthought or a consequence of sin. Instead, government seems to have been a natural part of Creation. From the very beginning, God invited humans to share in the ruling of

the world (Genesis 1:28). Paul seconds this idea in Romans 13:1 when he says that the authorities that exist have been established by God, though that certainly doesn't mean that God approves of what a particular government may do with its power.

✔ **Christians are to submit to a just government.** A consistent theme throughout the Bible is that, although exceptions exist, God's faithful are to be submissive to the government. Paul says this most explicitly in Romans 13:1–8:

> *Let every follower be in submission to the higher authorities, for there is no authority except from God, and those who exist are ordained by God. Therefore he who resists the authority, withstands the ordinance of God; and those who withstand will receive to themselves judgment . . . Therefore you need to be in submission, not only because of the wrath, but also for conscience' sake. For this reason you also pay taxes, for they are servants of God's service, attending continually on this very thing. Give therefore to everyone what you owe: taxes to whom taxes are due; customs to whom customs; respect to whom respect; honor to whom honor.*

Jesus backed up Paul's teaching when the crowd questioned him about paying taxes to the Roman occupiers (Matthew 22:21): "Give to Caesar the things that are Caesar's, and to God the things that are God's."

Therefore, although at times a Christian may need to support civil disobedience or outright revolution (see the next bullet), the foremost call is simply to submit.

✔ **Christians are to obey God first, government second.** Although Paul focuses on the importance of submitting to the government in Romans 13 (see the preceding bullet), Christians may run into situations where they must be willing to step away from specific acts should the government go against the higher authority of God.

The Old and New Testaments show several examples of civil disobedience. In the Old Testament, Moses disobeyed Pharaoh and demanded the release of slaves. The Old Testament prophet Daniel refused to obey a law that said he couldn't pray to God. King Nebuchadnezzar threw Shadrach, Meshach, and Abednego into a fiery furnace after they refused to bow down before a false god. (Don't sweat it — God rescued the trio. Read the story in Daniel 3.) Similarly, the New Testament apostles were law-abiding citizens, but when the authorities told them that they couldn't preach the gospel to others, they felt a moral obligation to disobey earthly rulers and serve the Lord instead by continuing to preach. In each of these instances, the motivations weren't selfish, but were responses to laws that were direct offenses to God.

✔ **Political reform is important, but transformed, godly lives are always most important.** God demonstrated many times in the Old Testament that he's concerned with oppression, social ills, and the needy. The ministry of Jesus parallels this concern as he healed many people and cared

for them. But, at the same time, Jesus and his apostles weren't political activists or political revolutionaries. Frankly, from what the Bible says, they actually talked very little of politics. Therefore, although Christians disagree on the extent to which reform should be sought after, the Bible indicates that Jesus' and the apostles' foremost priority was working to transform individual lives with the gospel.

Interpreting the Bible in regard to government: Five key understandings

Although the Bible provides general principles and guidelines for how a Christian relates to the government, I've never found a *Christian Citizens For Dummies* section packed inside my Bible. Given that reality, it's not surprising that Christians come to different conclusions on this issue. These groups and their perspectives parallel the five approaches I discuss in the "Living Out Christ's Calling in Different Ways" section earlier in the chapter:

- ✔ **Road Runners:** This separatist approach says that Christians should stay away from the government and politics altogether, because if they didn't, they'd only get their hands dirty. Supporters of this view believe that although God installed government out of necessity to keep order (because government is better than anarchy), he didn't endorse it or give it his seal of approval. Therefore, the Christian response is to accept powerlessness, avoid interaction with government, and disobey it as one's conscience requires (although accepting the consequences of such disobedience).

- ✔ **World Huggers:** This approach claims that the government's purpose is to improve the lives of its citizens. Therefore, proponents take an activist view, often emphasizing social justice issues, and look to Christ as a model for their advocacy because he was a supporter of the down-and-out and saved his hard words for the established "powers-that-be."

- ✔ **Brothers in Arms:** This approach says that government was not only created to keep order, but also to improve people's lives. People in power are true public servants, committed to the needs of others and leading society to virtue. These Christians believe that they should respect the government's laws, but if a law goes counter to God's Word, then it's no longer a law, but a perversion — and they don't follow it.

- ✔ **Tightrope Walkers:** Although this "balancing act" perspective doesn't forbid being involved in politics or government, it does see politics more pessimistically than the other approaches do (except the Road Runners). Advocates of this view don't expect much from the government, other than to preserve order so people can live their lives. As a result, they don't see social reform as a major priority, and they see the ideals put forth in the Bible as largely irrelevant to how a secular society works.

✔ **Transformers:** This view has a more positive, activist view of government, charging that the government should do more than just keep order, bringing Christian virtues into how it rules. Christians have acted out several examples of this transformer model within the past two hundred years. First, Christians spearheaded the anti-slavery movements in Britain and the United States. William Wilberforce (see Chapter 18), for example, was a strong evangelical Christian who worked for decades in British parliament in the 19th century to abolish slavery on moral grounds. Second, African American church leaders led the civil rights movements in the United States during the 1950 and 1960s. Third, a large part of the unsung credit of the fall of the Iron Curtain in Eastern Europe goes to Orthodox and Catholic pastors who headed nonviolent disobedience efforts during the late 1980s. In each of these examples, Christians responded with the belief that they were called by God to transform the unjust system that was before them.

Table 14-1 shows a summary of each of these perspectives on various issues of political involvement.

Was the Apostle Paul pro-slavery?

Similar to 19th century America's version, slavery was a widespread evil in the Roman Empire during the first century. As a result, part of the audience for Paul's letters included both slaves and slave owners. Some people have charged the Apostle Paul as being pro-slavery because he never condemns the institution of slavery in his writings. However, it's important to remember two realities. First, unlike the democracies that are prevalent today, Christians in Paul's day had no political power to change the system. Therefore, inspiring churches to political action or rebellion would be pointless in such a context and would only serve to weaken the Church's priorities of spreading the gospel through the region. Second, although Paul didn't speak out for or against the institution of slavery, one can't necessarily conclude that he didn't care about his society's evils. Instead, his actions simply make it clear that he was *more* concerned about the salvation of the individual slaves and slave owners than he was about changing the temporary sinful systems on earth.

Table 14-1		Spectrum of Christian Perspectives on Politics			
View	*Are politics and government good or bad?*	*Should laws be based on Christian principles?*	*What is the purpose of government?*	*Is civil disobedience justified?*	*Is political involvement compatible with Christian faith?*
Road Runners	Bad	No	Primarily order	Yes	No
World Huggers	Good	Conditional	Justice	Yes	Yes
Brothers in Arms	Good	Yes	Order	Yes, but rarely	Yes
Tightrope Walkers	Neutral	Ambivalent	Order (no expectation of justice)	Very rare for Christians	Yes (but an irrelevant question)
Transformers	Good	Possible	Order and justice	Yes, but rarely	Yes! (a Christian duty)

Tossing political hot potatoes

If you've read or seen *The Lord of the Rings,* you know that Sam the Hobbit likes to prepare potatoes by boiling 'em, mashing 'em, and sticking 'em in a stew. Humans, on the other hand, seem to enjoy heating up potatoes in the oven and then throwing them into the political arena for everyone to burn their hands on.

Within the world of politics, certain "hot potato" issues seem to always divide society, and to some extent, the Church as well. Three issues in particular that often come up in debates within the Church include war, the death penalty, and abortion.

War and peace

Talking about the Christian response to war is timely given the war on terrorism at the turn of the millennium and the crises that always seem to rise up in the Middle East. And though the world faces these new challenges at the dawn of the 21st century, the issues of war have been around since the first nations were formed.

Jesus and the apostles didn't provide crystal clear direction to Christians, though the Church can make many decisions based on the indirect teaching available in the scriptures. Traditionally, different parts of the Church tend to come down on opposite sides of the fence, one side arguing against any war at all, the other side claiming that just wars are morally permissible. I explain these positions in more detail in the following sections.

Keeping the peace

Some Christians read the Gospels and conclude that Jesus Christ both teaches and lives out pacifism. (*Pacifism* is the belief that all forms of violence are wrong, regardless of the reason or justification behind it.) They point to his teaching in the Sermon on the Mount, in which he tells his followers, "Whoever strikes you on your right cheek, turn to him the other also" (Matthew 5:39).

Christian pacifists also highlight Jesus' reaction when he was arrested in the Garden of Gethsemane. He not only refused to be disobedient in being arrested, but he also chastised Peter for attempting to offer a defense (Matthew 26:50–52):

> *Then they came and laid hands on Jesus, and took him. Behold, one of those who were with Jesus stretched out his hand, and drew his sword, and struck the servant of the high priest, and struck off his ear. Then Jesus said to him, "Put your sword back into its place, for all those who take the sword will die by the sword."*

Christ consistently indicated through his teaching and his life that God requires Christians to give up defending themselves, even when it's considered legitimate to do so. As I discuss in Chapter 13, all Christians believe that Jesus calls his disciples to surrender their lives to him. Given that, Christian pacifists say that pacifism lives out that principle within the context of war.

Holders of the Just War perspective (see the following section) often use the Israelites in the Old Testament as an example of God's support for war. Christian pacifists counter by saying that war was not God's original intention and came about only due to sin. What's more, they say that when Jesus came, he permanently put to rest any need of God's people to wage war because God's people were now a Church, not a political nation.

Defending by fighting

The opposite position Christians have held through the centuries is that, although all war is an evil and terrible business, sometimes it's necessary to prevent an even worse evil. St. Augustine and, later, Thomas Aquinas searched the Bible for answers and then devised a criteria to determine what types of wars are legitimate for a Christian to support. Their ideas have become popularly known today as the *Just War Theory* and include seven main criteria:

- ✔ **Just cause:** The war must be for a just cause. It should be defensive, and never any type of unprovoked violence. During the War on Terrorism in Iraq, for example, many Christians debated whether the United States had just cause to enter the war, because the United States invaded Iraq. The proponents of the war said that the United States was acting out of protection and defense, and that Iraq's chemical weapons caused hostility and provoked the war.

- ✔ **Just intentions:** The intention of the war must be just. The objective of the war must be to secure peace, and not to go to battle purely for money, land, or politics. Greater good must result because of the war than it would as the result of not acting in the war. Therefore, for example, when Great Britain and the United States fought Nazi Germany in World War II, nearly all Christians saw both Britain's and the United States' motivation as just to prevent Hitler's evil from spreading across the planet.

- ✔ **Last possible resort:** War must be a last resort. The government should exhaust all possible attempts to resolve the problem through economics or diplomacy before going to war.

- ✔ **Limited objectives:** The war must have objectives that are targeted and identifiable. The goal of the war must be peace, not complete annihilation of the enemy.

- ✔ **Proportional response:** The weapons used should be in proportion to what's needed to secure peace. In other words, you shouldn't use a sledgehammer if a ballpoint hammer will do the trick effectively.

- ✔ **Backed by legitimate authority:** A legal authority must formally declare the war. Only legitimate governments and officeholders have the right to declare war, not any band of mercenaries or terrorist groups.

- ✔ **Innocents protected:** The military should ensure, as much as is possible, that non-combatants are unharmed. Government and military targets are acceptable, but civilian targets are out of question.

Supporters of the Just War Theory believe that the pacifist position (see the preceding section, "Keeping the peace") misunderstands biblical teaching on this issue, saying:

- ✔ **The Sermon on the Mount is for individuals.** They believe they aren't overlooking Jesus' instructions in the Sermon on the Mount ("turn the other cheek"), but believe that it specifically applies to individuals, not governments.

- ✔ **God promotes peace *and* war.** They also suggest that the God of the New Testament is the same as the God of the Old Testament, who mandated war at times for the nation of Israel. Therefore, promoting only just peace or just war and wholly dismissing the other option doesn't square with what the Bible says.

- ✔ **God calls people to administer justice.** The Bible commands God's people to defend those who can't defend themselves. For example, Psalm 82:3–4 says, "Defend the weak, the poor, and the fatherless. Maintain the rights of the poor and oppressed. Rescue the weak and needy. Deliver them out of the hand of the wicked." But in order to be obedient to that command, one must sometimes use legitimate force.

Punishing criminals with the death penalty

The death penalty is a second political issue that tends to split Christians and different parts of the Church. After all, how can a person who professes to serve a God of forgiveness and peace justify killing a person, regardless of his or her offense? Both sides point to the Bible to back their position:

- ✔ **Supporting the death penalty:** Christians who defend the death penalty hold that God's justice, whether on heaven and earth, requires a proportionate response for the offense. It's not a matter of revenge, but a matter of administering proper justice. They point to the Old Testament Law in Israel that permitted capital punishment, or as Exodus 21:23 memorably says, "Life for life, eye for eye, tooth for tooth." They also believe that Paul implicitly supports capital punishment in Romans 13:4 ("If you do wrong, be afraid, for the government doesn't bear the sword for nothing") and in his response to the Roman ruler Festus in Acts 25, when he says that he won't argue against being put to death if he's guilty of any crime worthy of that punishment. Churches that tend to support some usage of the death penalty include Southern Baptists and the Lutheran Missouri Synod.

✔ **Arguing against the death penalty:** Christians who argue against the death penalty say that capital punishment goes smack against the sanctity of life that God ordained when he created human life. Pointing to the Sermon on the Mount, they believe that Jesus spoke against taking the life of another when he said, "You have heard that it was said, 'An eye for an eye, and a tooth for a tooth.' But I tell you, don't resist him who is evil; but whoever strikes you on your right cheek, turn to him the other also" (Matthew 5:38–39). They also highlight Jesus' forgiving response when the religious leaders were about to stone an adulterous woman. When the leaders asked Jesus what they should do, he replied, "He who is without sin among you, let him throw the first stone at her" (John 8:7). Churches that have taken a stand against the death penalty include the Catholic, Orthodox, Evangelical Lutheran Church of America, American Baptist, United Methodist, Presbyterian, and Episcopal Churches.

Aborting unwanted pregnancies

The debate over abortion is far more one-sided within the Christian Church than war and the death penalty are. Christians on both sides of the other two issues justify their position using the Bible, because they both deal with gray area issues that the Bible isn't always clear on. However, if you believe that the fetus is a human being, then it's frankly impossible to justify abortion by pointing to any passage in the Bible. In fact, the Bible implicitly affirms the humanness of the fetus in Jeremiah 1:5: "Before I formed you in the belly I knew you, and before you came forth out of the womb I sanctified you."

Consequently, biblical Christians predominately favor the pro-life position on abortion. A minority of Christians is against abortion personally and considers it morally wrong, but, based on political beliefs, argues against the government itself getting involved in regulating such matters. (World huggers often have this perspective.) Some Christians see a provision for allowing abortion in cases of incest, rape, or potential danger to the mother, but they emphasize that the Bible holds the sanctity of life as being one of the most precious of all God's gifts (see 1 Corinthians 3:16, Matthew 19:18, Numbers 35).

Although the Bible doesn't mention abortion by name, the early Church had to start dealing with this issue when Roman law began permitting abortion during that era. An early second-century document on Christian teaching explicitly states, "Thou shalt not murder a child by abortion." Through the years, some of the best-known Christian heavyweights explicitly spoke against abortion, including Augustine, Aquinas, Luther, and Calvin (see Chapter 18 for more on all those guys).

Chapter 15

Tackling Thorny Issues in the Church

*I*f you ever watch a political debate, chances are that a candidate will dance the political two-step. You know the routine. A candidate is asked a hardball question. The politician smiles and starts the response with "Good question; I'm glad you asked that. . . ." Then he or she spends the next several minutes dancing all around the question without ever really answering it. Just once, I'd love to hear someone be honest and just confess, "I haven't the foggiest notion." I'd vote for that candidate on the spot!

Although politicians have perfected the art of dodging issues, voters don't take candidates who make a habit of it too seriously. In the same way, you won't pay Christianity much attention if Christians greet tough questions with a Fred Astaire foxtrot. Therefore, in this chapter, I dive into some of the thorniest issues that non-Christians and Christians raise about the Christian faith, dealing with issues inside the Church. (For thorny issues outside of the Church, flip to Chapter 16.) And as I explore these topics, you don't have to worry about me doing any dancing. My wife's sore feet tell you that I have two lefties, so I pledge to leave my dancing shoes at home.

Observing Hypocrisy

Hypocrisy is everywhere. You see it on the news — corrupt televangelists back in the 1990s and scandalous priests in the 2000s. You see it in the cinema — Christians portrayed as saying one thing and then acting to the contrary. Whether it's from the media, the movies, or your meddling

neighbor, all too often you encounter people proclaiming faith on a Sunday morning, but then utterly failing to live it out during the rest of the week. When this occurs, you easily become disappointed, discouraged, and even downright disgusted.

Sadly, this hypocrisy is enough of a turn-off to get many people to dismiss the Christian faith outright. Christianity's worst enemy many times seems to be Christians themselves, because most don't seem to be able to practice what they preach. Yet, as real of a problem as hypocrisy is, is it legit to hold this issue against the Christian faith itself? Or, in a grand irony, does hypocrisy actually help prove the core teachings of Christianity?

Considering two types of hypocrites

The word *hypocrite* actually comes from the Greek word for actor. Basically, hypocrites are people pretending to be what they're not; in regard to Christianity, hypocrites are people who call themselves Christians, but whose actions don't follow suit. I divide these hypocrites into two groups:

- ✔ **Weak-kneed double-talkers:** Those who talk the talk, but don't walk the walk

- ✔ **Pharisee wannabes:** Those who walk the walk, but don't do it out of true love for and devotion to God

People often fall victim to one of these forms of hypocrisy or even to a combination of both of them.

Weak-kneed double-talkers: Constantly sinning and calling themselves Christians

The first category of hypocrites includes those who believe all the right stuff but are inconsistent in living out that belief. They're weak in saying no to sin. They know that what they're doing is wrong, but they do it anyway. But hypocrisy goes beyond moral failure; instead, it's moral failure that Christians cover up and keep hidden. Weak-kneed people are the disgraced Christians who make the headlines: the pastor who has an affair with someone he's counseling or the secretary who gets caught stealing the church funds. The weak-kneed aren't usually prideful people. In fact, they're often ashamed and saddened at their inability to do what's holy and pure.

Temptation hits people at the exact spot in which they're weakest. Therefore, to some extent, every Christian falls victim to being weak-kneed on certain sins in his or her life. However, weak-kneed double-talkers constantly struggle to give over an area of sin in their lives to God. When left unchecked, they create an entire private life of sin that lies just below the surface of their "normal" life.

Pharisee wannabes: Living by the rules and condemning others

Chapter 4 introduces you to the *Pharisees,* the dominant religious teachers of first-century Palestine. Many Christians today fall into the same trap of *legalism* (self-righteous and rigid practice of the outward acts of the faith) that the Pharisees did 2,000 years ago. These Pharisee wannabes are consumed with outer purity by following rules, but ignore inner qualities like love, grace, and humility. Unlike the weak-kneed, the modern-day Pharisees behave outwardly in a moral and upright manner. In fact, looking at their actions alone, they appear to be model Christians. But because they're so consumed with following the rules, they develop a hardness of heart that takes them even farther away from God as they live their lives.

Similarly, the original Pharisees were so obsessed with following the Hebrew Law that they rejected Jesus' message of love and grace. Outward morality became more important to them than true devotion to God. In fact, perhaps the greatest paradox of Jesus' ministry was that he endlessly clashed with the outwardly pure Pharisees, not with the blatant sinners of his day. Jesus points out the dead ends of their legalism in Matthew 23:27–28:

> *Woe to you, scribes and Pharisees, hypocrites! For you are like whitened tombs, which outwardly appear beautiful, but inwardly are full of dead men's bones, and of all uncleanness. Even so you also outwardly appear righteous to men, but inwardly you are full of hypocrisy and iniquity.*

The point that Jesus was trying to make was that the Pharisees loved following their rules in the name of God more than they actually loved God — so much so that when God dwelled in their midst as Jesus Christ, they rejected him. Their black-and-white rules couldn't handle Jesus' radical claims of grace, mercy, and love.

Pharisaism is a disease, however, that not only plagued first-century Jews in Palestine, but has also afflicted portions of the Christian Church throughout its history. This age-old bent towards Pharisaism leaves people striving to follow God through behavior rather than through love.

Pharisaism produces a selfish pride that negatively impacts one's relationships with God and others. First, with a focus on behavior, modern-day Pharisees give lip service to grace, but subconsciously, their pride coaxes them to believe that their "righteous" behavior is what saves them. Second, this group of hypocrites easily falls susceptible to treating others who don't measure up to their standards with disdain. If you walk across their path and don't make the grade, then watch out! Ouch!

Legalism is a trap that appeals to many people because it allows them to draw boundaries that, if they meet the expectations, God considers them acceptable. In a weird sort of way, the black-and-white world of legalism seems easier for many people, even though it's restrictive. Although some people rebel against boundaries, others actually cling to them for security.

TIP

A dose of anti-hypocrite medicine

If you're a Christian, you too may find hypocrisy creeping up at times in your own life. If you're one of the weak-kneed, doing the following may help steer you away from hypocrisy:

✔ Be honest with yourself and God and recognize hidden traps of sin in your life.

✔ Confess your sin, profess your earnest desire to rid yourself of those trappings, and give God permission to deal with those areas in your life.

✔ Spend time daily with the Lord through prayer and Bible reading (see Chapter 14).

✔ Find someone whom you can open up to and ask that person to hold you accountable (sharing openly your struggles, temptations, and victories) for your actions.

✔ If you screw up, ask for forgiveness and move on.

On the other hand, if you struggle with being legalistic, keep in mind the following:

✔ Recognize the hold that legalism has on your life and your temptation to focus on the external rather than on what God wants you to do.

✔ Confess your sin, profess your earnest desire to rid yourself of legalism, and give God permission to deal with those areas in your life.

✔ Spend time reading the Gospels, contrasting how Jesus lived compared to the Pharisees, identifying what's true Christianity (the message of Jesus' grace) and what's false (the Pharisees' idea that they could earn their way to heaven).

✔ Make your motto "What would Jesus do?" (WWJD), not "What would the Pharisees do?" (WWPD).

✔ If your legalism has caused you to treat others harshly, seek forgiveness from those individuals.

✔ Be accountable with another Christian to ensure that you stay on track. An accountability relationship is also a way to keep you humble and not self-righteous, because when you form a relationship like this, you give that person permission to shoot straight with you.

Weighing hypocrisy against Christianity's truth claims

Although the fact that hypocrites are part of the Church is sad and regrettable, Christians believe that this fact doesn't in any way undermine the truth claims of Christianity. In this section, consider the relationship between hypocrisy and the Christian faith.

Examining examples of the relationship between hypocrisy and truth

Hypocrisy describes an inconsistency between a person's beliefs and his or her outward actions. But it doesn't have anything to do with the validity of that person's beliefs. Consider two make-believe illustrations:

✔ A scientist recently discovered that Teletubby-like creatures inhabited the planet of Mars. However, he didn't have the photographic proof to convince his colleagues, because the Teletubbies always hid behind rocks when he tried to take a picture of them with his photographic telescope. In desperation, the scientist doctored up a few photos to come up with all the proof needed to further fund his research.

Although these rigged photographs perhaps prove that the guy is a crooked scientist who can't be trusted, his poor decisions don't have anything to do with the reality that Teletubbies do exist on Mars. In other words, the facts that the scientist knew in his head are independent of his actions.

✔ I first heard of the musical group called Swino when I saw some teenagers wearing Swino T-shirts and snorting at everyone as they walked down the street. Because the fans were obnoxious, I was immediately turned off to the musical group and wrote them off as a bunch of punks. But later, while driving my car, I scanned the radio searching for a tune to listen to and heard a catchy song that I couldn't get out of my head. When the DJ came back on, he informed me that none other than Swino performed the song.

I realized at that point that my disgust was pointed at the wrong place: My problem wasn't with Swino, but with some of their obnoxious fans. If I hadn't realized my error, I would've needlessly deprived myself of enjoying a catchy tune.

As you see from these hypothetical examples, one's behavior isn't always in synch with the truth claims of what that person believes. The examples illustrate two ideas:

✔ **Truth claims aren't automatically negated by problem behavior.** Like the scientist, Christians often make mistakes, but their behavior doesn't affect the truth of their claims.

✔ **God isn't a party to a Christian's wrongful behavior.** Like the Swino fans I encountered, some Christians are obnoxious, but as a reaction, you can't simply dismiss God, or you simply point your disdain in the wrong direction.

Understanding how hypocrisy supports Christian truth

If Christianity were a faith based on works — where God saves only the good people — then hypocrisy would prove that Christianity's unrealistic or perhaps even a scam, because a lifelong pattern of outward moral purity and inner submission to God seems a tall feat, to say the least. But biblical Christianity says that hypocritical behavior can and will happen, and that no one should be surprised when it does. In fact, hypocrisy only serves to *reinforce* two fundamental truths of Christianity:

- ✔ Sin is real and exists in every human, no matter how good he or she appears to be (see Chapter 4).

- ✔ Only by God's grace are people saved (flip back to Chapter 3). Every other option is a dead end. Rules and regulations simply produce modern-day Pharisees. Will power alone also falls short; well-intentioned people see the truth, but time after time, their will power alone fails them and they can't live it out consistently.

Dissing Nice-Guy Thinking

I've been to a few funerals over the course of my lifetime, and it seems like I always hear words to the effect of, "He was a really, really nice guy," referring to the guest of honor. Being a nice guy may be a nice compliment to hear, but from a Christian perspective, it's not an automatic ticket to heaven. In other words, being a good person isn't enough. When you read the New Testament and listen to the words of Jesus, you begin to discover that everyone, even really, really nice guys, needs the saving grace of Jesus Christ. (Check out Chapter 3 for more on this.)

Although the idea that a person's goodness earns salvation isn't biblical, it sure comes naturally to people. In fact, it seems to me that most everyone would opt for individuals getting what they deserve as the best way to deal with eternal fate. In general, this idea says that if you're a good person, you should be rewarded. But if you're a bad person, you deserve to be punished. Society loves fairness, and this way of thinking seems the fairest way to deal with a person.

I see the principle of getting what you deserve lived out on an everyday basis. Upon misbehaving, each of my boys is quite observant as to whether his punishment is in proportion to his brother's. And in the movies, so many films — *The Count of Monte Cristo, The Unforgiven, Tombstone,* and *The Italian Job,* to name a few — portray someone getting even with a bad person after he or she commits an evil deed. In fact, usually the loudest cheers in a crowded theater come when the hero ultimately kills the bad guy in the film's climax. This whole notion of getting what's coming to us seems to be in human blood. Despite this fact, Christianity sees it as a flawed perspective and one that's fundamentally at odds with the message of Jesus Christ.

Pointing out fundamental flaws of the Nice Guy approach

Modern-day society embraces the idea of getting what we deserve as the basis for explaining eternity. I call this perspective *Nice Guy Thinking;* the basic gist of this belief is that most people are generally good, and for the good folks, heaven awaits, because God wouldn't send someone good to hell. However, the bad people — the murdering, molesting, tyrannical types — will be punished for their evil deeds. The idea of good people being rewarded and bad people being punished may be the most instinctive of all solutions, but Christianity says that you better not stake your eternity on it.

Christians identify three fundamental flaws to this line of thinking, which I discuss in this section.

Nice Guy Thinking has too narrow a view of what's good

If you asked the average person what makes someone good, the typical response would be something like: "A good guy is someone who's a fine neighbor, father, and husband. He helps out his neighbors and friends during times of trouble, raises his family the best he can, and is a hard, dedicated worker." In this case, morality is restricted to meaning decent, kind behavior toward others. These people wink at other actions that don't seem to hurt anyone else. The deeds may be mischievous, but they're not anything to get worked up over.

The problem with this perspective is that it defines goodness in terms of other people — I am either better or worse than my neighbor. In doing so, it completely ignores how one treats God and dismisses the notion that one's behavior toward God even matters.

Consider a parallel: Suppose that I have neighbors who I've lived next to for years and have become close friends with. When my wife runs short on sugar, we don't hesitate to run over and ask to borrow some from them. I see the couple being actively involved with their children, attending PTA meetings, coaching soccer and baseball teams, and even helping to raise money for needy families during the Christmas season. The couple have seemingly met every criteria for being good and moral people. However, one morning, when I turn on CNN, I'm shocked to discover that my neighbors were arrested as spies working for a terrorist group from the Middle East.

Although the couple were good neighbors, I couldn't call them good citizens of the country, because they were flat-out traitors. My earlier notion of what *good* meant was inadequate, because it failed to take into account the bigger picture — my neighbors' loyalty to their country. When my neighbors stand trial, I could testify on behalf of their neighborliness, but my testimony is ultimately irrelevant to their traitorous actions.

In the same way, a woman may truly be a good neighbor, mother, and wife, but those qualities alone don't make her good before God. Instead, goodness from God's perspective only comes through his grace.

Nice Guy Thinking grades on a curve

One of my biggest tendencies when I slip up is to compare myself with someone else. Sure, I did something bad, but I justify that I'm at least a better person than that guy down the street or in the next pew. Like others, I prefer to grade my behavior on a curve. Billy Graham and Mother Teresa are the A+'s, and Hitler and Stalin are the Fs. As long as I measure up closer to Mr. Graham and Mother Theresa, I'm all set.

But Christianity forces you to look beyond the Hitlers and Stalins, because God doesn't grade on a curve. Christians believe that God is completely holy and can't even look upon sin. Therefore, although a 99 percent is good enough in human terms, from God's standpoint, it's still fundamentally flawed, because it's less than perfect.

On first take, it seems like God is overly picky, but this is only because it's tough to realize how deeply sin affects one's nature. To illustrate, imagine a 16-ounce glass of pure water. Suppose someone poured a single drop of super-duper lethal poison into the glass and offered you a drink. The person tells you not to worry about the poison, because it's just a drop, which you can overlook. But if you know what's good for you, you know that reality is different: The single drop changes the entire nature of the liquid. You can't just drink the 99.9 percent of pure water and ignore the 0.1 percent of poison. They've merged — the glass is now 100 percent poison. In the same way, as Chapter 4 details, sin isn't just a series of isolated acts that can be overlooked. Instead, it changes a person's very nature into something a holy God can't be near without a thorough cleansing of those sins.

Therefore, in Christianity, grading on a curve makes no sense. It's all or nothing from God's standpoint. If I'm thirsty, I want to know whether water is poison or not. In the same way, God looks on a person as either sin-free (through Jesus Christ) or not.

Nice Guy Thinking says that consequences are proportional to their causes

The expression "The punishment should fit the crime" is common sense wisdom today, whether the situation involves a parent trying to determine the discipline for a missing cookie or a jailor dealing with a prisoner who tried to break out. Most people naturally think that an action should have a direct, proportional relationship with its consequence. Therefore, it only makes sense to send a mass murderer to hell, but to send my really-really-nice-guy-of-a-friend to the same place just doesn't make any sense.

As logical as this may seem, this proportional relationship between action and consequence doesn't often exist even in fairy tales, let alone the real world. A small kiss turns a frog into a handsome prince. The prick of a needle causes a beautiful lady to sleep for decades. A single lottery ticket gives a lazy woman millions, while her hard-working sister struggles to make her mortgage payment. A boy chases a small ball into the street, but does so at the very moment a semi barrels down the road. In each of these scenarios, the causes were minor, almost trivial. But the results of these small actions had life-changing consequences. In the same way, a single sin, no matter how trivial it appears, has devastating costs.

Finding out how to be good enough for God

When you start to read the Bible in an attempt to find out what's good enough for God, you get a splash of cold water in the face: God's idea of what's acceptable is far different from the human idea of what's acceptable. Paul is brutally straightforward about humans' ability to be "good enough" for God in Romans 3:10,18:

> *There is no one righteous;*
> *no, not one.*
> *There is no one who understands.*
> *There is no one who seeks after God. . . .*
> *There is no fear of God before their eyes.*

Sobering words indeed! But what Paul is trying to emphasize here is that all people are sinful, no matter how good they may be compared to others.

The Apostle John agrees when he writes in 1 John 1:8–10:

> *If we say that we have no sin, we deceive ourselves, and the truth is not in us. If we confess our sins, he is faithful and righteous to forgive us the sins, and to cleanse us from all unrighteousness. If we say that we haven't sinned, we make him a liar, and his word is not in us.*

Like Paul, John makes it clear that all people are sinners and don't measure up to God's definition of holiness. However, he adds that so long as people confess their sins and trust in his forgiveness, God will clean up that sin from their lives.

If people aren't good on their own, being really, really nice guys and girls amounts to nothing more than shuffling the deck chairs on the Titanic: They're just performing superficial actions that don't have long-term significance. Instead, God wants to transform this mistaken Nice Guy Thinking into Graced Guy Thinking. For Christians believe that a most holy God considers them good only because of his grace (see Chapter 3).

Playing Salvation Monopoly

Unless you're the lucky one on top, you probably resent monopolies. Many people consider Bill Gates and Microsoft the Evil Empire in the software world, given their dominance over the competition. Political monopolies are rare in a democracy, because if one party gets too powerful, the electorate often prefers to quickly balance things out. The most successful sports teams are also the ones that are the most despised. It's not surprising, then, that this resentment toward monopolies often carries over to resentment of the exclusive claims that Christians make about their faith.

Indeed, in this age of tolerance, one of Christianity's claims that rub many people the wrong way is that Jesus Christ is the *only* way to salvation. It seems so presumptuous, self-righteous, and intolerant to buy into this idea. But Christians say that this belief is the exact opposite of what it seems.

Questioning whether all roads lead to heaven

People often use an old Eastern story to illustrate that all religions are more or less the same. It tells of an elephant standing in a room and a group of blindfolded men each taking turns touching it and describing what they find. The point of the story is that religions are like the blindfolded men, each telling a portion of the full truth (which the elephant represents).

That analogy may seem clever, but it has a big problem. A group of blindfolded men describing an elephant express many differences, but because they're all touching the same animal, the descriptions have much in common — the feel of the skin, the presence of hair, a sense of the creature's immensity, and so on. Though one man grabs a tail, another the trunk, and another the stomach, there remains a common unity to what they're touching.

In contrast, the major religions of the world have no single elephant, no common foundation of unity to speak of. Although *God* is a term religious people use in a generic sense, the Hebrew, Christian, Muslim, and Buddhist concepts of God are irreconcilably different from each other. I liken it to a group of blindfolded men — one describing a zebra, another a giraffe, the third an elephant, and the last one a lion. In this scenario, the only way to make their descriptions a part of the same creature is to ignore reality. Similarly, when you attempt to claim that all religions are equally valid, you inevitably reduce God into some sort of primordial sci-fi being that adapts to people's whims and fancies.

Similarly, Christianity says that you can talk about other ways to salvation all you want, but when all is said and done, Jesus Christ is the only solution out there. In doing so, the faith then goes out on a limb and says that you have to decide whether you believe it's true or false. If false, then move on. But if Jesus' claims are true, then by definition all other religions must be false. There's no other way around it. Like it or not, Jesus made it a zero-sum game; he didn't leave the window open for alternative worldviews or religions to be equally true.

Understanding why Christians say Jesus is the only way

The Christian belief that Jesus is the only way to salvation is deeply rooted in the Bible, which claims this idea in a variety of ways, including

- **Jesus is the way, the truth, and the life.** In John 14:6, Jesus makes the definitive statement:

    I am the way, the truth, and the life. No one comes to the Father, except through me. If you had known me, you would have known my Father also.

    Those aren't the words of someone who intended to be a moral compass or role model for followers of God. His claim encompassed everything of importance in all of life — he is the *only* route to God, the *lone* source of truth, and the *exclusive* means for obtaining eternal life.

- **Jesus is the front man for God.** The Bible calls Jesus the "image of the invisible God" (Colossians 1:15) and the only one who has ever seen God the Father (John 1:18).

- **Jesus is the lone mediator between God and humans.** Although Christians believe that God wants everyone to be saved, Paul makes it clear that this salvation only comes from one source — Jesus Christ. 1 Timothy 2:5–6 says, "For there is one God, and one mediator between God and men, the man Christ Jesus, who gave himself as a ransom for all."

- **No alternative routes are available.** Peter dismisses the possibility of other roads to God in Acts 4:12: "There is salvation in none other, for neither is there any other name under heaven, that is given among men, by which we must be saved!"

- **Jesus is the sheep's door.** Jesus compares himself to a sheep's door in John 10:7–9, differentiating between himself and everyone who came before him: "Most certainly, I tell you, I am the sheep's door. All who came before me are thieves and robbers, but the sheep didn't listen to them. I am the door. If anyone enters in by me, he will be saved, and will go in and go out, and will find pasture."

See Chapter 5 for more of the claims that Jesus made about himself as the one and only way to God.

The Christian claim that Jesus is the only way to reach God and experience salvation isn't a matter of arrogance. Instead, to the Christian, salvation simply doesn't make sense if Jesus isn't the sole means to God. As Chapter 3 describes, Christianity says that people only receive salvation from God because of the sacrifice that Jesus made by dying on the cross. This sacrifice wasn't an optional exercise that God did just to show his love. He did it out of necessity.

Accounting for people who've never heard of Jesus

Because Christianity plainly states that Jesus is the only way to salvation, the logical follow-on question is: What about those people who've never heard of him? Are the natives in the jungles of Borneo, for example, doomed to hell for being unfortunate enough not to have lived in a place where they could've heard of the Christian gospel?

The Bible says that no one can claim ignorance as an excuse (see Chapter 8). Paul alludes to the fact that people intuitively know the existence of God by what's around them. In Romans 1:20, he says:

> For the invisible things of him since the creation of the world are clearly seen, being perceived through the things that are made, even his everlasting power and divinity; that everyone is without excuse.

Creation in some way testifies as to who God is. So, even though a person may not know the name of Jesus Christ, he or she can know God and, therefore, is considered without excuse. The problem, Paul continues, is that people have denied what they know to be true. According to Romans 1:21, "Because, knowing God, they didn't glorify him as God, neither gave thanks, but became vain in their reasoning, and their senseless heart was darkened."

If no one can claim ignorance as an excuse, what does this mean for the natives of Borneo? Because the Bible is largely silent about this issue, Christians are left to speculate on exactly how God deals with people who've never heard the gospel. The Christian Church holds two major perspectives on this issue. Some Christians believe that salvation requires explicit knowledge of Jesus Christ, while others believe that God, in his mercy, makes some allowances for people who haven't heard the gospel. Check out the two views in more detail:

> ✔ **Nothing saves humans apart from an understanding of the gospel message of Jesus Christ.** Therefore, you must have explicit knowledge of the Good News of Jesus Christ in order to be saved. Unless you have

consciously believed in Jesus Christ and his saving work, then you've rejected him, whether purposefully or not. St. Augustine (see Chapter 18) and John Calvin (see Chapters 11 and 18) held this position, as do many within the Church today.

✔ **Knowledge of Jesus is critical, but some middle ground is possible.** In other words, people are saved if they respond to God based on the information available to them. In this scenario, Jesus Christ does the saving, but he makes allowances for people who've not heard of him specifically. Within this perspective, Christians have varying positions, such as

- If any person desires God's favor, he will be saved by Christ even if he doesn't realize how it's all done.

- If any person desires to know God, an opportunity will present itself to her sometime during her life. Many people argue that God will send a messenger (perhaps a human or even an angel) to someone who really wants to know about him.

- God speaks to people's hearts and reveals what's needed to receive saving grace, causing everyone to have an opportunity to accept or reject Christ.

People including Justin Martyr (an early Church father), author C.S. Lewis, Thomas Aquinas (see Chapter 18), and John Wesley (see Chapters 11 and 18) have held various forms of this viewpoint.

For some reason, God deliberately decided not to show his cards on this issue and left it an open question. Many Christians believe that the reason must be that God wants people to trust him on this issue and to work hard to reach all parts of the world with his Good News. However, because God is all-loving and completely fair, Christians have the assurance that his response to the natives in Borneo will be consistent with who he is.

Jesus, however, does warn people not to dwell too much on these what-if scenarios. When a disciple asked Jesus how many people would be saved, Jesus replied, "Strive to enter in by the narrow door, for many, I tell you, will seek to enter in, and will not be able" (Luke 13:24). In other words, Jesus was saying to mind your own business, making sure that *you* focus on your salvation and let *him* deal with the people who've never heard. Obviously, in light of the Great Commission (see Chapter 19), Jesus wasn't telling Christians to keep to themselves and forget about others. Instead, he was making it clear that God is the one who deals with each person's eternal fate, not other people's speculation.

Chapter 16

Taking On Tough Issues Raised in the Real World

. . . .

In This Chapter

▶ Sorting through the problem of evil

▶ Uncovering absolute and relative morality

▶ Viewing Darwinism from a Christian perspective

. . . .

Have you ever had poison ivy? Just the thought of it makes me itch all over. If the truth be told, I've never had poison ivy — a fact I attribute in large part to a story my mom told me growing up. When she was young, one of her friends was so convinced that she wasn't allergic to poison ivy that she put on a bathing suit, found a patch of it, and proceeded to roll through it, covering her entire body. Unfortunately for her, like most everyone, she was allergic to the three-leafed plant o' poison. Breaking out all over in an itchy rash, she spent the next few days in the local hospital recovering. Growing up, I learned two lessons from that story. First, never take poison ivy lightly. Second, my mom didn't always pick the most intelligent of friends.

As I explore tough issues related to Christianity and the world, I take the same approach as I do with poison ivy — I don't treat them lightly. The world has some thorny questions that you can't playfully roll around in. This chapter focuses on three important topics that non-Christians and Christians raise concerning Christianity. (Flip back to Chapter 15 for a discussion on three Church-related thorny issues.)

Wondering Why Bad Things Happen

There will come one day a personal and direct touch from God when every tear and perplexity, every oppression and distress, every suffering and pain, and wrong and injustice will have a complete and ample and overwhelming explanation.

—Oswald Chambers, *Shade of His Hand* (Discovery House Publishers, 1991)

If you turn on the evening news, you see bad things happening every day. A 4-year-old boy gets a rare virus that has no cure. Sweet 6-year-old Janice gets deathly sick when she accidentally eats cleaning detergent. A 34-year-old mother of four is tragically killed in a car crash. Terrorists hijack a plane and cause the deaths of hundreds of innocent people.

The problem for Christians is how to reconcile the inescapable fact of evil in the world with the God they believe is in control. After all, as I discuss in Chapter 7, the Bible says that God is all-powerful, all-loving, and all-knowing. But how can evil coexist with a God who has these awesome qualities? If you turn to the Bible for answers, you see that it tells how evil came into the world and how to deal with it (see Chapter 4), but it doesn't talk much about why God allows the bad stuff to happen. Consequently, from a logical standpoint, one can explain this dilemma in one of five ways:

- ✔ God wants evil to happen. So he's not all-loving.

- ✔ God hates evil, but he can't do anything to prevent it. So he's not all-powerful.

- ✔ God hates evil and would like to prevent it, but doesn't know when it's going to happen. So he's not all-knowing.

- ✔ God hates evil and actively prevents it from occurring. So the evil that you and I experience must, therefore, not be real but must be an illusion.

- ✔ God hates evil and has the power and foresight to stop it, but to achieve a greater good or for some other reason, he doesn't stop all evil from occurring.

None of the first three are consistent with biblical teaching. And compared to the wealth of evidence that supports a God who is all-powerful, all-loving, and all-knowing, no compelling reason to assume their validity exists. The fourth option isn't realistic, because evil is very tangible, and every person experiences it at some point. That leaves the final option — that God can stop evil, but he doesn't always do it. And that's what biblical Christianity claims is true.

Christians believe that God hates evil and that evil is never part of his *deliberate will* (what he intentionally accomplishes). However, because of the nature of the universe, he permits evil to occur through his *permissive will* (what he allows to happen). At the same time, he's not a God who has his hands tied behind his back. When a circumstance is contrary to his deliberate will, God intervenes in the world and overrides an evil from occurring or cancels out its effects. The Bible shows time and time again that prayer is a definite factor in God's intervention in the world with evil and suffering. To see how this plays out, check out another of my books, *Christian Prayer For Dummies* (Wiley).

Specifying two types of evil

Bad stuff happens. I see it all around me. Sometimes, I blame it on myself, but sometimes, I feel like a helpless victim. Think of the bad stuff (evil) that I encounter in two different forms:

- ✔ **Moral evil** is a natural consequence of human free will. Because God created people with the ability to choose, moral evil is the result of a person choosing wrong over right. Chapter 4 gives you the lowdown on this nasty stuff called sin.

- ✔ **Natural evil** is a byproduct of the first moral evil that Adam and Eve committed (known as the *Fall of man;* see Chapter 4) and includes evils that people after the Fall haven't caused by sinning. These include diseases, aging, natural disasters, polyester, leisure suits, and so on.

Christianity says that neither of these types of evil existed before Adam and Eve sinned. Rather, the first sinful act that the original dynamic duo committed unleashed a fury of evil onto the rest of the world that continues through the present day. However, Christianity goes on to say that the days of evil are numbered. Eventually, after the Second Coming of Jesus Christ (see Chapter 9), God will eliminate these evils once and for all in the new heaven and new earth.

Understanding why evil exists

So why would an all-loving, all-powerful, and all-knowing God allow this kind of evil to exist? Christians give a variety of responses to this problem, including the following:

- ✔ **Evil is the result of free will.** God gave freedom to people, and he meant it. Because God wanted to give true free will to humans, he had to allow for the possibility of evil to occur. In other words, when you take a risk in order to achieve the greatest good, you also open yourself to settling with the worst bad.

  As a comparison, suppose your softball team got a chance to play in the league championship. Would you take it? The opportunity to succeed is great, but you also open yourself up to losing as a natural byproduct of that decision to play. God seems to believe that the possibility of winning, even with the downside of losing, is greater than not playing in the game at all.

- ✔ **Evil is the result of original sin.** The suffering that evil causes is a direct consequence of sin. Therefore, because all people have sinned (see Romans 3:23), the argument holds that I have no one to blame but myself, even if the evil that affects me is not directly the result of my specific sin. In this role, I am much like the getaway driver of a bank robbery that

turned deadly. Even though I didn't pull the trigger, I still receive punishment, because I was part of the crime. In the same way, Christians believe that every person is directly or indirectly an accomplice to all the sin of the world (see Chapter 4).

✔ **Evil sometimes achieves good.** God hates evil but temporarily uses the suffering that results from evil to mold his believers into the kind of people that he wants them to be. Through suffering, Christians can develop qualities that last for eternity: joy regardless of circumstances, humility through knowledge of one's limitations, and obedience in spite of the costs. Take note of how these play out in a Christian's life:

- **Pain forces Christians to depend solely on God rather than on their own resolve.** As they experience suffering, God takes them into a deeper relationship with him as they trust him for sustaining grace and power.

- **Pain provides an opportunity for God to display his power in a Christian's life.** The Apostle Paul, for example, experienced suffering (he called it a "thorn in his flesh"), but Paul understood that this problem was a way for God's power to be displayed through his own weakness. In other words, Paul saw these moments as opportunities to glorify God: "For when I am weak, then I am strong" (2 Corinthians 12:7–10).

- **Pain brings spiritual joy.** Paul said that he *delighted* in the suffering he went through — not because he was a masochist, but because instances of pain were opportunities for Jesus to be glorified in his life, so long as he kept focusing and relying on the Lord in the process. Take but one example: When he was jailed for his faith, he used the situations to preach to other prisoners — and even the jailors — to help bring them to a saving faith in Jesus Christ.

✔ **The existence of evil allows for the best of all possible worlds.** Even though it doesn't seem like it initially, Christians believe that this world is the best way to bring about the best of all possible worlds. In spite of the evil that exists, any other ways of creating the world and humans would've resulted in even less goodness. For example, suppose God didn't give free will to humans. In that case, the resulting robots that he created may have been programmed not to sin, making evil an impossibility. But to a loving God who desires relationships with his creation, a pre-programmed robot is far less good as compared to a human who chooses God on his or her own.

This argument may seem hard to stomach given the starving kids in third-world countries, the numerous hurricanes that have left many families with nothing and the terrorist tragedies that shake our world. However, a slightly different take on this argument is to look ahead and consider the grand scheme of eternity. With the new heavens and new earth (flip back to Chapter 9), God is planning the Ultimate of All Possible Worlds that his followers will enjoy for eternity. Given what's to

REMEMBER

come, the way that he created and ordered this present world — with free will and all its implications — is evidently the best way to achieve that future, in spite of the current suffering and evil that exists.

However, humans have an earthly-centered mindset that makes it hard to think with an eternal perspective. The goal of most everyone is to achieve the highest quality of life on earth for as long as possible. Yet, God clearly demonstrates in the Bible that this objective isn't what he's got in mind for humanity. Instead, the New Testament talks a heck of a lot about suffering, persecution, and hardship for people who follow Jesus Christ. Earthly life, therefore, seems much more like a training ground for what's to come. Just as football players have to go through much suffering and pain in summer training camp in order to prepare for the regular season, so too do people on this earth. Think about it — if a football team skipped training camp, they'd be unprepared to make it when the real games started. It seems clear that God feels the same way about his purpose for earthly life. Evidently, in order to have that Ultimate of All Possible Worlds — one that combines human free will with perfect obedience (see Chapter 9) — humans have to go through a considerable amount of blood, sweat, and tears on earth in order to be ready for that future.

In the end, although Christians offer up intellectual reasons for why God permits evil, you can't easily sweep this topic under the table. The problem of evil and suffering is a tough issue to understand, involving both head and heart when people encounter it.

Another tough issue that Christians have to face head-on is the issue of moral relativism. I cover this topic in the next section.

Debating Moral Relativism

It's all relative — or so common wisdom says. Most people in postmodern society, even many who identify themselves as Christians, believe morality is relative and that each individual ultimately decides what's wrong or right for himself or herself. Yet, how compatible is *moral relativism* — the belief that all values depend on an individual's own understanding and beliefs — with biblical Christianity? Before you answer this question, consider whether God allows each individual to decide what's good and what's bad, or whether he sets absolutes that are independent of what people think. I explore these ideas in the following sections.

Seeing why moral relativism is popular

According to Barna Research (2001), 75 percent of all Americans and a whopping 96 percent of all teenagers believe that morality is relative to individuals. It's easy to understand the stronghold that relativism has within society

today — it allows me to have a belief in God and the reward of heaven in the future, yet still live the way that I want to based on my own moral code. Not only is relativism convenient, but it's also a natural follow-on to other individualistic trends in modern society, including

- ✔ **Politics:** To many people, absolutes are passé, throwbacks to days gone by of monarchies and absolute governments, overbearing Church authority, and rigid public moral codes. With the fall of communism and the rapid spread of democracy, except for China and a few third world holdouts, the world is turning into a group of self-ruled democratic governments.

- ✔ **Culture:** Following close behind this spread of political freedom is *cultural individualism,* the practice of each person doing his own thing, going his own way. This individualistic perspective has given way to people not only doing whatever floats their boat, but also wanting to go the next step and claim final say on what is ultimately right or wrong in their lives. In this light, then, abortion is naturally a personal issue, not something that the state should be involved with.

- ✔ **Societal change:** The transient nature of society — frequent geographical moves and the turnstile job market — has further turned society from being community-based to being individual-oriented, in which one moves from place to place or job to job with little loyalty to anyone but himself or herself.

- ✔ **Entertainment:** The entertainment industry is also highly oriented toward the individual. Entertainment used to consist primarily of cinemas and three network TV stations. Today, DVDs, videos, and hundreds of cable TV stations allow you to pick out exactly what you want to watch rather than be forced to deal with a decision that the program manager of the TV network made.

- ✔ **Technology:** Technology advances also focus on empowering you to do more as an individual and rely less on others. The Internet is perhaps the best example of this. You can shop without leaving your home, become your own travel agent, publish your own book online, and access the latest data without traveling to the library. As a result, technology caters to your every whim.

Winston Churchill said that his fellow citizens had no permanent friends, just permanent interests. Contemporary society puts a twist on Churchill's statement; society says that no permanent marriages, friends, or jobs exist, just temporary interests. By and large, society has become a collection of rugged individualists, each doing his or her own thing, coming together for temporary relationships that serve their present self-interests and moving on when they decide that fulfillment lies somewhere else. In the next section, I show you how this reality, which is a clear indication of society's values, contrasts sharply with Christianity.

A must-read: *The Abolition of Man*

When all that says "it is good" has been debunked, what says "I want" remains.

—C.S. Lewis, *The Abolition of Man* (Touchstone, 1996)

A minority of people today believe in the existence of *absolute moral truth,* meaning certain rights and wrongs do exist. I suspect that if British scholar and author C.S. Lewis were alive today, he would question whether the majority really understand the practical consequences of relative truth. C.S. Lewis' *The Abolition of Man* is an essay that speaks to this issue, diving into the inevitable consequences of what happens when you try to remove values from education and absolutes from society.

The Abolition of Man is a bit of a challenge to read. And yet, I had to recommend it for two reasons. First, it's short — only about 100 pages, so I figure that even if it's hard, most everyone can make it through a short book. Second, Lewis shows that people may fancy the notion that truth is relative, but they can't really live by it because the logical result is the destruction of what makes humans uniquely human.

As his quote above points out, when you eliminate absolutes from society, people become nothing more than animals doing what they want based on impulse or instinct. Lewis believed that a relativistic society produces what he calls "men without chests." In other words, Lewis uses the human body to show that when you remove absolutes and a person's spiritual conviction (his chest), you also rip out virtues like valor, integrity, and dignity. And when you do so, the man becomes ruled and controlled by his appetites.

Ironically, while society produces these men without chests, it still expects to find virtue and goodness in them. Or, as Lewis so memorably writes, "We laugh at honor and are shocked to find traitors in our midst. We castrate and bid the geldings be fruitful."

The book was written in the 1940s, which makes Lewis read like a prophet, as society is now struggling with exactly these issues that he saw coming.

Sizing up moral relativism from a Christian view

In a theoretical sense, moral relativism means that you can do anything you believe to be right and I can do likewise. If I disagree with your standard, then I may protest because it doesn't suit my interests, but it makes no sense for me to claim that I'm right and you're wrong, because what's wrong to me may not seem wrong to you.

But consider the practical implications of the idea of people actually living out relativism in society. Suppose, for example, I'm a teacher, and you turn in a political science test on which you answered all the questions correctly. But a day later, when you receive the test back from me, you see a big, fat *F* on it. Your answers may have been technically accurate, but I decided to grade by the grammar and neatness of the answers rather than content. You

can protest all you want and even threaten to take me to the board, just as long as you don't utter the phrase, "You're wrong," (which is a moral judgment). Or suppose that your neighbor is held up in his home at gunpoint and he makes a deal with the criminals to take his children and spare his life. You can be outraged at his decision, but you can't call him immoral, cowardly, or selfish (which are all moral judgments). Finally, suppose a friend invites you out for a fun night on the town, but you discover en route that she's actually taking you to a pro-Nazi meeting. You can run out of that meeting quicker than you can say "Aryan nutcases," but you can't use the *W* word when talking with your friend about her opinions.

On the one hand, these examples are certainly extreme. Though they're unusual, they only serve to underscore the point that society is able to function only because people of all backgrounds accept certain common values as right and some as wrong. C.S. Lewis sums it up well in *Mere Christianity* (Harper San Francisco, 2001):

> *What was the sense in saying the Nazis were in the wrong unless Right is a real thing which they at bottom knew as well as we did and ought to have practiced? If they had no notion of what we mean by right, then, though we might still have had to fight them, we could no more have blamed them for that than for the color of their hair.*

> *If your moral ideas can be truer, and those of the Nazis less true, there must be something — some Real Morality — for them to be true about. The reason why your idea of New York can be truer or less true than mine is that New York is a real place, existing quite apart from what either of us thinks.*

If all values are equal and determined by each individual, then no difference exists between bravery and cowardice, honesty and cheating, and prejudice and tolerance. But people aren't wired to treat these extremes in an equal manner, writing them off as mere preferences or personal taste. Society is implicitly built on certain values that everyone assumes others will follow. It's not just a matter of law, but it's also an intuitive sense of an ultimate Right and Wrong.

For example, *postmodernism* is a philosophical term that people often use to describe the mindset of contemporary society, referring to the worldview that embraces moral relativism and values equality above everything else. Postmodernists hold up issues, such as homosexual rights, racial equality, environmentalism, and animal rights as moral values of the 21st century. Ironically, postmodernists oppose the idea of a traditional morality but argue for their progressive agenda with a moral fervor that would make a Pharisee (see Chapter 4) proud. In other words, they don't speak out against bigotry and homophobia as being mere differences of opinion. Instead, they speak strongly of such issues, referring to them as "evils" that must be eliminated from society. What's notable isn't the rightness or wrongness of postmodern values; the telling point is the fact that postmodernists hold up any issue as being "right" and condemn the opposite stance as being "wrong" — all the while claiming that universal right and wrong don't exist.

Moral relativism: New clothes for a modern-day society

Although moral relativism is mainstream, that doesn't necessarily mean that it's correct. In fact, Christians say that if you read the Bible with one eye and glance around at society with the other, you see an example of Hans Christian Andersen's *The Emperor's New Clothes* being played out right before you.

In case you're unfamiliar with the tale, I'll fill you in. Andersen wrote the story of an emperor who was obsessed with clothes and paid more attention to what he wore than to running his kingdom. One day, two swindlers came into town and persuaded the emperor into thinking that they could make him a new outfit out of a special material. According to the swindlers, this cloth was invisible to anyone who was unfit for his office or who was incredibly stupid.

This new material intrigued the king, so he sent the duo off to make the new digs for himself. The king soon sent a councilor to see the tailors' progress. The two swindlers acted as if they were preparing the new clothes on looms when the man arrived. The councilor saw the empty looms but didn't want to admit that he couldn't see anything, so he talked up the attire's beauty to the emperor. Later, he sent a second assistant, who pulled off the same act. Finally, the emperor went to see for himself, but he didn't see anything. He knew that if he confessed, he'd be admitting that he wasn't fit for the office of the king. So he went along with the ruse, even when the tailors put the invisible clothes on him for a parade through the kingdom. As he marched through the streets in the nude, no one would admit that they couldn't see his clothes; that is, until a lone boy said the obvious: The king had nothing on at all!

In the same way, a Christian sees moral relativism as the new (invisible) clothes of modern-day society. Contemporary culture embraces relative values just like the fictional emperor craved his fancy new attire. But Christians believe that despite the fact that it's hip and popular, relativism is spun from the same empty loom, having no substance to it. People can try it on and wear it down the street, but when they actually try to live in a truly relativist world, this splash of reality, much like that little boy in the story, exposes the nakedness of their beliefs.

As the section, "Sizing up moral relativism from a Christian view" explains, everyone searches, consciously or unconsciously, for some set of values to cover up with.

In order for people to consistently live out moral relativism, they may promote their issues and try to convince people that it's in their best interest to support the position, but the moment that they paint the debate in terms of right and wrong, they've adopted an absolute framework. What's more, although people may not like the fact that someone disagrees with their perspective, true relativists must shrug their shoulders and utter, "To each his own." Yet, I've not heard of one person who can actually pull that off consistently on every issue in life.

Author Francis Schaffer looked at contemporary society and concluded that many people today are forced to take a leap of faith. On one hand, they want

to believe that absolutes don't exist. But they find that they can't live there, so they take an irrational leap of faith toward absolutes that they profess don't exist. In other words, they claim to have no moral absolutes, yet live their lives holding on to them just the same.

Biblical, historical Christianity is wholly incompatible with the idea of relative right and wrong. In fact, you simply can't reconcile relativism with Christianity unless you completely change the meaning of one of those two words. Christianity says that morality and truth are based on God's unchanging character and holiness, as expressed in the Bible. It's also based on an absolute definition of sin; for if sin is in the eye of the beholder, then Christ didn't really need to die, and God can't judge the world. Ultimately, Christianity says that God has the final say and that humans are under his authority, making people accountable to his absolutes.

Considering Darwinism

Ever since Charles Darwin first published his book The Origin of Species (Gramercy, 1995) back in 1859, many have seen Christianity on the ropes in a fight with science. Over the years, the media and movies (such as *Inherit the Wind*) often portray religious people as dumb, ignorant, and resistant to the facts, while they show science as the playground for the intelligent and the open-minded. But much has changed over the past century. Today, because of the discoveries since Darwin first published his theory, one can get a much better perspective on whether Christianity is compatible with science or whether it's a worldview that's great for the pews, but irrelevant for the labs and classrooms.

But before doing so, it's critical to understand the tight relationship between Darwinism and contemporary science.

Noting the difference between Darwinism and science

Watch any science documentary on TV or flip through a science textbook and the odds are quite high that you see the Darwinian theory of evolution treated as an ironclad scientific fact, stated without any qualifications. Indeed, contemporary science and Darwinism have become so closely tied together in some people's minds that they seem inseparable. However, the validity of this marriage depends on one's definition of science.

Ever since the infamous Scopes trial over a hundred years ago, people have seen Christianity as science's enemy. However, that statement would surprise

some of the most renowned early scientists in history, such as Galileo. The early scientists based their scientific method entirely on the assumption of an ordered universe that God created and maintains. They saw science as

- ✔ Investigation through experiments that could be watched and controlled
- ✔ Unbiased conclusions based on the results

In this context, rather than being an enemy, Christianity is very much in synch with the scientific process.

However, the definition of science is entirely different to much of the modern scientific community. Science has become synonymous with *naturalism,* the belief that the physical universe exists without any God or spiritual realm. The logical conclusion is that because nature is all that's real, it's the only thing that people can have scientific knowledge of. As a result, science must assume that nature is a closed system and can't have any outside influences or dependencies. The very idea of God existing or having a role in nature isn't even a subject of debate, because naturalists consider God outside the focus of science.

In the process, however, the door gets closed on God before any debate of the facts: Because contemporary science doesn't allow for the existence of God, then matters regarding any such being are automatically considered subjective belief, regardless of any scientific facts that provide evidence for a Creator of the world.

Consider the problem with this situation through an illustration. Suppose you want to enter a race in which the first person to get his or her motorized vehicle from New York to California wins a million dollars. But when you show up with your jet airplane, you're disqualified because the judges insist that your form of transportation is invalid, in spite of the fact that rules don't stipulate on the type of vehicle allowed. Your jet airplane may, in fact, be a perfectly valid motorized form of transportation and may get there days ahead of the competition, but that's a mute point. The judge's arbitrary interpretation of what *transportation* means has eliminated you from getting off the ground. In the same way, when words such as *science* are defined on Darwinian terms, scientific conclusions are already decided upon, regardless of what the evidence might show.

Darwinian evolution is a belief held so strongly today in the scientific community because it's become the foundation on which science itself is built. Rejecting evolution has become synonymous with rejecting science itself. To abandon evolution, in spite of its problems, is unthinkable to many, because there'd be nothing to replace it — God isn't an option, and ignorance isn't possible, either. Therefore, Darwinian evolution must be protected. In a 1999 op-ed piece in the *Wall Street Journal*, Professor Phillip Johnson, one of the most articulate creationist thinkers, quoted a Chinese paleontologist who said, "In China, we can criticize Darwin, but not the government. In America, you can criticize the government, but not Darwin."

Survey says

If you watch nature programs on TV, you may think that everyone believes in evolution, because the scientific theory is so often treated as plain fact. But according to a Gallup Poll (1991), approximately 91 percent of Americans believe in some form of Creation, while just 9 percent of all Americans believe in pure Darwinian evolution.

Because Christians distinguish between Darwinism and science and because Christianity *is* indeed compatible with science, I spend the next two sections honing in on Darwinism, showing you how Christianity addresses the idea of evolution.

Distinguishing between two theories of evolution

The foundation of modern science is built on evolution. Yet *evolution* is one of those vague words that mean different ideas to different people. It actually has two meanings:

- ✔ *Microevolution* is the theory that organisms can adapt to changes in their surroundings and develop a limited amount of diversity based on their environment. Variation within a species is possible — such as a bird's beak getting larger or a moth's wings changing color — but it's limited in scope. Microevolution has a solid scientific basis, and no one disputes its occurrence in nature. It's entirely consistent with Christianity, and Christians consider it an example of the ingenious way that God created highly adaptable organisms.

- ✔ *Macroevolution* is another ballgame altogether. Also called *Darwinian evolution,* this theory takes the proven idea of limited change over time and attempts to explain all questions concerning the *origins* of life in the same manner: Simple organisms branched out over billions of years to create complex organisms like you see inhabiting the world today.

Macroevolution is driven by *natural selection,* a survival-of-the-fittest process that has no mind or purpose; organisms that adapt to their environment survive, and those that don't adapt become extinct. Natural selection causes such features as wings and eyes to develop over extended periods of time as

a way for organisms to better adapt to their environments. Staunch evolutionist Richard Dawkins memorably called this evolutionary process "the blind watchmaker." (See Chapter 2 for the opposing Christian view of God as a "seeing watchmaker.") Macroevolution, as an impersonal, purposeless process, is incompatible with the personal God of Christianity.

Although microevolution is a theory that evidence confirms, macroevolution is far more speculative. In fact, scientists have no more evidence today (and many argue less) to support macroevolution than Darwin did. To scientists who believe in a God as a designer and creator, the theory of evolution has never successfully answered the basic questions about how life first began or explained the mystery of the DNA code. They also point to recent discoveries as further evidence showing the need for a God as designer. For example, in Darwin's day, scientists originally thought the cell was a simple structure, but advances in molecular biology over the past 30 years have shown how complex the cell is, making the likelihood of natural selection at the molecular level seemingly impossible. (See the "Irreducibly complex" sidebar in this chapter for more on cell complexity.)

Irreducibly complex

If it could be demonstrated that any complex organ existed which could not possibly have been formed by numerous, successive, slight modifications, my theory would absolutely break down.

—Charles Darwin

Charles Darwin believed that the cell is a relatively simple structure that could've evolved through natural selection. But as the quote above illustrates, Darwin himself saw holes in his theory should cells be proven to be too structurally complex to have evolved on their own. Due to technological advances over the past 30 years, scientists no longer have to speculate on the cell. They now have the ability to view and understand a cell's composition in ways that were unheard of decades before.

With this newly discovered knowledge in tow, scientist Michael Behe writes in his book *Darwin's Black Box* (Free Press, 1998) that it's impossible for cells to have evolved through a gradual process, because they're *irreducibly complex*. In other words, a core set of parts has to be present in a cell in order for it to function in the first place. To explain his point, Behe uses the example of an ordinary mouse trap. Behe argues that a mouse trap is irreducibly complex, because all its pieces have to be present and in working order for it to function. You can't just put a piece of wood out in the attic and catch a mouse or two, then add a spring to snatch a second, and then assemble the hammer for even more. This incremental approach doesn't work. Instead, all these pieces must be assembled together and functioning properly before the challenge of mouse catching can even begin. In the same way, cells and other living organisms are irreducibly complex, which seems incompatible with the survival-of-the-fittest theory and suggests strong evidence that cells were designed by God.

Springing up life from nonliving matter

Darwinian evolution requires that living organisms evolved from nonliving matter. Yet research has shown that the chances of life coming from non-life are as likely as getting me to stop after just one plateful at a buffet. As a comparison, imagine a tornado sweeping through a junkyard and randomly assembling a perfectly formed 747 jet. The odds of this event occurring are ridiculously small, but the odds of a living organism evolving from nonliving elements are even more miniscule.

Think of the complexity of the modern 747 jet and the fact that everything must work together precisely or else you have a disaster on your hands. Yet as the history of aviation and space travel has shown, intelligent people have done their best, but accidents still occur and design flaws happen. But because of intelligence, humans can look at tragedies and intelligently deduce how to avoid them in the future. A mindless, purposeless creation process would have no such luxury, making the odds of sustained successes even lower.

Moreover, the popular assumption is that the fossil record proves that simple creatures evolved to become complex ones. But, in reality, the fossil record doesn't show the proof of any transitional forms of species that Darwinian evolution requires. Fossils consistently show up as sudden explosions of species with little changes taking place after that in the fossil record.

Ultimately, although Darwinian evolution is often held up as the logical conclusion of centuries of scientific research, it's really a belief system that requires faith to believe in, just like Christianity. Darwinian evolution is the required way to explain the origins of the world if you have a naturalistic worldview. (See Chapter 14 for more on worldviews.)

Exploring Christian alternatives to Darwinian evolution

Christianity is perfectly compatible with an open-minded version of science that looks for facts without any bias or preconditions and accepts both supernatural and natural explanations, such as *microevolution*. (See the section, "Distinguishing between two theories of evolution," earlier in this chapter for more on microevolution.) And though Darwinian evolution dominates the airwaves and classrooms, Christians offer several theories that explain the origins of life. The generic term that encompasses these beliefs is *creationism*, the theory that God created the world.

Young earth creationists believe that the world is relatively young — perhaps only 10,000 years old — and read the accounts of Genesis 1 and 2 literally, believing that God created it in a six-day period. They base much scientific attention on highlighting the inaccuracy of scientific dating that dates the earth to the millions of years. They also see many of the changes that have taken place on earth as the result of the Flood as recorded in the Book of Genesis, Chapters 6 through 8.

Another group of creationists, called *progressive creationists,* agree with their secular counterparts on the earth's age, but believe that Creation took place over a longer period rather than six days. These people (mostly Christians) believe, for example, that God intervened in nature at various points in time, creating new species.

A new, highly respected group of creationists that has developed over the past decade is known as *intelligent design (ID) theorists.* This group of scientists and academics has steered away from supporting a particular theory on the earth's age and has instead focused on proving that an intelligent designer must've created the world. Many design theorists are Christian but not all of them are.

Some Christians, on the other hand, have attempted to wave a white flag to the scientific community and try to accommodate Christianity with Darwinian evolution. The result is *theistic evolution,* which says basically that God created the world but used natural selection as the means by which he created it.

The biggest problem with theistic evolution is that the term itself appears to be an oxymoron. As I explain throughout this chapter, Darwinian scientists have relentlessly asserted that natural selection is a mindless and purposeless process. Therefore, at most, God would seem to be an unneeded part of the process and could be disposed of without any change in what happens. It seems unlikely to believe that if God had a purpose for creating the world, he would've done so using a mindless, purposeless process that could've just as easily produced a completely different world with different creatures.

Considering the intricate details of the world

The *anthropic principle* is a recent scientific theory that says that the physical order and structure of the world is exactly what's needed in order to successfully support life — from the structure of the solar system to the force of gravity, the composition of water, and the structure of atoms. For example, if the earth were slightly farther away from the sun, all water would freeze and the earth would be a huge popsicle. If the earth were slightly closer to the sun, then all water would evaporate and all life would become like those dancing California raisins. Many Christians use the anthropic principle to point back to the need for a Creator to design the precise physical order of the universe.

Part V
The Part of Tens

In this part . . .

What do the Metric system, Agatha Christie's little Indians, David Lettermen's lists, and this part have in common? Why, they're all based on "tens," of course. In this part, I provide a variety of resources to help round out your understanding of Christianity. In doing so, I also give you some ideas on how to dive into the Christian faith even deeper. I start off by highlighting ten Christian holidays. You then explore ten Christians who are worth knowing about because of their leadership, contribution, and/or Christlike example. Next, you get a glimpse of ten key passages in the Bible to pay particular importance to. Finally, if you look like a deer in headlights when you hear jargon like "born again," "new creature in Christ," or "prayer warrior," then flip on over to Appendix A for a glossary of Christian lingo and find out what these buzzwords mean. And check out Appendix B if you're interested in important dates that shaped the Christian Church.

Chapter 17

Ten Christian Holy Days, Holidays, and Seasons

●●

In This Chapter

▶ Observing holy days

▶ Celebrating traditional holidays

▶ Reserving seasons for contemplation

●●

Many in postmodern society downplay tradition. This change has rippled through some parts of the Church as well. However, tradition remains an important part of what the Christian faith is all about, because when the Church recognizes holy days, holidays, and seasons, it connects Christians of today with Christians throughout history. Special days and seasons also serve as annual reminders of key aspects of the Christian faith, be it Christ's death and resurrection or a day of prayer to humble ourselves as a nation before God.

In this chapter, you discover more about ten major Christian holy days, holidays, and seasons. Some of these holy days that follow in calendar order commemorate actual events that transpired during the life of Christ, although others are special times of reflection and self-examination.

Lent

When: Begins 40 days before Easter

Observance: Self-examination and preparation for Easter

Lent was first observed in the fourth century as the 40-day period between Ash Wednesday (see the "Ashes to ashes" sidebar in this chapter) and Easter. Its focus was on self-examination and self-denial, and Christians used *fasting* (abstaining from eating food) in the early years as a visible demonstration of this process.

Ashes to ashes

Back in the seventh century, Church leaders began the practice of marking foreheads with ashes to symbolize repentance and mortality on Ash Wednesday, referring to Genesis 3:19: "For you are dust, and to dust you shall return."

Many churches don't practice this tradition anymore, because it's a man-made tradition with no biblical roots. However, some Catholic and Anglican churches today continue in this tradition during Ash Wednesday services.

Over the centuries, Catholics have relaxed some of the strict fasting rules. Today, only Ash Wednesday, Good Friday, and all Fridays during Lent are considered fasting days. On these days, Catholics over the age of 14 are to refrain from eating meat. (Historically, this practice was meant to help unify people who could afford meat with poor people who couldn't.) In addition, on Ash Wednesday and Good Friday, those between the ages of 18 and 59 are to eat only one full meal and two smaller meals and aren't to eat between meals.

Orthodox Christians are far more rigorous in their observance of fasting during Lent, believing that regular fasting is a crucially important discipline for one's spiritual growth. Meat, dairy products, and eggs (which historically were considered more luxury foods than ordinary breads) aren't allowed, with some additional restrictions on certain days. They can only eat fish (which was historically considered less of a luxury than red meat) on the feasts of the Annunciation and Palm Sunday.

Some Protestant denominations observe Lent (such as Anglican and Episcopalian), but many Protestant churches attach less significance to the season of Lent than to the individual holy days leading up to Easter.

In addition to refraining from eating, Lent is often a time in which Christians give something pleasurable up (furthering the focus on self-denial), be it chocolate, meat, or — shudder the thought! — coffee.

Palm Sunday

When: Sunday before Easter

Observance: Jesus' entry into Jerusalem

Biblical reference: Matthew 21:1–11

Christians observe Palm Sunday on the Sunday before Easter, celebrating Jesus' triumphal entry into Jerusalem. The reason they call it Palm Sunday stems from the fact that when Jesus rode a donkey into Jerusalem, a large

crowd of people in the city spread out palm branches on the ground before him as a sign of his kingship. Throughout Jesus' three-year ministry, he down-played his role as Messiah and sometimes even told people whom he healed not to say anything about the miracle to others. Palm Sunday is the one exception in which his followers loudly proclaimed his glory to all.

Today, Christians often celebrate Palm Sunday in a joyous, triumphant manner during worship services, emphasizing the glory of Jesus Christ. Some churches spread palm branches at the front of the sanctuary as a way to commemorate the event.

Maundy Thursday

When: Thursday before Easter

Observance: The Last Supper of Jesus

Biblical reference: John 13–17

Within the midst of the Easter season, Maundy Thursday is one Christian holy day that many Christians and even many churches often overlook, yet it symbolizes a critically important truth of the Christian faith — Jesus as a suffering servant and the call for his followers to do the same. It also draws a connection between the Passover sacrifice, a Jewish tradition, and Jesus Christ's sacrificial role on the cross.

The night before Jesus was crucified, he had a Passover supper with his disciples. (*Passover* is a Jewish holy day that celebrates God's deliverance of the Israelites from their slavery in Egypt.) After supper, Jesus knew that this would be his final opportunity to instruct his disciples before the crucifixion, so he talked at length about his purposes, what his followers should do in response, and the promise of the Holy Spirit to come. He then washed his disciples' feet in an incredible demonstration of humility and servanthood. Finally, he gave bread and wine to his disciples and asked them to partake of it in remembrance of him. The act of partaking of bread and wine is called *Communion* (or the Last Supper) today (see Chapter 8).

The word *Maundy* (pronounced *mawn*-dee) comes from the Latin word *mandatum*, which means "command." The command that this holy day refers to is the one that Jesus gave to his disciples during the Last Supper:

> *A new commandment I give to you, that you love one another, just like I have loved you; that you also love one another. By this everyone will know that you are my disciples, if you have love for one another.*

> —John 13:34–35

Along this line, many churches perform foot-washing services on Maundy Thursday as a way to remember Jesus' command. I remember going to one of those services as a teenager, panicking that my feet would be all smelly when someone washed them! I was certain the next song played by the organist would be the Odor Eaters theme song.

During the Middle Ages, this holy day was sometimes called Shere Thursday; *shere* means "pure." In England during this time, bearded men found another reason for that name when they sheared their beards on Maundy Thursday as a symbol of the cleansing of body and soul before Easter.

Good Friday

When: Friday before Easter

Observance: Crucifixion of Jesus on the cross

Biblical reference: Luke 23

Good Friday marks the day on which Jesus Christ was crucified on the cross for the sins of the world. When I was growing up, the term *Good Friday* always seemed confusing, because I associated *good* with *happy*. Good Friday isn't a happy day, but its name is a reminder that humans can only be considered good because of what happened on that day. Some believe that its name was originally *God's Friday,* which, over the years, became its present name. In Germany, Christians call it *Quiet Friday* (from noon on Friday until Easter morning, church bells remain silent). Christians in other parts of Europe call it *Great Friday* or *Holy Friday.*

Good Friday is a day of mourning and sorrow over the sacrificial death of Jesus Christ and a reminder that the sins of all people made it necessary for him to die in the first place. It's also a day of gratitude for the supreme sacrifice that he made.

Protestant churches sometimes hold services between noon and 3:00 p.m. to commemorate Jesus' hours on the cross. Catholics often remove everything from the altar and kiss the crucifix as an expression of worship. Some churches even hold a *Service of Darkness* in which candles are extinguished until people are left sitting in total darkness, as a reminder of the darkness that covered the earth after Jesus died (Luke 23:44–46).

Easter

When: First Sunday after the first full moon after March 21

Which came first: The bunny or the name?

No one knows for certain where the term *Easter* came from, but one theory is that it's derived from the Anglo-Saxon goddess Eostre, who was connected with fertility and spring. If so, Christians named their high holy day *Easter* aiming to replace the pagan celebration of spring with their own holiday — like they did with Christmas. Easter is also often known as *Pasch*, which comes from the Hebrew word *Pesach*, meaning "Passover." Some Protestants prefer to call it simply *Resurrection Day* to remove the commercialized baggage that they see associated with the holy day.

In addition, the Easter bunny has pagan origins and has no real connection with the Christian celebration, although some churches use eggs as a metaphor for the new life Christians receive because of the Resurrection.

Observance: Resurrection of Jesus Christ

Biblical reference: Luke 24

Bar none, Easter is the single most important holy day of the Christian Church, for it celebrates the resurrection of Jesus Christ, the central event in Christianity. To Christians, the resurrection backs up Jesus' claim that he had the authority to die for the sins of the world and the power to come back to life again. It also gives hope to Christians that they too will experience a resurrected life in heaven.

The exact day of the year that Easter falls on is very confusing, and the logic seems pretty old-fashioned in this digital age, because it's based on the lunar calendar and tied to the start of the solar spring. But the Western Church (Catholic and Protestant) continues to observe it based on the rules of long ago — that it falls on the first Sunday after the first full moon after March 21. It can't come before March 22 or after April 25. In contrast, Orthodox Churches wanted to tie Easter to Jewish Passover, given the relationship between Passover and the day of Christ's resurrection. (See the "Maundy Thursday" section, earlier in this chapter.) Because the Jewish calendar determines the date that Jews celebrate Passover, Easter for the Orthodox Churches can vary by as much as five weeks from the Western Church.

Pentecost

When: 40 days after Easter

Observance: Coming of the Holy Spirit

Biblical reference: Acts 2

Originally, Pentecost was a Jewish holiday held 50 days after Passover. One of three major feasts during the Jewish year, it celebrated Thanksgiving for harvested crops. However, Pentecost for Christians means something far different. Before Jesus was crucified, he told his disciples that the Holy Spirit (which I discuss in Chapter 7) would come after him (see John 14:16). And 40 days after Jesus was resurrected (ten days after he ascended into heaven; see Luke 24:51), that promise was fulfilled when Peter and the early Church were in Jerusalem for Pentecost.

Although many North American Christians hardly notice Pentecost today, traditional European churches consider it a major feast day. Pentecost, also called *Whitsuntide* in parts of Europe, is just behind Easter in overall importance. For example, in Germany today on only three occasions does the observance of a national holiday span two days: Christmas (December 25 and 26), Easter (Sunday and Monday), and Pentecost (Sunday and Monday).

National Day of Prayer

When: First Thursday of May

Observance: Calling humbly before God as a nation (U.S.)

The National Day of Prayer is a relatively modern holiday for the United States, but it has historical ties dating back to the start of the country. In 1775, the Continental Congress asked the 13 colonies to pray for wisdom as they discussed forming a new nation. Abraham Lincoln continued this tradition in 1863 when he called for a day of prayer and fasting during the American Civil War. In 1952, Harry Truman declared a national day of prayer, and in 1988, Ronald Reagan formally acknowledged its observance to be held the first Thursday in May.

The purpose of the National Day of Prayer is fourfold:

- ✔ Humbly coming before God as a nation and together seeking his will

- ✔ Praying for the country's leaders to seek wisdom and guidance in their decisions

- ✔ Praying for the spiritual, moral, economic, and political health of the nation

- ✔ Calling all people to repentance for the sins the nation commits or allows

Many churches in Britain observe their own National Day of Prayer each October, but these are sanctioned by the Church of England, not the government. In addition, an International Day of Prayer is held by the Church annually to pray for persecuted Christians around the world.

All Saints' Day

When: November 1

Observance: Honors all Christian saints

Since the seventh century, many in the Western Church have observed All Saints' Day as a holy day on November 1, and the Orthodox Church has observed it on the first Sunday after Pentecost.

All Saints' Day is the day that Catholics, Orthodox Christians, and some Anglicans (see Chapter 11) remember, thank God for, and revere the saints in heaven for various helps. Some Protestant churches observe All Saints' Day as well, but on this date, they remember and thank God for *all* saints, both dead and living. Some churches hold special services to mark this holy day.

Advent

When: Period marked by the four Sundays before Christmas

Observance: Preparation for Christmas and Christ's Second Coming

Advent began in the early Church as a 40-day time of preparation and self-examination before *Epiphany,* a January holiday that observes the visit of the Magi to Jesus (by the Western Church, made up of the Catholic and Protestant Churches) and the Baptism of Jesus (by the Eastern, or Orthodox, Church). (For more on the Western and Eastern Churches, see Chapter 10.) During Advent, the Church welcomed new Christians into the Church to be baptized. Over the years, Advent was eventually tied to honoring Christ's birth and anticipating his Second Coming (see Chapter 9).

Advent started off as a time of solemn preparation like Lent (see the "Lent" section in this chapter), but by the fourth century, the season had evolved into a more celebratory occasion in the Western Church. In contrast, the Orthodox Church has always tended to observe Advent in a more reflective, somber manner.

The lighting of the Advent wreath is the most popular tradition performed during this season. An Advent wreath is a circle of evergreens with four candles, three of which are usually colored violet purple (symbolizing royalty in some churches and penance in others) and the fourth colored rose red or pink (representing the expectation that people have in the coming Messiah). One of the purple candles is lit during the service on the first Sunday (highlighting the theme of hope), a second the next Sunday (love), a third the next Sunday (joy), and the rose-colored candle on the final Sunday before Christmas (peace). Some wreaths also have a white candle (representing the purity and holiness of Jesus Christ) placed in the center, which Christians light on Christmas day.

The origin of the wreath started as a pre-Christian practice by Germanic peoples as a symbol of the hope of a coming spring. Christians kept the tradition but changed its meaning as they looked forward to Christ's return.

St. Francis of Assisi is credited as displaying the first Christmas nativity scene, a re-creation of the manger scene, during Advent in 1223.

Christmas

When: December 25

Observance: Birth of Jesus Christ

Biblical reference: Luke 2:1–20

Christmas is the observance of Jesus' humble birth to a virgin in a stable in Bethlehem. The holiday also celebrates the events surrounding his birth, such as an angel's appearance to shepherds, telling them to visit the newborn king.

Although the Church doesn't consider it the most important Christian holiday, Christmas is certainly the most popular, at least in terms of cultural and social significance. But the early Church, believing that events later in Jesus' life should be the focus, didn't even consider it all that significant. What's more, when Church leaders first discussed observing the birthday of Jesus, some argued against celebrating it like you would another great person in history. Nonetheless, the Church had enough pro-observance support to mark the calendar.

Neither the New Testament nor any historical record marks the exact date of Jesus' birth. As a result, the Church initially considered many different dates, including January 2, March 21, March 25, April 18, April 19, May 20, May 28, November 17, and November 20. The Western Church first observed December 25 in the fourth century, and eventually Eastern Churches followed suit.

Some people criticize that Christmas has its origins as a pagan holiday. Some truth lies in that notion, considering that the timing of December 25 was selected to line up with several pagan Roman holidays that celebrated the winter solstice and worship of the sun. However, Church leaders didn't see matching the date as compromising Christian teaching with the culture. Responding to any criticism, a fourth-century bishop remarked, "We hold this day holy, not like the pagans because of the birth of the sun, but because of him who made it."

Most of the traditional customs of Christmas, such as gift giving, tree decorating, light hanging, and feasting, come from sources other than the Church.

Chapter 18

Ten Christian Leaders You Should Know About

Trying to formulate a Top Ten list of Christians is a bit of an oxymoron. The truth is that probably the most Christlike and obedient of Christians are the ones whom you never hear about. They're too busy serving Christ and others in positions of humility around the world and throughout history that only their Father in heaven and a few people around them understand their true impact.

Nonetheless, many Christians over the past two thousand years have played important roles in the Church, in society, or both. In this section, you explore ten of these folks who are worth getting to know something about.

St. Augustine of Hippo

Augustine (354–430) remains one of the most significant early Christian thinkers and Church leaders who continues to have an influence to this day. Before Augustine became a Christian, he was an intellectual who sensed a battle inside of him between his body and spirit, but he initially dismissed the Bible and Christianity. He toyed with other beliefs but always found them insufficient in dealing with his struggle over what he knew was right and the desires he had to do wrong. Living in Milan, he heard much about the great sermons of Bishop Ambrose, so he started attending services to hear his preaching. Through Ambrose's sermons, Augustine came to believe that Christianity isn't simply a religion for the uneducated, but it's a faith that applies intelligent thought and has legitimate claims of truth.

Augustine constantly struggled with sexual temptation and was unable to find anything that helped conquer his lack of self-control. One day, when walking through his garden and mentally searching for answers, he claimed to have heard a voice from out of nowhere saying, "Take it and read." A copy of a New Testament was nearby, and Augustine started reading Romans 13:13–14, a passage that deals exactly with his struggles against lust. Through this mystical experience, Augustine became convinced of the truth of Christianity and became a believer. His book *Confessions* (Oxford Press, 1998) focuses on his personal struggles in coming to the Christian faith.

Augustine became involved in the Church and eventually became the Bishop of Hippo in North Africa. Perhaps his greatest literary work was *The City of God* (Penguin, 1984), a book that took him years to write. This philosophical work focused on the nature of the relationships between the Christian and the government. Augustine's work has had a major influence on Christian political thought since that time. Even today you hear about the Just War Theory (see Chapter 14), which has its roots in Augustine's thought.

St. Francis of Assisi

St. Francis of Assisi (1182–1226) is known as a Christian who truly lived out Christ's call to "die to self." His call was to transform the world by portraying Christlike humility.

St. Francis was born Giovanni Bernardone. He grew up in a wealthy Italian noble home and was destined for the knighthood. But after a brief stint as a knight, he decided that the knight's life was not for him. In stark contrast, St. Francis of Assisi felt that if he was going to live like Christ did, then he had to live a life of poverty, living out the principles that Jesus gave in the Beatitudes (see Chapter 19) and the charge to the rich young ruler in which Jesus said, "Sell all you have, give to the poor, and then come and follow me." As a result, he left home with little more than the clothes off his back and began living a life of poverty in service to the Lord.

St. Francis eventually went to the pope and requested approval to form a *brotherhood* (fellowship of brothers in Christ). The pope approved, and Francis and his group of followers became known as Friars Minor ("lesser brothers"). Today, this same order is known as the Franciscans, who remain a vibrant part of the Catholic Church to this day.

St. Thomas Aquinas

Thomas Aquinas (1224–1274) is arguably the most significant Catholic thinker of all time. Aquinas was a monk, highly educated, and of noble birth. He was an intellectual and valued reason, all the while aligning his intellectual views with the teachings of the Church. Although many Christians before him had no use for pagan Greek thought, Aquinas embraced many of Aristotle's principles and saw considerable consistency between them and Christianity.

In many ways, Aquinas is at the root of Catholic thought, much of which he expresses in his great work, *Summa Theologica*. His views on the role of the papacy, the role of the sacraments in salvation, the doctrine of purgatory, the relationship between the Church and government, and the doctrine of transubstantiation (see Chapter 8) are all held as Catholic doctrine today. All these ideas didn't necessarily originate with Aquinas, but he articulated them and put them into a framework that made sense.

Martin Luther

Martin Luther (1483–1546) is known as the father of the Protestant Reformation and founder of the Lutheran Church. Luther started off as a German monk but was consumed by a terror of God's wrath. He continued to look for the peace that was missing in his life. His mentor urged him to focus on the Bible's teachings concerning forgiveness. Eventually, he began studying Romans, and as he did so, he saw that the Good News of Jesus Christ means that people are saved by grace through faith alone, not by anything they do (Romans 10:9–10). And that freedom in Christ changed his life.

Luther was troubled, because this wasn't the teaching of the Catholic Church. What's more, the Church at that time was involved in a corrupt practice of selling indulgences, which essentially means that people had to buy forgiveness for their sins. That issue pushed Luther to take action. In today's world, Luther may have created a Web site or appeared on Larry King Live protesting the use of indulgences in this manner. But in his day, people nailed arguments (called *theses*) to church doors. That's exactly what Luther did on October 31, 1517, nailing his now famous Ninety-five Theses, which condemned the sale of indulgences, on a church door in Wittenberg, Germany. His action was a protest, but he didn't consider it outright revolution against the Catholic Church. However, that's exactly how it turned out, as the theses spread like wildfire throughout Germany, earning him instant notoriety. Luther went on for many years after that to formulate his theology, which I discuss further in Chapter 11.

William Tyndale

William Tyndale (1484–1536) was an Englishman who lived in a time during which only the religious leaders had access to the Bible. Part of the reason for this was that the available scriptures were written in Latin, not in the language of the common person — English. Also, the Church leaders didn't think they should allow the average man and woman to interpret the scriptures for themselves. From the Church's perspective at the time, the Church clergy was the sole interpreter of the Bible, as I discuss more in Chapters 10 and 11. Tyndale, a supporter of the Reformation, disagreed and spearheaded the translation of the Bible into English so that everyone could read it.

The Church of England felt threatened by this and persecuted Tyndale. He left England and began living elsewhere in Europe, all the while working on his English translation of the Bible, which he then began smuggling into England. Eventually, the Church of England found him in Europe and brought him back to England, where he died a martyr's death. Tyndale's dying words were, "Lord, open the king of England's eyes." His prayer was eventually answered as King Henry VIII authorized an English Bible not many years later. And, just a few years after that, King James authorized perhaps the most well-known Bible translation — the King James Bible.

John Calvin

John Calvin (1509–1564) was an early Protestant leader and the founder of the Reformed Protestant Church, which includes such denominations as Presbyterians, Reformed Churches, and most Congregationalist and Baptist Churches. Calvin was a highly educated native of Paris and eventually became a believer of the new Protestant movement that was sweeping through parts of the European continent.

Around this time, Calvin wrote his best-known work, *Institutes of the Christian Religion* (Wm. B. Eerdmans Publishing Co., 1995), which was the clearest explanation of Protestantism that was printed in the early years after the Reformation. The work propelled him to instant leadership within Protestant circles. He eventually took a hybrid church/state leadership role in Geneva, Switzerland in which strict and rigid adherence to discipline was civil law. Calvin had high expectations of himself and others. He had no tolerance for slackers or disobedient people. The climate of Geneva during his leadership assumed that personality. The city became a symbol of moral purity and a center for Christian training.

Calvin's theological core was an emphasis on God's sovereignty over human free will, meaning that God chooses people who will be saved (known as the

elect) rather than vice versa. This belief is known as *predestination*. His theology was eventually hammered out and explained as the Five Points of Calvinism:

- ✔ **Total depravity:** Sinful humans are totally unable to save themselves.

- ✔ **Unconditional election:** God's purpose for saving people isn't based on anything that people have done, but solely on his will.

- ✔ **Limited atonement:** Christ's death was sufficient to save all people but only actually saves the elect.

- ✔ **Irresistible grace:** Those who are elected by God will also choose him with their own human wills.

- ✔ **Perseverance of the saints:** Those people who are chosen by God will never opt out, but will persevere in their faith and receive salvation.

I discuss predestination and Calvinism further in Chapter 11.

John Wesley

John Wesley (1703–1791) was the founder of the Methodist Church (including its spin-offs, such as the United Methodist, Free Methodist, and Wesleyan Churches) and was one of the most effective, hardest-working preachers of all time. Wesley is credited as reaching over 120,000 people across Britain and North America.

Nicknamed the Little Giant, Wesley was small in stature, but exerted a powerful influence in his ministry. Wesley was the 15th of 19 kids in his family (no, that's not a misprint) and was influenced greatly by his mother's evangelical faith. He eventually went to Oxford and studied theology. He formed a group while at Oxford, known as the Methodists, who sought to live their lives like those in the early Church.

Early on, Wesley was convinced that perfection was the ultimate Christian goal. Yet, after some personal failings, perfection seemed so far away, and Wesley struggled to understand what faith was. He eventually realized that what he needed more than to strive for perfection was to simply experience the forgiveness of Christ in his life. He soon felt a real change occur in him, a sense of assurance that he was forgiven and that, as Luther discovered two hundred years earlier, salvation is attained by grace through faith. Unlike Calvin, Wesley was a strong proponent of human free will, believing that God's all-knowing nature enables him to know his elect, but that God lets each person make up his or her own mind.

Although Wesley wasn't the outdoor type, he eventually teamed up with another preacher named George Whitefield and preached to people in open fields. The impact was amazing, and the Methodist revival came out of it.

Wesley was a workhorse, traveling at least 4,500 miles per year around England by horseback. Over his lifetime, he is estimated to have traveled over 250,000 miles preaching the gospel to people across Britain.

I discuss Wesley in more detail in Chapter 11.

William Wilberforce

William Wilberforce (1759–1833) was an evangelical Christian who lived out his beliefs as a member of British parliament for decades. Wilberforce felt called by God to seek justice and righteousness in this world. He felt that the number one issue of his day was slavery, so he became the force behind the abolition movement in England.

Wilberforce started speaking against the slave trade in 1789 by giving a speech in the House of Commons. At that time, few listened — the commercial interests against his position were too strong. But Wilberforce's determination against the odds never wavered. Although it took him decades to build the support needed, he persevered. Finally, in 1807, the British Parliament voted to abolish the slave trade. Wilberforce saw that as the first victory in the complete abolition of slavery, so he immediately set out to end slavery itself in the British Empire. However, because of bad health, he was forced to leave Parliament — but not before getting another evangelical known as Thomas Fowell Buxton to take the reigns and continue the fight. Just four days before Wilberforce died, Britain outlawed slavery in its vast empire — thanks in large part to the personal conviction of one Christian attempting to live like Christ.

Dietrich Bonhoeffer

Dietrich Bonhoeffer (1906–1945) was a German Lutheran pastor in Nazi Germany during the 1930s and 1940s and was one of the few pastors with the courage to speak against Hitler and the German Church, which looked the other way regarding the evils of the Nazis.

This defiance wasn't by any means easy for Bonhoeffer. He grew up thinking of the Church and the government as having the same interests, and he struggled as Hitler rose to power and began implementing policies that directly opposed biblical teaching. He eventually came to the conclusion that he had to obey God first and Germany after that. After World War II started and the evils of the Nazi regime grew more apparent, Bonhoeffer became involved

in a doomed plot to assassinate Adolph Hitler. When the attempt failed, Bonhoeffer was charged, arrested, and ultimately hanged just before the end of the war.

Bonhoeffer is best known for his work *The Cost of Discipleship* (Touchstone, 1995), which I discuss further in Chapter 13.

Alexander Solzhenitsyn

Alexander Solzhenitsyn (1918–present) is one of the greatest intellectuals and political writers of the past century. He was detained for eight years (1945–1953) for writing a letter in which he criticized Joseph Stalin, the leader of the Soviet Union. While in prison, his life was transformed as he became a Christian due to the influence of another Christian he met in the labor camp.

After Solzhenitsyn was let out of prison, he wrote a book called *One Day in the Life of Ivan Denisovich* (Signet, 1998) that told the brutal nature of the Soviet Gulag (prison system). This book became widely known in the U.S. and Europe, and he quickly became world renowned for his nonconforming positions. He also wrote *The Gulag Archipelago* (Perennial, 2002) based on stories he memorized while in prison, each of which chronicled the horror of the realities of the Gulag. Although he had to leave the Soviet Union in the 1970s as a result of his outspokenness against the government, he continued to be a moral force as an author and ultimately helped bring down the Communist Soviet Union.

Chapter 19

Ten New Testament Teachings You Should Know About

. . . .

In This Chapter

▶ Reviewing New Testament authors' explanations of the faith

▶ Taking Christ's words to heart

▶ Living the Christian life and fighting spiritual battles

. . . .

C hristians should read all of the New Testament because it's important, but certain teachings stand out from the rest of the Bible and deserve special emphasis. In this chapter, I highlight ten of these teachings that have special importance. These aren't necessarily *the* ten most important teachings of the New Testament, but they all focus on key components of the Christian faith.

Walking Along the "Roman Road" to Salvation

Look It Up: Romans 1:20–21, 3:23, 5:8, 6:23, 10:9–10, 10:13, 11:36

You find the plan of salvation throughout the New Testament, but the Book of Romans provides a grand sequence of all the important steps. Commonly nicknamed the *Roman Road,* this series of successive steps begins with an awareness of your sin, explains how Christ meets your need, and shows you how you can receive salvation in Christ. (See Chapter 3 for more discussion on salvation.) These verses introduce you to the following Christian concepts:

> ✔ **All people know right and wrong (1:20–21).**
>
> *For the invisible things of him since the creation of the world are clearly seen, being perceived through the things that are made, even his everlasting power and divinity; that they may be without excuse. Because, knowing*

God, they didn't glorify him as God, neither gave thanks, but became vain in their reasoning, and their senseless heart was darkened.

✔ **All people have sinned (3:23).**

For all have sinned, and fall short of the glory of God.

✔ **God still loves people in spite of their sin (5:8).**

But God commends his own love toward us, in that while we were yet sinners, Christ died for us.

✔ **God provides a way out of consequences of sin by giving a gift (6:23).**

For the wages of sin is death, but the free gift of God is eternal life in Christ Jesus our Lord.

✔ **God's gives this gift (salvation) to whoever believes in him (10:9–10).**

If you will confess with your mouth that Jesus is Lord and believe in your heart that God raised him from the dead, you will be saved. For with the heart, one believes unto righteousness; and with the mouth, confession is made unto salvation.

✔ **Salvation is based on a simple call of faith (10:13).**

Whoever will call on the name of the Lord will be saved.

✔ **In response, people should make Jesus Lord of their lives (11:36).**

For of him, and through him, and to him, are all things. To him be the glory for ever! Amen.

Listening to the Sermon on the Mount

Look It Up: Matthew 5:1–7:28

The Sermon on the Mount is so named because Jesus gave the teaching on a hill near Capernaum. Perhaps some of the most difficult teaching of Jesus' entire ministry is contained in these chapters; in them, Jesus challenged the rigid legalism of the religious leaders of his day (the Pharisees and Sadducees), emphasizing that God desires obedience of the heart, not the appearance of obedience. Perhaps the most well-known section is known as the Beatitudes (which comes from the Latin word meaning "blessed"):

Blessed are the poor in spirit,
for theirs is the Kingdom of Heaven.
Blessed are those who mourn,
for they shall be comforted.
Blessed are the gentle,
for they shall inherit the earth.
Blessed are those who hunger and thirst after righteousness,

for they shall be filled.
Blessed are the merciful,
for they shall obtain mercy.
Blessed are the pure in heart,
for they shall see God.
Blessed are the peacemakers,
for they shall be called children of God.
Blessed are those who have been persecuted for righteousness' sake,
for theirs is the Kingdom of Heaven.

—Matthew 5:2–10

A common interpretation of these high expectations and the rest of the Sermon on the Mount's teachings is that Jesus painted the portrait of absolute perfection that God demands. Is this utterly impossible? Absolutely. That's why Jesus is required to bridge the gap between the perfection that God requires and the best of what humans have to offer.

Praying the Lord's Prayer

Look It Up: Matthew 6:5–12

The Bible treats it as a given that Christians pray, but it says little on *how* to pray. Jesus, however, in his Sermon on the Mount teaching, gives such instruction in what Christians call the *Lord's Prayer* (or *Our Father*):

Our Father in heaven, hallowed be thy name.
Let thy Kingdom come.
Let thy will be done,
on earth as in heaven.
Give us today our daily bread.
Forgive us our debts, as we also forgive our debtors.
Bring us not into temptation, but deliver us from the evil one.
For thine is the Kingdom, the power, and the glory forever.
Amen.

When you look at the prayer Jesus gives, you see that Jesus starts by worshiping God the Father. Because Christians believe that God is worthy to be worshiped, then it follows that they should surrender to his will. (See Chapter 16 for more on God's will.) Christians believe that after you've worshiped him and surrendered to his will, you are invited to ask God to provide for you, forgive your sins, and protect you from evil.

Although the Lord's Prayer is a great prayer to memorize and recite, it's even more helpful to think of the prayer as a blueprint or a model for how to pray.

Identifying with the Prodigal Son

Look It Up: Luke 15:11–32

The parable of the prodigal son is perhaps the most famous of all the parable teachings of Jesus (see Chapters 3 and 6). The parable expresses the sacrificial love and forgiveness of a father toward his wayward son. Christians find many important parallels between Jesus' death on the cross for sinners and the actions of the father in this story:

- ✔ While the prodigal son leaves the father to go off and do his own thing, the father continues to love his son. In the same way, humans willingly sin and separate themselves from God, but God is always hoping for each person to return "home."

- ✔ The father doesn't run after the son but has his arms open wide should the son choose to return. Likewise, God doesn't force himself on people, but should they choose to come to him, he wraps his arms around them like the father in the story does.

- ✔ In light of Middle Eastern culture, the father in the parable humiliates himself when he runs out to meet his returning son. In the same way, Jesus' death on the cross is the ultimate example of God willingly humiliating himself simply because he loves the people he created.

In this parable, Jesus offers hope to the most despicable of sinners, as Luke 15:32 says: "Your brother was dead and is alive again. He was lost and is found." He made it clear that no sin is ever too much for God. The same hope that the prodigal son experienced is available to anyone and everyone, even to the worst scoundrels around.

Detailing the Death and Resurrection of Jesus Christ

Look It Up: Matthew 27:32–28:15, Mark 15:25–16:8, Luke 23:32–24:53, John 19:17–21:25

Christians believe that the death and resurrection of Jesus Christ is the critical turning point in history (see Chapter 5), and it serves as the foundation for their faith. Although the Gospel accounts of Matthew, Mark, Luke, and John each have their own identity and emphasis on the events that occurred, all underscore the reality of Jesus as a literal, risen savior. Luke 24:6 boils the hope of Christianity down to a few words: "He is not here; he has risen!"

Going Out with the Great Commission

Look It Up: Matthew 28:18–20

Last words always carry special importance. Whether they're the last utterances of a dying loved one or the final words of parents to a babysitter before they go out for the evening, people tend to close with words they want the listener to remember. Therefore, just before Jesus ascends into heaven 40 days after his resurrection (see Chapter 5), he leaves the disciples with these very important words:

> *All authority has been given to me in heaven and on earth. Therefore go, and make disciples of all nations, baptizing them in the name of the Father and of the Son and of the Holy Spirit, teaching them to observe all things that I commanded you. Behold, I am with you always, even to the end of the age.*

Christians refer to this command as the "Great Commission" and as the underlying purpose of the Church.

Appreciating Ancestors in the Hall of Faith

Look It Up: Hebrews 11

Hebrews 11 is sometimes referred to as the "Hall of Faith" because it lists, one after another, Old Testament believers who lived by faith — from Abel (Adam and Eve's son), to Noah, to Abraham, and so on down to the prophets. Christians consider these faithful believers heroes of the faith, who stuck it out in the midst of uncertainty and hardship. Hebrews 11:1 defines this faith: "Now faith is assurance of things hoped for, proof of things not seen."

Mixing Faith with Deeds

Look It Up: James 2:14–19

The Book of James reminds Christians that faith is more than just saying you believe in Jesus. Instead, true faith means that you live out your salvation through a transformed life:

> *What good is it, my brothers, if a man says he has faith, but has no works? Can faith save him? And if a brother or sister is naked and in lack of daily food, and one of you tells him or her, "Go in peace, be warmed and filled;"*

and yet you didn't give him or her the things the body needs, what good is it? Even so faith, if it has no works, is dead in itself. Yes, a man will say, "You have faith, and I have works." Show me your faith without works, and I by my works will show you my faith. You believe that God is one. You do well. The demons also believe, and shudder.

As you see from this passage, James dismisses intellectual belief alone as being enough for a saving faith. In fact, he even says that Satan's helpers (demons) believe in God, though that's not going to do them any good in the end.

Promising the Coming of the Holy Spirit

Look It Up: John 14:16–17, Acts 2:1–4

The challenge of being faithful in a hostile world can make any Christian feel all alone. Yet, before Jesus finished his earthly ministry, he promised that no believer will ever be alone but will have the presence of the Holy Spirit:

I will pray to the Father, and he will give you another Counselor, that he may be with you forever — the Spirit of truth, whom the world can't receive; for it doesn't see him, neither knows him. You know him, for he lives with you, and will be in you.

Then, on the day of Pentecost (40 days after Jesus ascended into heaven), the Holy Spirit filled the disciples. As I discuss in Chapter 7, this same promise applies to Christians today.

Suiting Up with the Armor of God

Look It Up: Ephesians 6:13–18

In the Book of Ephesians, Paul reminds Christians that the struggle they face in this world is not against people and the powers of the visible world, but against invisible, spiritual forces of Satan. As a result, he calls Christians to put on battle gear and be prepared for spiritual war:

Put on the whole armor of God, that you may be able to withstand in the evil day, and, having done all, to stand. Stand therefore, having the utility belt of truth buckled around your waist, and having put on the breastplate of righteousness, and having fitted your feet with the preparation of the Good News of peace; above all, taking up the shield of faith, with which you will be able to quench all the fiery darts of the evil one. And take the helmet of salvation, and the sword of the Spirit, which is the spoken word of God; with all prayer and requests, praying at all times in the Spirit, and being watchful to this end in all perseverance and requests for all the saints.

Appendix A

Glossary of Christian Lingo

• •

*O*ver the years, Christians have developed a knack for using catch-phrases in church and when talking about their faith. Most of this lingo originates from a term or phrase in the Bible that people have picked up on and now use in conversation. The problem is that Christians can easily fall into the trap of talking about Christianity and their faith using this jargon — which can be terribly confusing if you aren't sure what it all means. Therefore, use this glossary as your guide through the world of Christian buzzwords. You don't find heaven or hell defined here, but finally you figure out what God bumps are!

amen: The common and traditional ending to a prayer. Literally means "so be it." When you use *amen* to close a prayer, you're affirming everything you just said with "Let it be so."

apostle: In general, the term means "a messenger." However, people use it most often to refer to the select group of people that Jesus entrusted to lead the early Church and spread the gospel. This group included the original disciples (except for Judas) and Paul.

atonement: Repayment for sin. The Atonement of Christ refers to the sacrificial death that he made for the sins of the world.

backsliding: When a Christian becomes absorbed with sin and neglects his or her faith.

"bear my cross": See *take up my cross*.

believer: Another term for Christian.

blasphemy: Showing disrespect toward or contempt for God.

"blood bought": Expresses the idea that Christians are bought and paid for (saved from punishment) because of the Blood of Christ. See also ***Blood of Christ***.

Blood of Christ: When Jesus died on the cross for the sins of the world, his blood became, in effect, the active ingredient that cleanses sin from Christians. Paul refers to the "saving" effect of the Blood of Christ in Romans 5:9: "Since we have been justified by his blood, we will be saved from God's wrath through him."

Blood of the Lamb: Another name for Blood of Christ. In the Old Testament, a lamb was sacrificed as a payment for sins. Jesus Christ is considered The Lamb, making it clear that the Old Testament sacrifices were only prototypes of the real and final sacrifice that Jesus made.

Body of Christ: Another name for the Christian Church.

Book of Life: See *Book of the Lamb*.

Book of the Lamb: According to Revelation 13, each Christian's name will be written in the Book of the Lamb as a guarantee of his or her fellowship in heaven. People whose names aren't in the Book of the Lamb will go to eternal punishment (commonly referred to as *hell*).

born again: To be spiritually reborn by committing your life to Jesus and entering into a personal relationship with him. Jesus said in John 3:3 that unless a person is *born again,* he or she won't see the Kingdom of God.

Bride of Christ: Nickname for the Christian Church, using the analogy of Jesus Christ as the bridegroom and the Church as the bride.

brothers and sisters in Christ: Term that describes fellow Christians. Paul calls Christians the "children of God" and "brothers and sisters of Christ."

Calvary: The name of the hill outside of Jerusalem where Jesus was crucified. The term comes from the Latin word *Calvaria,* which is translated from the Hebrew word *Golgotha* (meaning "the place of the skull").

Catholic and catholic: *Catholic* with a capital *C* refers to the Roman Catholic Church, while lowercase *catholic* is a term that means "universal."

charismatics: Refers to people who experience speaking in tongues. The term originates from *charisma,* the Greek word for "gift." Charismatics believe that speaking in tongues is one gift that Christians receive from the Holy Spirit. Other gifts include the ability to *prophesy* (or highlight biblical truths for a specific context), see visions, and heal both physical and emotional sicknesses.

Christian walk: The practice of living out one's faith by serving, obeying, and worshiping God and getting to know him better through Bible reading and prayer.

Christlike: Christians are called to live their lives like Christ did. Paul wrote that Christians should be imitators of Christ (Ephesians 5:1) and have the same attitude as that of Jesus (Philippians 2:5).

crucifixion: An agonizing method of execution that the Romans performed by nailing a prisoner to a cross. Death took several hours or even days, because the person died from suffocation. The person was also usually stripped naked to add to the humiliation of the execution.

devotional: A devotional is a book filled with daily readings that Christians often use as a supplement to Bible reading, aiding in meditation and reflection on some aspect of God's truth.

devotions: See *quiet time*.

disciple: Follower of Jesus Christ. During Jesus' three-year ministry on earth, he had 12 disciples. However, Christians still commonly use the term *disciple* to describe a dedicated follower of Christ.

"dive into the Word": Refers to studying the Bible and applying its truths to one's life.

"dying to self": Jesus Christ said that those people who want to follow him must give up their own wants, concerns, and rights and be totally loyal and obedient to him. *Dying to self* doesn't mean dying physically, but giving up what you hold dear. Jesus wants 100 percent of his disciples, not the leftovers. See also *take up my cross*.

End Times: Events surrounding the Second Coming of Christ.

evangelical: In short, a Christian who believes that people are saved by grace through faith alone (and not by good deeds) and believes the Bible is the inspired Word of God. A detailed definition, provided by Barna Research, is a Christian with the following beliefs: Being born again is necessary to be saved; faith is a top priority in everyday life; Christians have a personal responsibility to share their beliefs with non-Christians; Satan really exists; salvation is possible only through grace, not by being a good person; Jesus Christ lived a sinless life on earth; and God is an all-knowing (omniscient), all-powerful (omnipotent), perfect deity who created the universe and still rules it today.

evangelism: Sharing with others the gospel of Jesus Christ.

Evil One: Another name for Satan.

Fall of man: The original sin of Adam and Eve.

fellowship: Sharing together with other Christians in worship, communicating concerns with each other, and sometimes simply being together as a collective church body.

"filled with the Spirit": Christians receive the gift of the Holy Spirit living in their lives. This expression describes the completeness that Christians have when they have the Holy Spirit inside of them. Paul contrasted being controlled

by alcohol with being controlled by the Holy Spirit in Ephesians 5:18: "And don't be drunk with wine, but be filled with the Spirit." Also note that some charismatics believe that being filled with the Spirit is synonymous with speaking in tongues.

flesh, the: A term that many Christians and some versions of the Bible use to refer to humans' tendency to sin. See also *sinful nature*.

free will: The ability that God gave humans to choose whether to follow him and have a relationship with him or to go their own separate ways.

"freedom from bondage": Refers to the freedom that Christians have from sin. Paul says in Romans 6:17 that apart from Christ, humans are slaves to sin, but with Christ, they're freed from this bondage.

"Give it to God": See *laying it on the altar of God*.

"Give the glory to God": Christians believe that God is in control and engineers circumstances in this world. Therefore, they use this expression to give credit to God for something good that happens, because he either allowed or engineered it, rather than taking credit for it themselves. The Bible also calls Christians to give glory to God even when something bad happens, because he shows his grace and mercy through those times as well.

God bumps: A term that some Christians use to describe the sensations (like goose bumps) that they feel when they experience the Lord's presence. Other Christians consider it a rather tacky term.

God incarnate: God taking on the form of a human. Christians believe that Jesus Christ was God incarnate, fully God and fully human.

"God laid it on my heart": God speaks to Christians, not in an audible voice, but by planting thoughts in their minds, usually so quickly that they may wonder where the thoughts came from. Oftentimes, when the message is really from God, it impacts their hearts as well when they begin to focus on it. However, this doesn't mean that every message that a Christian believes is from God, in fact, is. A Christian should always examine something he or she has heard with what the Bible says and pray about it. See also *God told me*.

"God told me": The idea that God communicates directly with an individual about a particular issue. However, if someone tells you this, be discerning. God usually speaks nowadays through the Bible and the Holy Spirit, not in an audible manner. Unfortunately, many people misuse this phrase, causing others to become skeptical about the idea of hearing God. See also *God laid it on my heart*.

God's will: What God wants. God's will is formally called his *deliberate will*, which reveals who God is and what he wants to happen. On the other hand, God's *permissive will* is what he allows to happen. God doesn't want disease,

sin, suffering, or death, but he does permit them to happen as a natural consequence of the freedom that he gives all people. Many things that happen today aren't part of God's deliberate will, but all things that happen, be they good or bad, are part of his permissive will.

"going home": Christians typically use this to refer to their eventual, eternal home — heaven.

gospel: Literally, the "good news" that Jesus Christ died on the cross for the sins of the human race and rose from the dead, and that those who believe in him will be saved from sin.

Gospels: Refers to the first four books of the New Testament — Matthew, Mark, Luke, and John — that chronicle the life, death, and resurrection of Jesus Christ.

grace: Receiving something that's undeserved. Christians believe that it's only by God's grace that humans can be saved from punishment for their sin.

"growing in my faith": See *Christian walk*.

hallelujah: A term that Christians use to express praise and thanksgiving to God. It's often said that *hallelujah* is the only word that's the same in every language.

heresy: False teaching that's not in line with the Bible or historical Christian beliefs and seriously undermines all of Christianity.

"his mansion": Term that refers to heaven.

holiness: Turning away from sin and setting oneself apart for the Lord, being completely devoted to him in every aspect of one's life.

Holy Ghost: See *Holy Spirit*.

Holy Spirit: Third person of the Trinity.

"I have Jesus in my heart": The Bible talks a lot about Christ coming into the life of a Christian. Jesus says in Revelation 3:20, "Behold, I stand at the door and knock. If anyone hears my voice and opens the door, then I will come in to him, and will dine with him, and he with me." The Apostle Paul adds that if I'm a Christian, then I no longer live (see *dying to self*) but Christ lives in me.

"in his time": Expresses the idea that God engineers circumstances according to when he wants them to occur, not when you or I do.

"In the end, God wins": The belief that God will ultimately defeat evil and that Jesus Christ will reign forever.

"in the world, but not of the world": The model that Christians should follow while living on this earth — living in the world as Christlike examples (see also *salt and light*), but not compromising God's standards in the process.

incarnate: See *God incarnate*.

"inconceivable": Expression that Vizzini uses in *The Princess Bride* each time something happens that he hadn't planned on.

intercessor: Someone who pleads on behalf of another before a king. Through his sacrificial death on the cross, Jesus interceded for Christians (and continues to do so), taking their punishment upon himself. The Bible also calls Christians to intercede for others through prayer, making other people's requests known before God.

"Invite Jesus into your heart": This expression refers to the decision to become a Christian. See also *I have Jesus in my heart*.

Judgment Day: God will judge all people based on their thoughts and actions over the course of their lives. Those judged "sinful," as measured against God's perfect standard, are sentenced to hell. Those saved by the Blood of Christ will receive eternal life in heaven.

justification: The declaration by God that Christians are made acceptable to him because of the Blood of Christ. Christians aren't automatically considered worthy; instead, Christ's righteousness is credited to them. In addition, Christians have been justified (or made right with) God only through his grace, not due to good behavior or actions. See also *righteousness*.

koinonia: A Greek word that means literally "communion together in God's grace," or simply "fellowship."

Lamb of God: Another name for Jesus Christ. See also *Blood of the Lamb*.

"laying it at the foot of the cross": See *laying it on the altar of God*.

"laying it on the altar of God": The idea of giving up either a problem or something you hold dear and allowing God to have it.

Light of the world: Jesus is the symbolic light of the world, according to John 8:12.

Lord: A common term for God.

"making Jesus the Lord of your life": See *dying to self*.

martyr: A Christian who dies as a direct result of his or her witness for Christ.

mercy: Not receiving punishment that's deserved. Because of Christ's sacrificial death, God shows mercy to Christians by not punishing them for their sins.

minister: Generic term that often refers to the leader of a church.

"narrow road": Refers to the difficult path of being a Christian. Jesus, in Matthew 7:13–14, said, "Enter in by the narrow gate; for wide is the gate and broad is the way that leads to destruction, and many are those who enter in by it. How narrow is the gate, and restricted is the way that leads to life!"

"new creature in Christ": References the Apostle Paul's statement in 2 Corinthians 5:17: "Therefore if anyone is in Christ, he is a new creation. The old things have passed away. Behold, all things have become new."

New Testament: Part of the Bible that starts with the birth of Jesus Christ, provides teachings of the early Church, and ends with a description of what's going to happen in the future. See also *Old Testament*.

New Testament Church: The Christian Church from the period after the resurrection of Jesus through the death of John, the last living apostle (roughly between A.D. 33 and A.D. 100).

nonbeliever: See *non-Christian*.

non-Christian: Anyone who doesn't believe in Jesus Christ as being the Savior from sin.

Old Testament: Part of the Bible that begins at the creation of the world and chronicles the history of Israel, God's chosen people. See also *New Testament*.

"on fire for the Lord": Being excited about your relationship with God and obediently living out your faith, no matter the cost.

original sin: The first sin that Adam and Eve committed (see Genesis 3) and the consequences of this sin that affect every generation of humans.

Orthodox and orthodox: *Orthodox* with a capital *O* refers to Eastern Orthodox Christians, a division of the Christian Church, whereas lowercase *orthodox* is a term that refers to traditional, historical Christian beliefs.

pastor: Common name for the leader of a church, often a Protestant term.

penance: The sacramental act of confessing sins to a clergyperson for assurance of forgiveness. Catholic, Orthodox, and even Anglican Christians commonly practice penance.

personal relationship with Christ: An expression Christians use to describe the intimate relationship that they have with Jesus Christ. With a focus on a personal relationship, no person, minister, or institution should come between an individual Christian and Jesus.

"Praise the Lord": Common expression that says, in effect: "God, you are great!"

prayer: Simply, communicating with God. Christian prayer is more than just telling God your list of requests; it's also a way to get to know God and what he wants to do in your life and in the world.

prayer closet: A private place to pray and get away from the busyness of the world. The term comes from Matthew 6:6: "When you pray, enter into your closet, and having shut your door, pray to your Father who is in secret, and your Father who sees in secret will reward you openly." A prayer closet doesn't have to be a literal closet, but the idea is to find a place free from outside distractions.

prayer warrior: A term that describes someone who's especially diligent in prayer.

priest: Common name for the leader of a church, usually a Catholic term.

propitiation: In effect, a substitute. Jesus died on the cross (taking our place) as the payment required by God for the sins of humans.

quiet time: Dedicated time with God each day in prayer and Bible reading. Typically ranges anywhere from five minutes to two hours, but, of course, you can spend as much quiet time as you like!

rapture: The Bible says that when Jesus Christ returns to the earth (see *Second Coming of Jesus Christ*), Christians will be *raptured,* or taken from earth, and will go directly to heaven without dying first.

"redeemed by the blood of the Lamb": To *redeem* is to exchange one thing for another. Christians exchange their sin for eternal life because of the sacrificial death of Jesus. See also *Blood of Christ*.

regeneration: The act of being born again. Regeneration is the event that happens when a person becomes a Christian in which God gives him or her a new nature (see 2 Corinthians 5:17).

resurrection: To come back to life after you're dead. Christians believe that Jesus Christ rose from the dead three days after he was crucified (see Luke 24) and that he still lives.

reverend: Another title for the leader of a church.

righteousness: Holy living based on God's standard of holiness. See also *holiness*.

Sabbath: A day of rest; typically, Christians consider Sunday as the Sabbath Day.

"salt and light": Jesus tells his followers in Matthew 5 that they're the salt of the earth and the light of the world. Salt seasons food — bet you knew that already! In the same way, Christians are to season, or influence, the world they live in. *Light* refers to pointing the way to the Truth of Jesus Christ himself.

salvation: To experience salvation is to be freed from eternal punishment and hell. See also *saved*.

sanctification: To become progressively more holy and Christlike. Christians won't be perfect in this earthly life, but through the process of sanctification, they come closer to that goal.

saved: To be saved is to have faith in Jesus Christ and the work he did on the cross (see also *Blood of Christ*). A saved person is in a secure position, being freed from the punishment of sin and promised to be with God in heaven after death.

scripture: Another name for the Bible.

Second Coming of Jesus Christ: Term that Christians use to describe Christ's eventual return to the earth. Christ's first coming was some 2,000 years ago, when he was born as a human child. When he comes for the second time, he'll descend from the clouds (see Matthew 24:30).

secular: Worldly. Anything that isn't spiritual in nature.

seeker-sensitive churches: A trend within some churches to attract new people by focusing on their needs and making worship services more specifically relevant to everyday life. Seeker-sensitive churches often use marketing techniques to attract people to church and integrate multimedia and entertainment as part of the worship service experience. Supporters of this movement see it as a way to effectively present Christianity to the 21st-century person, but critics of the seeker-sensitive movement feel that this thrust to attract people waters down the Christian message.

"set free in Christ": See *freedom from bondage*.

sin: Any deliberate action, attitude, or thought that goes against God. People often think of sin as an obvious act, such as murder, adultery, or theft. However, sin is also wrongdoing that's far more subtle and even unnoticeable at times, such as pride, envy, or even worry. Sin can either be something you shouldn't have done, but did *(sins of commission),* or something you should've done, but didn't *(sins of omission).*

sinful nature: A tendency to sin that has been passed down to each human by Adam and Eve. See also *flesh, the* and *Fall of man*.

"sitting at the foot of the cross": Focusing on the reality of Christ's agony and sacrificial death on the cross as well as the eternal love that God has for humans, which led Christ to make this sacrifice.

"slave to sin": See *freedom from bondage*.

speaking in tongues: The phenomenon of an emotionally intense spiritual experience that prompts a person to start talking in a nonhuman speech. The tongues speaker believes that the words are an angelic language that the Holy Spirit gives so that he or she can pray spontaneously as directed by God. To a bystander, the words don't resemble any humanlike languages and seem like gibberish or babble when listened to from a purely human standpoint. See also *charismatics*.

Spirit-filled Christian: A buzzword that has different meanings to different parts of the Church. Charismatics use the term to mean a Christian who speaks in tongues, but non-charismatics generally use the term to describe an earnest, obedient disciple of Christ. See also *filled with the Spirit*.

spiritual gifts: Special gifts that the Holy Spirit gives to Christians for the purpose of doing God's work and building up the Church. Spiritual gifts include wisdom, knowledge, faith, healing, miraculous powers, prophecy, spiritual discernment, speaking in tongues, and interpretation of tongues, to name a few (see 2 Corinthians 12:8–10).

"surrender all": See *dying to self*.

"take up my cross": Refers to giving up one's personal wants and desires to Jesus and living only for him. Jesus said, "If any man would come after me, let him deny himself, and take up his cross, and follow me" (Mark 8:34). See also *dying to self*.

testament: Refers to either a witness or a covenant. The Bible is made up of the Old Testament and New Testament.

"that still, small voice": Refers to God speaking silently, not in an audible manner. See also *God laid it on my heart*.

"Thy will be done": Praying *thy will be done* means that you're asking God's will to be done in the world, not your own. Jesus taught his followers to pray this phrase in the Lord's Prayer (see Matthew 6). When you pray *thy will be done,* you're transformed, exchanging your will for his, forgetting about yourself, and turning over your needs and wants to God.

"turn the other cheek": Expression means to not stick up for your rights, but rather to submit to others, even when they've wronged you. Jesus said, "You have heard that it was said, 'An eye for an eye, and a tooth for a tooth.' But I tell you, don't resist him who is evil; but whoever strikes you on your right cheek, turn to him the other also" (Matthew 5:38–39).

"walk with Christ": See *Christian walk*.

"walking through the valley of the shadow of death": Trusting God in the midst of difficult circumstances. Refers to Psalm 23:4: "Even though I walk through the valley of the shadow of death, I will fear no evil, for you are with me. Your rod and your staff, they comfort me."

"walking with the Lord": See *Christian walk*.

"washed in the Blood of Christ": Refers to the cleansing power of the Blood of Christ. If a person has been *washed in the Blood of Christ,* he or she has been cleansed of his or her sins. See also *Blood of Christ*.

Western Church: The Christian Church that formed in the western part of the ancient world and became headquartered in Rome. The Western Church became the Catholic Church. The Protestant Church came out of the Western Church during the Reformation.

"What would Jesus do?": A phrase that Charles Sheldon's 1896 novel *In His Steps* focuses on and that became a popular craze among Christian youths in the late 1990s and early 2000s. The idea behind the phrase is to ask yourself what Jesus would do in your situation and then do it, regardless of the consequences. The Apostle Paul urges Christians to live their lives like Jesus did, because he's the perfect, sinless model on which to base your life. See also *Christlike*.

Word, the: Term that refers to Jesus (see John 1) as well as the Bible.

works: Good behavior or actions. Jesus Christ made it clear that humans aren't saved by good works, but only by the grace of God.

"wrath of God": God's judgment on sinners.

WWJD: See *What would Jesus do?*

Timeline of Christian History

● ●

*1*n some ways, biblical Christianity is the same as it was back when the apostles walked on the earth in the first century. Yet, over time, the Christian Church has been profoundly affected by events that have taken place along with the people who influenced them over the past 2,000 years. In this appendix, I give you the scoop on some of the milestones that helped shape the Christian Church and tell you when they happened.

6–0 B.C. (approximate)

Jesus Christ is born in a stable in the town of Bethlehem to Mary and Joseph. Mary, a virgin, conceived Jesus through the miraculous power of the Holy Spirit. (See Luke 1–2.)

A.D. 27 (approximate)

Jesus begins his public ministry. During a three-year span, he travels around the Palestine area (modern-day Israel) proclaiming the Good News of his coming — that he came to free humanity from sin and make salvation possible for all. He also selects 12 disciples to equip and teach for ministry and to minister alongside him.

30 (approximate)

Jesus Christ is crucified on a hill outside Jerusalem called Golgotha (Luke 23–24). Roman officials seal his body in a tomb, but Jesus rises from the dead three days later. Jesus appears several times to his disciples over the next 40 days and then ascends into heaven (Acts 1). Forty days after Christ's ascension, the Holy Spirit comes to the apostles at *Pentecost* (Acts 2), a Jewish festival, empowering them and equipping them for ministry.

30–70

The *apostles*, who were appointed as Church leaders by Jesus himself, lead the Church in tremendous growth throughout the Mediterranean region. The Apostle Paul goes on missionary journeys to Asia Minor (modern-day Turkey), Greece, and Rome. Many of the New Testament books are written during this period, including (dates are approximate): Galatians (A.D. 49), James (49), 1 and 2 Thessalonians (51–52), 1 and 2 Corinthians (55), Romans (57), Gospel of Mark (58–60), Ephesians (60), Colossians (60), Philemon (60), Philippians (61), Gospel of Matthew (61–64), Gospel of Luke (61–64), 1 Timothy (64), Titus (64), 1 Peter (64–65), Jude (65), Acts (66–68), 2 Timothy (66–67), 2 Peter (66–68), and Hebrews (68–70).

64–312

Periodic waves of persecution against Christians occur in the Roman Empire during this time period. The worst period is between 186 and 312. Emperor Maximus Thrax (235–238), for example, seeks to decapitate the Church by arresting and executing its bishops. Emperor Decius (249–251) goes even further, killing anyone even accused of being a Christian. Emperor Diocletian (284–305) of the Eastern Roman Empire caps it off by torturing and executing Christians — including men, women, children, and the elderly. The Christians are executed in a variety of grizzly ways, including being burned, stoned, skinned alive, fed to wild animals, drowned, and crucified.

70–73

After Jewish rebels attempt to overthrow Roman authority, Romans capture Jerusalem and destroy the Jewish Temple in A.D. 70. Jews disperse from Jerusalem and scatter throughout the Roman Empire. In A.D. 73, the Romans defeat the final Jewish resisters at Masada. Because of these events, the Christian Church (which emerged from Judaism) is no longer based in Jerusalem and begins to branch out throughout the Mediterranean region and beyond into parts of Asia and Africa.

85–95

The Apostle John writes the final books of the New Testament. He writes the Gospel of John in approximately A.D. 85, completing 1, 2, and 3 John between 85 and 90. John pens the final book, Revelation, around A.D. 95.

271–272

Recognized as the first Christian monk, Anthony of Coma (known today as St. Anthony) converts to Christianity and moves to the Egyptian Desert to live as a hermit. Most people consider Anthony to be the father of Christian monasticism.

313

Emperor Constantine legalizes Christianity in the Roman Empire, officially ending Christian persecution that's happened off-and-on since the first century.

324

Bishop Eusebius of Caesarea writes the first Church history book, called *The History of the Church.*

325

A council of all bishops in the Church meet at Nicaea and develop the Nicean Creed (often referred to as the Nicene-Constantinopolitan Creed by Orthodox Christians) as a statement against *Arianism* (a heretical teaching that rejected the belief that Jesus is God).

374–430

Augustine (see Chapter 18) becomes a Christian in A.D. 374 and later becomes the bishop in the town of Hippo in North Africa. Augustine also writes many influential books during this timeframe, including *Confessions* and *City of God.*

380

Emperor Theodosius declares Christianity to be supreme and names himself the chief enforcer of Christian truth. Thus Christianity becomes the official state religion of the Roman Empire.

393–397

In A.D. 393, a council of bishops that meets in Hippo officially recognizes the New Testament canon. In A.D. 397, another council in Carthage does likewise.

403–461

In A.D. 403, Irish slave traders enslave a boy named Patrick, who is around 16 years old at the time. While a slave, Patrick becomes a Christian, and after he escapes from Ireland, he travels to Britain to study in a monastery. He eventually returns to Ireland in A.D. 432 as a missionary bishop and has an extremely fruitful ministry converting Irish people from Druidism to Christianity. Now known as "St. Patrick," according to tradition he died on March 17, 461.

429

A visiting monk to Rome, Telemachus witnesses a gladiator fight in the Roman Coliseum and goes into the arena to stop the fighting. Gladiators kill him when he tries to break up the match, and his martyrdom has a profound influence on the public's and emperor's opinions regarding gladiator fights. Emperor Honorius bans gladiator fights altogether that same day.

451

Although the Nicean Creed addresses the divine nature of Jesus, the issue of his humanness was never completely settled at the council of Nicaea. To deal with this issue, a council of bishops meets in Chalcedon and declares, in what is known today as the Chalcedonian Creed, that Jesus is one person with two natures: He's fully God and fully man.

1054

Centuries of tension between the Western and Eastern Churches come to a boil when the Bishop of Rome (or the *pope*) excommunicates the Patriarch of Constantinople (the leader of the Eastern Church) after the patriarch closes the Western-oriented churches in his area. The event is later known as The Great Schism, discussed more in Chapter 10.

1095–1270

Pope Urban II responds to a request from the Byzantine Emperor in 1095 to save Christians from Muslim invaders in the Holy Land. This is the first of a series of eight separate Crusades that conclude in failure in 1270.

1208

Francis of Assisi (see Chapter 18) commits himself to following Jesus' commands as strictly as is humanly possible. He gives up literally all his possessions and works among the poor in cities and towns. In the process, he accumulates numerous followers who become an order of monks (or friars), known as the Franciscans, though they call themselves the "friars minor," or the "little brothers."

1382

John Wycliffe becomes the first person to translate the Bible into English. After a number of years of work, he finishes the New Testament by 1380 and the entire Bible by 1382. The authorities in England don't welcome his Bible, so he has to translate it in France and then smuggle it into England.

1382–1415

While translating some of John Wycliffe's works from English into Czech, John Huss — a Catholic priest from Bohemia — becomes convinced of many of the same doctrinal issues that later inspire Martin Luther to lead the Protestant Reformation. Religious authorities imprison Huss in 1414 and burn him at the stake for his radical beliefs in 1415.

1427

Thomas à Kempis, a German monk, writes one of the most popular Christian books of all time: *The Imitation of Christ*. He was also part of The Brothers and Sisters of the Common Life, a group that took no formal vows but lived a life of poverty and strict obedience.

1457

The Moravian Brethren Church is founded by followers of John Huss, who died 42 years before. The Moravians focus on many of the same issues that later characterize the Protestants (such as justification by grace through faith alone and the need to be born again).

1517

Martin Luther, a German monk, nails his Ninety-five Theses to the door of the Wittenburg Cathedral to protest what he believes to be corruption in the Catholic Church. This act is the spark that ignites the Protestant Reformation.

1525

William Tyndale (see Chapter 18) translates the Bible into English and, like John Wycliffe a century and a half before him, begins to smuggle copies into England. The British authorities finally catch up with him while he's living in Brussels, Belgium; they send him back to England and execute him.

1532–1534

Because of his failure to secure approval from the pope for a divorce, King Henry VIII of England breaks from the Catholic Church and forms the Church of England. In 1534, the Parliament passes an Act of Supremacy, which makes this action official and binding.

1536

John Calvin (see Chapter 18) publishes his influential *Institutes of the Christian Religion* and later moves to Geneva to accept a position of leadership as Professor of Sacred Scripture.

1530–1540s

The Catholic Church begins to recognize the need for reform. The internal reforms and changes that the Catholic Church makes during this post-Reformation era help produce a rejuvenated, invigorated Catholic Church.

1540

The Catholic Church founds the Jesuit order (or Society of Jesus, S.J. for short). This order of monks is a part of the Catholic Church's response to the Reformation by allowing them to be more independent than other groups. Driven by a devotion to God and to learning, they establish missions and universities around the world. The same ideals continue to characterize the order today. If you meet a person with "S.J." after his name, you can bet he's both a priest and a scholar.

1609

John Smyth founds the Baptist Church in England.

1670

Philip Jacob Spener, a Lutheran pastor, founds the Pietist movement, which stresses the importance of the Christian faith starting with a new birth in Christ. Pietism impacts many Protestant Christians during this era, including such people as John Wesley.

1703–1791

John Wesley (born in 1703 — see Chapter 18) founds the Methodist Church in 1744. He travels for decades around England on horseback, preaching the gospel outdoors to the poor and underprivileged who would feel uncomfortable in a formal church setting. He maintains an active ministry, which includes opposition to slavery, until his death in 1791.

1734

The *Great Awakening* (a Christian revival in which many people are convicted of their sin and commit themselves to Jesus Christ) starts in the American colonies in 1734, triggered by the preaching of Jonathan Edwards, a New England pastor. Over the next 30 years, the Great Awakening moves southward throughout the colonies, having a significant influence on the spiritual life of the colonists and bringing many to Christianity. Some estimates say that around 80 percent of all colonists developed a common biblical Christian faith as a result of the Great Awakening.

1789

The leaders of the French Revolution rebel against Church authority. This rebellion against the Church emerges as a sign of modern secularism.

1793

Often considered the father of modern Protestant missions, William Carey, an evangelistic preacher, travels to India. He eventually translates the Bible into numerous Indian languages.

1820–30s

The Second Great Awakening in the United States begins as Charles Finney preaches throughout western New York. His mixture of preaching and showmanship lights a spark that starts to spread across the nation. The revival moves southward into the Appalachians and comes up with a new revival style — the camp meeting, in which a preacher holds a revival for several days and provides shelter for people far from home who attend. These old-fashioned revivals often involve entire towns and counties. As it continues to spread westward, Baptist and Methodist churches grow exponentially as a result of the revival. Churches continue having these meetings to the present day, calling their evangelistic meetings *revivals,* and some still calling them *camp meetings.* However, they're usually restricted to a few days within just one local church.

1901

The Protestant Pentecostal movement begins in Topeka, Kansas in 1901 when Pastor Charles Fox Parham leads a woman into an ecstatic experience, which he calls "the baptism of the Holy Spirit," and she starts to speak in tongues. The Pentecostals emerge as the first modern-day group of Christians to promote speaking in tongues. See Chapter 12 for more on this topic.

1962–1965

Pope John XXIII and his successor Paul VI assemble a council known as Vatican II that helps the Catholic Church reach out to a modern population without changing their core beliefs. The 16 documents that emerge from Vatican II both restate traditional Catholic teaching and offer extensive teaching on contemporary social issues.

1978

Pope John Paul II is elected pope.

1950–present

Billy Graham founds the Billy Graham Evangelistic Association and begins his ministry of preaching in evangelistic crusades. Graham is believed to have preached the Good News of Jesus Christ to more people throughout his ministry than anyone else in the history of the world has.

Index

• M •

• N •

Notes

Notes

Notes

Notes

Notes

Notes

Christianity For Dummies®

Cheat Sheet

Comparing Beliefs Across the Christian Church

This handy table helps you keep straight some of the major differences among the largest groups of the Christian Church.

Church	What's the means of salvation? (Chs 3 and 10)	How should Christians worship? (Ch 12)	What sacraments and ordinances does the Church observe?	How's the Church organized, and who heads it up?	Does the Church ordain women?	Who can be baptized? (Ch 8)
Anglican/ Episcopalian	God's grace by faith alone	Traditional style through liturgy; contemporary liturgy is possible	Baptism, Lord's Supper (Regard the other five that Catholics observe as "minor sacraments.")	Episcopal (Clergy in local churches presided over by bishop.)	Yes	Infants and professing Christians
Assembly of God	God's grace by faith alone	Non-liturgical (free) worship; sometimes contemporary	Baptism, Lord's Supper	Mixture of Congregational and Presbyterian (Local churches largely govern themselves, but don't have complete autonomy.)	Yes	Only professing Christians
Baptist	God's grace by faith alone	Non-liturgical (free) worship; sometimes contemporary	Baptism, Lord's Supper	Congregational (Local churches are self-governing.)	Depending on the convention (division of churches)	Only professing Christians
Catholic	God's grace, which Christians receive by faith and by observing the sacraments	Traditional style through liturgy; contemporary liturgy is possible	Baptism, Eucharist (Lord's Supper), Penance, Confirmation, Marriage, Holy Orders, Anointing of the Sick	Papal/Episcopal (Clergy in local churches presided over by bishop. The pope [the Bishop of Rome] is the ultimate Church leader.)	No	Infants and professing Christians
Lutheran	God's grace by faith alone	Traditional style through liturgy; contemporary worship is possible	Baptism, Lord's Supper	Mixed (Congregational, Presbyterian, and Episcopal structures exist.)	Depending on the synod (council)	Infants and professing Christians
Methodist	God's grace by faith alone	Traditional style through liturgy; contemporary worship is possible	Baptism, Lord's Supper	Episcopal (Clergy in local churches presided over by bishop.)	Yes	Infants and professing Christians
Orthodox	God's grace received through faith and ongoing participation in the work of one's salvation	Traditional style through liturgy	No official position, but often observes the Catholic sacraments	Episcopal (Clergy in local churches presided over by bishop.)	No	Infants and professing Christians
Presbyterian	God's grace by faith alone	Traditional style through liturgy	Baptism, Lord's Supper	Presbyterian (A graded organizational system by presbyters or elders.)	Yes	Infants and professing Christians

Christianity For Dum

D0100302

The Nicean Creed

The Nicean Creed (or the Nicene-Constantinopolitan Creed as Orthodox Christians call it) was developed in the fourth century and serves as the definitive statement on who exactly God is according to the Christian Church. This creed expresses common belief among all parts of the Church and is often recited in churches.

We believe in one God, the Father, the Almighty, Maker of heaven and earth, of all that is, seen and unseen.

We believe in one Lord, Jesus Christ, the only Son of God, eternally begotten of the Father, God from God, light from light, true God from true God, begotten, not made, of one Being with the Father; through him all things were made. For us and for our salvation he came down from heaven, was incarnate of the Holy Spirit and the Virgin Mary and became truly human. For our sake he was crucified under Pontius Pilate; he suffered death and was buried. On the third day he rose again in accordance with the scriptures; he ascended into heaven and is seated at the right hand of the Father. He will come again in glory to judge the living and the dead, and his kingdom will have no end.

We believe in the Holy Spirit, the Lord, the giver of life, who proceeds from the Father [and the Son], who with the Father and the Son is worshiped and glorified, who has spoken through the prophets. We believe in one holy catholic and apostolic Church. We acknowledge one baptism for the forgiveness of sins. We look for the resurrection of the dead, and the life of the world to come. Amen.

Christianity in a Nutshell

Like any religion, Christianity has tons of different beliefs about tons of different subjects, as well as ideas that stem from those beliefs, and so on, resulting in countless specific convictions. All in all, though, Christians agree on the basic ideas of salvation, which are

- God loves and wants a relationship with each person.
- Everyone is born with a tendency to sin. And this sin, whether it's large or small, separates people from God.
- God came to earth in human form (as Jesus Christ) and paid the costly penalty for sin by dying on the cross for all people. He rose from the dead three days later, triumphing over death.
- God offers forgiveness to everyone.
- Anyone who accepts this gift of forgiveness and believes in Jesus Christ receives salvation.

Keys to Christian Worship

Worship is the act of showing God that you're in awe of and devoted to him. It not only honors God, but it also empowers the worshiper. Keep in mind the following six keys to worship:

- Worship in reverence.
- Worship intentionally and with focus; don't simply go through the motions.
- Worship by letting the Holy Spirit work in your heart.
- Worship by giving to God with abandon.
- Worship constantly; it's not a once-a-week activity, but a way of life.

For Dummies: Bestselling Book Series for Beginners